Landmark IP Decisions of the European Court of Justice (2019-2024)

Landmark IP Decisions of the European Court of Justice (2019-2024)

Authors:

António Andrade, Claes Angvall, Huib Berendschot,
Margarida Castillo Silva, Roderick Chalmers Hoynck van Papendrecht,
Emma Dekeuwer, Isaline d'Hoop de Synghem, Ina Donvil,
Manuel Durães Rocha, Patrycja Gierdal, Marta Gimeno,
Eva Gostiša, Victoria Heinen, Pedro Hemsworth,
Urša Horvat Kous, Karel Janssens, Åsa Krook, Marie Manhaeve,
Lucia Martin-Sanz Barrachina, Dilan Mienert, Ewa Nagy,
Marion Nuytten, Matilde Ortins de Bettencourt, Ana Panão,
Jonna Rask, Maria Rubina Silva, Leonor Sá e Frade, Julia Selbmann,
Felix Suihko, Louise Thorning Ahle, Kerim Uzman, Lena van Bracht,
Bram Woltering, Barbara Załęcka-Wysocka

Editors:

Huib Berendschot, Karel Janssens,
Bram Woltering, Marie Manhaeve

LARCIER INTERSENTIA

Intersentia
Lefebvre Sarrut Belgium SA
Rue Haute 139/6
1000 Bruxelles
Belgium
Email: contact@larcier-intersentia.com

FSC
www.fsc.org
MIX
Paper | Supporting responsible forestry
FSC® C004472

Distribution for the UK, Ireland and
Rest of the World (excl. France, Belgium and Luxembourg)
Ingram Publisher Services UK
1 Deltic Avenue, Rooksley
Milton Keynes MK13 8LD
United Kingdom
Tel: +44 1752 202 301 | Fax: +44 1752 202 331
Email: ipsuk.customercare@ingramcontent.com

Distribution for France and Rest of the World (excl. Ireland and the UK)
Interforum Editis
92 avenue de France
75013 Paris
France

Distribution for Belgium and Luxembourg (exl. France, Ireland and the UK)
Larcier-Intersentia
Rue Haute, 139/6
1000 Bruxelles
Belgium

ISBN 978-1-83970-425-3
D/2025/06040/0061
NUR 827

British Library Cataloguing in Publication Data. A catalogue record for this book is available from the British Library.

Content

Introduction

The rapid pace of technological advancements continues to reshape the landscape of Intellectual Property law. New challenges and opportunities are emerging as technology evolves, with innovations impacting industries across the board. However, these advancements also give rise to complex legal questions within the domain of IP law, and the European Court of Justice (CJEU) continues to play a pivotal role in interpreting the legislation in light of these developments. This book provides an in-depth review of the most significant IP decisions issued by the European Court between 2019 and 2024.

The harmonisation of IP law within the European Union remains at the forefront of ensuring a unified legal framework that fosters innovation while protecting rights across the vast single market. As in previous years, customs surveillance and anti-counterfeiting efforts continue to underscore the importance of consistent and effective enforcement mechanisms, reinforcing the EU's commitment to a robust IP regime. Through its case law, the CJEU has been instrumental in promoting further harmonisation of IP laws across Member States, ensuring greater coherence in the legal framework.

While the CAPIP association no longer exists, the spirit of cooperation it nurtured persists. The close relationships between member firms, spread across multiple European jurisdictions, remain a cornerstone of the ongoing fight against counterfeiting and the promotion of further harmonisation in IP law. This continued cooperation has enabled the publication of this new – and third – edition of *Landmark IP Decisions of the European Court of Justice*, which builds on the success of its previous editions by offering critical insights into the most impactful IP rulings of the European Court from 2019 to 2024. As each of the decisions covered in this book stems from disputes before national courts, we have once again sought to provide expert commentary from those familiar with the legal landscape in the relevant jurisdictions.

The rapid rise of Artificial Intelligence will undoubtedly affect the future of IP practice and enforcement. This and other developments will continue to require ongoing attention and legal adaptation. We already look forward to the Court's case law in the coming years, and the next edition of this book.

COURT OF *JUSTICE* 14 MARCH 2019

ON WHETHER THE CONCEPT OF 'SHAPE' AS AN ABSOLUTE GROUND FOR REFUSAL COVERS OTHER CHARACTERISTICS, SUCH AS PATTERNS, APPLIED TO A SPECIFIC LOCATION ON A TWO-DIMENSIONAL PRODUCT

Case C-21/18

Summary and Analysis by Åsa Krook and Jonna Rask[1]

Parties:

Textilis Ltd and Ozgur Keskin

v

Svenskt Tenn AB

1. Background and History

Svenskt Tenn Aktiebolag ('Svenskt Tenn') is a Swedish interior design store that markets and sells furniture and furnishing fabrics as well as other decorative accessories. During the 1930s, Svenskt Tenn started a cooperation with an architect, Joseph Frank, who designed various patterns for furnishing fabrics for Svenskt Tenn, including a pattern called MANHATTAN, which Svenskt Tenn markets and sells and in respect of which Svenskt Tenn claims to be the holder of rights under copyright law.

On 4 January 2012, Svenskt Tenn filed an application for registration of an EU trade mark with the European Union Intellectual Property Office (EUIPO). The figurative mark, designated MANHATTAN, was registered under number 010540268 in classes 11, 16, 20, 21, 24, 27 and 35 under the Nice Classification of Goods and Services, including among other things bed and table covers, wallpaper and furniture.

1 Åsa Krook is an IP partner at the Finnish law firm Waselius & Wist and is a member of the Finnish Bar Association. Jonna Rask is an Associate Lawyer at the Finnish law firm Waselius & Wist.

The figurative mark MANHATTAN is represented as follows:

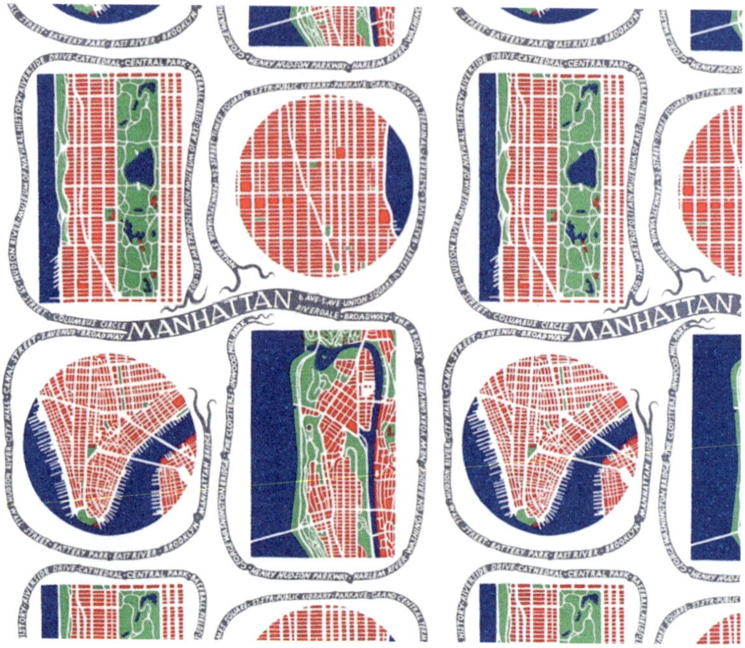

Textilis Ltd ('Textilis') was at the time of the proceedings a company incorporated under English law. It was owned by Mr Ozgur Keskin, who had been active in online trading since 2013. The company marketed fabrics and goods for interior decoration bearing patterns similar to those of the figurative mark MANHATTAN.

Svenskt Tenn brought an action in Stockholm District Court, Sweden (Stockholms tingsrätt) against Textilis and Mr Keskin for infringement of its EU trade mark MANHATTAN and of its copyright. Svenskt Tenn also applied for an order that Textilis and Mr Keskin, on pain of a penalty, be prohibited, first, from marketing or distributing in any other way to the Swedish public certain designated objects and, second, from using the MANHATTAN trade mark in Sweden for fabrics, cushions, and furniture.

In response to these actions, Textilis and Mr Keskin brought a counter-claim for a declaration that the trade mark MANHATTAN be invalidated, on the grounds that, first, it lacked distinctive character and, second, having regard to the way in which it is used, it was made up of a shape which gave substantial value to the goods, within the meaning of Article 7(1)(e)(iii) of Regulation No 207/2009.

The Stockholm District Court dismissed the counterclaim on the grounds that first, under Article 4 of Regulation No 207/2009, all signs capable of being represented graphically may be EU trade marks, provided that they have a distinctive character and, second, the mark MANHATTAN was not a shape within the meaning of Article 7(1)(e)(iii) of that regulation. The District Court also ruled that Textilis and Mr Keskin had infringed the trade mark MANHATTAN and, simultaneously, the copyright to the MANHATTAN pattern.

Based on an appeal against the District Court's judgment by Textilis and Mr Keskin, the Patent and Market Court of Appeal, which is a division of the Svea Court of Appeal (Svea hovrätt, Patent- och marknadsöverdomstolen), sought to ascertain whether a figurative mark such as MANHATTAN, which consists of a two-dimensional representation of two-dimensional goods, such as a fabric, can be regarded as a shape within the meaning of Article 7(1)(e)(iii) of Regulation No 207/2009. It underlined in this respect that it is clear from Article 7(1)(e)(iii) that the ground for invalidity provided for in that provision applies to three-dimensional and two-dimensional marks representing three-dimensional shapes.[2]

The Patent and Market Court of Appeal decided to stay the proceedings and refer the following questions to the CJEU for a preliminary ruling:

> '1. *Is Article 4 of [Regulation 2015/2424] to be interpreted as meaning that Article 7(1)(e)(iii), in its new wording, is applicable to a court's assessment of invalidity (under Article 52(1)(a) of the Trade Marks Regulation) that is made after the entry into force of the amendment, namely after 23 March 2016, even if the action concerns a declaration of invalidity where the action was brought before that date and therefore concerns a trade mark registered before that date?*
>
> 2. *Is Article 7(1)(e)(iii) of [Regulation No 207/2009], in the version applicable, to be interpreted as meaning that its scope covers a sign which consists of the two-dimensional representation of a two-dimensional product, for example fabric decorated with the sign in question?*
>
> 3. *If the answer to question 2 is in the affirmative, according to what principles is the wording "signs which consist exclusively of the shape (or another characteristic) which gives substantial value to the goods" in Article 7(1)(e)(iii) of [Regulation No 207/2009, as amended,] to be interpreted, in a situation where the registration covers a wide range of classes of goods and goods and the sign may be affixed in different ways to the goods? Is the assessment to be made in accordance with more objective/general criteria, for example with the starting point of how the mark appears and how it is possible to affix it to different goods, that is to say without regard to the manner in which the trade mark proprietor may de facto have affixed or may intend to affix the sign to various goods?*'

---

2 These include, e.g. the representation of a sculpture or a vase, as held by the EFTA Court in paras. 110 to 115 of its judgment of 6 April 2017, *Norwegian Board of Appeal for Industrial Property Rights* – appeal from the municipality of Oslo (E-05/16), or as the Court of Justice held in the judgment of 18 June 2002, *Philips* (C-299/99, EU:C:2002:377).

2. Decision

1. Article 7(1)(e)(iii) of Council Regulation (EC) No 207/2009 of 26 February 2009 on the [European Union] trade mark, as amended by Regulation (EU) 2015/2424 of the European Parliament and of the Council of 16 December 2015, must be interpreted as meaning that it is not applicable to marks registered before the entry into force of Regulation No 207/2009, as amended by Regulation 2015/2424.

2. Article 7(1)(e)(iii) of Regulation No 207/2009 must be interpreted as meaning that a sign such as that at issue in the main proceedings, consisting of two-dimensional decorative motifs, which are affixed to goods, such as fabric or paper, does not 'consist exclusively of the shape', within the meaning of that provision.

3. Motivation and Analysis

First, the CJEU interpreted Article 7(1)(e)(iii) of Regulation No 207/2009. The CJEU stated that, in order to ensure observance of the principles of legal certainty and the protection of legitimate expectations, the substantive rules of EU law must be interpreted as applying to situations existing before their entry into force only in so far as it clearly follows from their terms, objectives or general scheme that such effect must be given to them.[3] The court also noted that it is not apparent from the purpose or the scheme of Regulation 2015/2424 that the EU legislature intended to confer retroactive effect on Article 7(1)(e)(iii) of Regulation No 207/2009.[4] As no express provision of this nature was included in Regulation No 2015/2424, the CJEU held that Article 7(1)(e)(iii) of Regulation No 207/2009 is not applicable to EU trade marks registered before the entry into force of that amended regulation. Consequently, the CJEU held that the answer to the first question was that Article 7(1)(e)(iii) of Regulation No 207/2009, as amended, must be interpreted as meaning that it is not applicable to marks registered before the entry into force of the amended regulation.[5]

Regarding the second question, the CJEU assessed the concept of 'shape'. The CJEU referred to the recent decision in the Louboutin red sole case.[6] The Court has consistently held that the meaning and scope of the concept of shape must be determined by considering its usual meaning in everyday language, while

---

3 Case C-4/10, 14 July 2011, *Bureau national interprofessionnel du Cognac*, para. 26.

4 Such an interpretation also emerges from Rec. 12 of Reg. 2015/2424, which recalls the importance which the EU legislature attaches to the principle of legal certainty.

5 Paras. 30-33 of the annotated judgment.

6 Case C-163/16, 12 June 2018, *Louboutin and Christian Louboutin*.

also taking into account the context in which it occurs and the purposes of the rules of which it is part.[7] The CJEU held that in the context of trade mark law, the concept is usually understood as a set of lines or contours that outline the product concerned.[8]

In applying the above considerations, the CJEU has previously held that the application of a particular colour to a specific location of a product does not mean that the sign at issue consists of a 'shape' within the meaning of Article 3(1)(e)(iii) of Directive 2008/95, whose wording is similar to that of Article 7(1)(e)(iii) of Regulation No 207/2009, where it is not the form of the product or part of the product that a registration of the mark seeks to protect, but only the application of a particular colour in a specific location.[9] The CJEU pointed out that as the European Commission has indicated in its observations, it is common ground that, unlike a sign relating to a colour per se, the sign at issue in the main proceedings, which was made up of two-dimensional and decorative motifs and which was affixed to goods such as fabric or paper, contained lines and contours. However, the CJEU held that the sign could not be regarded as consisting '*exclusively of a shape*' within the meaning of Article 7(1)(e)(iii) of Regulation No 207/2009.[10]

Furthermore, according to the CJEU, although the sign represented shapes that were formed by the external outline of drawings representing stylised parts of geographical maps, it was clear that the sign also '*contain[ed] decorative elements situated both inside and outside those outlines*,' including words such as 'Manhattan'. Thus, a sign consisting of two-dimensional decorative motifs is not 'indissociable' from the shape of the goods where that sign is affixed to goods whose form differs from such decorative motifs. Accordingly, the exclusion laid down in Article 7(1)(e)(iii) of Regulation No 207/2009 cannot apply to such a sign, and a sign such as the one at issue in the main proceedings does not consist '*exclusively of a shape*.'[11] The CJEU finally pointed out that the fact that the sign at issue was also protected by copyright had no bearing on whether or not it consisted exclusively of a 'shape', within the meaning of Article 7(1)(e)(iii) of Regulation No 207/2009.

As regards the third question, the CJEU referred to its answer to the second question and considered it unnecessary to provide a separate response for it.[12]

---

[7] With regard to Dir. 2008/95/EC of the European Parliament and of the Council of 22 October 2008 to approximate the laws of the Member States relating to trade marks (OJ 2008 L 299, p. 25), Case C-163/16, 12 June 2018, *Louboutin and Christian Louboutin*, para. 20.

[8] Case C-163/16, 12 June 2018, *Louboutin and Christian Louboutin*, para. 21.

[9] Case C-163/16, 12 June 2018, *Louboutin and Christian Louboutin*, para. 24.

[10] Paras. 37-39 of the annotated judgment.

[11] Paras. 40-43 of the annotated judgment.

[12] Para. 47 of the annotated judgment.

The ruling by the CJEU further clarifies the scope of Article 7(1)(e)(iii) of Regulation No 207/2009. It could be said that the ruling provides a rather restrictive interpretation of Article 7(1)(e)(iii) of Regulation No 207/2009. It confirms that the CJEU recognises neither patterns of a product nor colours applied to a specific location of a product as falling under the scope of 'shape' for the purpose of Article 7(1)(e)(iii). Regulation No 207/2009 has since been replaced by the new Regulation No 2017/1001, but the ruling is equally important for interpretation under the new regulation. Hence, the list of characteristics that do not fall within the concept of 'shape' continues to expand[13] and the scope of the provision is further clarified.

---

[13] 'EU–CJEU–Does the concept of "shape" as an absolute ground for refusal cover other characteristics, such as patterns, applied to a specific location on a two-dimensional product?' *The Trademark Reporter, Annual Review of EU Trademark Law*, 2019, p. 478.

COURT OF JUSTICE 27 MARCH 2019

ON THE DISTINCTION OF GROUNDS FOR APPLYING FOR A COLOUR MARK AND A FIGURATIVE MARK

Case C-578/17

Summary and Analysis by Åsa Krook and Jonna Rask[1]

Parties:

Oy Hartwall Ab

v

Patentti- ja rekisterihallitus

1. Background and History

Oy Hartwall Ab is a beverage company based in Helsinki, Finland. The company was founded in 1836 when Victor Hartwall established a mineral water production plant in Helsinki.[2] Hartwall is known for its mineral water, long drinks and malt liquors.

Hartwall applied to the Finnish Patent and Registration Office (*Patentti- ja rekisterihallitus*, 'PRH')[3] to register the sign represented below as a figurative trade mark. Following a preparatory decision of the PRH, the company clarified that it was applying for the registration of the mark at issue as a 'colour mark', not a figurative mark, described as follows: '*The colours of the sign are blue (PMS 2748, PMS CYAN) and grey (PMS 877)*' in class 32: 'Mineral waters'. The mark applied for is a blue ribbon with a grey outline.

[1] Åsa Krook is an IP partner at the Finnish law firm Waselius & Wist and is a member of the Finnish Bar. Jonna Rask is an Associate Lawyer at the Finnish law firm Waselius & Wist.

[2] The production plant was the first in the Nordic countries.

[3] Patentti- ja rekisterihallitus ('PRH') is the Intellectual Property Office of Finland. E.g. the PRH permits and renews trade marks and patents as well as maintaining the Trade Register.

By its decision of 5 June 2013, the PRH rejected Hartwall's application on the ground that the trade mark applied for lacked distinctive character. In that regard, the PRH highlighted that the exclusive right to register certain colours cannot be granted if it is not established that the colours in respect of which protection is sought have acquired distinctive character through significant long-term use. The PRH also noted that a market study produced by Hartwall showed that the reputation of the mark at issue was established not with regard to the colours as such, but with regard to the figurative sign, the contours of which are defined and determined. The colour combination for which protection was sought had not been established through use nor gained a distinctive character by the date on which registration was sought.[4]

Hartwall appealed PRH's decision to the Finnish Market Court (*markkinaoikeus*). The Market Court dismissed the appeal, notably on the ground that the graphic representation of the sign in respect of which protection was sought did not include a systematic arrangement associating the colours concerned in a predetermined and uniform way, and, therefore, that the mark did not satisfy the requirements of graphic representation of a sign as laid down by the Finnish Trademarks Act (7/1964).[5]

Hartwall filed an appeal against the decision of the Market Court to the Supreme Administrative Court in Finland (*korkein hallinto-oikeus*). The Supreme Administrative Court stated that, to its knowledge, the Market Court had not yet settled the question whether a sign represented as a colour drawing can be registered as a 'colour mark'. It added that the Market Court had not ruled on the effect of the classification of a mark as a colour mark on the assessment of that mark's distinctive character.

The Supreme Administrative Court highlighted the importance of the answer to that question in the matter brought before it, in so far as the PRH was of the view that, as regards colour marks, the distinctive character of a colour mark must be proved by evidence of long-term significant use of the sign. However, the consequences of the classification of the sign by the person seeking protection of that sign remained unclear under applicable trade mark law.

In these circumstances, the Supreme Administrative Court decided to stay the proceedings and to refer the following questions to the Court of Justice of the European Union (CJEU) for a preliminary ruling:

> '1. *For the interpretation of Article 2 of Directive [2008/95] and the condition relating to the distinctive character of a trade mark within the*

---

[4] In 2021, the PRH found, *inter alia*, that the colour mark of the confectionery company Cloetta Suomi Oy had become distinctive as a trade mark through decades of use.

[5] Market Court of Finland, 31 March 2015, MD:238/15.

meaning of Article 3(1)(b) thereof, is it of relevance whether the trade mark is to be registered as a figurative mark or a colour mark?

2. If the classification of the mark as a colour mark or figurative mark is of importance in the assessment of its distinctive character, is the mark, regardless of its representation as a drawing, to be registered as a colour mark in accordance with the trade mark application, or can it be registered only as a figurative mark?

3. If it is possible to register, as a colour mark, a mark represented in the form of a drawing in the trade mark application, is it necessary for the registration as a colour mark of a mark which has been graphically illustrated in the trade mark application with the accuracy required by the case-law of the Court of Justice relating to colour marks (and which is not the registration as a mark of a colour in itself, abstract, without shape or contours), is it necessary to submit in addition solid evidence of use as required by the [Intellectual Property Office] or any such evidence?'

2. Decision

1. Articles 2 and 3(1)(b) of Directive 2008/95/EC of the European Parliament and of the Council of 22 October 2008 to approximate the laws of the Member States relating to trade marks must be interpreted as meaning that the classification as a 'colour mark' or 'figurative mark' given to a sign by the applicant on registration is a relevant factor among others for the purpose of establishing whether that sign can constitute a trade mark within the meaning of Article 2 of the directive and, if so, whether it is distinctive within the meaning of Article 3(1)(b) of that directive, but does not release the competent trade mark authority from its obligation to carry out a global assessment of distinctive character by reference to the actual situation of the mark considered, which means that that authority cannot refuse registration of a sign as a mark on the sole ground that that sign has not acquired distinctive character through use in relation to the goods or services claimed.

2. Article 2 of Directive 2008/95 must be interpreted as precluding, in circumstances such as those in the main proceedings, the registration of a sign as a mark due to an inconsistency in the application for registration, which it is for the referring court to ascertain.

3. Motivation and Analysis

The CJEU stated that it should be borne in mind that Directive 2008/95 does not establish categories of marks and Article 2 and Article 3(1)(b) of the Directive make no distinction between different categories of trade marks.[6] Thus, it is for the Member States to determine what form the procedures concerning the registration and invalidity of trade marks are to take and they remain entirely free to adopt rules governing those procedures in that field.[7] Such freedom should not, however, run counter to the harmonised definition of the notion of 'trade mark' and to the criteria governing the distinctive character of a mark, both deriving from Articles 2 and 3(1) of Directive 2008/95, which could deprive the Directive of its effectiveness and be detrimental to the proper functioning of the system of trade mark registration.

First, the CJEU assessed the effect of the categorisation of a sign as a 'colour mark' or 'figurative mark' on the assessment of distinctive character. In that regard, the Court held that the fact that the registration of a sign is sought as a 'colour mark' or 'figurative mark' is relevant in order to determine the subject matter and scope of the protection conferred by trade mark law for the purpose of applying Article 2 of Directive 2008/95. As for the effect of the categorisation, the Court found that it must be held that when a competent authority examines a trade mark application, it must, in order to determine whether the sign in respect of which protection is sought under trade mark law has distinctive character within the meaning of Article 3(1)(b) of Directive 2008/95, carry out an examination by reference to the actual situation, taking into account all circumstances of the case and in particular any use which has been made of the sign.[8] The examination of the distinctive character of a mark can therefore not be carried out in the abstract.[9]

The Court has previously considered that the criteria of assessment of the distinctive character of colour marks are the same as those applicable to the other categories of marks. Although the criteria remain the same, it is apparent from the CJEU's case law that the perception of the relevant public is not necessarily the same in the case of a sign consisting of a colour per se as it is in the case of a word mark or figurative mark.[10] While the public is accustomed to perceiving word marks or figurative marks instantly as signs identifying the commercial origin of certain goods or services, a colour per se is not normally inherently capable of distinguishing the goods or services of a particular undertaking.

The CJEU has also previously held that, in the case of a colour per se, distinctiveness without any prior use is inconceivable save in exceptional circumstances and, even if a colour per se does not initially have any distinctive character,

---

6 Case C-217/13 and C-218/13, 19 June 2014, *Oberbank and Others*, para. 46.

7 Rec. 6 of Dir. 2008/95.

8 Case C-104/01, 6 May 2003, *Libertel*, para. 76; Case C-363/99, 12 February 2004, *Koninklijke KPN Nederland*, paras. 31-35; Case C-49/02, 24 June 2004, *Heidelberger Bauchemie*, para. 41.

9 Case C-363/99, 12 February 2004, *Koninklijke KPN Nederland*, para. 31.

10 Case C-104/01, 6 May 2003, *Libertel*, para. 65.

it may acquire such character in relation to the goods or services in respect of which registration of the mark is sought following the use made of it.[11]

Moreover, in assessing the potential distinctive character of a colour per se or a colour combination as a trade mark, regard must be had to the general interest in not unduly restricting the availability of colours for the other traders who offer for sale similar goods or services as those for which registration is sought.[12]

Advocate General Mr Saugmandsgaard Øe held in point 45 of his Opinion delivered on 22 November 2018 that it is of relevance whether the mark is to be registered as a figurative mark or a colour mark in the sense that the specific characteristics of colour marks require that they be taken into account in assessing whether a colour mark has distinctive character. In that connection, it must be borne in mind both that a colour mark seldom has distinctive character initially and that there is a public interest in not unduly restricting the availability of colours for other operators who offer for sale goods or services of the same type.

However, the Court held that its case law does not release competent trade mark authorities from the obligation to carry out an examination of distinctive character by reference to the actual situation, taking into account all circumstances of each case. Thus, it would run counter to such an examination if those authorities could establish the distinctive character of a colour per se or a colour combination solely on account of such a colour sign being used in relation to the goods or services claimed.[13] Furthermore, if the registration of a sign as a trade mark involves a combination of colours designated in the abstract and which lacks clear contours, established CJEU case law dictates that the graphic depiction of these colours should be systematically arranged by linking them in a predetermined and consistent manner.[14]

Thus, in the overall analysis of distinctive character by reference to the actual situation, the CJEU found that it is necessary to examine whether and to what extent the systematically arranged colour combination is capable of conferring inherent distinctive character on the sign in question. The Court thereby held that the competent trade mark authority cannot refuse registration of a sign as a trade mark on the sole ground that that sign has not acquired distinctive character through use in relation to the goods or services claimed.[15]

---

11 Case C-104/01, 6 May 2003, *Libertel*, paras. 66-67.

12 Case C-104/01, 6 May 2003, *Libertel*, para. 60; Case C-49/02, 24 June 2004, *Heidelberger Bauchemie*, para. 41.

13 Para. 32 of the annotated judgment.

14 C-49/02, 24 June 2004, *Heidelberger Bauchemie*, para. 33.

15 Para. 35 of the annotated judgment.

As regards the second question, the CJEU assessed whether there is an obstacle to the registration as a colour mark of a trade mark such as the one in question, which is represented as a figurative mark in the trade mark application. In that regard, it should be noted that, according to the CJEU's settled case law, a sign may be registered as a trade mark only if the applicant provides a graphic representation in accordance with the requirement in Article 2 of Directive 2008/95, with the effect that the subject matter and scope of the protection sought are clearly and precisely determined.[16] However, the verbal description of the sign serves to clarify the subject matter and scope of the protection sought under trade mark law.[17]

As Advocate General Mr Saugmandsgaard Øe set out, in essence, in points 60 to 63 of his Opinion, the Court held that when a trade mark application contains an inconsistency between the sign protection of which is sought in the form of a drawing, and the classification given to the mark by the applicant, the consequence of which is that it is impossible to determine exactly the subject matter and scope of the protection sought under trade mark law, the competent authority must refuse registration of the mark on account of the lack of clarity and precision of the trade mark application. In the case in question, the CJEU found that there was an inconsistency showing that the application for protection under trade mark law was unclear and imprecise. Consequently, the answer to the second question was that Article 2 of Directive 2008/95 must be interpreted as precluding, in circumstances such as those in the main proceedings, the registration of a sign as a trade mark due to an inconsistency in the application for registration, which it is for the referring court (i.e. the Finnish Market Court) to ascertain.

In view of the answer to the second question, the Court found no need to assess the third question.

The CJEU confirmed that the criteria for assessing the distinctive character of a colour mark are the same as for other types of trade marks. In a situation where, in a trade mark registration application, there is a conflict between the figurative mark for which protection is sought and where the classification of the mark indicated by the applicant makes it impossible to define with sufficient precision the subject matter and scope of protection of the mark applied for, the competent authority must reject the trade mark registration on the ground that the application is not sufficiently precise. Furthermore, the CJEU pointed out that the mark for which Hartwall applied for protection was presented as a figurative mark, whereas the word description only concerned protection for the colours grey and blue. Hartwall also specified in its application that the application was for registration of a colour trade mark. Based on this, the CJEU

[16] Case C-104/01, 6 May 2003, *Libertel*, para. 29.

[17] Case C-283/01, 27 November 2003, *Shield Mark*, para. 59; C-49/02, 24 June 2004, *Heidelberger Bauchemie*, para. 34.

found that there was a conflict in the application, which led to the application not being considered sufficiently clear.

The Finnish Trade Marks Act (544/2019)[18] does not contain a requirement for graphic representation. Instead, it is required that the representation be clear and precise. The requirement for clear and precise representation was equally not met in the case at hand. The Supreme Administrative Court held that the subject matter of the registration applied for remained unclear within the meaning of the CJEU's judgment and that this constituted an obstacle for registration.

The appeal was therefore dismissed by the Supreme Administrative Court and the Market Court judgment remained unchanged. The new claims made by Hartwall in the Supreme Administrative Court after the judgment of the CJEU, according to which the decisions by the previous instances should be annulled and the trade mark application referred to PRH for registration as a position mark or, failing this, as a figurative trade mark, were not considered by the Supreme Court.[19]

The CJEU ruling confirmed that when applying for a colour mark, the terminology and description of the mark must be accurate already at the application stage. Directive 2008/95, which has now been replaced by Directive 2015/2436, did not establish categories of marks and Member States have the freedom to determine registration procedures as long as they adhere to the harmonised definition of a trade mark and criteria for distinctive character. Since the PRH categorises trade marks as 'colour marks' and 'figurative marks', the lack of clarity of the explanation (the conflict between the description of the application as a colour mark and presentation of the object of application as a position mark) at the application stage was critical in the present case.

Finally, the ruling underlines the CJEU's view that the public perceives colour marks differently from figurative marks. Consumers rarely depend on the colour itself in order to identify a product's or service's commercial origin, but rather the figurative mark incorporating those colours. Furthermore, it needs to be noted that the scope of protection provided to a colour mark differs from the scope of protection conferred to a position mark. Therefore, a trade mark registration needs to be precise and clear in order for the public to be able to understand the scope of exclusive rights conferred by a specific registration.

---

[18] Similarly to Dir. (EU) 2015/2436 of the European Parliament and of the Council of 16 December 2015 to approximate the laws of the Member States relating to trademarks and Reg. (EU) 2017/1001 of the European Parliament and of the Council of 14 June 2017 on the European Union trademark.

[19] The Finnish Supreme Administrative Court judgment KHO:2019:100.

COURT OF *JUSTICE* 2 MAY 2019

ON THE USE OF SIGNS CAPABLE OF EVOKING THE REGION WITH WHICH A PROTECTED PDO IS ASSOCIATED AND WHETHER THE CONCEPT OF THE 'AVERAGE CONSUMER WHO IS REASONABLY WELL INFORMED AND REASONABLY OBSERVANT AND CIRCUMSPECT' REFERS TO EUROPEAN CONSUMERS OR CONSUMERS OF THE MEMBER STATE IN WHICH THE PRODUCT COVERED BY THE PDO IS MADE AND MAINLY CONSUMED

Case C-614/17

Summary and Analysis by Marta Gimeno[1]

Parties:

Fundación Consejo Regulador de la Denominación de Origen Protegida Queso Manchego

v

Industrial Quesera Cuquerella SL (IQC)
Juan Ramón Cuquerella Montagud

1. Background and History

In 2012, the company Industrial Quesera Cuquerella SL ('ICQ') launched several cheeses in Spain using images and references to various iconic characters and elements of La Mancha (a Spanish region), such as Don Quixote, his bony horse or the traditional windmills located there. These products were produced in the area concerned, but not covered by the PDO 'queso manchego'.[2]

The Queso Manchego Foundation, which was in charge of the management and protection of the PDO, decided to bring an infringement action against Juan Ramón Cuquerella Montagud and the IQC before the Spanish commercial courts. By means of this action, the claimant sought a declaration that both the labels used by IQC in order to identify and market the cheeses 'Adarga de Oro'[3], 'Super Rocinante' and 'Rocinante'[4] and the use of the words 'Quesos Rocinante' infringed the PDO 'queso manchego' in that those labels and those words constituted an unlawful evocation of the PDO within the meaning of Article 13(1)(b) of Regulation No 510/2006 of 20 March 2006 on the protection

---

[1] Partner and Head of the Litigation Department of Herrero & Asociados, S.L.

[2] 'Manchego' is a Spanish term that refers to people or products that come from La Mancha.

[3] 'Golden shield' (the word *adarga* is now obsolete in Spanish).

[4] Name of Don Quixote´s horse.

of geographical indications and designations of origin for agricultural products and foodstuffs ('Regulation 520/2006').[5]

The court of first instance dismissed the action on two main grounds:
- the signs and denominations used by IQC were not visually or phonetically similar to the PDOs 'queso manchego' or 'La Mancha'; and
- the use of signs such as the name 'Rocinante' or the image of the literary character Don Quixote de La Mancha evoked the region of La Mancha and not the cheese covered by the PDO 'queso manchego'.

The Foundation appealed against this decision, but without any success: the Superior Court confirmed that the uses carried out by ICQ evoked La Mancha and not necessarily the PDO 'queso manchego'.

Faced with this outcome, the Queso Manchego Foundation decided to file a cassation appeal before the Spanish Supreme Court[6], arguing that all the references to Don Quixote and La Mancha made by the counterparty would evoke in the mind of the consumer the products protected by the PDO 'queso manchego' and that such terms and figurative elements infringed the PDO, since IQC´s products were not covered by it.

In these circumstances, the Spanish Supreme Court decided to stay the proceedings and to refer the following questions to the Court of Justice for a preliminary ruling:

> *'1) Must the evocation of a [PDO], prohibited by Article 13(1)(b) of Regulation No 510/2006 necessarily be brought about by the use of a name visually, phonetically or conceptually similar to the [PDO] or may it be brought about by the use of figurative signs evoking the [PDO]?*
>
> *2) When the [PDO] is of a geographical nature (Article 2(1)(a) of Regulation No 510/2006) and when the products are the same or comparable, can the use of signs evoking the region with which a [PDO] is associated constitute evocation of the [PDO] itself, within the meaning of Article 13(1)(b) of Regulation No 510/2006, which is prohibited even when the user of those signs is a producer established in the region associated with the [PDO], but whose products are not protected by [that PDO]*

[5] Reg. (EC) No 510/2006 of 20 March 2006 on the protection of geographical indications and designations of origin for agricultural products and foodstuffs (*OJ L* 93, 31.3.2006, p. 12-25). This Regulation is no longer in force as it was repealed by Reg. (EU) 2024/1143 of the European Parliament and of the Council of 11 April 2024 on geographical indications for wine, spirit drinks and agricultural products, as well as traditional specialities guaranteed and optional quality terms for agricultural products, amending Regs (EU) No 1308/2013, (EU) 2019/787 and (EU) 2019/1753 and repealing Reg. (EU) No 1151/2012.

[6] Tribunal Supremo.

because they do not meet the requirements set out in the product specification, apart from the geographical provenance?

3) Must the concept of the average consumer who is reasonably well informed and reasonably observant and circumspect, to whose perception the national court has to refer in order to assess whether there is "evocation" within the meaning of Article 13(1)(b) of Regulation No 510/2006, be understood to cover European consumers or can it cover only consumers of the Member State in which the product giving rise to evocation of the protected geographical indication is produced or with which the PDO is geographically associated and in which the product is mainly consumed?'

2. Decision

1. Article 13(1)(b) of Council Regulation (EC) No 510/2006 of 20 March 2006 on the protection of geographical indications and designations of origin for agricultural products and foodstuffs must be interpreted as meaning that a registered name may be evoked through the use of figurative signs.

2. Article 13(1)(b) of Regulation No 510/2006 must be interpreted as meaning that the use of figurative signs evoking the geographical area with which a designation of origin, as referred to in Article 2(1)(a) of that regulation, is associated may constitute evocation of that designation, including where such figurative signs are used by a producer established in that region, but whose products, similar or comparable to those protected by the designation of origin, are not covered by it.

3. The concept of the average consumer who is reasonably well informed and reasonably observant and circumspect, to whose perception the national court has to refer in order to assess whether there is 'evocation' within the meaning of Article 13(1)(b) of Regulation No 510/2006, must be understood as covering European consumers, including consumers of the Member State in which the product giving rise to evocation of the protected name is made or with which that name is geographically associated and in which the product is mainly consumed.

3. Motivation and Analysis

<u>i) First question on whether a registered name can be evoked through the use of figurative signs</u>

By its first question, the referring court asked whether Article 13(1)(b) of Regulation No 510/2006 must be interpreted as meaning that a registered name may be evoked by the use of figurative signs.

According to this specific provision, PDOs are protected against:

> '*(b) any misuse, imitation or evocation, even if the true origin of the product is indicated or if the protected name is translated or accompanied by an expression such as "style", "type", "method", "as produced in", "imitation" or similar;*
>
> *(c) any other false or misleading indication as to the provenance, origin, nature or essential qualities of the product, on the inner or outer packaging, advertising material or documents relating to the product concerned, and the packing of the product in a container liable to convey a false impression as to its origin;*'

In this regard, the CJEU[7] pointed out that the interpretation of EU legislation must be based not only on the text itself, but also on its context and purpose,[8] which in the case of the PDO is to enable consumers to identify correctly the origin and characteristics of the products, as well as to ensure fair competition and grant the products protected by a PDO a certain degree of credibility.[9]

The CJEU recognised that several of its decisions had held that the concept of 'evocation' covers a situation where the term used to designate a product incorporates part of a registered name,[10] but this did not imply that a figurative sign cannot evoke, in the mind of the consumer, products whose designation is protected.[11]

Moreover, the wording of Article 13(1)(b) does not limit the scope of that provision solely to the names of the products covered by those names. On the contrary,

---

7 Para. 16 of the annotated judgment.

8 Case C-325/16, 17 May 2018, *Industrias Químicas del Vallés*, para. 27, and Case C-44/17, 7 June 2018, *Scotch Whisky Association*, para. 27.

9 Recs 5 and 6 of Reg. No 510/2006:
'*[…]. In view of their specific nature, additional special provisions should be adopted for agricultural products and foodstuffs from a defined geographical area requiring producers to use the appropriate Community symbols or indications on packaging. The use of such symbols or indications should be made obligatory in the case of Community designations, on the one hand, to make this category of products and the guarantees attached to them better known to consumers and, on the other, to permit easier identification of these products on the market so as to facilitate checks. A reasonable length of time should be allowed for operators to adjust to this obligation.*
Provision should be made for a Community approach to designations of origin and geographical indications. A framework of Community rules on a system of protection permits the development of geographical indications and designations of origin since, by providing a more uniform approach, such a framework ensures fair competition between the producers of products bearing such indications and enhances the credibility of the products in the consumer's eyes.'

10 Case C-87/97, 4 March 1999, *Consorzio per la tutela del formaggio Gorgonzola*, para. 25.

11 Paras. 18-21 of the annotated judgment.

as the Advocate General[12] pointed out, the provision refers to protection against 'any' evocation, even where the protected designation is accompanied on the packaging of the product concerned by an expression such as 'style', 'type', 'method', 'as produced in' or 'imitation', with the result that figurative elements can indeed fall within the prohibition included in the article.

The decisive criterion is whether, when the consumer is confronted with a disputed image/designation, the image triggered directly in his or her mind is that of the product whose geographical indication is protected.[13]

It should also be noted that one of the purposes of this Regulation is to ensure that the consumer receives clear and precise information about the origin of a product, which can only be guaranteed if possible evocations include figurative elements as well as denominations.

Consequently, the CJEU[14] concluded that a PDO may be evoked through the use of figurative signs, although it reminded the referring court that the decision on the merits of the case (i.e. whether the uses carried out by IQC evoked the PDO 'queso manchego' and therefore constituted an infringement of that PDO) rested with the Spanish court.

ii) Second question: whether the use of figurative signs evoking the geographical area with which a designation of origin is associated may constitute an evocation of that designation

The Court then went on to examine the second question raised by the referring court, which was essentially whether the use of figurative signs evoking the geographical area to which a designation of origin relates may constitute an evocation of that designation, even if those figurative signs are used by a producer established in that region whose products, though similar or comparable to those protected by the designation of origin, are not covered by it.

In this regard, the Court[15] recalled that Regulation No 510/2006[16] does not contain any exception allowing a producer to use figurative signs evoking the geographical area whose name is part of a PDO and, accordingly, allowing it to take unfair advantage of the reputation of that designation. The CJEU's conclusion on this point was blunt: the fact that a producer of similar or comparable

12 Opinion of Advocate General G. Pitruzzella of 10 January 2019, para. 28.

13 Para. 21 and Case C-44/17, 7 June 2018, *Scotch Whisky Association*, para. 5.

14 Para. 32 of the annotated judgment.

15 Para. 34 and 35 of the annotated judgment.

16 In this sense, Art. 13 1(b) of the Reg. states:
'*Registered names shall be protected against: [...](b)any misuse, imitation or evocation, even if the true origin of the product is indicated or if the protected name is translated or accompanied by an expression such as "style", "type", "method", "as produced in", "imitation" or similar.*'

products to those protected by a designation of origin is established in a geographical area associated with that designation cannot exclude that producer from the scope of Article 13(1)(b) of Regulation No 510/2006.[17]

Once again, and before proceeding with the analysis of the last referred question, the Court highlighted that it was for the referring court[18] (in this case, the Spanish Supreme Court) to decide whether the use of the controversial signs (i.e. the illustrations of a character resembling Don Quixote de La Mancha, a bony horse and landscapes with windmills and sheep) were capable of creating conceptual proximity with the PDO 'queso manchego', with the result that the image immediately produced in the consumer's mind was that of the product protected by that PDO.

The Court explained that, in determining whether there was an infringement, the national court must primarily consider how consumers were likely to react. This involved establishing whether a connection was likely to be made between the disputed elements, such as figurative signs representing a geographical area, and a registered name. The national court should evaluate if this link was clear enough to associate the registered name directly with the presence of these elements. The assessment hinged on whether there was clear conceptual proximity between the disputed signs and the protected designation of origin (PDO), in this case, 'queso manchego', which referred to the La Mancha region. Specifically, the national court needed to ascertain if the figurative signs, including illustrations reminiscent of Don Quixote, a horse, windmills, and sheep, were capable of creating a direct association with 'queso manchego'. It might also consider the necessity of examining all figurative and word signs on the products to make an informed decision, as suggested by the Advocate General.[19]

<u>iii) Third question: whether the concept of the average consumer, to whose perception the national court has to refer, must be understood as covering European consumers or only consumers of the Member State in which the product is made or mainly consumed</u>

Finally, the referring court asked whether the concept of the average consumer who is reasonably well informed and reasonably observant and circumspect, to whose perception the national court must refer in order to assess whether there is 'evocation', must be understood as covering European consumers or only consumers of the Member State in which the product giving rise to the alleged evocation of the protected name is manufactured or with which that name is geographically associated and in which that product is mainly consumed.

---

[17] Para. 36 of the annotated judgment.

[18] Para. 37 of the annotated judgment.

[19] Paras. 38-42 of the annotated judgment.

In this regard, the Court[20] indicated that it had already held that, in order to determine whether there is an 'evocation' of a registered geographical indication, the referring court must ascertain whether, when confronted with the disputed designation, the *average European consumer* who is reasonably well informed and reasonably observant and circumspect, immediately conjures up in his or her mind the image of the product whose geographical indication is protected.[21]

The CJEU[22] recalled that Article 16(b) of Regulation No 110/2008 protects registered geographical indications against any evocation *throughout the territory of the European Union* and that it covers all European consumers.[23]

Thus, as the Advocate General[24] correctly observed, while the effective and uniform protection of registered names means that circumstances which may lead to the conclusion that there is no 'evocation' in relation to consumers in only one Member State must be disregarded, that does not mean, on the other hand, that evocation assessed in relation to consumers of a single Member State is not sufficient to trigger the protection provided in Article 13(1)(b) of Regulation No 510/2006.

Once again, the CJEU[25] stated that it was for the referring court to assess whether both the figurative and word elements of the product at issue in the main proceedings evoked the image of a registered name *in the minds of the consumers in Spain* (the country where the products were produced and mainly consumed); if this was the case, those elements must be protected against evocation wherever it might occur *throughout the territory of the European Union.*

Finally, the CJEU[26] concluded that the concept of the average consumer, to whose perception the national court must refer in order to assess whether there is 'evocation', must be understood as covering European consumers, including consumers of the Member State in which the product giving rise to alleged evocation of the protected name is made or with which that name is geographically associated and in which the product is mainly consumed.

* *
*

---

20 Para. 45 of the annotated judgment.

21 See, to that effect Case C-44/17, 7 June 2018, *Scotch Whisky Association*, para. 56.

22 Para. 46 of the annotated judgment.

23 Case C-75/15, 21 January 2016, *Viiniverla*, paras. 27 and 28, and Case C-44/17, 7 June 2018, *Scotch Whisky Association*, para. 59

24 Opinion of Advocate General G. Pitruzzella of 10 January 2019, para. 51.

25 Para. 49 of the annotated judgment.

26 Para. 50 of the annotated judgment.

Having taken note of this decision of the CJEU, the Spanish Supreme Court, in its ruling dated 18 July 2019,[27] unsurprisingly concluded that the figurative elements consisting of the figure of Don Quixote, windmills, etc. had a sufficiently direct and unequivocal conceptual proximity to the region of La Mancha, so that the sight of these signs on a cheese, as a reference image, caused the consumer to think of the PDO 'queso manchego'.

As a result, the defendants were obliged to cease the use of the controversial labelling in the course of trade.

One striking feature of this particular case was that ICQ had held the registered trademark RACIONERO since 1968 (earlier than the PDO), which the Supreme Court did not take into account in its ruling.

As for the future of PDOs in general, this ruling will undoubtedly be an extremely important milestone in the fight against labelling which, subtly and with the intention of misleading consumers, includes graphic elements, symbols, maps, and other figurative elements directly linked to geographical areas associated with products of different quality.

---

27 STS 451/2019, 18 July 2019 on proceeding 3250/2014.

Court of Justice 12 June 2019

On what effect a disclaimer should have on the extent of protection of an earlier trade mark when likelihood of confusion is evaluated in relation to a younger trade mark application

Case C-705/17

Summary and Analysis by Claes Agnvall[1]

Parties:

Patent- och registreringsverket (PRV)

v

Mats Hansson

1. Background and History

On 16 December 2015 Mr Mats Hansson filed an application for a national trade mark registration for the word mark ROSLAGSÖL for goods in Class 32, including non-alcoholic beverages and beers. On 14 July 2016 the PRV (Swedish Patent and Registration Office) rejected the application because it considered there to be a likelihood of confusion with the following earlier figurative national trade mark, registered in 2007 by the Swedish company Norrtelje Brenneri Aktiebolag for alcoholic beverages:

The PRV reasoned that the signs started with the descriptive term ROSLAGS and that this dominant element would not be outweighed by other words or figurative elements in the signs. Since the signs furthermore referred to similar or identical goods, the PRV concluded that there was a likelihood of confusion.

---

1 Claes Agnvall is senior partner at the Swedish law firm Zacco.

The earlier registration was accompanied by a disclaimer, stating that no exclusive right was granted over the word *RoslagsPunsch*. The PRV had requested the disclaimer as a condition for registration, since 'Roslags'[2] refers to a geographical area of Sweden and 'Punsch'[3] is the name of an alcoholic beverage.

Mr Hansson appealed the decision of the PRV of 2016 before the Swedish Patents and Market Court and claimed that there was no likelihood of confusion between the signs in question. The PRV argued before the Patents and Market Court that an element of a registration which had been excluded from protection by means of a disclaimer should in principle be regarded as not distinctive. It noted that the disclaimer requested in the earlier registration had been granted because the trade mark included a term that was descriptive of a geographical region, 'Roslags'.[4]

However, in view of the CJEU's judgment of 4 May 1999 in the Windsurfing Chiemsee case[5], the practice of the PRV regarding the non-distinctive character of geographical names had developed in the meantime.[6] Geographical names could now be considered as distinctive and the term 'Roslags' could in itself be capable of registration as a trade mark. As such, it could influence the overall impression created by the earlier mark and its scope of protection. The PRV held that the relevant trade could perceive the relevant signs as originating from the same commercial source.

Contrary to the position of the PRV, the Patents and Market Court concluded that there was no likelihood of confusion and approved the registration of Mr Hansson's sign as a trade mark. The purpose of the disclaimer was according to the court, to clarify that the exclusive right did not extend to the words as such. Despite the disclaimer, the words should be considered when evaluating the likelihood of confusion as they could influence the overall perception of the earlier sign.

The PRV appealed the decision to the Patents and Market Court of Appeal, Stockholm, Sweden.[7]

In the view of the Patents and Market Court of Appeal (the referring court), the substantive rules on the protection of national trade marks were in principle fully harmonised in EU law. This was confirmed by the implementation of

---

2 Roslags would be understood as something referring to or originating from the Roslagen region in Sweden.

3 Punsch is a type of liqueur in Sweden

4 Para. 22 of the annotated judgment.

5 Cases C-108/97 and C-109/97, 4 May 1999, *Windsurfing Chiemsee*, paras. 31 and 32

6 Case 10/292, *Nacka Forum*, 30 December 2011, the Swedish Court of Patent Appeals.

7 Para. 24 of the annotated judgment.

Directive 2008/95[8] and related case-law. However, procedural rules lay within the competence of the Member States.

The referring court therefore asked if a national rule allowing a disclaimer to be made could be considered as a *procedural rule* even if it could have the effect of changing the criteria used in the global assessment of the likelihood of confusion within the meaning of Article 4(1)(b) of said directive.[9]

In respect of the settled case-law of the CJEU according to which the assessment of the likelihood of confusion must be based on an overall impression and the perceptions of consumers played a dominant part in the global assessment of that likelihood, the Patent and Market Court of Appeal was uncertain if it could interpret Article 4(1)(b) of Directive 2008/95 as meaning that a disclaimer could affect that assessment because it expressly excluded an element of the earlier trade mark from protection at the time of registration, so that that element must be given less importance in the analysis of the overall impression than it would have had in the absence of the disclaimer.

If the Directive 2008/95 precluded a disclaimer from influencing the overall assessment by giving an element less importance, the question would then arise whether the Directive could allow a disclaimer to have the effect that the element to which it related should be considered not to have been subject of the registration of the earlier trade mark? If this were allowed, did this mean that the element to which the disclaimer related did not enjoy the protection of that mark, so that it could be excluded from the analysis of the likelihood of confusion within the meaning of Article 4(1)(b) of the Directive 2008/95? In addition, the referring court noted that the effect of a disclaimer in national case-law was not uniformly assessed when evaluating the likelihood of confusion according to Article 4(1)(b) of the Directive 2008/95. It further noted that the practice of the EUIPO when applying the now repealed Article 37(2)[10] of

---

8 Dir. 2008/95/EC of the European Parliament and of the Council of 22 October 2008 to approximate the laws of the Member States relating to trade marks, *OJ L* 299, p. 25-33. Dir. 2008/95 is no longer in force as it has been replaced by Dir. 2015/2436 of 16 December 2015 to approximate the laws of the Member States relating to trade marks, *OJ L* 336, p. 1-26.

9 Para. 25 of the annotated judgment. Art. 4(1)(b) Dir. 2008/95 states that: '*A trade mark shall not be registered or, if registered, shall be liable to be declared invalid if because of its identity with, or similarity to, the earlier trade mark and the identity or similarity of the goods or services covered by the trade marks, there exists a likelihood of confusion on the part of the public; the likelihood of confusion includes the likelihood of association with the earlier trade mark.*'

10 Art 37.2 was repealed through Reg. 2015/2424 of the European Parliament and of the Council of 16 December 2015 amending Council Reg. (EC) No 207/2009 on the Community trade mark and Commission Regulation (EC) No 2868/95 implementing Council Regulation (EC) No 40/94 on the Community trade mark, and repealing Commission Regulation (EC) No 2869/95 on the fees payable to the Office for Harmonization in the Internal Market, *OJ L* 341, p. 21-94.

Regulation 207/2009[11] reflected the view that the excluded element was devoid of any distinctive character.

Under those circumstances, the Patents and Market Court of Appeal decided to stay the proceedings and to refer the following questions to the Court of Justice for a preliminary ruling:

> *'(1) Must Article 4(1)(b) of [Directive 2008/95] be interpreted as meaning that the global assessment of all relevant factors which is to be made in an assessment of the likelihood of confusion may be affected by the fact that an element of the trade mark has expressly been excluded from protection on registration, that is to say, that a so-called disclaimer has been entered on registration?*
>
> *(2) If the answer to the first question is in the affirmative, can the disclaimer in such a case affect the global assessment in such a way that the competent authority has regard to the element in question but gives it a more limited importance so that it is not regarded as being distinctive, even if the element would de facto be distinctive and prominent in the earlier trade mark?*
>
> *(3) If the answer to the first question is in the affirmative and the answer to the second question in the negative, can the disclaimer even so affect the global assessment in any other way?'*

2. Decision

Article 4(1)(b) of Directive 2008/95/EC of the European Parliament and of the Council of 22 October 2008 to approximate the laws of the Member States relating to trade marks must be interpreted as precluding national legislation making provision for a disclaimer whose effect would be to exclude an element of a complex trade mark, referred to in that disclaimer, from the global analysis of the relevant factors for showing the existence of a likelihood of confusion within the meaning of that provision, or to attribute to such an element, in advance and permanently, limited importance in that analysis.

3. Motivation and Analysis

Before delving into the matter at hand, the Court reiterated the fundamental role of a trade mark: to ensure that consumers can reliably identify the origin

---

11 Council Regulation (EC) No 207/2009 of 26 February 2009 on the Community trade mark *OJ L 78*, p. 1-42.

of goods or services, thereby distinguishing them clearly from those originating elsewhere, without any potential for confusion.[12]

The Court noted that Directive 2008/95 primarily concerns trade marks for goods or services in respect of which a registration or application process occurs within a Member State. The Directive aims to harmonise national laws that significantly impact the internal market. It is fundamental that uniform protection for registered trade marks across all Member States is ensured, while allowing flexibility for Member States to determine *procedural aspects*, including registration conditions.[13]

The Court stated that Directive 2008/95 neither requires Member States to implement provisions in their national laws allowing the registration of a trade mark accompanied by a disclaimer, nor prohibits them from doing so. Additionally, Directive 2008/95 does not detail the impact such a disclaimer would have on assessing the likelihood of confusion as per its requirements.[14]

Provided that a disclaimer would not risk undermining the effectiveness of the provisions of the Directive by which proprietors of earlier rights are given protection against signs which could give rise to a likelihood of confusion, the CJEU stated that Member States are in principle free to allow disclaimers in their national law. However, such a disclaimer must not conflict with or call into question the objectives expressed in Directive 2008/95.[15]

The Court underscored that the risk of confusion meant the risk of a belief arising in the common origin of goods or services, as per Article 4(1)(b) of Directive 2008/95.

With respect to the analysis of the likelihood of confusion within the meaning of Article 4(1)(b) of Directive 2008/95 and the influence a disclaimer could have on it, the referring court in the present case set out three possible effects of a disclaimer.[16] National law could thus be interpreted in the following three ways according to the referring court:

1. The element of a complex mark which is subject to a disclaimer should be excluded from the analysis of likelihood of confusion.

---

[12] Para. 31 of the annotated judgment.

[13] Case C-348/04, 26 April 2007, *Boerhringer Ingelheim and others*, paras. 58 and 59; Cases C-217/13 and C-218/13, 19 June 2014, *Oberbank and others*, paras. 66 and 67; Case C-482/09, 22 September 2011, *Budějovický Budvar*, paras. 30 and 32.

[14] Para. 36 of the annotated judgment.

[15] Paras. 37-38 of the annotated judgment.

[16] Para. 39 of the annotated judgment.

2. The element subject to a disclaimer should be taken into consideration in such an analysis, but its importance must be limited even if it is the distinctive or dominant element of that mark.

3. The element subject to a disclaimer should be taken into account in the analysis of the likelihood of confusion in a manner consistent with the principles applicable to that analysis identified in the settled case-law of the Court.

The Court recalled that a likelihood of confusion within the meaning of Article 4(1)(b) of Directive 2008/95 exists when there is a risk that the public might believe that the goods or services in question come from the same undertaking or, as the case may be, from economically linked undertakings.[17]

The existence of likelihood of confusion depends on numerous elements.[18] Settled case-law points in particular to the recognition of the trade mark on the market, the association which may be made with the used or registered sign, the degree of similarity between the trade mark and the sign and the degree of similarity between the goods or services identified. A global assessment taking into account all relevant factors in a particular case is thus required to identify the likelihood of confusion.[19] A further factor to consider is the distinctiveness of the earlier mark, as this determines the scope of protection.[20] The likelihood of confusion will be greater the more distinctive the earlier mark is.[21]

A global assessment of the likelihood of confusion implies some interdependence between the relevant factors.[22] In particular, the degree of similarity between the signs and between the goods or services is relevant. Consequently, a lesser degree of similarity between those goods or services may be offset by a greater degree of similarity between the trade marks, and vice versa.[23]

In addition, according to the Court's case-law, the weak distinctiveness of a trade mark does not exclude the likelihood of confusion, in particular where the signs and the goods and services covered are similar.[24]

---

[17] Para. 40 of the annotated judgment. Case C-39/97, 29 September 1998, *Canon*, para. 29; Case C-591-12 P, 8 May 2014, *Bimbo v OHIM*, para. 19.

[18] Para. 41 of the of the annotated judgment.

[19] Case C-39/97, 29 September 1998, *Canon*, para. 16; Case C-342/97, 22 June 1999, *Lloyd Schuhfabrik Meyer*, para. 18; Case C-102/07, 10 April 2008, *adidas and adidas Benelux*, para. 19.

[20] Para. 42 of the annotated judgment.

[21] Case C-43/15, 8 November 2016, *BSH v EUIPO*, para. 62.

[22] Para. 43 of the annotated judgment.

[23] Case C-39/97, 29 September 1998, *Canon*, para. 17; Case C-342/97, 22 June 1999, *Lloyd Schuhfabrik Meyer*, para. 19.

[24] Para. 44 of the annotated judgment. Case C-43/15, 8 November 2016, *BSH v EUIPO*, para. 63.

In respect of the similarity between the signs the global assessment must be based on the overall impression created by them taking into consideration their visual, phonetic, and conceptual similarity.[25] The perception of the signs by the average consumer plays a decisive role; moreover, the Court noted that the average consumer perceives a mark as whole[26] and does not analyse its various details.[27]

On the basis of these principles the Court dealt with the first possible effect of a disclaimer as set out by the referring court, namely that '*the element of a complex mark which is subject of a disclaimer should be excluded from the analysis of likelihood of confusion.*' The Court stated that such an interpretation would not be compatible with the requirements of Article 4(1)(b) of Directive 2008/95 reasoning that an exclusion from the analysis of likelihood of confusion would lead to an incorrect assessment both of the similarity between the signs at issue and of the distinctiveness of the earlier trade mark, and hence to a distorted global assessment, in particular as those factors considered in the overall assessment are interdependent.[28]

Dealing with the factor 'assessment of similarity' first, the Court recalled that one cannot take a single component of a complex mark and compare it with another mark: on the contrary, the marks should be compared as whole taking into account their distinctive and dominant elements.[29,30] One must analyse the relative weights of the components of a sign in the eyes of the public in order to determine the overall impression it makes. It follows that descriptive elements of signs cannot by default be excluded from the assessment of similarity.[31,32]

---

25 Para. 43 of the annotated judgment.

26 Thus, it is imperative to scrutinise the elements of a sign and their respective significance in public perception, to ascertain the overall impression created by the signs in question, considering the specific circumstances of each case.

27 Case C-251, 11 November 1997, *Sabel*, para. 23; Case-342/97, 22 June 1999, *Lloyd Schuhfabrik Meyer*, para. 25.

28 Para 47 of the annotated judgment.

29 Para 48 of the annotated judgment.

30 See further the Opinion of Advocate General Pitruzzella, 6 March 2019, para. 31 for a summary of factors for assessing degree of similarity.

31 Para. 49 of the annotated judgment.

32 See further the Opinion of Advocate General Pitruzzella, 6 March 2019, para 38: '*[...] given that the rules relating to perception must be observed in the assessment of the similarity between conflicting signs and the fact that that assessment must be strictly objective, I think the existence of a disclaimer covering just one element of a mark for which protection is sought should not alter the parameters of that assessment: it should result in neither the exclusion of that element from consideration, nor the attribution to that element of a value within the sign or a distinctive character other than that which it actually has. The determination, through a synthesis of all the factors, of the overall impression conveyed by the mark as a whole must, even in such a case, be arrived at solely by reference to the perception of the relevant public.*'

Second, in respect of the factor 'distinctiveness', the Court's case-law indicates that the level of distinctiveness depends on the inherent characteristics of the mark, considering the presence or absence of descriptive elements in relation to the goods or services concerned.[33] The power of a mark to identify goods or services and to identify a commercial origin must be assessed in relation to the mark as a whole with all its components.[34] The exclusion of an element of a mark from the analysis of distinctiveness could thus have an effect on the extent of protection of the mark.[35,36]

Turning to the second possible effect of a disclaimer which the referring court had set out, namely that the element that is the subject of a disclaimer should be taken into consideration in such an analysis, but its importance must be limited even if it is the distinctive or dominant element of that mark, the Court stated by analogy with paragraphs 48 to 51 of its judgment that it would be incompatible with Article 4(1)(b) of Directive 2008/95 for national law to lead to a practice where such an element was automatically considered to lack distinctiveness, with the consequence that it was given limited importance in the analysis of likelihood of confusion.[37]

The Court clarified first that weakly distinctive elements of a complex mark, irrespective of whether they had been mentioned in a disclaimer or not, would generally be given less weight than more distinctive elements when analysing the

---

33 Case C-342/97, 22 June 1999, *Lloyd Schuhfabrik Meyer*, paras. 20, 22 and 23.

34 See further the Opinion of Advocate General Pitruzzella, 6 March 2019, para. 43, where he states '*To expunge from that assessment one of the elements of a complex mark, or to ascribe to it a weight other than that which it actually has, could affect the global assessment of the identifying power of the mark. That identifying power depends of how capable the sign is of conveying a message which the public will associate with the goods of services covered. While that message will be conveyed principally by the more distinctive and dominant elements of the mark, it is with reference to the sign viewed as a whole, and therefore in the light of all of its components, that it is necessary to evaluate its capacity to identify the origin of the goods or services.*'

35 Para. 51 of the annotated judgment.

36 See further the Opinion of Advocate General Pitruzzella, 6 March 2019, para. 47: '*To exclude from the assessment of the degree of distinctiveness of a mark which must be carried out when assessing the likelihood of confusion pertaining to one of its elements for the sole reason that, in the examination that was carried out at the time of registration, that element was regarded as devoid of distinctive character, thus necessitating the use of a disclaimer, would mean that no account could be taken of how the perception of the mark might have changed between the time when it was registered and the time when the assessment of the likelihood of confusion is carried out, or indeed of any other factor arising subsequently to registration that could influence that assessment.*'

37 Para. 52 of the annotated judgment.

similarity between the signs.[38] It recalled, however, that the analysis could not be subject to general presumptions and that the individual assessment of each sign in order to determine its overall impression must be made in light of the particular circumstances of the case.[39]

Further, in the global assessment of likelihood of confusion, the Court accepted that the likelihood of confusion was not often found where the signs to be compared coincided in an element that was weakly distinctive for the relevant goods or services. However, the Court added that a finding of likelihood of confusion could not be ruled out in advance, as consideration had to be given to the interdependence of the relevant factors of the case.[40,41]

It followed that even though the relevant public's perception of elements of marks which were the subject of a disclaimer would sometimes be consistent with a possible general rule whereby limited weight would be afforded to the disclaimed element, this would not always be the case.[42] Should there be such a general rule as suggested by the referring court, this could lead to situations where younger marks could be registered despite being perceived as causing a likelihood of confusion among the relevant public in accordance with Article 4(1)(b) of Directive 2008/95.

In view of the Court's interpretations of the first and second possible effects, the Court finally touched upon the question of whether it would be incorrect to take a disclaimed element of a mark into consideration when evaluating likelihood of confusion according to the principles behind Article 4(1)(b) of Directive 2008/95. The Court's interpretation could be alleged to lead to a situation where an element of mark covered by a disclaimer would enjoy a protection it could not have.[43]

The Court stated however that its interpretations could not be called into question for that reason. This was because a finding of likelihood of confusion granted protection for a combination of elements of a mark, and should an element

---

38 Para. 53 of the annotated judgment; Case C-251, 11 November 1997, *Sabel*, para. 23; Case C-235/05 P, 27 April 2006, L'Oreal vs. OHIM, not published, para. 43.

39 Para. 54 of the annotated judgment; Case C-591/12 P, 8 May 2014, *Bimbo vs. OHIM*, para. 36

40 Case C-42/12 P, 29 November, *Hrbek v OHIM*, not published, para. 63; Case C-42/15 P, 8 November 2016, *BHS v EUIPO*, paras. 48 and 61-64.

41 See also the Opinion of Advocate General Pitruzzella, 6 March 2019, para. 48, where he stated that to exclude an element from the global assessment '*would not only stand in the way of determining the identifying power of the mark in current, effective and specific terms, as is required for the purposes of examining of the likelihood of confusion, but could also, given the interdependence of the various factors that enter into consideration, result in an incorrect appraisal of the likelihood of confusion.*'

42 Para. 56 of the annotated judgment.

43 Para. 57 of the annotated judgment.

covered by a disclaimer be one of the elements in that combination it would not be protected as such.[44] Consequently, a complex mark would not confer an exclusive right to a sole element, whether that sole element was subject to a disclaimer or not. In addition to this, and referring to the Opinion of the Advocate General,[45] the Court stressed that Article 3(1)(c) of the Directive 2008/95 in any case ensured that marks consisting only of descriptive terms would not be registered or could be invalidated and could therefore be freely used by other economic operators.[46] A further argument in support of the CJEU's interpretation was that it followed from Article 6(1)(b) of the Directive 2008/95 that the exclusive right conferred by a mark did not allow the holder to prohibit third parties from using descriptive indications for the relevant goods or services.[47]

As a final argument in support of its interpretations, the CJEU stressed that the same protection for a sign against likelihood of confusion must be provided in all Member States and that the analysis of a likelihood of confusion should be based on the same criteria. Directive 2008/95 warrants a unified practice in the Member States which was highly relevant in the case under consideration, as some states did not offer the possibility to register trademarks with a disclaimer, and if they did, the effect of disclaimers may vary.[48]

With the above considerations the CJEU confirmed that the third possible interpretation as outlined by the referring court reflected an approach supported by Article 4(1)(b) of Directive 2008/95 and the case-law developed by the CJEU.

* *
*

Both the CJEU's judgment and the Advocate General's Opinion[49] state that Member States are in principle free to have provisions in their national law allowing disclaimers. However, a disclaimer must not negatively influence the process of finding a likelihood of confusion in accordance with Directive 2008/95;

---

[44] Para. 58 of the annotated judgment; see, by analogy, orders Cases C579/08 P, 15 January 2010, *Messer Group v Air Products and Chemicals*, para. 73 and C-422/12 P, 30 January 2014, *Industrias Alen v The Clorox Company*, para. 45.

[45] Case C-705/17, 6 March 2019, Opinion of Advocate General Pitruzzella, para. 26, where the Advocate General referred to Art. 6 (1)(b) of the Dir. 2008/95 and pointed out in general terms that descriptive elements of a complex mark '– *which are not in themselves registrable as trade marks – remain available for use even if they are elements of a composite or complex sign that has been registered as a mark*.'

[46] Para. 59 of the annotated judgment.

[47] Para. 60 of the annotated judgment; Cases C-108/97 and C-109/97, 4 May 1999, *Windsurfing Chiemsee*, paras. 25 and 28; and C-102/07, 10 April 2008, *adidas AG and adidas Benelux*, paras. 46 and 47; and C-51/10 P, 10 March 2011, *Agencja Wydawnicza Technopol*, paras. 59 and 62.

[48] Para 61 of the annotated judgment.

[49] Case C-705/17, 6 March 2019, Opinion of Advocate General Pitruzzella, para. 26.

in particular, it should not influence the protection given to holders of earlier rights when analysed in relation to younger marks. Equally important is that the conditions for obtaining registration of a trade mark are the same in all Member States and that equal protection is offered for trade marks under the legal systems in all Member States.

The CJEU judgment, which is firmly grounded in Article 4(1)(b) of Directive 2008/95 and other provisions, navigates through all relevant aspects of the subject matter and reaches a finding that defines the effects of a disclaimer on the examination of the likelihood of confusion. This clarifies that descriptive elements of a complex mark, whether they are covered by a disclaimer or not, will be equally considered in all Member States based on established case-law in combination with the interpretation of Directive 2008/95.

In view of the CJEU judgment, it is natural to wonder if there is any future for provisions allowing disclaimers. A disclaimer may well serve its purpose at the time when an application is examined on absolute grounds, making it clear that in complex marks certain elements do not meet the threshold for adding distinctiveness to a sign. Such a disclaimer will thus clarify the elements on which the registration is actually based, and provide useful information for anyone analysing the registration and seeking to understand the reasoning behind the official examination.

In the past, disclaimers were frequently recorded by the PRV as soon as there were verbal elements in the signs which lacked distinctiveness. The purpose was to clarify the basis of registration.

The practice of requesting disclaimers has however changed over time and the PRV's practice of requesting disclaimers could be described today as almost obsolete. One reason for this is that a disclaimer adds little leverage except at the time for registration and is of no use in subsequent scenarios such as analysis of likelihood of confusion. In the process of analysing a likelihood of confusion and with the influence of the Directive 2008/95 and EU case-law, which stresses the global assessment, the disclaimer has no purpose since all the relevant factors of the case, including the level of distinctiveness, will be analysed on their own merits. The CJEU judgment is therefore welcome as it clarifies the non-existent role of a disclaimer in relation to assessments of likelihood of confusion.

Less and less use of disclaimers will probably be made in future. The Patents and Market Court of Appeal concluded in view of the CJEU judgment that a disclaimer lacked independent legal effect. The Swedish court continued with a question in its judgment if the rule should remain in the Trade Mark Act.[50] Its existence in law might only lead to misunderstandings and problems regarding

[50] Case PMÖÅ 9778-16, 16 March 2020, Patents and Market Appeal Court, *Roslagsöl / Roslags Punch*, p. 8, para. 5.

how and when it should be applied. Whether or not the rule should be removed is a question for the legislature, but, in my personal opinion, there is no reason for keeping it.

On the topic of the future of disclaimers, the CJEU judgment was also important as practice with regard to distinctiveness is not static, but constantly under development.[51] The registration for ROSLAGS PUNSCH was a good example of this. Geographical indications such as ROSLAGS had earlier been considered to lack distinctiveness; under a change of approach[52] in accordance with the CJEU judgment in Windsurfing Chiemsee,[53] they are now considered distinctive provided the geographical indication will not be associated by the relevant trade with the goods/services in question and that such a connection is not likely in the future. Since ROSLAGS is not connected with alcoholic beverages, and is not likely to be so connected in the future, that element of the sign should be attributed distinctive character contrary to what the existing disclaimer might say. The correctness of the CJEU judgment is clear from this example: ROSLAGS must be interpreted on its own merits and in line with the considerations behind Article 4(1)(b) of Directive 2008/95 despite the existence of a disclaimer.[54]

A further consideration which conveys the importance of the CJEU's finding is that the perception of signs by the average consumer of the goods or services in question plays a decisive role in the global assessment of the likelihood of confusion. As pointed out in paragraph 56 of the annotated judgment, in some situations the perception of signs by the relevant public could be consistent with a disclaimer in a complex trade mark whereby an element is held to be non-distinctive. However, this will not necessarily be so in every case. The public's perception of a sign as strong/distinctive in respect of a particular element that is subject to a disclaimer could lead to a situation where, if disclaimers are taken into account in the analysis of likelihood of confusion, a younger sign could be accepted for registration despite there being a likelihood of confusion in the eyes of the public.[55]

---

51 See also Opinion of Advocate General Pitruzzella, 6 March 2019, paras. 44 and in particular 45: '*Indeed, it cannot be ruled out that an element of a complex mark which, at the time when the mark was registered, was devoid of distinctive character, being merely descriptive, will have become distinctive with the passage of time, for example, as a result of the use that has been made of the mark, and especially where the importance within the mark of the element in question is not merely negligible or even dominates the overall impression which the mark conveys to the relevant public.*'

52 Case-10/292, 30 December 2011, *Nacka Forum*, Swedish Court of Patent Appeals.

53 Cases C-108/97 & C-109/97, 4 May 1999, *Windsurfing Chiemsee*, paras. 31-32.

54 See also Opinion of Advocate General Pitruzzella, 6 March 2019, para 46.

55 Para 56 of the annotated judgment.

Court of Justice 29 July 2019

On the concept of samples as reproductions and infringement of the phonogram producer's exclusive rights

Case C-476/17

Summary and Analysis by Julia Selbmann[1]

Parties:

Pelham GmbH
Moses Pelham
Martin Haas

v

Ralf Hütter
Florian Schneider-Esleben

1. Background and History

Ralf Hütter and Florian Schneider-Esleben ('Hütter and Others') are the founders of the German electropop band Kraftwerk. In 1977, Kraftwerk released a phonogram featuring a song called 'Metall auf Metall'; Hütter and Others were the producers of the phonogram as well as the performers of the song. In 1997, Pelham GmbH, a company governed by German law, produced and released a phonogram featuring a song written by Moses Pelham and Martin Haas ('Pelham and Others'). In this song, two seconds of a rhythm sequence from the song 'Metall auf Metall' were copied, slowed down, and incorporated ('sampled') as a continuous loop without consent from Hütter and Others.

Hütter and Others claimed that Pelham and Others had infringed the related right they held as producers of the phonogram in question under Paragraph 85(1) of the German Act on Copyright and Related Rights Act (UrhG)[2] transposing

---

1 Julia Selbmann, LL.M. is an IP/Commercial lawyer at the German law firm GÖRG Partnerschaft von Rechtsanwälten mbB and is a member of the Berlin Bar.

2 Para. 85(1) sentence 1 of the German Copyright and Related Rights Act states: '*The producer of an audio recording has the exclusive right to reproduce, distribute and make available to the public that audio recording.*'

Article 2(c) of Directive 2001/29/EC[3] and Article 9 of Directive 2006/115/EC,[4] and thus requested termination of the infringements, damages, provision of information and surrender of the phonograms for the purposes of destruction.

The Regional Court of Hamburg as court of first instance upheld the action in 2004; the appeal brought by Pelham and Others was unsuccessful. According to the courts, the law does not provide for a minimum threshold for the extraction of sound parts, which means that every sampling is also an infringement.

Upon appeal on a point of law, the German Federal Court of Justice annulled the decision of the appeal court (Higher Regional Court of Hamburg) and referred the matter back to it for further examination with regard to the sampling in question potentially being so-called free use of the work. According to the old version of Paragraph 24 UrhG, artists were allowed to use copyrighted works as inspiration for their own works without the author's consent if the used work 'faded', i.e. differed enough from the new work. The German Federal Court of Justice applied this principle by analogy to the related rights of producers of a phonogram. However, it established an exception to this free use where the artist using the sample could have recreated and recorded the sequence with reasonable effort and therefore was not dependent on the use of an existing work. The reason behind this exception was the consideration of property rights protected under Article 14 of the German Basic Law (GG) of the producer on the one hand and artistic freedom protected under Article 5, Section 3 GG on the other.

Based on this exception, the appeal court dismissed the appeal again in 2011, claiming Pelham and Others could have recorded the sequence themselves. Upon a second appeal on a point of law, the German Federal Court of Justice dismissed the appeal in 2012, confirming that Pelham and Others did not depend on using the sample.

However, this decision was annulled by the German Federal Constitutional Court, which referred the matter back to the German Federal Court of Justice. The German Federal Constitutional Court found an unjustified violation of Pelham and Others' artistic freedom due to the restrictive application of Paragraph 24 UrhG (old version) and the exception established by the Constitutional Court: sampling must also be possible and thus count as free use, even

---

3 Dir. 2001/29/EC on the harmonisation of certain aspects of copyright and related rights in the information society, Art. 2(c) states: '*Member States shall provide for the exclusive right to authorise or prohibit direct or indirect, temporary or permanent reproduction by any means and in any form, in whole or in part: […] (c) for phonogram producers, of their phonograms.*'

4 Dir. 2006/115/EC on rental right and lending right and on certain rights related to copyright in the field of intellectual property, Art. 9(1): '*Member States shall provide the exclusive right to make available to the public, by sale or otherwise, the objects indicated in points (a) to (d), including copies thereof, hereinafter 'the distribution right': […] (b) for phonogram producers, in respect of their phonograms.*'

if a sound sequence could be recreated, if the sampling was not (economically) detrimental to the property of the author/producer of the older work, as is the case with very short rhythm sequences.

In those circumstances, the German Federal Court of Justice decided to stay the proceedings and to refer the following questions to the Court of Justice for a preliminary ruling:

> '1. *Is there an infringement of the phonogram producer's exclusive right under Article 2(c) of Directive 2001/29 to reproduce its phonogram if very short audio snatches are taken from its phonogram and transferred to another phonogram?*
>
> 2. *Is a phonogram which contains very short audio snatches transferred from another phonogram a copy of the other phonogram within the meaning of Article 9(1)(b) of Directive 2006/115?*
>
> 3. *Can the Member States enact a provision which – in the manner of Paragraph 24(1) of [the UrhG] – inherently limits the scope of protection of the phonogram producer's exclusive right to reproduce (Article 2(c) of Directive 2001/29) and to distribute (Article 9(1)(b) of Directive 2006/115) its phonogram in such a way that an independent work created in free use of its phonogram may be exploited without the phonogram producer's consent?*
>
> 4. *Can it be said that a work or other subject matter is being used for quotation purposes within the meaning of Article 5(3)(d) of Directive 2001/29 if it is not evident that another person's work or another person's sdubject matter is being used?*
>
> 5. *Do the provisions of EU law on the reproduction right and the distribution right of the phonogram producer (Article 2(c) of Directive 2001/29 and Article 9(1)(b) of Directive 2006/115) and the exceptions or limitations to those rights (Article 5(2) and (3) of Directive 2001/29 and the first paragraph of Article 10(2) of Directive 2006/115) allow any latitude in terms of implementation in national law*
>
> 6. *In what way are the fundamental rights set out in [the Charter] to be taken into account when ascertaining the scope of protection of the exclusive right of the phonogram producer to reproduce (Article 2(c) of Directive 2001/29) and to distribute (Article 9(1)(b) of Directive 2006/115) its phonogram and the scope of the exceptions or limitations to those rights (Article 5(2) and (3) of Directive 2001/29 and the first paragraph of Article 10(2) of Directive 2006/115)?*'

2. Decision

1. Article 2(c) of Directive 2001/29/EC of the European Parliament and of the Council of 22 May 2001 on the harmonisation of certain aspects of copyright and related rights in the information society, must, in the light of the Charter of Fundamental Rights of the European Union, be interpreted as meaning that the phonogram producer's exclusive right under that provision to reproduce and distribute his or her phonogram allows him to prevent another person from taking a sound sample, even if very short, of his or her phonogram for the purposes of including that sample in another phonogram, unless that sample is included in the phonogram in a modified form unrecognisable to the ear.

2. Article 9(1)(b) of Directive 2006/115/EC of the European Parliament and of the Council of 12 December 2006 on rental right and lending right and on certain rights related to copyright in the field of intellectual property must be interpreted as meaning that a phonogram which contains sound samples transferred from another phonogram does not constitute a 'copy', within the meaning of that provision, of that phonogram, since it does not reproduce all or a substantial part of that phonogram.

3. A Member State cannot, in its national law, lay down an exception or limitation, other than those provided for in Article 5 of Directive 2001/29, to the phonogram producer's right provided for in Article 2(c) of that directive.

4. Article 5(3)(d) of Directive 2001/29 must be interpreted as meaning that the concept of 'quotations', referred to in that provision, does not extend to a situation in which it is not possible to identify the work concerned by the quotation in question.

5. Article 2(c) of Directive 2001/29 must be interpreted as constituting a measure of full harmonisation of the corresponding substantive law.

3. Motivation and Analysis

According to Article 2 Directive 2001/29/EC, copyright holders and related right holders enjoy the exclusive right to authorise or prohibit the reproduction of their works. However, the concept of '*reproduction, [...] in whole or in part*' is not defined in Directive 2001/29/EC and therefore to be determined by considering the usual meaning in everyday language, as well as taking into account the context in which it occurs and the purpose of the rules of which it is part.[5] Directive 2001/29/EC aims at guaranteeing a high level of protection of copyrights

[5] Case C-201/13, 3 September 2014, *Deckmyn and Vrijbridsfod*, para. 19.

and related rights as well as of the phonogram producer's investment.[6] Therefore, the CJEU concluded that even taking a very small sample of a work such as a phonogram is a reproduction in part within the meaning of the provision, and thus falls within the exclusive right granted to the producer of such a phonogram under that provision.[7]

However, if the sample is used in a new work in a modified form and is therefore unrecognisable to the ear, such use cannot be prohibited by the copyright holder and related right holder on the basis of the exclusive right granted under Article 2(c) of Directive 2001/29/EC.[8] This limitation to the exclusive rights of copyright holders and related right holders granted under Article 2 Directive 2001/29/EC creates a fair balance between the protection of copyright and related rights and other fundamental rights and freedoms,[9] including freedom of the arts (Art. 13 ECHR) and freedom of expression (Art. 11 and Art. 10(1) ECHR). It has to be considered that sampling for the creation of a new work is a common technique and form of artistic expression. Further, the use of an audio fragment and alteration to the point of unrecognisability contradicts the concept of a mere reproduction or copy as well as the meaning of the term in everyday language. Additionally, the use of a very small fragment of a work in that manner does not interfere with the opportunity of copyright holders and related right holders to realise satisfactory returns on their investment. They should therefore not be able to prohibit such use of their work, as their economic interests are not affected.[10]

Article 9(1)(b) Directive 2006/115/EC grants the producer of a phonogram the exclusive right to make the phonogram available to the public. However, the concept of 'copy' is not defined in Directive 2006/115/EC and therefore likewise to be determined with reference to its usual everyday meaning, the context in which it occurs and the purpose of the rules of which it is part. The protection guaranteed by Article 9(1)(b) Directive 2006/115/EC is aimed at protecting the investment of the producer, particularly against pirated production and distribution to the public of counterfeit copies of phonograms. Only an article which reproduces all or a substantial part of the sounds recorded in a phonogram is, by its nature, intended to replace lawful copies of that phonogram and, therefore, capable of constituting a copy of that phonogram within the meaning of Article 9(1) Directive 2006/115/EC.[11]

---

[6] Rec. 10 in the preamble to Dir. 2001/29/EC.

[7] Para. 29 of the annotated judgment.

[8] Para. 31 of the annotated judgment.

[9] Recs 3 and 31 in the preamble to Dir. 2001/29/EC; Case C-161/17, 7 August 2018, *Renckhoff*, para. 41.

[10] Paras. 37, 38 of the annotated judgment.

[11] Paras. 45, 46 of the annotated judgment.

Sound samples, especially in a modified form, transferred from a phonogram for the purposes of creating a new and distinct work from that phonogram do not constitute a copy of a phonogram within the meaning of Article 9(1) Directive 2006/115/EC.[12]

The referring court had noted that paragraph 24(1) UrhG allows the creation of an independent work using the work of another person without the consent of the author or phonogram producer of the work used, as this constitutes free use. The right to free use under paragraph 24 UrhG is not a derogation from copyright as such but rather an inherent limitation to its scope of protection, based on the idea that cultural creation always builds upon the previous work of other authors.[13]

The CJEU drew on its answer to the second question stating that a reproduction such as that at issue does not fall within the scope of Article 9(1)(b) Directive 2006/115/EC, in its assessment of the third question on whether a Member State may, in its national law, lay down an exception or limitation, other than those provided for in Article 5 Directive 2001/29/EC, to the phonogram producer's right provided for in Article 2(c) Directive 2001/29/EC.

The CJEU had already previously concluded that the list of exceptions and limitations contained in Article 5 Directive 2001/29/EC is exhaustive.[14] Directive 2001/29/EC aims to harmonise the safeguarding of a fair balance between the interests of holders of copyright and related rights as well as the interests and fundamental rights of users of protected subject matter and public interests.[15] This requires that the exceptions and limitations provided for in Article 5(1) to (4) Directive 2001/29/EC be applied only in certain special cases which do not conflict with a normal exploitation of the work or other subject matter and do not unreasonably prejudice the legitimate interests of the right holder.[16]

Deviations from this legal framework through national law endanger the effectiveness of the harmonisation of copyright and related rights by Directive 2001/29/EC, as well as the objective of legal certainty pursued by it.[17] Direct negative effects on the functioning of the internal market of copyright and related rights due to national differences in the exceptions and limitations to certain restricted acts[18] are prohibited by the exhaustive list of the exceptions

---

[12] Para. 55 of the annotated judgment.

[13] Para. 56 of the annotated judgment.

[14] Case C-301/15, 16 November 2016, para. 34, Case C-161/17, 7 August 2018, *Renckhoff*, para. 16.

[15] Rec. 32 in the preamble to Dir. 2001/29/EC.

[16] Para. 62 of the annotated judgment.

[17] Case C-466/12, 13 February 2014, *Svensson and Others*, para. 34, 35.

[18] Rec. 31 in the preamble to Dir. 2001/29/EC.

and limitations set out in Article 5 Directive 2001/29/EC and its consistent application to ensure the proper functioning of the internal market.

Article 5(3)(d) Directive 2001/29/EC allows Member States to provide for exceptions or limitations to the exclusive rights of reproduction and of communication to the public referred to in Articles 2 and 3 Directive 2001/29/EC in the case of quotations for purposes such as criticism or review. This requires that they relate to a work or other subject matter which has already been lawfully made available to the public, and that, if impossible, the source, including the author's name, is indicated, and finally, that their use is in accordance with fair practice, and to the extent required by the specific purpose.[19] This means that the use at issue for the purposes of quotation must not go beyond what is necessary to achieve the informative purpose of that particular quotation.[20]

However, the concept of 'quotation' is not defined in Directive 2001/29/EC and therefore to be determined by considering the usual meaning in everyday language. The CJEU therefore established that a quotation in accordance with Article 5(3)(d) Directive 2001/29/EC consists of the use of a work or of an extract from a work by a user other than the copyright holder, for the purposes of illustrating an assertion, defending an opinion or allowing an intellectual comparison between that work and the assertions of that user, with the intention of entering into dialogue with that work.[21]

As the sample in question is unrecognisable to the ear and therefore not identified as an extract from the work concerned by the quotation, it cannot cause an interaction between the work used and the new work created with the extract from the used work. Consequently, Article 5(3)(d) Directive 2001/29/EC must be interpreted as meaning that the concept of 'quotations', referred to in that provision, does not extend to a situation in which it is not possible to identify the work concerned by the quotation in question.[22]

Regarding the fifth question on whether Directive 2001/29/EC and Directive 2006/115/EC allow any latitude in terms of implementation in national law, the CJEU recalled the principle of primacy of EU law. This means that rules of national law, even of a constitutional order, cannot be allowed to undermine the effectiveness of EU law in the territory of that State. Only in situations in which action of the Member States is not entirely determined by EU law do Member States retain discretion in the application of national standards of protection of fundamental rights by national authorities and courts. However, they have to

[19] Para. 67 of the annotated judgment.

[20] Para. 69 of the annotated judgment.

[21] Paras. 70-71 of the annotated judgment.

[22] Para. 74 of the annotated judgment.

ensure that the level of protection provided for by the Charter and the primacy, unity and effectiveness of EU law are not compromised.[23]

Directive 2001/29/EC aims to harmonise only certain aspects of the law on copyright and related rights, granting the Member States a degree of discretion with regard to the implementation of the directive. However, Article 2(c) Directive 2001/29/EC defines the exclusive rights of reproduction of a phonogram producer. This provision is not qualified by any condition, nor is it subject, in its implementation or effects, to any measure being taken in any particular form. Article 2(c) Directive 2001/29 therefore constitutes a measure of full harmonisation of the corresponding substantive law, not allowing any latitude in terms of implementation in national law.[24]

The CJEU ruling expressly stated the objective of an EU-wide consistent balance of the (economic) interests of holders of copyrights and related rights on the one hand, and artistic freedom and other interests and fundamental rights on the other hand.

However, this ruling puts a special focus on the intention of full harmonisation of copyright and related rights. As this decision has shown, the legal framework set out in Directive 2001/29/EC does not allow for national limitations of these rights such as found in paragraph 24 UrhG, no matter whether the Member States consider them actual limitations or mere delineations of the scope of protection. As a result, this ruling essentially strengthens the position of holders of copyrights and related rights.

On the other hand, the ruling has set a high threshold for the use of work (fragments) as quotations by defining the requirements, and in particular that of an interaction with the used work. This does not take account of the common practice of sampling and remixing in the music industry, which is generally interested in incorporating recognisable fragments of other artists' music into work without any restriction on the content and context, such as an obligation to enter into a dialogue with the work the fragment was taken from.[25]

In fact, the CJEU concluded from its consideration of the usual meaning in everyday language that taking a sample of a work is a reproduction in part within the meaning of Article 2(c) of Directive 2001/29/EC. Regardless of the fact that it does not specify the uniform usual meaning of the word in everyday language in all 24 official languages of the European Union,[26] it seems obvious

---

23 Case C-399/11, 26 February 2013, *Melloni*, para. 60; Case C-617/10, 26 February 2013, *Åkerberg Fransson*, para. 29.

24 Paras. 84, 85 of the annotated judgment.

25 See R. Hauck, Copying or quoting – On the copyright permissibility of sampling, *GRUR-Prax* 2019, 385.

26 See A. Stumpf, Case note, *GRUR Int.* 2019, p. 1086-1095.

that a sample unrecognisable as such will hardly be considered a reproduction (in part) of a work due to a lack of association.

This further shifts the point of assessment of whether or not to assume a violation of Article 2(c) of Directive 2001/29/EC to the outcome rather than the action: using a sample of an existing work is – according to the CJEU – *per se* a reproduction (in part) of the work. Therefore, taking an extract of a work is the act that Article 2(c) of Directive 2001/29/EC restricts. However, whether the reproduction is, in fact, considered a violation of copyright and related rights will depend on what happens next to the sample taken, i.e. whether it is subject to sufficient modification to the point where it is not recognisable to the ear. The assessment of a reproduction in the sense of Article 2(c) of Directive 2001/29/EC will, therefore, exclusively be determined by the auditory impression of the fragment as it appears in the new work.

Hence, the CJEU makes the unrecognisability of a sample as deriving from a work a criterion for non-violation of Article 2(c) of Directive 2001/29/EC. This raises the question of when unrecognisability is to be assumed. The CJEU has not equipped the national courts with further information as to how the assessment of recognisability should be carried out, such as with reference to benchmarks of degrees of resemblance, or to whom the sample taken should appear recognisable. Whose ear should matter? A layman's ear? A well-informed genre enthusiast's ear? The judge's ear? A musicologist's ear? The – probably biased – ear of the phonogram producer whose phonogram the sample is taken from? This criterion – as objective as it may sound at first – will lead to very subjective evaluations of whether a fragment in the original is different enough from the fragment in the derived work.

With the introduction of this criterion, the CJEU further seems to assume a causal link between a modification of the fragment, or the degree thereof, and its unrecognisability in the new work. The CJEU fails to consider that recognisability may often not depend on whether the fragment has been modified, as in the case at hand (where it is slowed down and continuously looped), but rather on how the fragment is embedded in the new work, its artistic context and prevalence.

This ruling will therefore leave it to the national courts, to – subjectively – assess whether or not a sample is recognisable as such to 'the ear' in order to count as a reproduction or not. However, the CJEU has expressed its tendency to strengthen copyright and related rights with the ruling that even the smallest copied fragments are reproductions, that unrecognisability of samples excludes a violation and that national law cannot deviate from the scope of protection of copyright and related rights.

COURT OF JUSTICE 12 SEPTEMBER 2019

ON THE RIGHT TO APPROPRIATE COMPENSATION FOR LOSSES CAUSED BY PROVISIONAL MEASURES

Case C-688/17

Summary and Analysis by Eva Gostiša[1]

Parties:

Bayer Pharma AG

v

Richter Gedeon Vegyészeti Gyár Nyrt.
Exeltis Magyarország Gyógyszerkereskedelmi Kft.

1. Background and History

The central issue in the case at hand was whether or not a party, a pharmaceutical company launching its medicinal product at risk,[2] is automatically entitled to a compensation when a patent holder has enforced a preliminary injunction against it that has been granted but subsequently revoked.

On 8 August 2000, Bayer filed a patent application with the Szellemi Tulajdon Nemzeti Hivatal (National Intellectual Property Office, Hungary, 'the Office') relating to a pharmaceutical product containing a contraceptive active ingredient. The patent was granted on 4 October 2010.

Richter, in November 2009 and August 2010, and Exeltis, in October 2010, began marketing in Hungary products that, according to Bayer, infringed its patent ('the Products').

On 8 November 2010, Richter applied to the Office for a declaration of non-infringement, seeking to establish that its Products did not infringe the applicant's patent. On 8 December 2010, Richter and Exeltis also submitted an application for the patent to be revoked.

On 9 November 2010, Bayer applied to the referring court for provisional measures to prevent Richter and Exeltis from placing the Products on the market.

---

1 Eva Gostiša is a partner at the Slovenian law firm Jadek & Pensa d.o.o., specialising in IP law among other fields, and is a member of the Slovenian Bar Association.

2 In short, launching a product 'at risk' means launching it prior to the expiry/revocation of a patent/patent application.

That application was dismissed because it did not demonstrate a credible infringement. On 11 August 2011, Bayer also brought infringement proceedings before the referring court against Richter and Exeltis. These proceedings were suspended pending a final decision being made in the proceedings for the declaration of the invalidity of the patent.

Pursuant to new applications for provisional measures submitted by Bayer, by enforceable orders of 11 July 2011 which came into force on 8 August 2011, the referring court, by means of provisional measures, prohibited Richter and Exeltis from placing their Products on the market. The companies complied with their obligations voluntarily and withdrew their Products from the market.

In appeals brought by Richter and Exeltis, the Fővárosi Ítélőtábla (Budapest Regional Court of Appeal, Hungary), by orders of 29 September 2011 and 4 October 2011, set aside the 11 July 2011 orders on grounds of procedural defects and referred the case back to the referring court. By orders of 23 and 30 January 2012, made in the new proceedings, the referring court dismissed Bayer's applications for provisional measures, taking the view that, having regard in particular to the advanced phase of the proceedings for a declaration of invalidity of Bayer's patent and for revocation of an equivalent European patent, granting these measures could no longer be seen as proportionate in terms of the public interest. The Fővárosi Ítélőtábla (Budapest Regional Court of Appeal) confirmed these orders.

The provisional measures were therefore in force from 8 August 2011 to 4 October 2011 with respect to Richter and from 8 August 2011 to 29 September 2011 with respect to Exeltis.

By a decision of 13 September 2012, the Office revoked the patent in its entirety. After setting aside this decision and amending an earlier decision of the Office that partially revoked the patent, the referring court, in turn, declared the patent to be invalid in its entirety, by an order of 9 September 2014. The Fővárosi Ítélőtábla (Budapest Regional Court of Appeal) confirmed this order by its order of 20 September 2016.

By a counterclaim submitted on 22 February 2012 and an application submitted on 6 July 2017 (which were joined in the main proceedings), Richter and Exeltis both applied for Bayer to be ordered to compensate for the losses caused by the provisional measures.

Bayer, on the other hand, submitted that these claims should be rejected, arguing that Richter and Exeltis had themselves caused the losses they claimed to have suffered by having intentionally and unlawfully placed the products in question on the market. In accordance with Article 340(1) of the Civil Code, there was therefore no justification for their claim for compensation for these losses.

Hungarian law contains no substantive rules that relate explicitly to the situations under Article 9(7) of Directive 2004/48.[3]

Against this background, by a decision of 9 November 2017, the Fővárosi Törvényszék (Budapest High Court) stayed the proceedings pending before it and referred the following questions for a preliminary ruling:

'1) Should the expression "provide [...] appropriate compensation" referred to in Article 9(7) of Directive [2004/48] be interpreted to mean that Member States must establish the substantive rules of law on the liability of parties and the amount and method of compensation, by virtue of which the courts of the Member States can order applicants to compensate defendants for losses caused by measures which the court subsequently revoked or which subsequently lapsed due to an act or omission by the applicant, or in cases in which the court has subsequently found that there was no infringement or threat of infringement of an intellectual property right?

2) If the answer to the first question referred for a preliminary ruling is in the affirmative, does Article 9(7) of Directive [2004/48] preclude opposition to the legislation of a Member State by virtue of which the rules to be applied to the compensation referred to in that provision of the Directive are the general rules of that Member State on civil liability and compensation according to which the court cannot oblige the applicant to provide

---

3 In relation to this case the following provisions of Hungarian law applied: Art. 18(1) and (2) of Találmányok szabadalmi oltalmáról 1995. évi XXXIII. törvény (Law No XXXIII of 1995 on the protection of inventions by means of patents) provides that '*the protection conferred by a patent commences on publication of the application and its effects are retroactive to the date of the application. That protection is provisional and becomes final only once the applicant obtains a patent for his invention.*'
Art. 156(1) of Polgári perrendtartásról szóló 1952. évi III. törvény (Law No III of 1952 on Civil Procedure) provides that '*[T]he court may order a provisional measure applied for in an application or counterclaim or an application for provisional measures, where such a measure is necessary to prevent imminent loss or to preserve the status quo of the matter in dispute, or to preserve a better right of the applicant, where the loss caused by the measure does not outweigh the expected benefit of the measure. [...] The applicant must demonstrate that the facts on which the application is based are plausible.*'
Under Art. 339(1) of the polgári törvénykönyvről szóló 1959. évi IV. törvény (Law No IV of 1959, on the Civil Code; 'the Civil Code'): '*Any person who unlawfully causes harm to another must provide a remedy for that harm. A person is relieved of that obligation if it is demonstrated that the person concerned acted as would generally be expected in the circumstances in question.*'
Art. 340(1) of the Civil Code provides: '*The injured party is under an obligation to act as would generally be expected in the circumstances in question in order to avoid or to mitigate the loss. A party shall not be compensated for loss resulting from the injured party's failure to comply with that obligation.*'

> *compensation for losses caused by a provisional measure which was subsequently held to be unfounded due to the invalidity of the patent, and which were incurred as a result of the defendant's failure to act as would generally be expected in the circumstances in question, or losses for which the defendant is responsible for that same reason, provided that, when requesting the provisional measure, the applicant acted as would generally be expected in those circumstances?'*

2. Decision

Article 9(7) of Directive 2004/48/EC of the European Parliament and of the Council of 29 April 2004 on the enforcement of intellectual property rights, in particular, the concept of 'appropriate compensation' referred to in that provision, must be interpreted as not precluding national legislation which provides that a party shall not be compensated for losses which he has suffered due to his not having acted as may generally be expected in order to avoid or mitigate his loss and which, in circumstances such as those in the main proceedings, results in the court not making an order for provisional measures against the applicant obliging him to provide compensation for losses caused by those measures even though the patent on the basis of which those had been requested and granted has subsequently been found to be invalid, to the extent that that legislation permits the court to take due account of all the objective circumstances of the case, including the conduct of the parties, in order, *inter alia*, to determine that the applicant has not abused those measures.

3. Motivation and Analysis

A crucial point of discussion in this case was whether Article 9(7) of Directive 2004/48[4] automatically grants an entity, here a pharmaceutical company, launching a medicinal product at risk, a right to damages where the patent on which the preliminary measure was based is later on revoked.

Advocate General Pitruzzella in his Opinion[5] took the position that the concept of 'appropriate compensation' in Article 9(7) cannot be interpreted as indicating any specific regime for the applicants' liability. The expression, and in particular the use of the adjective 'appropriate', merely requires an

---

4 Art. 9(7) of Dir. 2004/48 states: '*Where the provisional measures are revoked or where they lapse due to any act or omission by the applicant, or where it is subsequently found that there has been no infringement or threat of infringement of an intellectual property right, the judicial authorities shall have the authority to order the applicant, upon request of the defendant, to provide the defendant appropriate compensation for any injury caused by those measures.*'

5 Delivered on 11 April 2019.

assessment of whether the compensation payable to the defendant is in line with the loss actually suffered and the circumstances of the case, in accordance with the principles set out in Recital 17 of Directive 2004/48. According to this recital, '*the measures, procedures and remedies provided for in this Directive should be determined in each case in such a manner as to take due account of the specific characteristics of that case, including the specific features of each intellectual property right.*'

According to Advocate General Pitruzzella, this means that it is for each Member State to determine the substantive rules that govern how the defendant should be compensated for the injury incurred as a result of the adoption of provisional measures in the situations under Article 9(7) of Directive 2004/48, provided nevertheless that those rules make it possible to achieve the objective of that Article, that is to say, that each national legal system should set up a regime of effective legal remedies enabling defendants to obtain appropriate compensation for any injury suffered, following a fitting and fair assessment within the framework of the national law on liability. However, he pointed out that the Member States must also ensure that the regime they set does not discourage the holders of intellectual property rights from applying for the measures under Article 9(1) and (2) of Directive 2004/48. The Advocate General therefore supported the automatic entitlement to damages, while pointing out that the system may not unduly burden the right holders, thus seeking a balance between the interests of the parties involved.

As to the second question posed by the Budapest High Court, the Advocate General reiterated his above-stated position, explaining that it would be contrary to the wording and the objectives of Article 9(7) of Directive 2004/48 if Member States could systematically exclude any right to compensation for a defendant where that defendant accessed the market in infringement of the patent for whose protection the provisional measures were adopted, without first waiting for it to be found to be invalid.

In essence, Advocate General Pitruzzella explained that the provisions of Directive 2004/48, like those of the TRIPS Agreement, seek a balance between two objectives, i.e. protecting the interests of the holders of intellectual property rights on the one hand and preserving legitimate trade against any unjustified obstacle on the other. Were it sufficient, in order for the applicant to escape its obligation to compensate for loss caused by provisional measures adopted on the basis of an intellectual property right that was subsequently found to be invalid with retroactive effect, for the applicant to rely on the fact that the right in question was valid at the time those measures were adopted, neither of the two objectives referred to above would be served – neither that of protecting intellectual property, since there would never have been a valid right that justified its holder being given exclusivity, nor that of protecting legitimate trade, because no compensation would be awarded for an unjustified obstacle.

According to Advocate General Pitruzzella, a 'launch at risk' is therefore not a factor that can by itself rule out the defendant's right to appropriate compensation. The national court can nevertheless take such behaviour into account, together with other relevant circumstances, when determining the compensation to be awarded to the defendant.

The CJEU took a different position. It held that, firstly, the concept of 'appropriate compensation' must be regarded as an autonomous concept of EU law which must be given a uniform interpretation throughout the territory of the European Union.[6] Therefore, the Member States must give their national courts the authority to provide the defendant with appropriate compensation in accordance with Article 9(7) of Directive 2004/48. Consequently, it is up to the national courts to assess the specific circumstances of the case before them in order to decide whether it is appropriate to order the applicant to pay to the defendant compensation which must be 'appropriate', that is to say, justified in the light of the circumstances.[7]

In particular, while the exercise of their authority to grant such compensation is strictly subject to the condition that either (i) the provisional measures have been repealed or ceased to apply, or (ii) it is subsequently found that there is no infringement or threat of infringement of an intellectual property right, the fact that those conditions are satisfied in a specific case does not mean that the competent national courts will automatically be obliged to order the applicant to pay compensation for any losses suffered by the defendant as a result of the measures. To put it simply, according to the CJEU there is no automatic entitlement to compensation. Rather, the national courts have to assess, considering the circumstances of the particular case, whether the applicant is entitled to it.

The CJEU then touched on the second question, i.e. whether Article 9(7) of Directive 2004/48, in particular, the concept of 'appropriate compensation' referred to in that provision, precludes the application, in such circumstances, of national legislation which in essence excludes the defendant from being able to obtain compensation for the losses which he has suffered due to the fact that he did not act as would generally be expected of a person in the situation concerned in order to prevent or mitigate such losses, to the extent that the applicant, when requesting the provisional measures, has himself acted as would generally be expected of a person in the situation concerned.

---

6 Paras. 41 and 49 of the annotated judgment.

7 Para. 52 of the annotated judgment.

In this regard the CJEU based its decision on Recital 22 of Directive 2004/48,[8] explaining that a finding that an application for provisional measures is unjustified presupposes, primarily, that there is no risk that irreparable harm may be caused to the holder of an intellectual property right in the event of delay in the adoption of the measures sought by him. Therefore, where defendants market their products even though a patent application has been submitted or there is a patent hindering marketing, which is for the referring court to ascertain, such conduct may, *prima facie*, be regarded as objectively indicative of the existence of a risk for the holder of the patent of irreparable harm if the adoption of the measures sought by the patent holder is delayed. Consequently, the application for provisional measures submitted by the latter in response to such conduct cannot be regarded *a priori* as 'unjustified'.[9]

Further, the fact that the provisional measures in the main proceedings have been repealed cannot be regarded in itself as a decisive factor in proving the unjustified nature of the application which gave rise to the provisional measures which have been set aside.[10] A different conclusion could have the effect, in circumstances such as those of the main proceedings, of discouraging the patent holder from availing himself of the measures referred to in Article 9 of Directive 2004/48 and would thus run counter to the directive's objective of ensuring a high level of protection of intellectual property.[11]

There is, however, one important point which it is for the competent national courts to establish, and that is whether, in a given case, the applicant has abused those measures and procedures.[12] This follows from Article 3(2) of Directive 2004/48, according to which the measures, procedures, and remedies necessary to ensure the enforcement of the intellectual property rights covered by that directive are to be applied in such a manner as to avoid the creation of barriers to legitimate trade and to provide for safeguards against their abuse. In assessing whether abuse exists, the court must take due account of all the objective circumstances of the case, including the conduct of the parties.[13]

---

8 Rec. 22 of Dir. 2004/48 states: *'It is also essential to provide for provisional measures for the immediate termination of infringements, without awaiting a decision on the substance of the case, while observing the rights of the defence, ensuring the proportionality of the provisional measures as appropriate to the characteristics of the case in question and providing the guarantees needed to cover the costs and the injury caused to the defendant by an unjustified request. Such measures are particularly justified where any delay would cause irreparable harm to the holder of an intellectual property right.'*

9 Para. 63 of the annotated judgment.

10 Para. 64 of the annotated judgment.

11 Para. 65 of the annotated judgment.

12 Para. 69 of the annotated judgment.

13 Para. 70 of the annotated judgment.

* *
*

At first glance it would indeed seem that, as suggested by Advocate General Pitruzzella, Article 9(7) of Directive 2004/48 provides an automatic entitlement to compensation where the provisional measure, based on a granted patent, is later on revoked since the patent has been found invalid, and the only question which is to be dealt with by the national court is the amount of compensation to be awarded to the defendant, taking into account all circumstances of the particular case. It should also be noted that, in his Opinion, the Advocate General managed to achieve a balance between the interests of the patent holder and the protection of legitimate trade.

The CJEU's approach, on the other hand, tends more towards the protection of intellectual property rights and their owners, imposing on national courts a requirement to establish whether the measures have been abused. In Slovenia, the right to appropriate compensation stems from the Enforcement and Security Act.[14] It also stems from settled case-law that the abuse of procedural rights means acting contrary to the principles of conscientiousness and fairness. How the Slovenian courts will apply the guidance provided by the CJEU remains to be seen.

---

[14] *Zakon o izvršbi in zavarovanju*, Official Gazette of the Republic of Slovenia, No. 51/98, as amended, states in Art. 279: '*A debtor shall have the right to demand compensation from the creditor for damage suffered as a consequence of an interim injunction which was unfounded or which the creditor was unable to justify.*'

Court of Justice 12 September 2019

On the requirement under national law of a significant aesthetic visual effect for copyright protection

Case C-683/17

Summary and Analysis by António Andrade and Pedro Hemsworth[1]

Parties:

Cofemel – Sociedade de Vestuário, SA

v

G-Star Raw, CV

1. Background and History

G-Star and Cofemel are two well-known companies active in the creation, production and sale of clothing.

G-Star exploits several trade marks, such as *G-STAR, G-STAR RAW, G-STAR DENIM RAW, GS-RAW, G-RAW* and *RAW,* whilst Cofemel sells its products under the trade mark *TIFFOSI.*

In August 2013, G-Star filed a lawsuit in a Portuguese court against Cofemel, requesting that it be ordered to cease acts constituting infringements of its copyright and acts of unfair competition committed against the company, and seeking compensation for the harm suffered and, in the event of any new infringement, the payment of a periodic penalty until the infringements ceased.

In its legal action, G-Star claimed that Cofemel had been producing and commercialising jeans, t-shirts, and sweatshirts identical to G-Star's ARC and ROWDY models. G-Star also claimed that these clothing items were original intellectual creations and, as such, should be classified as 'works', thus benefiting from the protection of copyright under applicable legislation. A few examples of the products in question are shown below:

[1] António Andrade is a partner at Abreu Advogados in Portugal. Pedro Hemsworth is a trainee lawyer at Abreu Advogados in Portugal.

Cofemel contested these claims, alleging that the models could not be classified as 'works' and as such did not benefit from this protection. The court of first instance partly upheld G-Star's action and ordered Cofemel, *inter alia*, to cease its infringement of G-Star's copyright, to pay the latter a sum corresponding to the profits obtained from the sale of the clothing produced in breach of that copyright and to pay it a daily penalty payment in the event of a further infringement.

Cofemel then presented an appeal to Tribunal da Relação de Lisboa (the Court of Appeal), which confirmed the decision and stated that Article 2(1)(a) of the Portuguese Code on Copyright and Related Rights must be understood in the light of Directive 2001/29, as interpreted by the Court of Justice in cases C-5/08, EU:C:2009:465 (*Infopaq International*) and C-145/10, EU: C:2011:798, in the sense that the protection of copyright conferred on applied artworks, industrial models and works of design depends on their originality, due to the fact that they are the result of the intellectual creation of their author, without any particular degree of aesthetic or artistic value being required. Further, the Court recognised that G-Star's ARC and ROWDY models were works that benefited from copyright protection.

Cofemel finally appealed to the Supreme Court of Justice of Portugal. This Court considered that the G-Star models that were the object of the appeal were created by designers (employed by G-Star), who had contractually transmitted the copyright to G-Star. The Court also considered that these models were the result of designs and a manufacturing process that was recognised as being innovative in the fashion industry and that had been partially utilised by Cofemel for the production of clothing for its brand.

Secondly, the Court noted that while Article 2(1)(i) of the Code on Copyright and Related Rights clearly includes works of applied art, industrial designs and works of design in the list of works protected by copyright, it does not specify the level of originality required for such subject matter to be granted that protection. The Court also stated that there was no consensus in Portuguese case-law and legal theory on this issue, which was at the heart of the dispute between Cofemel and G-Star. For that reason, it was uncertain whether it should be held, in the light of the interpretation of Directive 2001/29 adopted by the Court in the judgments of 16 July 2009, *Infopaq International* (C-5/08, EU:C:2009:465), and of 1 December 2011, Painer (C-145/10, EU:C:2011:798), that the protection ensured by copyright extends to such subject matter in the same way as to any literary and artistic work, and therefore subject to the condition of originality, in the sense that it is the result of the author's own intellectual creation, or whether it is possible to hold that a prerequisite of such protection is the existence of a specific degree of aesthetic or artistic value.

The Court therefore referred the following questions to the CJEU for a preliminary ruling:

> *'(1) Does the interpretation by the Court of Article 2(a) of Directive 2001/29 preclude national legislation – in the present case, the provision in Article 2(1)(i) of the Code on Copyright and Related Rights – which confers copyright protection on works of applied art, industrial designs and works of design which, over and above their practical purpose, create their own visual and distinctive effect from an aesthetic point of view, their originality being the fundamental criterion which governs the grant of protection in the area of copyright?*

(2) Does the interpretation by the Court of Article 2(a) of Directive 2001/29 preclude national legislation – in the present case, the provision in Article 2(1)(i) of the Code on Copyright and Related Rights – which confers copyright protection on works of applied art, industrial designs and works of design if, in the light of a particularly rigorous assessment of their artistic character, and taking account [of] the dominant views in cultural and institutional circles, they qualify as an "artistic creation" or "work of art"?'

2. Decision

Article 2(a) of Directive 2001/29/EC of the European Parliament and of the Council of 2 May 2001 on the harmonisation of certain aspects of copyright and related rights in the information society must be interpreted as precluding national legislation from conferring protection, under copyright, to designs such as the clothing designs at issue in the main proceedings, on the ground that, over and above their practical purpose, they generate a specific, aesthetically significant visual effect.

3. Motivation and Analysis

In its analysis the CJEU began by stating that the term 'work' used throughout the Directive has a settled case-law basis that allows it to be understood as an autonomous EU concept, which must be interpreted and applied uniformly, requiring two cumulative conditions to be satisfied, as follows:

a) There must be an original subject matter, in the sense of being the author's own intellectual creation.

b) Classification as work is reserved to the elements that are an expression of such creation (which in this case would be the manufactured clothes).[2]

On this matter, the CJEU considered that if a subject matter is to be capable of being regarded as original, it is both necessary and sufficient for it to reflect the personality of the author, as an expression of his or her free and creative choices. This is questionable from the Portuguese perspective, in an environment where designers are subject to guidelines and limitations in creating works that reflect a whole aesthetic approach of the company that has durability and is sustained by its trade marks. However, it is possible that designers are provided enough freedom in order to fulfil this criterion.

---

2 Para. 29 of the annotated judgment.

The CJEU added that '*when the realisation of a subject matter has been dictated by technical considerations, rules or other constraints, which have left no room for creative freedom, that subject matter cannot be regarded as possessing the originality required for it to constitute a work*.'[3] This reflects the reality of the fashion industry, as mentioned in the previous paragraph, meaning that it is possible that the design of a certain clothing item by an internal designer of a trade mark with an already very recognisable identity and aesthetic is not subject to the protection of copyright. However, this formulation is merely hypothetical since, as mentioned earlier, the manufacturing company usually has contractual ownership of the copyright.

On the other hand, we note that the CJEU also stated that the work that is the subject of the Directive necessarily entails the existence of a subject matter that is identifiable with '*sufficient precision and objectivity*', for two reasons. First, the authorities responsible for ensuring the exclusive rights inherent to copyright must be able to identify, clearly and precisely, the subject matter protected. Second, it is necessary to ensure that there is no element of subjectivity, which is detrimental to legal certainty, in the process of identifying the subject matter, and this means that that subject matter must have been expressed in an objective manner.[4]

The CJEU also stated that the EU legislature had opted for a system in which the protection reserved for designs and the protection ensured by copyright are not mutually exclusive and that it must be held that designs are capable of classification as 'works' within the meaning of Directive 2001/29. It added that it should be further examined whether classification as 'works' is possible for designs such as the clothing designs at issue, which over and above their practical purpose, generate, according to the referring court, a specific and aesthetically significant visual effect. The CJEU stated that the doubts of that court concerned the issue of whether such a factor of aesthetic originality constitutes the central criterion for the granting of protection provided for by Directive 2001/129.[5]

The Advocate General had also stated that the purpose of the protection of designs is to protect subject matter which, '*while being new and distinctive, is functional and liable to be mass-produced. Further, that protection is to apply for a limited time, but sufficient time to ensure a return on the investment necessary for the creation and production of that subject matter, without thereby excessively restricting competition*.'[6]

Finally, the CJEU noted that the aesthetic effect that may be produced by a design is the product of an intrinsically subjective sensation of beauty experienced

---

[3] Para. 31 of the annotated judgment.

[4] Paras. 32-34 of the annotated judgment.

[5] Paras. 47-49 of the annotated judgment.

[6] Para. 50 of the annotated judgment.

by each individual who may look at that design. Consequently, that subjective effect does not, in itself, permit a subject matter to be characterised as existing and identifiable with sufficient precision and objectivity.[7]

That said, in our opinion the CJEU almost ends on a very positive note, stating that aesthetic considerations play a part in creative activity, but that the circumstance that a design may generate an aesthetic effect does not, in itself, make it possible to determine whether that design constitutes an intellectual creation reflecting the freedom of choice and personality of its author.

Due to all the above, the CJEU concluded, rightly in our view, that a specific, aesthetically significant visual effect is not the key criterion for the classification of designs such as clothing designs as 'works' over and above their practical purpose.

Whilst we consider that G-Star's claim is very understandable and *prima facie* seems to be fair, one must understand that these criteria are extremely relevant to a clearly definition of the concept of copyright (which needs to be further harmonised in the future) and also to determining its interaction with industrial property rights, as the CJEU very clearly outlined. The protection of designs and models follows a fundamentally different purpose from copyright and the fact that design/fashion generates an aesthetic effect cannot by itself mean that a work of applied art can automatically also be subject to the protection of copyright. The Portuguese courts have already adopted this understanding in case-law.[8]

---

7 Paras. 53-54 of the annotated judgment.

8 Case 279/18.1YHLSB.L1-PICRS, made available at www.dgsi.pt/jtrl.nsf/33182fc732316039802565fa00497eec/2e5cfd03c403bb7980258553002c75a0?OpenDocument.

COURT OF JUSTICE 21 NOVEMBER 2019

ON PROVISIONAL AND PROTECTIVE MEASURES AND JURISDICTION OF NATIONAL COURTS OF FIRST INSTANCE

Case C-678/18

Summary and Analysis by Huib Berendschot[1]

Parties:

Spin Master Ltd, Toronto, Canada

v

High5 Product B.V., Waalwijk, the Netherlands

1. Background and History

This request for a preliminary ruling concerned the interpretation of Article 90(1) of Regulation 6/2002 on Community designs ('CDR').[2]

The request was made in proceedings between Spin Master Ltd ('Spin Master') and High5 Products B.V. ('High5') concerning the jurisdiction of national courts other than the designated Community Trade Mark Court to render judgments in provisional measure proceedings.

Spin Master Ltd is a company which has its registered office in Toronto (Canada) and operates in the toy sector. Under the brand name 'Bunchems', it markets a toy consisting of small plastic balls which bunch together and are available in eight colours. These balls make it possible to create all kinds of shapes and figures.

On 16 January 2015 a Community design was registered for that toy in the name of Spin Master under number 002614669-0002.

---

1 Huib Berendschot is an attorney-at-law and partner at AKD, the Netherlands, and works within the Intellectual Property & Technology practice group.

2 Council Regulation (EC) No 6/2002 of 12 December 2001 on Community designs, *OJ L* 3, 5.1.2002, p. 1-24.

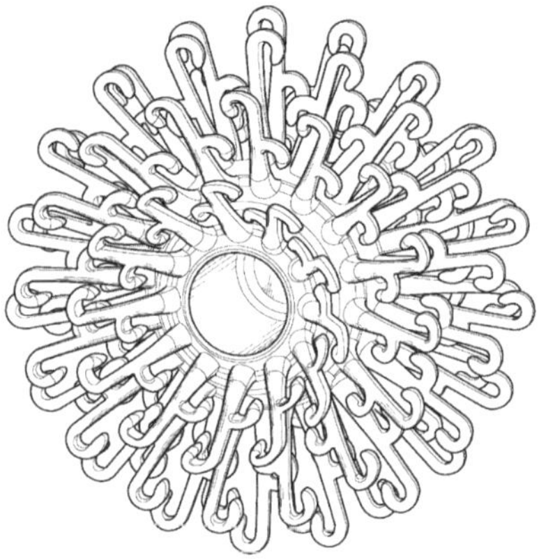

High5 is a company based in Waalwijk (Netherlands) which distributes, under the name 'Linkeez', a similar toy consisting of small plastic balls which bunch together, also available in eight colours.

By letter of 18 November 2016, Spin Master served formal notice on High5 to bring an end to the infringement of the abovementioned Community design.

As High5 did not comply with the formal notice, Spin Master brought an application for interim relief before the judge of the District Court, Amsterdam, by which it sought an order prohibiting the marketing of the toy distributed by High5 Products. The Court of Amsterdam is not a Community Design Court within the meaning of Article 80(1) CDR.[3]

A plea of lack of jurisdiction having been raised in respect of the application, the judge of the District Court, Amsterdam, dealing with applications for interim relief held, in a decision of 12 January 2017, that he had jurisdiction to deal with the application for interim relief which had been submitted to him. He based his decision on the fact, first, that Netherlands law conferred jurisdiction on him to rule on a similar request based on a Benelux design and, secondly, that Article 3 of the law of 4 November 2004 did not mean that he did not have jurisdiction in interim proceedings giving rise to an application for an injunction limited to the territory of the Netherlands, such as the application before him.

On 31 August 2018, the Attorney General at the Supreme Court in the Netherlands lodged a so-called appeal in the interest of the law against that decision before the Hoge Raad der Nederlanden (Supreme Court of the Netherlands) on the ground that, in the Attorney General's view, the judge of the District Court

---

[3] Art. 80(1) CDR states that: '*The Member States shall designate in their territories as limited a number as possible of national courts and tribunals of first and second instance (Community design courts) which shall perform the functions assigned to them by this Regulation.*'

of The Hague dealing with applications for interim measures, as the court designated under Article 80(1) CDR, had exclusive jurisdiction in Community design matters, including provisional and protective measures.

The referring court stated that the question raised before it was whether Article 90(1) CDR precluded the legislation of a Member State from providing that the exclusive jurisdiction of the courts designated under Article 80(1) CDR also extended to provisional measures, including protective measures, within the meaning of Article 90(1) CDR.

The referring court pointed out that, by adopting Article 3 of the Law of 4 November 2004, the Netherlands legislature had sought to make use of the specific intellectual-property expertise of the District Court, The Hague and of the Court of Appeal, The Hague, Netherlands. It observed that the question of the exclusive jurisdiction of the courts designated under Article 80(1) CDR in respect of provisional measures, including protective measures, had given rise to divergent assessments in case-law and academic legal writing, including in Member States other than the Kingdom of the Netherlands.

The referring court was uncertain as to the proper interpretation of Article 90(1) CDR. According to one interpretation, the EU legislature, by that provision, introduced a mandatory exception to the wish, otherwise expressed therein, to promote specialisation in the courts, since Member States were not free to confer exclusive jurisdiction on Community design courts to hear all applications for provisional measures, including protective measures, in design matters. According to a second interpretation, the EU legislature, by that provision, sought merely to allow Member States to provide, in their national legislation, that jurisdiction to hear such applications was also to be conferred on other courts with jurisdiction to adopt such measures in cases relating to national designs.

The referring court also contemplated the possibility that, in so far as Article 81 CDR established on a mandatory basis the domestic jurisdiction of the Community design courts for the claims referred to in that article, Article 90 CDR applied only to provisional measures, including protective measures, of another kind.

Finally, the referring court stated that the setting-aside of a decision following an appeal in the interest of the law brought by the Attorney General had no influence on the legal situation of the parties concerned by that decision, as the proceedings in that event related only to a point of law raised in numerous cases and forming the subject of divergent assessments.

In those circumstances, the Supreme Court of the Netherlands decided to stay the proceedings and to refer the following question to the Court of Justice for a preliminary ruling:

> *'Must Article 90(1) CDR be interpreted as requiring the mandatory granting, to all courts and tribunals of a Member State referred to therein, of jurisdiction to grant provisional and protective measures, or does it leave the Member States – in full or in part – free to delegate jurisdiction*

to grant such measures exclusively to the courts and tribunals which, in accordance with Article 80(1) CDR, have been designated as courts (of first and second instance) for Community design?'

2. Decision

Article 90(1) of Council Regulation (EC) No 6/2002 of 12 December 2001 on Community designs must be interpreted as meaning that the courts and tribunals of the Member States with jurisdiction to order provisional measures, including protective measures, in respect of a national design also have jurisdiction to order such measures in respect of a Community design.

3. Motivation and Analysis

As the CJEU commonly does, it reformulated the questions of the referring court, noting that the national court by its question was essentially asking whether Article 90(1) of Regulation No 6/2002 must be interpreted as meaning that the courts or tribunals of the Member States with jurisdiction to order provisional or protective measures in respect of a national design also have jurisdiction to order such measures in respect of a Community design or whether the Member States are free, either wholly or in part, to confer jurisdiction in that respect exclusively on the courts designated as Community design courts (now called EU Trade Mark Courts).[4]

The referring court's question related in particular to the determination of the courts and tribunals with jurisdiction within each Member State that are competent to order provisional measures, including protective measures, in respect of a Community design.

The article of which interpretation was requested, Article 90(1) of Regulation No 6/2002, reads as follows:

> *'Application may be made to the courts of a Member State, including Community design courts, for such provisional measures, including protective measures, in respect of a Community design as may be available under the law of that State in respect of national design rights even if, under this Regulation, a Community design court of another Member State has jurisdiction as to the substance of the matter.'*

It follows from the wording of the article that a claimant may apply for provisional measures, including protective measures, in respect of a Community

[4] Para. 28 of the annotated judgment.

design not only to the Community design courts of the Member State, but also to any court or tribunal in that State with jurisdiction to adopt such measures in respect of national designs.[5]

The CJEU in the first place referred to the opinion of the Advocate General that the use of the word 'including' confirmed that that court does not necessarily have to be a specialised court.[6]

Secondly, the CJEU considered that the previous finding was not affected by the use of the word 'may' in Article 90(1).[7] The use of that word cannot be regarded as meaning that that provision gives Member States a discretionary power as to the attribution of jurisdiction concerning provisional measures, including protective measures, in respect of a Community design. As the Advocate General observed in point 66 of his Opinion, the word 'may' thus refers only to litigants who wish to bring an action before a court for a provisional or protective measure relating to one of the actions listed in Article 81 of Regulation No 6/2002.

Contrary to the observations submitted by the Netherlands Government, provisional measures, including protective measures, in respect of a Community design, referred to in Article 90(1) of Regulation No 6/2002, relate to infringement or invalidity actions, set out in Article 81 of that regulation and may be ordered by the courts of a Member State which have jurisdiction to adopt such measures in respect of national designs.[8]

Thirdly, in the case of court proceedings the substance of which concerns infringement or invalidity actions, the EU legislature also pointed out, in Recital 29 of Regulation No 6/2002, that the exercise of the rights conferred by a design must be enforced in an efficient manner throughout the territory of the European Union. The EU legislature was therefore able to ensure that, in the case of requests for provisional measures, including protective measures, concerning infringement or invalidity, the requirements of proximity and efficiency should prevail over the objective of specialisation.[9]

The effect of such provisional measures, in the CJEU's opinion, is by its nature limited in time and the granting of them by the court having jurisdiction in the matter cannot prejudge the outcome of the action for infringement or invalidity brought on the substance, which falls within the exclusive jurisdiction of the Community design courts. So, there is no objection to allowing a wider range of court to grant provisional measures in respect of Community designs.

---

5 Para. 32 of the annotated judgment.

6 Opinion of Advocate General Campos Sánchez-Bordona of the annotated judgment, para. 41.

7 Para. 33 of the annotated judgment.

8 Para. 38 of the annotated judgment.

9 Para. 41 of the annotated judgment.

* *
*

The judgment is significant, as it is also relevant in the field of EU trade marks. The EUTM Regulation[10] has a regime for infringement proceedings that is identical to the one described above for Community designs. That means that the EUTM Regulation must be interpreted as meaning that the courts and tribunals of the Member States with jurisdiction to order provisional measures, including protective measures, in respect of a national trade mark also have jurisdiction to order such measures in respect of an EU trade mark.[11]

The meaning for legal practice in the Netherlands is that courts in 11 districts may grant provisional measures in relation to Community designs, whereas only the court of The Hague is allowed to grant measures in proceedings on the merits.

In the Netherlands there is a lot of pressure on the court of The Hague, as the majority of intellectual property cases relating to designs, trade marks and patents are dealt with by that court. This affects the length of proceedings from issuance of a writ until judgment.

To the extent that cases in which provisional measures are granted by courts other than the court of The Hague and are subsequently settled on the basis of the judgment in the preliminary proceedings, some pressure is taken off the court in The Hague.

The same may occur in other jurisdictions which have only one court that may deal with proceedings on the merits, as is the case in the majority of EU Member States.[12]

---

10 Reg. (EU) 2017/1001 of the European Parliament and of the Council of 14 June 2017 on the European Union trade mark, *OJ L* 154, 16.6.2017, p. 1-99.

11 See annotation by D.W.F. Verkade, *NJ* 2020/209.

12 See publication of the lists of EU trade mark courts and Community design courts in accordance with Art. 123(3) of Reg. (EU) 2017/1001 of the European Parliament and of the Council on the European Union trade mark and Art. 80(4) of Council Regulation (EC) No 6/2002 on Community designs (2020/C-327/06).

COURT OF JUSTICE 21 NOVEMBER 2019

ON THE LIMITATION OF TRADEMARK RIGHTS IN CONSEQUENCE OF ACQUIESCENCE

Case C-466/20

Summary and Analysis by Bram Woltering[1]

Parties:

HEITEC AG

v

HEITECH Promotion GmbH,
RW

1. Background and History

This request for a preliminary ruling concerns the interpretation of Article 9 of Directive 2008/95/EC of the European Parliament and of the Council of 22 October 2008 to approximate the laws of the Member States relating to trade marks (OJ 2008 L 299, p. 25), and Articles 54 and 111 of Council Regulation (EC) No 207/2009 of 26 February 2009 on the Community trade mark (OJ 2009 L 78, p. 1).

The request was made in proceedings between, on the one hand, HEITEC AG ('Heitec') and, on the other, HEITECH Promotion GmbH ('Heitech') and RW concerning the use by the latter of the trade name HEITECH Promotion GmbH and trade marks containing the word element 'heitech'.

The applicant in the main proceedings, Heitec, is the proprietor of the EU word mark HEITEC, applied for on 18 March 1998, with seniority claimed as from 13 July 1991, and registered on 4 July 2005. Heitec was entered in the commercial register in 1984 under the name Heitec Industrieplanung GmbH. Its name was changed in 1988 to Heitec GmbH. Since the year 2000, it has been operating under the name of Heitec AG.

Heitech, of which RW is the managing director, was entered in the commercial register on 16 April 2003.

Heitech is the proprietor of a German figurative mark containing the word element 'heitech promotion', applied for on 17 September 2002 and registered on

[1] Bram Woltering is an attorney-at-law at AKD, the Netherlands, and works within the Intellectual Property & Technology practice group.

4 February 2003, which it uses since 29 September 2004 at the latest, and of an EU figurative mark containing the word element 'heitech', applied for on 6 February 2008 and registered on 20 November 2008, which it uses since 6 May 2009 at the latest.

The further events as established in the national proceedings are as follows:

- By letter of 29 November 2004, Heitech contacted the representatives of Heitec to ask whether the latter would agree to conclude a coexistence agreement.
- On 7 July 2008, Heitec became aware of Heitech's application for registration of the EU figurative mark containing the word element 'heitech'.
- By letter of 22 April 2009, Heitec sent Heitech a warning letter regarding the latter's use of its trade name and the EU trade mark containing the word element 'heitech'. In its reply of 6 May 2009, Heitech again proposed the conclusion of a coexistence agreement.
- On 31 December 2012, the Landgericht Nürnberg-Fürth (Regional Court, Nuremberg-Fürth, Germany) received, by fax, the application initiating proceedings, submitted by Heitec against Heitech and RW. This application was dated 15 December 2012. By decision of 4 January 2013, Heitec was asked to pay an advance on the costs of the proceedings.
- On 12 March 2013, that court pointed out to Heitec's representative that this advance payment had not been made and that the originals of the application initiating proceedings had not been lodged.
- By letter of 23 September 2013, Heitec informed Heitech that it refused to conclude a coexistence agreement and proposed to conclude a licence agreement while stating that it had initiated legal proceedings.
- By letter of 29 December 2013, Heitec informed Heitech that it was relying on its trade name and that it was the proprietor of the EU trade mark HEITEC. It stated that the legal proceedings were pending.
- On 30 December 2013, the court of lower instance received written submissions from Heitec dated 12 December 2013, together with a cheque for court fees and a new application initiating proceedings bearing the date 4 October 2013.
- On 14 January 2014, that court drew Heitec's attention to the fact that it was also necessary to serve the application initiating proceedings of 15 December 2012, and Heitec was therefore asked to lodge the original documents. These originals were received by the court on 22 February 2014. On 24 February 2014, the court alerted Heitec to the fact that the heads of claim in the originals of the application initiating proceedings received on 22 February 2014 were not consistent with the heads of claim in the initiating application submitted on 31 December 2012.
- On 16 May 2014, the lower instance court opened the preliminary written procedure and ordered that copies, drawn up by that court, of the initiating application of 15 December 2012 be served on the defendants in the main proceedings. Notice was finally served on 23 May 2014.

In its action, Heitec brought claims based on the infringement of the rights conferred by its trade name HEITEC and its EU trade mark HEITEC. In addition to the regular request for a prohibition order it also brought claims for information, for a finding of an obligation to pay compensation, for the destruction of goods and for the payment of the costs of sending the warning letter.

The court of first instance rejected the main claims brought by Heitec. Heitec appealed before the Oberlandesgericht Nürnberg (Higher Regional Court, Nuremberg, Germany). The court of appeal held that Heitec's action was unfounded on the ground that Heitec was time-barred. In that regard, it noted that Heitech had used its later signs for an uninterrupted period of at least five years and that Heitec had acquiesced in such use, since, although it was aware of the use, it had not taken sufficient measures to stop it. The court action had not interrupted the period of limitation, since it had been served on Heitech and RW only after five years had elapsed since the warning letter which preceded that action.

Heitec brought a further appeal before the referring court. That court noted that the outcome of the appeal depended on whether Heitec was time-barred from bringing its claim for an injunction and its ancillary claims. It also noted that the Oberlandesgericht Nürnberg (Higher Regional Court, Nuremberg) did not err in law in finding that there was 'use' in the present case from 6 May 2009 at the latest and that Heitec had become aware of that by means of the letter of 6 May 2009 which Heitech had sent to it. It was, moreover, common ground that Heitech was not accused of having acted in bad faith.

In these circumstances, the Bundesgerichtshof (Federal Court of Justice, Germany) decided to stay the proceedings and to refer the following questions to the Court of Justice for a preliminary ruling:

> *'(1) Can acquiescence within the meaning of Article 9(1) and (2) of [Directive 2008/95] and Article 54(1) and (2) and Article 111(2) of Regulation No 207/2009 be excluded not only by means of an administrative or court action, but also through conduct not involving a court or administrative authority?*
>
> *(2) If Question 1 is answered in the affirmative:*
>
> *does the sending of a warning letter, in which the proprietor of the earlier sign, before initiating legal proceedings, requires the proprietor of the later sign to agree to refrain from using the sign, and to enter into an obligation to pay a contractual penalty in the event of an infringement, constitute conduct precluding acquiescence within the meaning of Article 9(1) and (2) of [Directive 2008/95] and Article 54(1) and (2) and Article 111(2) of [Regulation No 207/2009]?*
>
> *(3) When seeking judicial redress, is the bringing of the action before the court or the receipt of the action by the defendant decisive for calculating*

the five-year acquiescence period for the purposes of Article 9(1) and (2) of [Directive 2008/95] and Article 54(1) and (2) and Article 111(2) of [Regulation No 207/2009]? Is it significant in this regard that receipt of the action by the defendant is delayed beyond the expiry of the five-year period through the fault of the proprietor of the earlier trade mark?

(4) Does the limitation of rights in accordance with Article 9(1) and (2) of [Directive 2008/95] and Article 54(1) and (2) and Article 111(2) of [Regulation No 207/2009] encompass consequential claims under trade mark law, for example, claims for compensation, provision of information or destruction, as well as prohibitory injunctions?'

2. Decision

1. Article 9 of Directive 2008/95/EC of the European Parliament and of the Council of 22 October 2008 to approximate the laws of the Member States relating to trade marks and Articles 54, 110 and 111 of Council Regulation (EC) No 207/2009 of 26 February 2009 on the Community trade mark must be interpreted as meaning that an act, such as a warning letter, by which the proprietor of an earlier mark or other earlier right opposes the use of a later mark without taking the necessary steps to obtain a legally binding solution does not stop acquiescence and, consequently, does not interrupt the period of limitation.

2. Article 9 of Directive 2008/95 and Articles 54, 110 and 111 of Regulation No 207/2009 must be interpreted to mean that the limitation in consequence of acquiescence referred to in those provisions may not be prevented by the bringing of a court action in which the proprietor of an earlier mark or other earlier right sought a declaration of invalidity of a later mark or opposed the use of that mark, where the application initiating proceedings, although filed before the date of expiry of the period of limitation, did not, owing to a lack of diligence on the part of the applicant, satisfy the requirements of the applicable national law for service and was rectified only after that date for reasons attributable to the applicant.

3. Article 9 of Directive 2008/95 and Articles 54, 110 and 111 of Regulation No 207/2009 must be interpreted as meaning that, where the proprietor of an earlier mark or other earlier right, within the meaning of those provisions, is time-barred from seeking a declaration of invalidity of a later mark and from opposing the use of that mark, that proprietor is also time-barred from bringing ancillary or related claims, such as claims for damages, the provision of information or the destruction of goods.

3. Motivation and Analysis

The European Court of Justice (hereinafter: 'the Court') noted that the referring court by its first and second questions was in essence asking whether Article 9 of Directive 2008/95 and Articles 54 and 111 of Regulation No 207/2009 (now replaced by Art. 9 of Dir. 2015/2436 and Art. 61 and 138 of Reg. No 2017/1001 respectively) must be interpreted as meaning that an act, such as a warning letter, whereby the proprietor of an earlier mark or other earlier right opposes the use of a later mark without bringing an administrative or judicial appeal, is capable of ending acquiescence within the meaning of those provisions.

The Court recalled that the regime for limitation in consequence of acquiescence provided for in the EU trade mark legislation pursues the objective of striking a balance between the interest which the proprietor of a trade mark has in safeguarding its essential function, on the one hand, and the interests of other economic operators in having signs capable of denoting their goods and services, on the other.[2] In particular, by setting a period of limitation in consequence of acquiescence of five consecutive years with knowledge of the use of the later trade mark, the EU legislature sought to ensure that the protection conferred by an earlier trade mark on its proprietor remains limited to cases where the proprietor shows itself to be sufficiently vigilant by opposing the use of signs by other operators likely to infringe its mark.[3]

More specifically the Court clarified that the rule on limitation in consequence of acquiescence is intended to safeguard legal certainty. Where the proprietor of an earlier mark or other earlier right has knowingly 'acquiesced' in the use of a later mark applied for in good faith for a continuous period of five years, the proprietor of the later mark must be certain in law that such use can no longer be challenged by the proprietor of that earlier mark or other earlier right.[4]

The Court pointed out that the concept of 'acquiescence' has the same meaning in the directive and in the regulation, namely that the proprietor of that earlier mark or other earlier right remains inactive even though it is aware of the use of a later mark which it would be in a position to oppose. It has 'acquiesced' by failing to take measures open to it to remedy that situation.[5]

Accordingly, the proprietor of an earlier mark or other earlier right is time-barred from seeking a declaration of invalidity or opposing the use of a later mark applied for in good faith, where, for a period of five consecutive years,

---

[2] Para. 46 of the annotated judgment, with reference to judgments of 27 April 2006, *Levi Strauss*, C-145/05, EU:C:2006:264, para. 29, and of 22 September 2011, *Budějovický Budvar*, C-482/09, EU:C:2011:605, para. 34.

[3] Para. 46 of the annotated judgment, with reference to judgment of 27 April 2006, *Levi Strauss*, C 145/05, EU:C:2006:264, para. 30.

[4] As noted in recital 12 of Directive 2008/95, see para. 48 of the annotated judgment.

[5] Para. 49 of the annotated judgment, also referring to the judgment of 22 September 2011, *Budějovický Budvar*, C 482/09, EU:C:2011:605, paras. 35 and 44.

while being aware of such use, it has failed to carry out an act that clearly expresses its wish to oppose that use and to remedy the alleged infringement of its rights.[6] The Court notes that such an interpretation also applies to Article 110 of Regulation No 207/2009 (now Art. 138 of Reg. No 2017/1001).[7]

The Court recalled that, in any event, the bringing of an administrative or court action before the expiry of that period ends acquiescence and consequently prevents limitation (see, to that effect, the judgment of 22 September 2011, *Budějovický Budvar*, C-482/09, EU:C:2011:605, para. 49).[8] Bringing such an action unequivocally expresses a wish to oppose the use of the later mark and to remedy the alleged infringement of rights.[9]

The Court noted that where the bringing of that action was preceded by the sending of a warning letter, with which the proprietor of the later mark did not comply, that warning letter may interrupt the period of limitation in consequence of acquiescence provided that, following the unsatisfactory response to that warning letter, the proprietor of the earlier mark or other earlier right continues to express its opposition to the use of the later mark and takes the measures available to it to enforce its rights.[10] In contrast, if the proprietor of the earlier mark or other earlier right, having expressed its opposition to the use of the later mark by a warning letter, does not, after noting the refusal of the addressee of that letter to comply with it or to enter into negotiations, pursue its efforts within a reasonable period in order to remedy that situation, where appropriate by bringing an administrative or court action, it must be inferred that the proprietor has failed to take the measures available to it to put an end to the alleged infringement of its rights.[11]

The Court explained that any interpretation to the effect that sending a warning letter is sufficient, in itself, to interrupt the period of limitation would allow the proprietor of the earlier mark or other earlier right to circumvent the regime for limitation in consequence of acquiescence by repeatedly sending a warning letter approximately every five years. This would undermine the objectives of the regime for limitation in consequence of acquiescence, and would deprive that regime of its effectiveness.[12]

As to the third question, the Court noted that the referring court was in essence asking if acquiescence may be prevented by the bringing of a court action in

6 Para. 50 of the annotated judgment.

7 Para. 51 of the annotated judgment.

8 Para. 52 of the annotated judgment, with reference to judgment of 22 September 2011, *Budějovický Budvar*, C 482/09, EU:C:2011:605, para. 49

9 Para. 53 of the annotated judgment.

10 Para. 54 of the annotated judgment.

11 Para. 55 of the annotated judgment.

12 Para. 56 of the annotated judgment.

which the proprietor of an earlier mark or other earlier right seeks a declaration of invalidity of a later mark or opposes the use of that mark, but where the application initiating proceedings, although filed before the expiry date of the period of limitation, was not, owing to a lack of diligence on the part of the applicant, served on the defendant until after that date.

For the question of when a court action has been 'brought', the Court found it prudent to look at the interpretation of rules adopted in the field of judicial cooperation in civil matters. From these, it follows that a court action has been 'brought' on the date on which the application initiating proceedings was lodged, although the court concerned can be deemed to be seized at that time only if the applicant has not subsequently failed to take the steps it was required to take to have service effected on the defendant.

The lodging of the application initiating proceedings normally reflects the genuine and unambiguous wish of the applicant to assert its rights, which is sufficient, in principle, to end acquiescence and, consequently, to interrupt the period of limitation.[13]

The conduct of that party may nevertheless, in certain cases, raise doubts as to that wish and the serious nature of the action brought before the court seized. That is the case, in particular, where, owing to a lack of diligence on the part of the applicant, the application initiating proceedings is not rectified in good time when it fails to meet the formal requirements of national law for service on the defendant.[14] In such circumstances, which are attributable to the applicant, the latter cannot claim to have put an end to the acquiescence of the use of the later mark by lodging the application initiating proceedings. It is only by rectifying that application, in accordance with the requirements of the applicable national law, that the applicant is to be regarded as having unequivocally expressed a clear and serious intention to assert its rights and that, consequently, the action may be deemed to have been effectively initiated.[15]

The Court noted that it is for the referring court to ascertain the date on which the application initiating proceedings was rectified in such a way as to enable the court seized to commence the proceedings and to serve that document on the defendants in the main proceedings. If the rectification did not take place until after the expiry of the period of limitation in consequence of acquiescence, it is for the referring court to assess whether that fact is mainly due to conduct on the part of the applicant in the main proceedings which may be characterised as a lack of diligence. If that court were to take the view that that was the case, it would have to conclude that its action must be regarded as time-barred.[16]

---

[13] Para. 62 of the annotated judgment.

[14] Para. 63 of the annotated judgment.

[15] Para. 64 of the annotated judgment.

[16] Para. 67 of the annotated judgment.

The fourth question according to the Court in essence concerned whether Article 9 of Directive 2008/95 and Articles 54 and 111 of Regulation No 207/2009 must be interpreted as meaning that, where the proprietor of an earlier mark or other earlier right, within the meaning of those provisions, is time-barred from seeking a declaration of invalidity of a later mark and from opposing the use of that mark, that proprietor is also time-barred from bringing ancillary or related claims, such as claims for damages, the provision of information or the destruction of goods.

The Court, not surprisingly, answered this in the affirmative. It explained that it would be contrary to and undermine the objectives of the regime for limitation in consequence of acquiescence, most notably the safeguarding of legal certainty, to allow, in such a situation, that proprietor to bring an action against the proprietor of that later mark after the end of that period of five consecutive years seeking that the latter be ordered to pay damages or seeking injunctions against the latter.[17]

* *
*

The CJEU's ruling is of importance for the reason that it provides practical guidance on situations of acquiescence.

The Court opts for a rigid approach. If an older trade mark proprietor has become aware of a younger trade mark, it must in principle bring proceedings within five years in order not to forfeit its rights.

This ruling drew particular attention from Dutch scholars on the grounds that (i) the approach might be too rigid, and (ii) the ruling seemed to put an end to a Dutch practice under which reasonableness and fairness play an important role in assessing the limitation of rights.[18]

As to the rigid approach, it was noted that there can be situations in which an older proprietor does not initiate proceedings within five years against a younger proprietor, but where, however, it is unambiguously clear to the younger proprietor that the older proprietor does not wish to relinquish its rights. Examples of such a situation that were given in the literature include the following:

- the situation where the older and younger trade mark holders are still negotiating a possible coexistence of the two trade marks. The annotated decision sheds no direct light on how such a situation must be regarded.
- the situation where an infringement initially only takes place on a (very) small scale. From a procedural and economic point of view it might often

[17] Paras. 70-73 of the annotated judgment.

[18] Most notably, annotations of S.L.H. Bergsma, in *Berichten Industriële Eigendom* 2022/4, no. 8, p. 191-199, and J. Vrielink, in *Intellectuele Eigendom en Reclamerecht (IER)*, 2023/12.

> not make sense to initiate costly legal proceedings. The extent of the infringement may, however, increase over time, making it necessary to take legal action against it. From the annotated ruling it seems to follow that, in such a case, the trade mark proprietor has nevertheless forfeited its rights, if for five years it has been aware of the prior infringement (even if it is only a minor one) but did not take legal action against it.[19]

In Dutch legal practice, reasonableness and fairness have traditionally played an important role in assessing the limitation of rights in trade mark law. In 1993, the year of entry into force of the Community Trade Mark Regulation and three years before the implementation of the Trade Mark Directive in the Benelux, the Dutch Supreme Court ruled that the '*delay in exercising rights or a lack of diligence in asserting judicial rights*' by itself does not provide sufficient grounds for a limitation of right in trade mark law.[20] The starting point of the Dutch practice is that the mere lapse of time is not sufficient to assume a limitation of right. Even after the implementation of the Trade Mark Directive, Dutch courts included the aspect of reasonableness and fairness in their assessment whether there was a situation of acquiescence in the younger trade mark (also in relation to acquiescence in the use of signs that were not registered as a trade mark).

Since the term 'acquiescence' according to the Court has the same meaning in the regulation and the corresponding provision of the directive, such a liberal approach no longer seems possible when assessing whether the right of an older proprietor to act against a younger trade mark is limited.[21] Strictly speaking, there is still room for the earlier Dutch practice where the case does not concern actions against the use of signs that are not registered as a trade mark. However, it is conceivable that judges may be inclined to follow the annotated judgment in applying a more rigid approach now that the CJEU has made it apparent that safeguarding legal certainty for the proprietor of the later mark is paramount.

To conclude, trade mark owners should be aware that merely sending a summons letter may not be sufficient to prevent limitation of the right to take action and that one has to follow up with proceedings. For the sake of certainty, it is advisable to initiate proceedings even when there is a minor infringement and/or when negotiations are ongoing around the end of the five-year period since the trade mark owner was aware of the younger trade mark.

---

19 S.L.H. Bergsma, in *Berichten Industriële Eigendom* 2022/4, no. 8, p. 191-199.

20 Dutch Supreme Court 17 December 1993, ECLI:NL:HR:1993:ZC1186 (*Michelin*).

21 S.L.H. Bergsma, in *Berichten Industriële Eigendom* 2022/4, no. 8, p. 191-199, and J. Vrielink, in *Intellectuele Eigendom en Reclamerecht (IER)*, 2023/12.

Court of Justice 19 December 2019

On second-hand e-books and the right of communication to the public

Case C-263/18

Summary and Analysis by Bram Woltering[1]

Parties:

Nederlands Uitgeversverbond
Groep Algemene Uitgevers

v

Tom Kabinet Internet BV
Tom Kabinet Holding BV
Tom Kabinet Uitgeverij BV

1. Background and History

This request for a preliminary ruling concerned the interpretation of Articles 2[2], 4(1) and (2)[3] and 5[4] of Directive 2001/29/EC of the European Parliament and of the Council of 22 May 2001 on the harmonisation of certain aspects of copyright and related rights in the information society.

---

1 Bram Woltering is an attorney-at-law at AKD, the Netherlands, and works within the Intellectual Property & Technology practice group.

2 Art. 2 of Dir. 2001/29, entitled 'Reproduction right', provides: '*Member States shall provide for the exclusive right to authorise or prohibit direct or indirect, temporary or permanent reproduction by any means and in any form, in whole or in part: (a) for authors, of their works: […].*'

3 Art. 4 Dir. 2001/29, entitled 'Distribution right', reads as follows: '*1. Member States shall provide for authors, in respect of the original of their works or of copies thereof, the exclusive right to authorise or prohibit any form of distribution to the public by sale or otherwise. 2. The distribution right shall not be exhausted within the Community in respect of the original or copies of the work, except where the first sale or other transfer of ownership in the Community of that object is made by the rightholder or with his consent.*'

4 Art. 5 Dir. 2001/29, entitled 'Exceptions and limitations', states, in para. 1:
'*Temporary acts of reproduction referred to in Article 2, which are transient or incidental, which are an integral and essential part of a technological process and the sole purpose of which is to enable:*

(a) a transmission in a network between third parties by an intermediary, or
(b) a lawful use

of a work or other subject matter to be made, and which have no independent economic significance, shall be exempted from the reproduction right provided for in Article 2.'

The request was made in proceedings between, on the one hand, Nederlands Uitgeversverbond ('NUV') and Groep Algemene Uitgevers ('GAU') and, on the other hand, Tom Kabinet Internet BV ('Tom Kabinet'), Tom Kabinet Holding BV and Tom Kabinet Uitgeverij BV, concerning the provision of an online service consisting of a virtual market for second-hand e-books.

NUV and GAU, associations whose purpose is to defend the interests of Dutch publishers, were mandated by several publishers to protect the copyrights granted to them by copyright holders by means of exclusive licences.

Tom Kabinet Holding is the sole shareholder of Tom Kabinet Uitgeverij, a publisher of books, e-books, and databases, and also of Tom Kabinet. Tom Kabinet operates a website on which it launched an online service consisting of a virtual market for second-hand e-books on 24 June 2014.

In 2014, NUV and GAU brought an action against Tom Kabinet, Tom Kabinet Holding and Tom Kabinet Uitgeverij before the urgent applications judge at the Rechtbank Amsterdam (District Court, Amsterdam, the Netherlands) in respect of that online service. The District Court dismissed the action on the ground that there was no infringement of copyright.

NUV and GAU appealed against that decision before the Gerechtshof Amsterdam (Court of Appeal, Amsterdam, Netherlands), which, by its judgment of 20 January 2015, upheld the decision but prohibited Tom Kabinet from offering an online service enabling the sale of unlawfully downloaded e-books. No appeal on a point of law was lodged against that judgment.

As of 8 June 2015, Tom Kabinet changed the services it had previously offered and replaced them with the 'Tom Leesclub' (Tom reading club, 'the reading club'), in which Tom Kabinet acted as an e-book trader. In return for a fee, the reading club offered its members second-hand e-books which had either been purchased by Tom Kabinet or donated to Tom Kabinet free of charge by members of the club. In the latter case, these members had to provide the download link for the book in question and declare that they had not kept a copy of the book. Tom Kabinet then uploaded the e-book from the retailer's website and placed its own digital watermark on it, which served as confirmation that it was a legally acquired copy.

Initially, the e-books available through the reading club could be purchased at a fixed price of EUR 1.75 per e-book. After payment, the member could download the e-book from Tom Kabinet's website and subsequently resell it to Tom Kabinet. Membership of the reading club was subject to payment by members of a monthly subscription fee of EUR 3.99. Any e-book provided free of charge by a member entitled that member to a discount of EUR 0.99 on the following month's subscription.

From November 2015, the payment of a monthly subscription was no longer a prerequisite for membership of the reading club. On the one hand, the price of every e-book was now set at EUR 2. On the other hand, the members of the reading club also needed 'credits' in order to be able to purchase an e-book through the reading club; credits could be obtained by making an e-book available to the club, either for a fee or free of charge. Such credits could also be purchased when making an order.

NUV and GAU requested the Rechtbank Den Haag (District Court, The Hague, Netherlands) for an injunction prohibiting Tom Kabinet, Tom Kabinet Holding and Tom Kabinet Uitgeverij from infringing the copyright of NUV's and GAU's affiliates by making available or reproducing e-books. They argued that Tom Kabinet was making an unauthorised communication of e-books to the public.

In an interim judgment of 12 July 2017, the referring court found that the e-books at issue were to be classified as works, within the meaning of Directive 2001/29, and that Tom Kabinet's offer, in circumstances such as those at issue in the main proceedings, did not constitute a communication to the public of those works, within the meaning of Article 3(1) of that Directive.[5]

However, the referring court observed that the answers to the questions whether making an e-book available at a distance by downloading it for use for an unlimited period in return for payment could constitute an act of distribution within the meaning of Article 4(1) of Directive 2001/29, and whether the right of distribution could thus be exhausted, within the meaning of Article 4(2) of that Directive, were unclear. It also wondered whether, in the event of a resale, the copyright holder might object, on the basis of Article 2 of that Directive, to the acts of reproduction necessary for the lawful transmission between subsequent purchasers of the copy in respect of which any distribution right had been exhausted. According to the national court, the answer to that question was not apparent from the case-law of the Court of Justice.

In those circumstances, the District Court decided to stay the proceedings and to refer the following questions to the CJEU for a preliminary ruling:

> *'(1) Is Article 4(1) of [Directive 2001/29] to be interpreted as meaning that "any form of distribution to the public by sale or otherwise of the original of their works or copies thereof" as referred to therein includes the making available remotely by downloading, for use for an unlimited period, of e-books (being digital copies of books protected by copyright)*

---

[5] Art. 3 Dir. 2001/29, entitled 'Right of communication to the public of works and right of making available to the public other subject matter', provides, in paras. 1 and 3:
'*1. Member States shall provide authors with the exclusive right to authorise or prohibit any communication to the public of their works, by wire or wireless means, including the making available to the public of their works in such a way that members of the public may access them from a place and at a time individually chosen by them. [...] 3. The rights referred to in paragraphs 1 and 2 shall not be exhausted by any act of communication to the public or making available to the public as set out in this Article.*'

at a price by means of which the copyright holder receives remuneration equivalent to the economic value of the work belonging to him?

(2) If question 1 is to be answered in the affirmative, is the distribution right with regard to the original or copies of a work as referred to in Article 4(2) of [Directive 2001/29] exhausted in the European Union, when the first sale or other transfer of that material, which includes the making available remotely by downloading, for use for an unlimited period, of e-books (being digital copies of books protected by copyright) at a price by means of which the copyright holder receives remuneration equivalent to the economic value of the work belonging to him, takes place in the European Union through the rightholder or with his consent?

(3) Is Article 2 of [Directive 2001/29] to be interpreted as meaning that a transfer between successive acquirers of a lawfully acquired copy in respect of which the distribution right has been exhausted constitutes consent to the acts of reproduction referred to therein, in so far as those acts of reproduction are necessary for the lawful use of that copy and, if so, which conditions apply?

(4) Is Article 5 of [Directive 2001/29] to be interpreted as meaning that the copyright holder may no longer oppose the acts of reproduction necessary for a transfer between successive acquirers of the lawfully acquired copy in respect of which the distribution right has been exhausted and, if so, which conditions apply?'

2. Decision

The supply to the public by downloading, for permanent use, of an e-book is covered by the concept of 'communication to the public' and, more specifically, by that of 'making available to the public of [authors'] works in such a way that members of the public may access them from a place and at a time individually chosen by them,' within the meaning of Article 3(1) of Directive 2001/29/EC of the European Parliament and of the Council of 22 May 2001 on the harmonisation of certain aspects of copyright and related rights in the information society.

3. Motivation and Analysis

The CJEU reformulated the questions of the referring court, noting that the national court was essentially asking whether the supply of an e-book by way of downloading for permanent use falls within the concept of 'communication to the public' within the meaning of Article 3(1) of Directive 2001/29, or within the concept of 'distribution to the public', as referred to in Article 4(1) of that Directive.

As is apparent from Article 3(1) of Directive 2001/29, authors have the exclusive right to authorise or prohibit any communication to the public of their works, by wire or wireless means, including the making available to the public of their works in such a way that members of the public may access them from a place and at a time individually chosen by them.

Article 4(1) of that Directive, on the other hand, provides that authors have, in respect of the original of their works or of copies thereof, the exclusive right to authorise or prohibit any form of distribution to the public by sale or otherwise, that right being, under Article 4(2) of that Directive, exhausted where the first sale or other transfer of ownership in the European Union of the original or of a copy of the work is made by the rightholder or with his or her consent.

According to the CJEU,[6] neither these provisions nor any other provision of Directive 2001/29 can, on the basis of their wording alone, determine whether the supply of an e-book by downloading it for permanent use constitutes a communication to the public, in particular a making available to the public of a work in such a way that members of the public may access it from a place and at a time individually chosen by them, or an act of distribution for the purposes of that Directive.

The CJEU explained that an interpretation of a provision of EU law requires that account be taken not only of its wording, but also of its context, the objectives pursued by the rules of which it is part and, where appropriate, its origins.[7] Given that, as is apparent from Recital 15 of Directive 2001/29,[8] the Directive serves, *inter alia*, to implement a number of the European Union's obligations under the WIPO Copyright Treaty (WCT), the concepts of 'communication to the public' and 'distribution to the public' must, as far as possible, be interpreted in accordance with the definitions contained in the WCT.[9]

In this regard the CJEU concluded that making an e-book available to the public by downloading it for permanent use is covered by the concept of 'communication to the public'.

---

6 Para. 37 of the annotated judgment.

7 Para. 38 of the annotated judgment, referring to *inter alia* Case-3-97/16 and C-435, *Acacia and D'Amato*, para. 31, and Case C-621/18, 10 December 2018, *Wightman and Others*, para. 47, and Case C-572/17, 19 December 2018, *Syed*, C-572/17, para. 20 and the case-law cited.

8 Rec. (15) Dir. 2001/29, provides: '*The Diplomatic Conference held under the auspices of the World Intellectual Property Organisation (WIPO) in December 1996 led to the adoption of two new Treaties, the 'WIPO Copyright Treaty' and the 'WIPO Performances and Phonograms Treaty', dealing respectively with the protection of authors and the protection of performers and phonogram producers. [...] This Directive also serves to implement a number of the new international obligations.*'

9 Para. 39 of the annotated judgment.

First of all, the CJEU noted that the relevant Articles 6 and 7 in the WCT (and the explanation of those articles) provide that the distribution right only covers copies that can be put into circulation as tangible objects.[10]

Secondly, the CJEU inferred from the Commission's explanatory memorandum to the proposed Directive that distribution refers only to tangible copies, and that a communication to the public refers to any communication of a work to the public. The explanatory memorandum made clear the intention to distinguish between electronic and tangible distribution of protected materials.[11]

Thirdly, such an interpretation is supported by the aim of that Directive, as set out in its preamble, and by the context of Articles 3(1) and 4(1) of that Directive. In this respect, the CJEU referred, *inter alia,* to Recitals 28 and 29 of Directive 2001/29. These relate to the distribution right, and state that this right includes the exclusive right to control '*distribution of the work incorporated in a tangible article*' and that the question of exhaustion of the right does not arise in the case of services and, in particular, online services, making it clear that, unlike a CD-ROM or a CD-I, where the intellectual property is incorporated in a material medium, namely an item of goods, any online service is in fact an act which should be subject to authorisation where the copyright or related right so provides.[12]

Fourth, an interpretation of the distribution right referred to in Article 4(1) of Directive 2001/29 as applying only to the distribution of works incorporated in a material medium also follows from Article 4(2) of that Directive in relation to the exhaustion of that right. It will be recalled that the CJEU had earlier ruled that the EU legislature, by using the terms 'tangible article' and 'that object' in Recital 28 of that Directive, wished to give authors control over the initial marketing in the European Union of each tangible object incorporating their intellectual creation.[13]

The CJEU then needed to address its own *UsedSoft* ruling.[14] Admittedly, as the CJEU noted, the CJEU held, in relation to the exhaustion of the right of distribution of copies of computer programs referred to in Article 4(2) of Directive 2009/24, that it does not follow from that provision that exhaustion is limited to copies of computer programs on a physical medium, but that, on the contrary, that provision, by referring without further specification to

---

10 Para. 40 of the annotated judgment.

11 Paras. 41-45 of the annotated judgment.

12 Paras. 46-51 of the annotated judgment.

13 Para. 52 of the annotated judgment, referring to Case C-419/13, 22 January 2015, *Art & Allposters International*, C-419/13, para. 37.

14 Case C-128/11, 3 July 2012, *UsedSoft*.

the '*sale […] of a copy of a program*,' makes no distinction as to the tangible or intangible form of the copy in question.[15]

The CJEU resolved the apparent discrepancy by following the Advocate General's opinion[16] and pointing out that an e-book is not a computer program, so that the provisions of the Software Directive, a *lex specialis*, do not need to be applied to it. In addition, the CJEU considered that the sale of software on a tangible medium and the sale of software by download are economically equivalent, whereas this cannot be assumed in the case of a book on a tangible medium and an e-book. The quality of digital copies does not deteriorate, and their exchange requires no effort or cost, implying that the impact of a second-hand market on the ability of the rightholder to obtain appropriate remuneration will be much greater.[17]

In its interlocutory judgment, the national court held that the mere fact that the e-book was offered for sale did not constitute disclosure of the content of the protected work and that there was no public since the e-book was made available only to one member of the reading club.

On the contrary, the CJEU held that Tom Kabinet was making the works concerned available to anyone who was registered with the reading club's website, that person being able to access the site from a place and at a time individually chosen by him or her. Accordingly, the supply of such a service must be considered to be the communication of a work within the meaning of Article 3(1) of Directive 2001/29.[18]

The CJEU distinguished two cumulative elements on this point, namely an act consisting of a communication of a work and its communication to a public. As to the latter, the Court recalled that the concept of communication must be interpreted broadly.[19]

The CJEU noted that 'communication to the public' includes any transmission or retransmission of a work to the public not present at the place where the communication originates, by wire or wireless means. As regards the concept of 'making available to the public', the CJEU recalled that it had held that such an act implies that members of the public may access the protected work from

15 Para. 53 of the annotated judgment.

16 Opinion of Advocate General Spzunar for C-263/18, 10 September 2019, *Tom Kabinet*, para. 67.

17 Paras. 54-59 of the annotated judgment.

18 Para. 65 of the annotated judgment.

19 Para. 61 of the annotated judgment, referring to Case C-610/15, 14 June 2017, *Stichting Brein*, C-610/15, para. 24 and the case-law cited therein.

a place and at a time individually chosen by them,[20] irrespective of whether the persons comprising that public avail themselves of that opportunity.[21,22]

Applying this to the reading club, the CJEU considered that Tom Cabinet was making the e-books available to anyone who signed up, and that those persons could therefore access them at a place and time individually chosen by them. This was considered to be 'the communication of a work', without those persons having to make use of that possibility by actually retrieving the e-book from the website. Given that the concept of 'public' involves a certain *de minimis* threshold[23] the CJEU did take into account the number of persons who could access the same work at the same time, as well as the number who could access it successively. This threshold was met because any interested person could become a member of the reading club, and for this reason, there was no security mechanism to ensure that only one copy could be downloaded or that the copy was no longer usable after the expiry of the period of use.[24]

Finally, the CJEU considered that Tom Kabinet appealed to a new public. Tom Kabinet was addressing an audience that the publishers had not already considered. The rationale here was that the provision of an e-book is accompanied by a user licence, which only allows the user to read it on their own devices.[25]

* *
*

This was a highly anticipated judgment. In 2012, the CJEU issued its famous UsedSoft judgment, which interpreted the Software Directive, and held that it was possible to resell lawful copies of computer programs downloaded from the internet, if the contractual operation in question was tantamount to a sale (it formally concerned a 'licence' which had the characteristics of a 'sale'). In the light of UsedSoft, the question was whether the same conclusion should be reached for other copyright subject matters in digital format under the InfoSoc Directive, including e-books, audiobooks, music and audiovisual files, etc.

The answer to the question of whether the exhaustion principle applies has major implications. The effect of the annotated judgment is that the exhaustion principle does not apply to the supply of e-books by online download for permanent use. Such a supply is covered by the right of communication to the public. Therefore, rightholders can, in principle, stop the resale of their e-books

---

20 Case C-297/13, 26 March 2015, *C More Entertainment*, paras. 24 and 25.

21 Case C-610/15, 14 June 2017, *Stichting Brein*, C-610/15, para. 31 and the case-law cited therein.

22 Paras. 62-64 of the annotated judgment.

23 Case C-610/15, 14 June 2017, *Stichting Brein*, C-610/15, para. 31 and the case-law cited therein.

24 Paras. 66-69 of the annotated judgment.

25 Para. 71 of the annotated judgment.

that have been supplied in this way. The judgment was met with some mixed reactions in the Dutch legal literature, which noted that from a practical point of view, it is not easy to distinguish between downloads of different 'used' digital products[26] and that the way in which the Court framed the economic and functional difference between e-books and software was not entirely convincing.[27]

The judgment is obviously of great importance to the e-book market, but also affects other types of work, such as digital films and music. It seems evident from the ruling that the reselling of digital music or digital films also constitutes an infringement of copyright.

The judgment of the Court meant the end of Tom Kabinet's business model for second-hand e-books. Following the decision, Tom Kabinet decided to end its activities. On a national level, the case was not pursued any further as the parties terminated the proceedings.

Undoubtedly, digital content and the various (future) different technical means to make such content available to consumers, under various business models, will be a recurrent subject before the CJEU.

---

[26] M. Weij, Tijdschrift voor Internetrecht 2020, nr. 2, p. 58, and V. Tweehuysen, '*Digitale exemplaren in het auteursrecht*', NTBR 2020/31.

[27] V. Tweehuysen, 'Digitale exemplaren in het auteursrecht', *NTBR* 2020/31.

COURT OF JUSTICE 29 JANUARY 2020

ON THE IDENTIFICATION OF THE GOODS OR SERVICES COVERED BY THE REGISTRATION, FAILURE TO COMPLY WITH THE REQUIREMENTS OF CLARITY AND PRECISION, AND BAD FAITH OF THE APPLICANT

Case C-371/18

Summary and Analysis by Bram Woltering[1]

Parties:

Sky plc
Sky International AG
Sky UK Ltd

v

SkyKick UK Ltd
SkyKick Inc

1. Background and History

The request for a preliminary ruling in this case concerned the interpretation of EU trade mark law and the approximation of the Member States' laws on trade marks.

It was made in proceedings between Sky plc, Sky International AG and Sky UK Ltd (together, 'Sky and Others'), and SkyKick UK Ltd and SkyKick Inc. (together, 'the SkyKick companies'), concerning the alleged infringement by the SkyKick companies of EU trade marks and a national United Kingdom trade mark belonging to Sky and Others.

Sky and Others, belonging to a well-known broadcasting group, were the proprietors of four Community figurative and word marks and one national United Kingdom word mark which included the word 'Sky' (together, 'the trade marks at issue in the main proceedings'). Those trade marks were registered in respect of a large number of goods and services in a number of classes of the Nice Classification, in particular Classes 9 and 38.

Sky and Others brought an action for infringement of the trade marks at issue in the main proceedings against the SkyKick companies (suppliers of cloud

---

[1] Bram Woltering is an attorney-at-law at AKD, the Netherlands, and works within the Intellectual Property & Technology practice group.

migration software) before the referring court, the High Court of Justice (England & Wales), Chancery Division (United Kingdom).

For the purposes of their action for infringement, Sky and Others relied on the registration of the trade marks at issue in the main proceedings in respect of goods in Class 9, namely computer software, computer software supplied from the Internet, computer software and telecommunications apparatus to enable connection to databases and the Internet, and data storage. They additionally relied on the services in Class 38, namely telecommunications services, electronic mail services, internet portal services, and computer services for accessing and retrieving information, messages, text, sound, images and data via a computer or computer network. Not every trade mark at issue in the main proceedings was registered in respect of those goods and services.

The referring court also stated that Sky and Others made extensive use of the trade marks at issue in the main proceedings in relation to a range of goods and services relating to their core business areas of television broadcasting, telephony, and broadband provision. It was not in dispute that those trade marks were a household name in the United Kingdom and Ireland in those areas. However, Sky and Others did not offer email migration or cloud backup goods or services, nor was there any evidence that they planned to do so in the immediate future. The three main products offered by the SkyKick companies were based on Software as a Service (SaaS) and concerned cloud migration, cloud backup and cloud management.

In the context of those proceedings, the SkyKick companies filed a counterclaim for a declaration that the trade marks at issue in the main proceedings were invalid. In support of that counterclaim, they contended that those trade marks were registered in respect of goods or services that were not specified with sufficient clarity and precision. The SkyKick companies relied in that regard on the judgment of 19 June 2012, *Chartered Institute of Patent Attorneys* (C-307/10, EU:C:2012:361).

In that context, the referring court questioned, in the first place, whether such a ground for invalidity could be asserted against a registered trade mark. In that regard, it recalled that the Court had held, in the cited judgment, that an applicant for a trade mark must designate with sufficient clarity and precision the goods and services in respect of which protection for the trade mark is sought in order to enable the competent authorities and third parties to determine the extent of the protection conferred by the trade mark. If the applicant fails to do so, the national office or the European Union Intellectual Property Office (EUIPO) should refuse to allow the application to proceed to registration without the specification being amended to make it sufficiently clear and precise.

The referring court considered that it did not, however, follow from the case-law arising from that judgment that the trade mark concerned could be declared invalid after registration on the ground that the specification lacked clarity or precision.

It stated that, in the case of an EU trade mark, Article 128(1) of Regulation 2017/1001 provides that a counterclaim for a declaration of invalidity '*may only be based on the grounds for [...] invalidity mentioned in this Regulation.*' In the present case, the SkyKick companies were relying on the ground provided for in Article 59(1)(a) of that regulation, read in the light of Article 4 and Article 7(1)(a) of the regulation, which do not require that the specification of goods and services in an EU trade mark application be clear and precise. The position was the same in relation to a national trade mark.

In the second place, if such a ground could be asserted, the referring court was uncertain whether the specifications of the goods and services could be objected to in respect of all of the trade marks at issue in the main proceedings. It stated that the SkyKick companies were contending that, in the case in the main proceedings, the identification of the goods and services covered by those trade marks lacked clarity and precision, except for 'telecommunications services' and 'electronic mail services' in Class 38. The SkyKick companies and Sky and Others disagreed as to whether the specifications 'computer software', 'computer software supplied from the Internet' and 'computer software and telecoms apparatus to enable connection to databases and the Internet' were clear and precise.

In that regard, the referring court considered that registration of a trade mark for 'computer software' was too broad and, therefore, contrary to the public interest because it conferred on the proprietor a monopoly of immense breadth which could not be justified by a commercial interest. However, in the referring court's view, it did not necessarily follow that the term 'computer software' was lacking in clarity and precision. Nonetheless, it was uncertain to what extent the indications in the European Trade Mark and Design Network (ETMDN) Common Communication on the Common Practice on the General Indications of the Nice Class Headings, of 28 October 2015, in relation to 'machines' in Class 7 within the meaning of the Nice Classification, could not equally apply to 'computer software'.

In the third place, the referring court was uncertain whether the validity of the trade marks at issue in the main proceedings could be affected by the trade mark applicant's bad faith at the time of filing the application for protection. The SkyKick companies had contended before the court that the trade marks at issue in the main proceedings had been registered in bad faith because Sky and Others did not intend to use them in relation to all of the goods and services covered by the registration of those trade marks. The trade marks should, therefore, all be cancelled or, at the very least, cancelled in part as regards the goods and services for which Sky and Others had no intention to use those marks.

In the referring court's view, to register trade marks without actual use of them being required would facilitate the registration process and enable brand owners to obtain protection of their trade marks more easily in advance of a commercial launch. However, facilitating registration or allowing it to be obtained too broadly would have the effect of creating barriers to market entry for third parties and eroding the public domain. Accordingly, the possibility of registering a trade mark without the intention to use it in relation to all or some of the specified goods and services would enable abuse, which would be harmful, if there were indeed no possibility of challenging an abusive registration by relying on the bad faith of the proprietor of the trade mark concerned. The referring court noted that, in their case-law, the United Kingdom courts and tribunals had focused more closely on the requirement of intention to use the trade mark concerned for the goods and services specified in the application for registration, because of the existence of Section 32(3) of the Trade Marks Act 1994 in that Member State's law.

The referring court was uncertain whether that provision was compatible with EU law. Assuming that it was compatible with EU law, the referring court was also uncertain as to the scope of the condition relating to the intention to use the trade mark for the goods and services for which it was registered.

First, although there was no express requirement of an intention to use in EU law, and a registered trade mark could not, as the law currently stood, be revoked for non-use until five years had expired, the case-law of the Court of Justice and of the General Court of the European Union suggested that, in certain circumstances, applying to register a trade mark without any intention to use it in relation to the specified goods or services might constitute bad faith on the part of that trade mark's proprietor at the time the application for protection was filed.

Secondly, it was apparent from the case-law that the fact that the applicant had applied for registration of the trade mark in question in respect of a broad range of goods or services was not sufficient to demonstrate bad faith if the applicant had a reasonable commercial rationale for seeking such protection having regard to that trade mark's use. Nor was the fact that the applicant might potentially use the trade mark sufficient to demonstrate the absence of good faith.

Thirdly, the case-law permitted the inference that, in an appropriate case, the applicant could have made the application partly in good faith and partly in bad faith, if it intended to use the trade mark solely in relation to some of the goods or services in respect of which it was registered.

If a trade mark applicant made the application for registration in bad faith in so far as the application with respect to some goods and services, but in good faith with respect to others, the referring court enquired whether the invalidity must be total or partial.

It considered that, in the case in the main proceedings, there was evidence showing that, at the time of registration of the trade marks at issue, Sky and Others did not intend to use them in relation to all of the goods and services covered by the registrations. Those registrations covered goods and services for which Sky and Others had no commercial rationale for seeking protection, so that the inclusion of such goods and services formed part of their strategy of seeking very broad protection of the trade marks.

In those circumstances, the High Court of Justice (England & Wales), Chancery Division decided to stay the proceedings and to refer the following questions to the Court of Justice for a preliminary ruling:

> '*(1) Can an EU trade mark or a national trade mark registered in a Member State be declared wholly or partially invalid on the ground that some or all of the terms in the specification of goods and services are lacking in sufficient clarity and precision to enable the competent authorities and third parties to determine on the basis of those terms alone the extent of the protection conferred by the trade mark*
>
> *(2) If the answer to question (1) is yes, is a term such as "computer software" too general and covers goods which are too variable to be compatible with the trade mark's function as an indication of origin for that term to be sufficiently clear and precise to enable the competent authorities and third parties to determine on the basis of that term alone the extent of the protection conferred by the trade mark?*
>
> *(3) Can it constitute bad faith simply to apply to register a trade mark without any intention to use it in relation to the specified goods or services?*
>
> *(4) If the answer to question (3) is yes, is it possible to conclude that the applicant made the application partly in good faith and partly in bad faith if and to the extent that the applicant had an intention to use the trade mark in relation to some of the specified goods or services, but no intention to use the trade mark in relation to other specified goods or services?*
>
> *(5) Is section 32(3) of the UK Trade Marks Act 1994 compatible with [Directive 2015/2436] and its predecessors?*'

2. Decision

1. Articles 7 and 51 of Council Regulation (EC) No 40/94 of 20 December 1993 on the Community trade mark, as amended by Council Regulation (EC) No 1891/2006 of 18 December 2006, and Article 3 of First Council Directive 89/104/EEC of 21 December 1988 to approximate the laws of the Member States relating to trade marks must be interpreted as meaning that a Community

trade mark or a national trade mark cannot be declared wholly or partially invalid on the ground that terms used to designate the goods and services in respect of which that trade mark was registered lack clarity and precision.

2. Article 51(1)(b) of Regulation No 40/94, as amended by Regulation No 1891/2006, and Article 3(2)(d) of First Directive 89/104 must be interpreted as meaning that a trade mark application made without any intention to use the trade mark in relation to the goods and services covered by the registration constitutes bad faith, within the meaning of those provisions, if the applicant for registration of that mark had the intention either of undermining, in a manner inconsistent with honest practices, the interests of third parties, or of obtaining, without even targeting a specific third party, an exclusive right for purposes other than those falling within the functions of a trade mark. When the absence of the intention to use the trade mark in accordance with the essential functions of a trade mark concerns only certain goods or services referred to in the application for registration, that application constitutes bad faith only in so far as it relates to those goods or services.

3. First Directive 89/104 must be interpreted as not precluding a provision of national law under which an applicant for registration of a trade mark must state that the trade mark is being used in relation to the goods and services in relation to which it is sought to register the trade mark, or that he or she has a bona fide intention that it should be so used, in so far as the infringement of such an obligation does not constitute, in itself, a ground for invalidity of a trade mark already registered.

3. Motivation and Analysis

The Court noted that the referring court by its first and second questions was in essence asking whether Articles 7 and 51 of Regulation No 40/94 and Article 3 of First Directive 89/104[2] must be interpreted as meaning that a Community trade mark or a national trade mark might be declared wholly or partially invalid on the ground that terms used to designate the goods and services in respect of which that mark was registered were lacking in clarity and precision. If that was the case, the referring court was enquiring whether the term 'computer software' met that requirement of clarity and precision.

---

2 Now replaced respectively by Art. 7 and 59 of Reg. (EU) 2017/1001 of the European Parliament and of the Council of 14 June 2017 on the European Union trade mark, *OJ L* 154, p. 1-99 and Art. 4 of Directive (EU) 2015/2436 of the European Parliament and of the Council of 16 December 2015 to approximate the laws of the Member States relating to trade marks, *OJ L* 336, p. 1-26.

To answer those questions the Court first needed to assess whether the lack of clarity and precision of the terms used to designate the goods and services covered by a trade mark constituted, in itself, an absolute ground for invalidity of a national trade mark or a Community trade mark. This was not the case according to the Court. Such a ground was not part of the exhaustive list of absolute grounds for invalidity.[3]

In addition, the Court explained that its earlier judgment in *Chartered Institute of Patent Attorneys*[4] could not be interpreted as meaning that the Court intended to recognise additional grounds for invalidity. This judgment merely provided clarifications on the requirements relating to new EU trade mark registration applications, and thus did not concern trade marks that were already registered at the date of the judgment's delivery.[5]

Furthermore, the concept of clarity and precision of the terms could not be understood to be part of the absolute ground on the requirement of graphic representability, given that the latter only concerned the sign of which the trade mark consisted.[6] Lastly and similarly, the lack of clarity and precision of the terms used to designate the goods and services in respect of which a trade mark had been registered was also not capable of providing a basis for invalidity on the ground that such a deficiency was contrary to public policy.[7]

The Court did, however, note that the rights of the proprietor of a trade mark might be declared to be revoked if, within a continuous period of five years, the trade mark had not been put to genuine use in the territory concerned in connection with the goods or services in respect of which it was registered. A national or Community trade mark registered for a range of goods and services designated in a manner which lacked clarity and precision could, in any event, only be protected in respect of the goods and services for which it was put to genuine use.[8]

The Court noted that the referring court by its third and fourth question was in essence asking whether Article 51(1)(b) of Regulation No 40/94 and Article 3(2)(d) of First Directive 89/104 (now replaced respectively by Article 59(1)(b) of Regulation No 2017/1001 and Article 4(2) of Directive 2015/2436) must be interpreted as meaning that a trade mark application made without any intention to use the trade mark in relation to the goods and services covered by the registration constituted bad faith within the meaning of those provisions and, if so, whether

---

3 Paras. 55-58 of the annotated judgment.

4 Case C-307/10, 19 June 2012, *Chartered Institute of Patent Attorneys*.

5 Para. 61 of the annotated judgment.

6 Paras. 62-64 of the annotated judgment.

7 Paras. 65-67 of the annotated judgment.

8 Paras. 68-70 of the annotated judgment.

Article 51(3) of Regulation No 40/94 and Article 13 of First Directive 89/104[9] must be interpreted as meaning that, when the absence of the intention to use a trade mark in accordance with its essential functions concerned only certain goods or services covered by the registration, the invalidity of that trade mark covered those goods or services only.

The Court recalled that a trade mark might be declared invalid where the applicant was acting in bad faith when it filed the application for the trade mark. Neither the Regulation nor the Directive provides a definition of the concept of 'bad faith'. The concept is an autonomous concept of EU law and, in the light of the need for a coherent application of the national systems and the EU system of marks, the concept of 'bad faith' must be interpreted in the context of the Directive in the same manner as in the context of the Regulation.[10] Referring to CJEU *Koton,*[11] the Courts noted that the concept of 'bad faith' presupposes the presence of a dishonest state of mind or intention, and that regard must be had, for the purposes of interpreting that concept, to the specific context of trade mark law, which is that of the course of trade. In that regard, the EU rules on trade marks are aimed, in particular, at contributing to the system of undistorted competition in the European Union, in which each undertaking must, in order to attract and retain customers by the quality of its goods or services, be able to have registered as trade marks signs which enable the consumer, without any possibility of confusion, to distinguish those goods or services from others which have a different origin. Bad faith applies where it is apparent from relevant and consistent indicia that the proprietor of a trade mark has filed the application for registration of that mark not with the aim of engaging fairly in competition but with the intention of undermining, in a manner inconsistent with honest practices, the interests of third parties, or with the intention of obtaining, without even targeting a specific third party, an exclusive right for purposes other than those falling within the functions of a trade mark, in particular the essential function of indicating origin.[12]

The bad faith of the trade mark applicant cannot be presumed on the basis of the mere finding that, at the time of filing its application, it had no economic activity corresponding to the goods and services referred to in the application. The reason for this is that the applicant for a trade mark is not required to indicate or even to know precisely, on the date on which its application for registration of a mark is filed or of the examination of that application, the use it will make of the mark applied for, and has a period of five years within which to begin actual use consistent with the essential function of the trade mark. However, the Court noted that the registration of a trade mark by an applicant without any

---

[9] Now replaced respectively by Art. 59(3) of Reg. No 2017/1001 and Art. 7 of Dir. 2015/2436.

[10] Para. 73 of the annotated judgment, in analogy referring to Case C-320/12, 27 June 2013, *Malaysia Dairy Industries.*

[11] Case 12 C-104/18, September 2019, *Koton Mağazacilik Tekstil Sanayi ve Ticaret v EUIPO.*

[12] Paras. 74-75 of the annotated judgment.

intention to use it in relation to the goods and services covered by that registration may constitute bad faith, where there is no rationale for the application for registration. Such bad faith may, however, according to the Court, be established only if there are objective, relevant and consistent indicia tending to show that, when the application for a trade mark was filed, the trade mark applicant had the intention either of undermining, in a manner inconsistent with honest practices, the interests of third parties, or of obtaining, without even targeting a specific third party, an exclusive right for purposes other than those falling within the functions of a trade mark.[13] When the absence of the intention to use a trade mark in accordance with its essential functions concerns only certain goods or services covered by the registration, the invalidity of the trade mark covers those goods or services only.[14]

Finally, the Court held that national law is not precluded from requiring a declaration by an applicant that it will use the mark (in good faith), as long as failure to do so does not constitute in itself a ground for invalidity.[15]

* *
*

The CJEU's ruling was highly anticipated as a source of further clarification regarding (i) the possible consequences for registered trade marks which have terms used to designate the goods and services that lack clarity and precision, and (ii) the concept of 'bad faith'.

The assessment of whether an application was made in bad faith inherently requires a factual assessment.

Sky's application for the trade mark in Class 9 and 38 came down to the question whether or not there were objective, relevant and consistent indicia tending to show that, when the application for the trade mark was filed, the trade mark applicant had the intention either of undermining, in a manner inconsistent with honest practices, the interests of third parties, or of obtaining, without even targeting a specific third party, an exclusive right for purposes other than those falling within the functions of a trade mark.

The course of proceedings after the referral illustrates this is not an easy task. The High Court (Lord Justice Arnold) held that Sky's trade marks had been partly filed in bad faith, *inter alia* in relation to 'computer software' and 'data storage'. The High Court found not only that Sky did not intend to use the trade marks, but that there was no foreseeable prospect that they would ever intend to use the trade marks in relation to such goods and services. Moreover, the

13 Paras. 76-78 of the annotated judgment.

14 Paras. 79-80 of the annotated judgment.

15 Paras. 83-87 of the annotated judgment.

High Court found that Sky had made the applications pursuant to a deliberate strategy of seeking very broad protection of the trade mark regardless of whether it was commercially justified. Sky had thus applied for the trade marks with the intention of obtaining an exclusive right for purposes other than those falling within the functions of a trade mark, namely purely as a legal weapon against third parties, whether in threats of infringement claims or actual infringement claims or opposition to third-party applications for registration.[16]

Interestingly, given that 'computer software' was a broad and vague category, the High Court divided it into subcategories for which the trade mark remained valid, as it held that subcategories such as 'computer software supplied as part of or in connection with any telecommunications apparatus or service' were not useful.[17] Given that Sky retained protection for key goods and services SkyKick was found to have infringed Sky's registrations in respect of the resultant specification. Both parties appealed.

The Court of Appeal decided that Sky had not act in bad faith with regard to its application for 'computer software.' Given that Sky intended to use its marks for a type of software, but not all types of software, the Court of Appeal held that this could not constitute bad faith. According to the Court of Appeal it was not wrong to file for a broad category of goods or services where the intention or commercial justification existed for at least one item within that category.[18] Following the judgment of the Court of Appeal SkyKick appealed to the UK Supreme Court on the issue of bad faith. At the time of writing[19] the matter is still pending before the UK Supreme Court.

Following Brexit, these questions in Sky versus SkyKick unfortunately will not end up before the CJEU again. It will be interesting to see which approach will be taken in the UK as to the interplay between the breadth of specification and vulnerability to the accusation of invalidity on the grounds of bad faith. Can an intention of use or commercial justification for a subcategory within a broad category prevent an application for the broader category as a whole being found to be in bad faith? The answer to this question has important implications: being able to retain a broad category rather than a narrowly trimmed down subcategory might be decisive for the outcome in infringement proceedings. It seems inevitable that courts in the EU will at some point be confronted with the same questions and will refer them to the CJEU for some welcome guidance.

---

16 England and Wales High Court (Chancery Division) [2020] EWHC 990 (Ch), [2020] RPC 16, paras. 19-21.

17 England and Wales High Court (Chancery Division) [2020] EWHC 990 (Ch), [2020] RPC 16, paras. 19-21.

18 England and Wales Court of Appeal (Civil Division), [2021] RPC 17, [2021] EWCA Civ 1121.

19 September 2024.

COURT OF JUSTICE 2 APRIL 2020

ON LIABILITY FOR STORAGE ON BEHALF OF THIRD PARTIES OF GOODS THAT INFRINGE A TRADE MARK

Case C-567/18

Summary and analysis by Lena van Bracht[1]

Parties:

Coty Germany GmbH

v

Amazon Services Europe Sàrl
Amazon Europe Core Sàrl
Amazon FC Graben GmbH
Amazon EU Sàrl

1. Background and History

Coty Germany GmbH ('Coty') is a listed perfume and cosmetics group. The Group owns various well-known cosmetics and skincare brands. Coty also sells perfumes, among other things. Coty holds a licence for the EU trade mark 'DAVIDOFF', which provides protection for '*perfumery, essential oils, body and beauty care products*.'[2]

Amazon Services Europe offers third-party sellers the opportunity to place sales offers for their goods on the website www.amazon.de in the 'Amazon Marketplace' section. The purchase contracts for the goods sold in this way are concluded between the third-party sellers and the buyers. Third-party sellers also have the option of participating in the 'Shipping by Amazon' programme, in which the goods are stored by Amazon Group companies, including Amazon FC Graben, which operates a warehouse. The goods are shipped via external service providers.[3]

A legal dispute over the fragrance of the 'DAVIDOFF' brand arose between Coty as the licence holder and the two companies Amazon Services Europe and Amazon FC Graben ('Amazon'). Coty accused Amazon of infringing trade mark rights by storing and shipping bottles of 'Davidoff Hot Water' perfume that were offered for sale by third-party sellers on the 'Amazon Marketplace', having

[1] Lena van Bracht is an IP/Commercial Litigation lawyer at the German law firm GÖRG Partnerschaft von Rechtsanwälten mbB and is a member of the Berlin Bar.

[2] www.coty.com/.

[3] www.amazon.de/gp/help/customer/display.html?nodeId=GEF528GN65XSJ7V8.

been placed on the market without Coty's consent. Amazon did not offer the perfumes for sale itself but took over the storage and dispatch of the goods for a third-party seller on the Amazon Marketplace.

Coty initially sued Amazon for injunctive relief in this regard before the German courts. Coty requested that Amazon be ordered to cease and desist from possessing or sending perfumes bearing the 'Davidoff Hot Water' trade mark in the course of trade in Germany for the purpose of placing them on the market or having them possessed or sent for the purpose of placing them on the market if the goods had not been placed on the market in the Union with its consent. Amazon was not aware that the goods infringed the trade mark.[4]

Both the claim and the subsequent appeal were dismissed. The courts were of the opinion that Amazon had neither possessed the goods in question for itself nor placed them on the market itself by shipping them for a third party.[5]

The case went all the way to the German Federal Court of Justice (BGH), which asked the Court of Justice of the European Union to interpret the provisions of Article 9(2)(b) of Regulation No 207/2009 and Article 9(3)(b) of Regulation No 2017/1001 on the EU trade mark, as this was decisive for the outcome of the decision. The BGH was clearly disinclined to attribute the purposes pursued by the indirect proprietor to the direct proprietor.[6] With this position, BGH was upholding the warehouse keeper's and freight forwarder's privilege.[7]

The BGH decided to stay the proceedings and to refer the following question to the Court of Justice for a preliminary ruling:

> *'Does a person who, on behalf of a third party, stores goods which infringe trade mark rights, without having knowledge of that infringement, stock those goods for the purpose of offering them or putting them on the market, if it is not that person himself but rather the third party alone which intends to offer the goods or put them on the market?'*

2. Decision

Article 9(2)(b) of Council Regulation (EC) No 207/2009 of 26 February 2009 on the [European Union] trade mark and Article 9(3)(b) of Regulation (EU) No 2017/1001 of the European Parliament and of the Council of 14 June 2017

4 Para. 12 of the annotated judgment.

5 Para. 13 of the annotated judgment.

6 BGH order of reference of 26 July 2018 – I ZR 20/17, BeckRS 2018, 19562.

7 BGH, judgment of 17 September 2009 – Xa ZR 2/08 (OLG Düsseldorf) MP3-Player-Import. Here too, the forwarder and carrier had no general duty to check for infringements of property rights by the transported goods.

on the European Union trade mark must be interpreted as meaning that a person who, on behalf of a third party, stores goods which infringe trade mark rights, without being aware of that infringement, must be regarded as not stocking those goods in order to offer them or put them on the market for the purposes of those provisions, if that person does not itself pursue those aims.

3. Motivation and Analysis

First of all, the CJEU stated that it was necessary to examine whether the storage of goods of a third party constitutes 'use' of the trade mark within the meaning of Article 9(1) of Regulation No 207/2009 and Article 9(1) and (2) of Regulation No 2017/1001 and, in particular, can be regarded as 'possession' of those goods for the purpose of offering them or putting them on the market within the meaning of Article 9(2)(b) of Regulation No 207/2009, the content of which has been incorporated into Article 9(3)(b) of Regulation No 2017/1001.[8] The forms of use listed in Article 9(2) of Regulation No 207/2009, the content of which has been incorporated into Article 9(3) of Regulation No 2017/1001, are not exhaustive.[9] Whether mere storage falls within them must be determined, the CJEU stated, according to whether such storage can be regarded as 'use' of the trade mark within the meaning of Article 9(1) of Regulation No 207/2009 and Article 9(1) and (2) of Regulation No 2017/1001 and, in particular, as 'possession' of those goods for the purpose of offering them or putting them on the market within the meaning of Article 9(2)(b) of Regulation No 207/2009, the content of which has been taken over in Article 9(3)(b) of Regulation No 2017/1001.[10]

The CJEU found that a company that merely stores goods only infringes a trade mark if, like the seller, it pursues the purpose of offering the goods for sale or putting them on the market. This is not the case with Amazon Marketplace. A company that stores goods for a third party without being aware of a trade mark infringement is not using the trade mark itself if, like the seller, it does not intend to offer the goods for sale or place them on the market.[11]

---

[8] Para. 35 of the annotated judgment.

[9] Para. 33 of the annotated judgment.

[10] Para. 35 of the annotated judgment.

[11] Para. 53 of the annotated judgment.

However, the Court pointed out that other provisions of Union law, in particular Article 14(1) of Directive 2000/31[12] or the first sentence of Article 11 of Directive 2004/48,[13] may give rise to claims by the trade mark proprietor.[14]

The CJEU thus followed the opinion of the BGH and agreed with its decision-making practice.[15] In line with its previous case-law on operators of trading platforms, it clarified that use within the meaning of this standard requires active conduct and direct or indirect control over the act of use. Similarly to a trading platform operator, this is not automatically the case for a warehouse keeper, who merely provides storage for third-party goods.

The Attorney General initially took a different view and wanted to hold Amazon responsible. This was mainly due to Amazon's economic interest in selling the products due to the sales fees.[16]

The decision shows that it is not the mere possession of the goods that is relevant, but rather why and for what purpose the goods are held. A strict distinction must be made between the interests of the warehouse keeper/freight forwarder and those of the seller. Only the person who wishes to sell the goods possesses the goods for that purpose and bears responsibility for them. The person who merely stores the goods for another person is not pursuing that purpose, but is merely providing a service, namely storage.

However, the court left open the question whether liability under the principles of '*Störerhaftung*' (breach of duty of care) could be considered, as this question was not the subject of the question referred by the BGH.

The court also did not address the question of whether a distinction should be made between a traditional logistics company and a company such as Amazon – a point also made by the Advocate General. Unlike a traditional logistics company, Amazon makes money from the sale of the goods in question. Amazon profits from the offers of third parties and is involved in the entire sales process. The question therefore arises as to whether the object and purpose of ownership

---

[12] Dir. 2000/31/EC of the European Parliament and of the Council of 8 June 2000 on certain legal aspects of information society services, in particular electronic commerce, in the Internal Market ('Dir. on electronic commerce').

[13] Dir. 2004/48/EC of the European Parliament and of the Council of 29 April 2004 on the enforcement of intellectual property rights.

[14] Para. 49 of the annotated judgment.

[15] Similar decisions had already been made in the past, likewise, focusing on the purpose of possession. E.g. a German court (Higher Regional Court Düsseldorf judgment of 19 October 2017 – I-20 U 29/17, BeckRS 2017, p. 130,901) ruled in 2017 that a freight forwarder that transports and delivers goods that infringe trade mark rights is not liable if it does not exercise actual control over the goods for the purpose of offering them or placing them on the market.

[16] Opinion of Advocate General of 28 November 2019 – C-567/18, GRUR-RS 2019, p. 29, 558.

is to be understood differently and more broadly where the profit from the sale of goods is shared than in the case of a traditional logistics company which has no interest in the sale of the products.

For the time being, however, it remains the case that knowledge of an infringement is decisive for liability.

Court of Justice 26 March 2020

On the revocation of a trade mark for lack of genuine use. Right of the trade mark proprietor to plead infringement of his or her exclusive rights as a result of the use by a third party of an identical or similar sign during the period preceding the date on which the revocation took effect

Case C-622/18

Summary and analysis by Huib Berendschot[1]

Parties:

AR

v

Cooper International Spirits LLC
St Dalfour SAS
Établissement Gabriel Boudier SA

1. Background and History

AR, the appellant in the main proceedings, markets alcohol and spirits.[2]

On 5 December 2005, AR filed an application for registration of the semi-figurative trade mark SAINT GERMAIN with the Institut national de la propriété industrielle ('INPI') in France.

That mark was registered on 12 May 2006 under number 3,395,502 for goods and services in classes 30, 32 and 33 of the so-called Nice Agreement,[3] corresponding in particular to alcoholic beverages (except beers), ciders, digestives, wines and spirits, as well as alcoholic extracts and essences.

On 8 June 2012, having learnt that Cooper International Spirits was distributing a liqueur manufactured by St Dalfour and Établissements Gabriel Boudier under the name 'St-Germain', the appellant in the main proceedings brought an action against those three companies before the Tribunal de grande instance de Paris (Regional Court, Paris, France) for trade mark infringement.

---

1 Huib Berendschot is an attorney at law at AKD, the Netherlands, and works within the Intellectual Property & Technology practice group.

2 Para. 15 of the annotated judgment.

3 Nice Agreement Concerning the International Classification of Goods and Services for the Purposes of the Registration of Marks of 15 June 1957.

In parallel proceedings, by judgment of 28 February 2013, the Tribunal de grande instance de Nanterre (Regional Court, Nanterre, France) revoked the appellant's trade mark SAINT GERMAIN with effect from 13 May 2011. That judgment was upheld by judgment of the Cour d'appel de Versailles (Court of Appeal, Versailles, France) of 11 February 2014, which became irrevocable.[4]

Before the Regional Court of Paris, the appellant in the main proceedings maintained its claims alleging infringement for the period prior to the revocation which was not time-barred, that is to say, from 8 June 2009 to 13 May 2011.

Those claims were dismissed in their entirety by judgment of the Regional Court of 16 January 2015, on the ground that the trade mark in question had not been used since it had been filed.

That judgment was upheld by judgment of the Court of Appeal of Paris of 13 September 2016.

As grounds for that judgment, the Court of Appeal found, *inter alia*, that the evidence relied on by the appellant in the main proceedings was not sufficient to demonstrate that the mark SAINT GERMAIN had actually been used.[5]

The Court of Appeal concluded that the appellant in the main proceedings could not successfully argue that the trade mark's function as a guarantee of origin had been adversely affected, or that the monopoly on use conferred by its mark had been adversely affected, or indeed that its investment function had been adversely affected, since the use of a sign identical with the trade mark by a competitor is not such, failing any use of that mark, as to impede its use substantially.[6]

The appellant in the main proceedings brought an appeal in cassation against that judgment, on the ground that the Court of Appeal had infringed Articles L 713-3 and L 714-5 of the Intellectual Property Code.

In support of that appeal, the appellant submitted that all its claims alleging infringement had been incorrectly dismissed on the ground that it had not demonstrated that the mark SAINT GERMAIN had actually been used, even though neither EU law nor the Intellectual Property Code provides that, during the five-year period following registration of a trade mark, the proprietor of that mark must prove that the mark has been used in order to benefit from trade mark protection. Moreover, as regards infringement, the likelihood of confusion on the part of the public must be assessed in the abstract, in the

---

4 Para. 19 of the annotated judgment.

5 Para. 20 of the annotated judgment.

6 Para. 21 of the annotated judgment.

light of the subject matter of the registration, and not in relation to a specific situation on the market.

Conversely, the respondents in the main proceedings contended that a trade mark performs its essential function only if it is actually used by its proprietor to indicate the commercial origin of the goods or services designated in its registration and that, if the trade mark is not used in accordance with its essential function, the proprietor cannot complain of any adverse effect on that function or any risk of its being adversely affected.

The Cour de cassation ('Court of Cassation', France) stated, as a preliminary point, that the appeal in cassation before it did not take issue with the fact that the Court of Appeal had examined the infringement not in the light of the reproduction of the mark but of its imitation, which presupposed that there was a likelihood of confusion on the part of the public. It pointed out that, under national law, the court hearing the case on the merits has sole jurisdiction to assess whether there is such a likelihood of confusion and the Court of Cassation, for its part, has jurisdiction only to assess whether the judgment under appeal correctly applies the law applicable.[7]

It observed that, with regard to infringement by imitation, the Court had held that use of a sign which is identical or similar to the trade mark which gives rise to a likelihood of confusion on the part of the public affects or is liable to affect the essential function of the mark.[8] The Court added that, although a trade mark's function of indicating origin is not the only function of the mark that is worthy of protection against injury by third parties,[9] the protection conferred against infringement by reproduction, in so far as it is absolute and reserved for injury caused not only to the mark's essential function, but also to other functions (in particular those of communication, investment or advertising), is broader than the protection provided against infringement by imitation. The application of this latter form of protection requires proof of a likelihood of confusion and, accordingly, the possibility that the essential function of the mark may be affected.[10]

The Court of Cassation also pointed out that the European Court of Justice had held that a trade mark is always supposed to fulfil its function of indicating origin, whereas it performs its other functions only in so far as its proprietor uses it to that end, in particular for the purposes of advertising or investment.[11]

---

7 Para. 30 of the annotated judgment.

8 Case C-533/06, 12 June 2008, *O2 Holdings and O2 (UK)*, para. 59.

9 Case C-323/09, 22 September 2011, *Interflora and Interflora British Unit*, para. 39.

10 Case C-487/07, 18 June 2009, *L'Oréal and Others*, paras. 58 and 59.

11 Case C-323/09, 22 September 2011, *Interflora and Interflora British* Unit, para. 40.

It added that, in the light of that case-law, it appears that, in the present case, since the issue is whether or not there is an infringement by imitation, it is only necessary to examine the alleged adverse effect on the essential function of the trade mark resulting from a likelihood of confusion.

In that regard, it pointed out that, in the judgment of the European Court of Justice of 21 December 2016, *Länsförsäkringar*,[12] the Court held that Articles 15(1) and 51(1)(a) of Regulation No 207/2009 ('EUTMR') confer on the proprietor of the trade mark a grace period within which to begin to make genuine use of its mark, during which it may rely on the exclusive rights which the mark confers, pursuant to Article 9(1) EUTMR, in respect of all the goods and services, without having to demonstrate such use. That meant that, during that period, the extent of the right conferred on the proprietor of the trade mark must be assessed by reference to the goods and services covered by the registration of the mark, not on the basis of the use which the proprietor was able to make of the mark during that period.

The Court of Cassation observed, however, that the case in the main proceedings differed from the case that gave rise to the *Länsförsäkringar* judgment, in that the trade mark proprietor's rights had been revoked as a result of the lack of use of the mark during the five-year period following its registration.[13]

The question then arose as to whether the proprietor of a trade mark who has never used it and whose rights in it have been revoked on expiry of the five-year period laid down in the first subparagraph of Article 10(1) of Directive 2008/95 ('the Directive') may claim that the essential function of its trade mark has been affected and, consequently, seek compensation for injury as a result of the alleged use by a third party of an identical or similar sign during the five-year period following registration of the mark.

In those circumstances, the Court of Cassation decided to stay proceedings and to refer the following question to the Court:

> *'Must article 5(1)(b) and articles 10 and 12 of the Directive be interpreted as meaning that a proprietor who has never (used his or her) trade mark and whose rights in it were revoked on expiry of the period of five years following publication of its registration can obtain compensation for injury caused by infringement, claiming an adverse effect on the essential function of (his or her) trade mark, caused by use by a third party, before the date on which the revocation took effect, of a sign similar to that trade mark to designate goods or services identical or similar to those for which that trade mark was registered?'*

---

[12] Case C-654/15, 21 December 2016, *Länsförsäkringar*.

[13] Para. 33 of the annotated judgment.

2. Decision

Article 5(1)(b), the first subparagraph of Article 10(1) and the first subparagraph of Article 12(1) of Directive 2008/95/EC of the European Parliament and of the Council of 22 October 2008 to approximate the laws of the Member States relating to trade marks, read in conjunction with recital 6 thereof, must be interpreted as leaving Member States the option of allowing the proprietor of a trade mark whose rights in that mark have been revoked on expiry of the five-year period from its registration because he or she failed to make genuine use of the mark in the Member State concerned in connection with the goods or services for which it was registered to retain the right to claim compensation for the injury sustained as a result of the use by a third party, before the date on which the revocation took effect, of a similar sign in connection with identical or similar goods or services that is liable to be confused with his or her trade mark.

3. Motivation and Analysis

As the CJEU commonly does, it rephrased the question of the referring court, the Court of Cassation. It found that the court was asking in essence whether Article 5(1)(b), the first subparagraph of Article 10(1) and the first subparagraph of Article 12(1) of the Directive must be interpreted as meaning that the proprietor of a trade mark whose rights in that mark have been revoked on expiry of the five-year period from its registration because it failed to make genuine use of the mark in the Member State concerned in connection with the goods or services for which it was registered retains the right to claim compensation for the injury sustained as a result of the use by a third party, before the date on which the revocation took effect, of a similar sign in connection with identical or similar goods or services that is liable to be confused with its trade mark.[14]

The CJEU considered that it had previously – in its *Länsförsäkringar* judgment – held that Article 15(1) and Article 51(1)(a) EUTMR confer on the proprietor of a trade mark a grace period within which to begin to make genuine use of that mark, during which it may rely on the exclusive rights which the mark confers, pursuant to Article 9(1) of the regulation, in respect of all the goods or services for which the mark is registered, without having to demonstrate such use.[15]

It stated that, under Article 9(1)(b) EUTMR, whether the goods or services of the alleged infringer are identical or similar to the goods or services covered by the EU trade mark at issue, the extent of the exclusive right conferred by virtue

---

[14] Para. 36 of the annotated judgment.

[15] Case C-654/15, 21 December 2016, *Länsförsäkringar*, para. 26.

of that provision should be assessed, during the five-year period following registration of the EU trade mark, in light of the goods and services covered by the mark's registration, and not in relation to the use that the proprietor has been able to make of the mark during that period.[16]

The CJEU added that in its *Länsförsäkringar* judgment it had held that, from the time when the five-year period following registration of the EU trade mark expires, the extent of that exclusive right may be affected by the finding– made following a counter-claim, or a defence as to the merits, lodged by the third party in infringement proceedings – that the proprietor had at that time not yet begun to make genuine use of its mark in respect of some or all of the goods and services for which it has been registered.[17]

The CJEU then concurred with the Court of Cassation that the case in the main proceedings was to be distinguished from the case that gave rise to the *Länsförsäkringar* judgment of 21 December 2016, in that it concerned the question of the scope of that exclusive right on expiry of the grace period. The CJEU then examined whether under the Directive, revocation of the rights conferred by a mark may have an effect on the possibility for the proprietor to rely, after expiry of the grace period, on infringements of the exclusive rights conferred by that mark which occurred within that period.[18]

The CJEU first considered that, in accordance with Recital 6 of the Directive which *inter alia* states that Member States should remain free to determine the effects of revocation or invalidity of trade marks, the Directive leaves the national legislature entirely free to determine the date on which revocation of a trade mark takes effect.

Secondly, it took the view that it follows from Article 11(3) of the Directive that Member States remain free to decide whether they wish to provide that, where a counter-claim for revocation is made, a trade mark may not be successfully invoked in infringement proceedings if it is established as a result of a plea that the trade mark can be revoked pursuant to Article 12(1) of the Directive.

In the present case, it noted that the French legislature had chosen to have the revocation of a trade mark for non-use take effect on expiry of the five-year period following registration of the mark. It had not made use of the option provided for in Article 11(3) of the Directive.[19]

---

[16] Case C-654/15, 21 December 2016, *Länsförsäkringar*, para. 27

[17] Case C-654/15, 21 December 2016, *Länsförsäkringar*, para. 28.

[18] Para. 42 of the annotated judgment.

[19] Art. 11(3) of the Dir.: '*Without prejudice to the application of Article 12, where a counter-claim for revocation is made, any Member State may provide that a trade mark may not be successfully invoked in infringement proceedings if it is established as a result of a plea that the trade mark could be revoked pursuant to Article 12(1).*'

French legislation therefore maintained the possibility, for the proprietor of a trade mark, of relying, after expiry of the grace period, on infringements of the exclusive rights conferred by that mark which occurred within that period, even though the proprietor had had its rights in the mark revoked.

As regards the award of damages, the CJEU referred to Directive 2004/48 (on the enforcement of intellectual property rights) and in particular to Article 13(1) thereof, under which such damages must be '*appropriate to the actual prejudice suffered by the proprietor of the trade mark.*'[20]

It added that although the fact that a trade mark has not been used does not, in itself, preclude compensation in respect of acts of infringement that have been committed, it remains an important factor to be taken into account in determining the existence and, as the case may be, the extent of the injury sustained by the proprietor and, accordingly, the amount of damages that it might claim.

These considerations led the court to answer the referring court's question by stating that Article 5(1)(b), the first subparagraph of Article 10(1) and the first subparagraph of Article 12(1) of the Directive, read in conjunction with Recital 6, must be interpreted as leaving Member States the option of allowing the proprietor of a trade mark whose rights in that mark have been revoked on expiry of the five-year period from its registration because it failed to make genuine use of the mark in the Member State concerned in connection with the goods or services for which it was registered to retain the right to claim compensation for the injury sustained as a result of the use by a third party, before the date on which the revocation took effect, of a similar sign in connection with identical or similar goods or services that is liable to be confused with its trade mark.[21]

* *
*

What is the meaning of this judgment for legal practice? The case is certainly interesting. It highlights the disparity in terms of jurisdictions being able to operate different regimes as to compensation for trade mark infringement. The judgment seems to have little effect on cases with similar underlying facts, however, as we will see.

The facts that gave rise to the referral by the Court of Cassation and to the CJEU judgment are rare. It is not common for a trade mark proprietor to pursue trade mark infringement in a situation where no use of the mark has been made. In this case, the defendant had used a mark nearly identical to the one registered by the proprietor, for goods identical to those for which it had been registered.

---

[20] Dir. 2004/48/EC of the European Parliament and of the Council of 29 April 2004 on the enforcement of intellectual property rights, *OJ L* 157, 30 April 2004, p. 45-86.

[21] Para. 48 of the annotated judgment.

The proprietor had not sued solely for trade mark infringement while knowing that its mark's protection had expired, but had also sought compensation.

From my perspective the case – on which judgment was given at a time when Directive 2015/2436[22] was not yet in place - might have taken a different course after the implementation of this latter directive. Article 17 of this directive provides for the possibility of a legal defence based on non-use of the trade mark that is invoked. Under that article, the proprietor of a trade mark is *entitled to prohibit the use of a sign only to the extent that the proprietor's rights are not liable to be revoked at the time the infringement action is brought*. If the defendant so requested, the proprietor of the trade mark must furnish proof that, during the five-year period preceding the date on which the action is brought, the trade mark has been put to genuine use in connection with the goods or services in respect of which it was registered and which are cited as justification for the action, or that there are valid reasons for non-use, provided that the registration procedure of the trade mark has at the date of bringing the action been completed for not less than five years.

If it had been able to rely on Directive 2015/2436, Cooper International Spirits LLC would probably have cited non-use as a defence in the infringement proceedings. If in that situation the court had judged (as it did in this case in separate proceedings) that the mark in question had not been put to genuine use, the proprietor would have lost its entitlement to sue for trade mark infringement. In that situation there would have been no basis for seeking compensation. Article 13 of Directive 2004/48 makes payment of damages dependent on a successful infringement claim. Directive 2015/2436 seems to leave no opportunity to sue for infringement in the period during which there was not yet an obligation to use the mark, if the action itself is brought at a time when the mark is liable to revocation.

The judgment of the CJEU is interesting since it left open the opportunity for the French court to award damages to the trade mark owner even though its trade mark rights had been revoked. In doing so, the CJEU effectively strengthened the position of trade mark owners during the so-called grace period, i.e. the first five years after registration.

The value of this judgment in other jurisdictions is strongly dependent on national rules[23] on compensation in similar situations and in particular on how Article 13 of Directive 2004/48 has been implemented and what compensation is considered appropriate for the actual prejudice suffered.

---

[22] Dir. 2015/2436 of the European Parliament and of the Council of 16 December 2015 to approximate the laws of the Member States relating to trade marks, *OJ L* 336, 23 December 2015, p. 1-26.

[23] For the Benelux countries this is determined by the rules on compensation laid down in the Benelux Convention on Intellectual Property.

Even if an infringement is established, it may in practice be difficult to determine the monetary amount of damages. The function of the mark may have been affected, but the estimation of the amount of damages may be difficult in the absence of use of the mark. In paragraph 47 of the judgment in the case between AR and Cooper International, the CJEU held that the fact that a trade mark has not been used does not, in itself, preclude compensation in respect of acts of infringement that have been committed, but that the lack of use remains an important factor to be taken into account in determining the existence and, as the case may be, the extent of the injury sustained by the proprietor and, accordingly, the amount of damages that may be claimed.

The final question is what happened in the proceedings in France when the matter was referred back to the Court of Appeal, Paris. Before the Regional Court, Paris and the Court of Appeal, Paris found that there was no trade mark infringement, primarily because the Saint German trade mark had not been put to use by the owner. The Court of Appeal – following the judgment of the CJEU – therefore had to decide on both the issue of infringement and the issue of damages.

By judgment of 25 March 2022 (two years after the judgment of the CJEU) the Court of Appeal ruled that the use of a highly similar mark by Cooper International c.s. for goods that identical to the ones for which AR had registered its mark constituted an infringement of the rights of AR in the period of two years prior to 13 March 2011 when Cooper International c.s. used the mark without the authorisation of AR, who at that time was still the legitimate owner of the mark.

On the question of compensation, the Court of Appeal considered that the infringement of the trade mark should be compensated.

AR sought to demonstrate that it had begun using the mark with two general and non-detailed testimonials from private individuals stating that they had consumed SAINT GERMAIN Cognac cream until 2008. The court held that these were not sufficient to show that the project went beyond the preparatory acts of 2006 and that the appearance of the infringing products on the market had dissuaded it from pursuing this project. It considered that the arrival on the market of the ST-GERMAIN product of Cooper International c.s of which AR became aware in 2010 could not be considered a valid reason for AR's failure to use its SAINT GERMAIN trade mark.

The Court of Appeal further found that, due to the absence of exploitation by AR of its trademark, AR could not claim compensation in the form of a licence fee.

In the light of the foregoing, the Paris Court of Appeal concluded that the award of a fixed annual fee was a more appropriate way of compensating AR for the loss it had actually suffered. It set this fee at an amount of EUR 10,000 for each year that the mark had been infringed, i.e. two years. It therefore awarded the sum of EUR 20,000, as well as ordering Cooper International c.s.t to pay legal costs of EUR 15,000.

COURT OF *JUSTICE 23 APRIL 2020*

ON TRADE MARK PROTECTION OF PRODUCT SHAPES

Case C-237/19

Summary and Analysis by Urša Horvat Kous[1]

Parties:

Gömböc Kutató, Szolgáltató és Kereskedelmi Kft.

v

Szellemi Tulajdon Nemzeti Hivatala

1. Background and History

The central issue in this case was the refusal by the Hungarian National Intellectual Property Office to register a three-dimensional shape, resembling a Gömböc, as a national trade mark. 'Gömböc' is a term used to represent a convex monostatic object made of a homogeneous material, which has a single point of stable equilibrium and a single point of unstable equilibrium, i.e. a total of two points of equilibrium, the shape of which itself ensures that the object always returns to its position of balance. Gömböc Kft. sought registration of the following shape for its decorative items, decorative crystalware and chinaware and toys[2]:

[1] Urša Horvat Kous is a managing associate at the Slovenian law firm Jadek & Pensa d.o.o., specialising in IP law among other areas, and is a member of the Slovenian Bar Association.

[2] Classes 14, 21 and 28 of the Nice Agreement concerning the International Classification of Goods and Services for the Purposes of the Registration of Marks of 15 June 1957, as revised and amended ('the Nice Agreement').

The case was adjudicated under the framework of Directive 2008/95/EC[3] (also referred to as the 'Directive'), focusing on Article 3(1)(e)(ii) and (iii). These clauses deal with the non-registrability of shapes which are necessary for achieving a technical result and shapes which add substantial value to the goods. The same provision was transposed into Hungarian law through Article 2(2)(b) of Law No XI of 1997 on the protection of trade marks and geographical indications (Magyar Közlöny 1997/27[4] ('the Law on Trade Marks')).

The Hungarian Office rejected the trade mark application on the ground that the shape of the Gömböc was an integral part of its technical function and that its distinct design contributed substantially to its value, arguing that the sign for which registration was sought represented a three-dimensional object which, due to its external design and the homogeneous material used, always returned to its position of balance, and that the shape of the object as a whole served to achieve its technical purpose of always regaining its equilibrium. The Hungarian Office assessed the application separately for each of the classes of goods and services in respect of which it was sought, namely:

(a) <u>Toys:</u> the Hungarian Office found that all the elements of the sign at issue were designed to achieve that technical result, that is to say, they served a technical function. Therefore, the informed and reasonable consumer would perceive the sign at issue as a shape necessary to obtain the technical result sought by the object represented by that sign.

(b) <u>Decorative items:</u> the Office stated that, although three-dimensional decorative objects could in principle not be denied protection under trade mark law, where the distinctive style of such objects determined their formal appearance, the value of the product lay in its shape.

This decision was challenged before the courts in Hungary, and the Supreme Court referred the matter to the CJEU for a preliminary ruling. According to the referring court, the relevant case-law of the CJEU[5] had so far failed to remove all doubt on the matter, leaving the court unable to reach a final decision in the case at hand. In particular, the referring court was uncertain whether such an assessment must be based solely on the graphic representation in the application for registration of the sign, or whether, in a situation where the product in question had become very well known, the perception of the relevant public could also be taken into account.

---

3 Dir. 2008/95/EC of the European Parliament and of the Council of 22 October 2008 to approximate the laws of the Member States relating to trade marks.

4 Original title: védjegyek és a földrajzi árujelzők oltalmáról szóló 1997. évi XI. Törvény.

5 Case C-205-13, 18 September 2014, *Hauck*, and Case C-13/15, 10 November 2016, *Simba Toys v EUIPO*.

The referring court furthermore sought guidance as to whether the knowledge of the public could influence the decision, and finally, about the relationship between trade marks and designs in cases where a visual representation of a product (more commonly protected as a design) is applied for as a trade mark.

In those circumstances, the Kúria (Supreme Court, Hungary) decided to stay the proceedings and to refer the following questions to the Court of Justice for a preliminary ruling:

> *'(1) Must Article 3(1)[(e)(ii)] of [Directive 2008/95], in the case of a sign consisting exclusively of the shape of the product, be interpreted as meaning that*
>
> > *(a) it is on the basis of the graphic representation contained in the register alone that it may be determined whether the shape is necessary to obtain the technical result sought, or*
> >
> > *(b) may the perception of the relevant public also be taken into account?*
> >
> > *In other words, is it permissible to take into account the fact that the relevant public is aware that the shape for which registration is sought is necessary in order to obtain the technical result sought?*
>
> *(2) Must Article 3(1)[(e)(iii)] of [Directive 2008/95] be interpreted as meaning that that ground for refusal is applicable to a sign that consists exclusively of the shape of the product where it is [only] by taking into account the perception or knowledge of the buyer as regards the product that is graphically represented that it is possible to establish that the shape gives substantial value to the product?*
>
> *(3) Must Article 3(1)[(e)(iii)] of [Directive 2008/95] be interpreted as meaning that that ground for refusal is applicable to a sign, consisting exclusively of the shape of a product*
>
> > *(a) which, by virtue of its individual character, already enjoys the protection conferred on designs, or*
> >
> > *(b) the aesthetic appearance of which gives the product a certain value?'*

2. Decision

1. Article 3(1)(e)(ii) of Directive 2008/95/EC of the European Parliament and of the Council of 22 October 2008 to approximate the laws of the Member States relating to trade marks must be interpreted as meaning that, in order to establish whether a sign consists exclusively of the shape of goods which is necessary to obtain a technical result, assessment does not have to be limited to the graphic representation of that sign. Information other than that relating to the graphic representation alone, such as the perception of the relevant public, may be used in order to identify the essential characteristics of the sign at issue.

However, while information which is not apparent from the graphic representation of the sign may be taken into consideration in order to establish whether those characteristics perform a technical function of the goods in question, such information must originate from objective and reliable sources and may not include the perception of the relevant public.

2. Article 3(1)(e)(iii) of Directive 2008/95 must be interpreted as meaning that the perception or knowledge of the relevant public as regards the product represented graphically by a sign that consists exclusively of the shape of that product may be taken into consideration in order to identify an essential characteristic of that shape. The ground for refusal set out in that provision may be applied if it is apparent from objective and reliable evidence that the consumer's decision to purchase the product in question is to a large extent determined by that characteristic.

3. Article 3(1)(e)(iii) of Directive 2008/95 must be interpreted as meaning that the ground for refusal of registration provided for in that provision must not be applied systematically to a sign which consists exclusively of the shape of the goods where that sign enjoys protection under the law relating to designs or where the sign consists exclusively of the shape of a decorative item.

3. Motivation and Analysis

A first key point of discussion was whether the assessment of whether a shape is necessary to achieve a technical result should be based solely on its graphic representation or whether the public's perception should also be taken into account. The CJEU clarified that while the graphic representation is fundamental, other objective and reliable sources,[6] such as for example the additional features relating to the function of the goods in question,[7] may be considered. However, it emphasised that the perception of the general public should not influence this technical assessment.[8,9,10]

---

6 Para. 34 of the annotated judgment.

7 See, by analogy, Case C-30/15, 10 November 2016, *Simba Toys v EUIPO*, para. 48.

8 Para. 35 of the annotated judgment.

9 As also already concluded by the court in the Case C-48/09, 14 September 2010, *Lego Juris v OHIM*.

10 Since '*the relevant public does not necessarily have the required expertise to enable it to determine with accuracy what the technical features of the product in question are and the extent to which the shape of that product forming the sign contributes to the technical result sought*' (para. 36 of the analysed judgment).

The CJEU emphasised[11] that the ground for refusal in Article 3(1)(e)(ii) of the Directive is intended to prevent the protection afforded by trade mark law from being extended beyond signs which serve to distinguish a product or service from those offered by competitors, so as to constitute an obstacle preventing competitors from freely offering for sale products incorporating such technical solutions or functional characteristics in competition with the proprietor of the trade mark.[12] In that assessment, one or more minor arbitrary features of a three-dimensional sign should not and do not alter the conclusion that the sign consists exclusively of the shape of goods which is necessary to obtain a technical result.[13,14]

Such an approach is absolutely necessary to prevent undertakings from using trade mark law to perpetuate exclusive rights relating to technical solutions indefinitely (which would not be possible through design or patent protection).[15] This approach also applies in cases where only part of the shape is visible.[16]

As part of the assessment of the second question, the CJEU examined whether the ground for refusal of registration provided for in Article 3(1)(e)(iii) of the Directive is applicable to a sign which consists exclusively of the shape of the goods and in respect of which it is only on the basis of the perception or knowledge of the relevant public as regards the product graphically represented that the competent authority reaches the view that the shape gives substantial value to that product.[17]

The CJEU held that the public's perception or knowledge of the product could be considered, especially to enable the competent authority to identify the essential characteristics of that sign.[18] However, it stressed that the refusal to grant trade mark protection must be based on concrete evidence showing that the shape heavily influences consumer purchasing decisions.[19]

The CJEU emphasised that when assessing the necessity of a shape for a technical result, authorities should not confine themselves to its graphic representation. However, they must avoid relying on the public's perception, as this introduces subjectivity and potential inaccuracies.[20] In contrast, when assessing whether a shape gives substantial value to goods, the CJEU allowed for

---

11 Para. 35 and 37 of the annotated judgment.

12 See, by analogy, Case C-299/99, 18 June 2002, *Philips*, para. 78.

13 Para. 26 of the annotated judgment.

14 See, by analogy, Case C-48/09, 14 September 2010, *Lego Juris v OHIM*, para. 52.

15 See, by analogy, Case C-48/09, 14 September 2010, *Lego Juris v OHIM*, para. 45.

16 Para. 32 of the annotated judgment.

17 Para. 38 of the annotated judgment.

18 Para. 44 of the annotated judgment.

19 Para. 41 of the annotated judgment.

20 Paras. 35 and 36 of the annotated judgment.

consideration of the public's perception. This reflects an understanding that the value attributed to a product by consumers may be influenced by factors beyond just its functional or technical characteristics.[21]

Thirdly, the CJEU also examined whether a shape which significantly influences the goods' value could be trademarked, especially if it already enjoys design protection.[22] The CJEU clarified that existence of design protection for a product's appearance does not automatically exclude it from trade mark protection.[23] This point is critical to understanding the independent yet overlapping scopes of design and trade mark law in the EU.

The ruling highlights that the existence of design protection does not preclude trade mark protection. The CJEU emphasised the need for a case-by-case analysis to determine whether the shape of a product already protected as a design is also eligible for trade mark protection. Article 16 of Directive 98/71[24] provides that this same directive '*shall be without prejudice to any provisions of [European Union] law or of the law of the Member State concerned relating to unregistered design rights, trade marks or other distinctive signs, patents and utility models.*'[25] It follows therefore that the legislators had no intention of preventing the coexistence of design and trade mark protection for the appearance of a product. However, the considerations and analysis of such appearance will be subject to different assessments and criteria, depending on whether it is applied for as a design or as a trade mark.[26]

* *
*

As the use of distinctive and non-traditional signs continues to evolve, this CJEU ruling has significant implications for EU trade mark law, particularly in relation to the protection of three-dimensional shapes. This ruling is not the first in which the CJEU has touched upon the question of registration of signs consisting exclusively of the shape of the goods. The CJEU has previously addressed the topic in the Lego Juris A/S v OHIM,[27] the Philips v Remington[28] and the Hauck GmbH & Co KG v Stokke A/S and Others[29] cases, among others. It is therefore clear that this has been an important question in the EU for the

---

21 Paras. 45 and 47 of the annotated judgment.

22 Para. 48 of the annotated judgment.

23 Para. 59 of the annotated judgment.

24 Directive 98/71/EC of the European Parliament and of the Council of 13 October 1998 on the legal protection of designs.

25 Para. 52 of the annotated judgment.

26 Para. 57 of the annotated judgment.

27 Case C-48/09 P, 14 September 2010.

28 Case C-299/99, 18 June 2002.

29 Case C-205/13, 18 September 2014.

past few decades. Throughout its practice the CJEU has had to find a balance between limiting the scope of applications of shape trade marks to prevent monopolies over shapes on the one hand and allowing companies to freely choose the most beneficial way of protecting their rights on the other. In certain cases, it has failed to define the boundaries and criteria comprehensively and clearly.[30] The annotated judgment represents a new step towards providing clear guidelines to intellectual property offices as well as companies.

Companies may want to opt for trade mark protection as opposed to design protection, as it allows unlimited renewal, is not influenced by prior disclosure or publication, and allows for application of standards such as the likelihood of confusion. The annotated judgment, which underscores the importance of an objective, detailed analysis when assessing whether a shape is necessary for a technical result or adds substantial value to goods, will therefore provide important guidance both to companies when deciding on an application, and to intellectual property offices when assessing it. It sets a precedent for how national intellectual property offices and courts should approach similar cases, balancing the need to protect technical solutions and functional characteristics of products with the exclusivity granted by trade mark rights.

This judgment serves as an important reference for legal practitioners and businesses in the EU, guiding them through the intricacies of registering three-dimensional shapes as trade marks. It clarifies the extent to which design protection interacts with trade mark law, fostering a better understanding of intellectual property rights within the European Union.

30 E.g. the term 'exclusively' in the Lego case, since the provision interpreted in it (which is essentially the same as the provision discussed in the annotated judgment) excluded registration of signs consisting *exclusively* of the shape of goods necessary to obtain a technical result.

COURT OF *JUSTICE* 22 OCTOBER 2020

ON THE CONCEPT OF GENUINE USE AND ITS INTERPRETATION, ESPECIALLY IN RELATION TO A NARROW AND LIMITED USE WITHIN A BROADER CATEGORY

Joined cases C-720/18 and C-721/18

Summary and Analysis by Urša Horvat Kous[1]

Parties:

Ferrari SpA

v

DU

1. Background and History

Ferrari is, among others, the proprietor of the following figurative trade mark registered both internationally and in Germany, relating to vehicles and relevant (spare) parts for such vehicles:

testarossa

The sign was registered as a trade mark with WIPO[2] and the German Patent and Trade Mark Office[3] in Class 12 of the Nice Agreement concerning the International Classification of Goods and Services for the Purposes of the Registration of Marks of 15 June 1957 ('the Nice Classification'). Both marks were registered not in respect of high-priced luxury sports cars, but generally in respect of motor cars and parts thereof.

Testarossa is a sports car manufactured by Ferrari, which went into production in 1984 as the successor to the Ferrari Berlinetta Boxer. Ferrari sold a sports car model under the designation 'Testarossa' between 1984 and 1991 and sold the

---

1 Urša Horvat Kous is a managing associate at the Slovenian law firm Jadek & Pensa d.o.o., specialising among others in IP law, and is a member of the Slovenian Bar Association.

2 For '*Vehicles; apparatus for locomotion by land, air or water, in particular motor cars and parts thereof*', registered on 22 July 1987.

3 For '*Land vehicles, aircraft and water vehicles and parts thereof; motors and engines for land vehicles; car components, i.e. tow bars, luggage racks, ski racks, mudguards, snow chains, air deflectors, head restraints, seat belts, child safety seats*', registered on 7 May 1990.

follow-up models 512 TR and F512 M until 1996. According to the referring court, in 2014, Ferrari produced a one-off piece with the model designation 'Ferrari F12 TRS'. In light of the limited scope of use (due to the fact that the trade mark was used for designation of luxury sports cars manufactured in limited quantities), several legal questions were raised following two sets of proceedings against Ferrari SpA concerning the revocation due to lack of genuine use of the two trade marks owned by Ferrari. It was expressly pointed out that while the marks at issue were in fact used in respect of high-priced sports cars, they were not registered for such a specific type of cars but for cars in general.

Directive 2008/95 to approximate the laws of the Member States relating to trade marks ('the Directive') and the German Law on the protection of trade marks and other distinctive signs of 25 October 1994 (BGBl. 1994 I, p. 3082; 'the Law on trade marks') provide the relevant legal context to the case at hand, namely the provisions on genuine use and the revocation of a trade mark if such genuine use is lacking. Articles 10 and 12 of the Directive set out the framework for revocation of a trade mark due to lack of genuine use: '*A trade mark shall be liable to revocation if, within a continuous period of five years, it has not been put to genuine use in the Member State in connection with the goods or services in respect of which it is registered, and there are no proper reasons for non-use.*' The said provisions have been transposed into German law in a similar way.[4] Article 13 of the Directive further provides that '*Where grounds for refusal of registration or for revocation or invalidity of a trade mark exist in respect of only some of the goods or services for which that trade mark has been applied for or registered, refusal of registration or revocation or invalidity shall cover those goods or services only.*'

The lower court in Germany ordered the cancellation of Ferrari's trade marks due to non-use over a continuous five-year period in Germany and Switzerland. Ferrari appealed, citing limited but genuine use of the trade marks for high-priced sports cars and associated parts.[5] The higher court questioned whether such limited use sufficed for trade mark maintenance, especially given that the marks were registered for a broad category of goods. Additional issues included whether the sale of used goods bearing the trade mark, the sale of replacement parts, and services relating to the goods but not using the trade mark count as genuine use. It was apparent from the order for reference that, during the period relevant to the assessment of the use of the marks at issue, Ferrari used those trade marks to identify replacement and accessory parts of very high-priced luxury sports cars previously sold under those trade marks.

---

4 Para. 49 of the Law on trade marks.

5 I.e. it had conducted resale of inspected used vehicles, replacement, and accessory parts in respect of the vehicles bearing the marks at issue and offered maintenance services for those vehicles. According to the findings of the court of first instance in Germany, between 2011 and 2016, the turnover from the sale of replacement parts was EUR 17,000.

Questions of a mostly procedural nature were also raised, the most important being that of the burden of proof, which usually (also in accordance with German law) lies with the applicant/claimant/plaintiff, whereas in the case of proof of genuine use it should (generally and as a rule, in accordance with the law) lie with the trade mark proprietor as the sole party in possession of the relevant evidence. Lastly, the question arose whether the application of the 1892 convention between Switzerland and Germany[6] is in line with the EU legislation, as it would allow use in Switzerland to be used as proof of use in Germany.

In these circumstances, the Oberlandesgericht Düsseldorf (Higher Regional Court, Düsseldorf) decided to stay the proceedings and to refer the following questions, which are identical in both cases, to the CJEU for a preliminary ruling:

> *'(1) When assessing the question of whether use is genuine in terms of nature and extent within the meaning of Article 12(1) of [Directive 2008/95] in the case of a trade mark which is registered in respect of a broad category of goods, in this case land vehicles, in particular motor cars and parts thereof, but is actually only used in respect of a particular market segment, in this case high-priced luxury sports cars and parts thereof, is account to be taken of the market for the registered category of goods overall or may account be taken of the particular segment? If the use in respect of the particular market segment is sufficient, is the trade mark to be maintained in relation to that market segment in cancellation proceedings due to revocation?*
>
> *(2) Does the sale of used goods which have already been released onto the market by the trade mark proprietor in the European Economic Area constitute use of the trade mark by the trade mark proprietor within the meaning of Article 12(1) of [Directive 2008/95]?*
>
> *(3) Is a trade mark which is registered not only in respect of a product, but also in respect of parts of that product also used in a right-maintaining manner in respect of the product if that product is no longer sold, but there are still sales of trademarked accessory and replacement parts for the trademarked product sold in the past?*
>
> *(4) When assessing whether there is genuine use, is consideration also to be given to whether the trade mark proprietor offers services which do not use the trade mark but are intended for the goods already sold?*

6 Convention between Switzerland and Germany concerning the Reciprocal Protection of Patents, Designs and Trademarks, signed in Berlin on 13 April 1892, as amended ('the Convention of 1892'), which in Art. (1) states that the legal disadvantages which, under the laws of the contracting parties, occur when a trade mark has not been used within a certain period of time are precluded if the use takes place in the territory of the other party.

(5) When examining the use of the trade mark in the Member State concerned (in this case Germany) within the meaning of Article 12(1) of [Directive 2008/95], pursuant to Article 5 of the [Convention of 1892], are uses of the trade mark in Switzerland also to be taken into consideration?

(6) Is it compatible with [Directive 2008/95] to require the trade mark proprietor against which action is being taken due to revocation of the trade mark to comprehensively explain the use of the trade mark, but to impose the risk of evidence not being furnished on the cancellation applicant?'

2. Decision

1. Article 12(1) and Article 13 of Directive 2008/95/EC of the European Parliament and of the Council of 22 October 2008 to approximate the laws of the Member States relating to trade marks must be interpreted as meaning that a trade mark registered in respect of a category of goods and replacement parts thereof must be regarded as having been put to 'genuine use' within the meaning of Article 12(1), in connection with all the goods in that category and the replacement parts thereof, if it has been so used only in respect of some of those goods, such as high-priced luxury sports cars, or only in respect of replacement parts or accessories of some of those goods, unless it is apparent from the relevant facts and evidence that a consumer who wishes to purchase those goods will perceive them as an independent subcategory of the category of goods in respect of which the mark concerned was registered.

2. Article 12(1) of Directive 2008/95 must be interpreted as meaning that a trade mark is capable of being put to genuine use by its proprietor when that proprietor resells second-hand goods put on the market under that mark.

3. Article 12(1) of Directive 2008/95 must be interpreted as meaning that a trade mark is put to genuine use by its proprietor where that proprietor provides certain services connected with the goods previously sold under that mark, on condition that those services are provided under that mark.

4. The first paragraph of Article 351 TFEU must be interpreted as allowing a court of a Member State to apply a convention concluded between a Member State of the European Union and a non-member State before 1 January 1958 or, for States acceding to the European Union, before the date of their accession, such as the Convention between Switzerland and Germany concerning the Reciprocal Protection of Patents, Designs and Trademarks, signed in Berlin on 13 April 1892, as amended, which provides that the use of a trade mark registered in that Member State in the territory of the non-member State must be taken into consideration in order to determine whether that mark has been put to 'genuine use' within the meaning of Article 12(1) of Directive 2008/95,

until such time as one of the steps referred to in the second paragraph of Article 351 TFEU makes it possible to eliminate any incompatibilities between the TFEU and that convention.

5. Article 12(1) of Directive 2008/95 must be interpreted as meaning that the burden of proof that a trade mark has been put to 'genuine use', within the meaning of that provision, rests on the proprietor of that mark.

3. Motivation and Analysis

The CJEU first tackled the first and third question,[7] thus determining the scope and extent of genuine use required to prevent the revocation of a trade mark. The CJEU was faced with an important question, needing to find a balance between protecting the rights of trade mark proprietors on the one hand and the interests of their competitors in using identical or similar sign for those goods or services.

This was not the first time the CJEU had encountered the question of whether the sale of goods previously placed on the market can be considered as genuine use of a trade mark. In its judgment on Case C-40/01, 11 March 2003, *Ansul*, the CJEU took the position that the sale of used goods can represent genuine use if certain criteria are met. In the *Ferrari v DU* case, the CJEU followed this case-law and again concluded[8] that the use by its proprietor of a registered trade mark in respect of replacement parts forming an integral part of the goods covered by that mark is capable of constituting 'genuine use' within the meaning of Article 12(1) of Directive 2008/95, not only for the replacement parts themselves but also for the goods covered by that mark. It is, according to the CJEU, irrelevant in that regard that the registration of that mark covers not only entire goods but also replacement parts thereof.

The CJEU clarified[9] that one of the most important questions[10] in that regard is whether a consumer who wishes to purchase a product or service falling within the category of goods or services covered by the trade mark in question will associate all the goods or services belonging to that category with that mark. In other words, a consumer who wishes to purchase a product or service in a category of goods or services that has been defined particularly precisely and narrowly, but within which it is not possible to make any significant sub-divisions,

---

[7] Paras. 30-53 of the annotated judgment.

[8] Para. 35 of the annotated judgment.

[9] Para. 37 of the annotated judgment.

[10] On the other hand, the referring court considered the concept of 'particular market segment'. The CJEU, however, concluded that the fact that the company which was the proprietor of the marks in question in the main proceedings had used those marks in respect of 'very high-priced luxury sports cars' (i.e. a subcategory of 'cars') does not show that the proprietor did not use the mark in respect of all goods protected by that mark.

should associate all the goods or services belonging to that category with a mark registered in respect of that category of goods or services, such that that trade mark will fulfil its essential function of guaranteeing the origin of those goods or services. Accordingly, proof of use of some of those goods and services in such a homogeneous category will suffice.[11,12]

The CJEU further considered the question of use of a trade mark registered for several categories of goods or services, in light of both the purpose of trade mark protection for the trade mark proprietor on the one hand, and the interest of competitors on the other. The CJEU concluded that if a broad category of goods can be sub-divided into several independent subcategories, it is necessary to require the proprietor of a mark registered in respect of that category of goods or services to adduce proof of genuine use of his mark for each of these independent subcategories. Failure to do so may result in partial trade mark revocation, as the interest of competitors must prevail. When determining whether subcategories can be created (or, on the other hand, if all goods must fall into one category) the criterion of the purpose and intended use of the goods or services at issue is the essential criterion for defining an independent subcategory of goods.[13,14]

Second, the CJEU considered whether Article 12(1) of the Directive must be interpreted as meaning that a trade mark is capable of being put to genuine use by its proprietor when that proprietor resells second-hand goods put on the market under that mark. The Court considered that resale, as such, of a second-hand product bearing a trade mark does not mean that that mark is being 'used' – the mark was used when it was affixed by the trademark proprietor onto the new product when that product was first put on the market. However, if the proprietor of the trade mark concerned actually uses the mark in accordance with its essential function, which is to guarantee the identity of the origin of the goods for which it was registered, when reselling second-hand goods, such use is capable of constituting 'genuine use' of the mark within the meaning of Article 12(1) of the Directive.[15]

Regarding the fourth question, the CJEU concluded that it cannot be excluded that the provision of services connected with the goods previously sold under a trade mark, also represents proof of genuine use. However, this is only the case if these services are actually provided by the proprietor under the trade mark.[16,17]

---

11 See, by analogy, Case C-714/18, 16 July 2020, *ACTC v EUIPO*, para. 42.

12 On the other hand, if such sub-categories can be created, failure to prove use in one such subcategory will result in a revocation of the mark for those goods and/or services (Art. 13 Dir. and para. 49(3) Law on trade marks).

13 Paras. 37 and 38 of the annotated judgment.

14 See, by analogy, Case C-714/18, 16 July 2020, *ACTC v EUIPO*, para. 44.

15 Paras. 54 - 60 of the annotated judgment.

16 Para. 64 of the annotated judgment.

17 As also per Case C-40/01, 11 March 2003, *Ansul*.

In responding to the fifth question, the CJEU concluded that the application of the Convention of 1892 by Germany might give rise to difficulties, in so far as a mark registered in Germany, while capable of being maintained in the register only on the basis of genuine use in the territory of the Swiss Confederation, could not be relied on to preclude the registration of an EU trade mark. Its reasoning was that, in a situation where a request is made for proof of genuine use of the trade mark in the context of opposition proceedings, the proprietor of the trade mark would not be in a position to provide such proof in the territory of the European Union alone.[18] The CJEU indicated that Germany will, in accordance with Article 351 of the TFEU, need to eliminate the incompatibility of the Convention of 1892 with EU law, but that until it has done so, the court of the Member State has no other option but to apply the Convention.[19]

Lastly, the CJEU tackled the question of the burden of proof. As a first step, it concluded that the question of the burden of proof in respect of genuine use, within the meaning of Article 12(1) of the Directive, in the context of proceedings relating to revocation of a trade mark for non-use, does not constitute a procedural provision that falls under the competence of Member States.[20,21] The reasoning behind this judgment is clear and logical, as any other conclusion would result in trade mark proprietors having different levels of protection depending on the legal system concerned, thus failing to achieve the fundamental objective of '*the same protection under the legal systems of all the Member States*' set out in recital 10 of the Directive. Many prior CJEU judgments had already emphasised that the burden of proof can only lie with the proprietor of the trade mark.[22]

* *
*

The decision in the Ferrari case by the CJEU has significant practical implications for trade mark law, particularly for businesses operating in the luxury goods sector and those with vintage or heritage brands. Such marks are usually used in a limited scope and could fall outside the scope of genuine use if construed too narrowly. The ruling clarifies that a trade mark can maintain its validity even if used only for certain goods within a broader category for which it is registered if such a category cannot be divided into subcategories. This interpretation is particularly beneficial for brands like Ferrari, which deal in high-end, luxury products with limited production runs. It provides leeway for such companies to continue benefiting from trade mark protection without

---

18 Para. 70 of the annotated judgment.

19 Para. 71 of the annotated judgment.

20 Para. 76 of the annotated judgment.

21 See, by analogy, Case C-217/13 and C-218/13, 19 June 2014, *Oberbank and Others*, para. 66.

22 Case C-610/11, 26 September 2013, *Centrotherm Systemtechnik v OHIM*, para. 61; Case C-217/13 and C-218/13, 19 June 2014, *Oberbank and Others*, para. 70.

the necessity of widespread or continuous use of the mark on new products. Furthermore, the judgment acknowledges the validity of trade mark use in the context of resale of second-hand goods and connected services, expanding the scope of trade mark use beyond first-sale scenarios.

The judgment also has strategic implications for how companies manage their trade marks. Companies with diverse product lines or those considering expanding into new market segments can be more confident in maintaining trade mark protection across a broad range of goods or services. This could encourage the preservation and revival of vintage or heritage brands, as the judgment essentially protects the trade marks of products no longer in production, provided they are still in use in some capacity, such as through replacement parts or associated services and provided that the consumers perceive them as one and the same category.

Lastly, the judgment contributes to the harmonisation of trademark law within the EU. By clarifying the interpretation of 'genuine use' and the burden of proof in trade mark revocation cases, the ruling aids in creating a more predictable and consistent legal landscape across EU Member States. This predictability is crucial for businesses operating in multiple EU countries, providing clearer guidelines on how to maintain and defend their trade mark rights within the single market.

Court of Justice 18 November 2020

On the communication to the public of an audiovisual work incorporating a phonogram or a reproduction of a phonogram and the possibility to claim a single equitable remuneration

Case C-147/19

Summary and Analysis by Marta Gimeno[1]

Parties:

Atresmedia Corporación de Medios de Comunicación, S.A.

v

Asociación de Gestión de Derecho Intelectuales (AGEDI)
Artistas Intérpretes o Ejecutantes, Sociedad de Gestión de España (AIE)

1. Background and History

On 29 July 2010, AGEDI and AIE (entities that manage the intellectual property rights of phonogram producers and performers respectively) brought an action before Commercial Court no. 4[2] in Madrid (Spain) against Atresmedia, the owner of several TV channels, seeking the payment of damages for (i) acts of communication to the public of phonograms published for commercial purposes, or reproductions of those phonograms, carried out between 1 June 2003 and 31 December 2009 via the television channels operated by Atresmedia, and (ii) the unauthorised reproduction of phonograms in connection with those acts of communication to the public.

It should be noted that the incorporation of the phonograms in the audiovisual recordings that were subsequently broadcast had been authorised by the rightholders and that Atresmedia had already paid a remuneration in return. The questions raised, therefore, related to the subsequent communication to the public and reproduction of those phonograms.[3]

The action was declared unfounded by the Commercial Court in Madrid, and both AGEDI and AIE brought an appeal against the court's decision before the Provincial Court in Madrid,[4] which upheld their application in its entirety.

---

[1] Partner and Head of the Litigation Department of Herrero & Asociados, S.L.

[2] Juzgado de lo Mercantil número 4 de Madrid.

[3] Para. 25 of the annotated judgment.

[4] Audiencia Provincial de Madrid.

Atresmedia brought an appeal on a point of law before the referring court (the Spanish Supreme Court[5]) against the judgment of the Provincial Court in Madrid. The appeal related exclusively to whether the communication to the public of audiovisual works carried out by Atresmedia via its television channels gave rise to the right to the single equitable fee provided for in Spanish law in Article 108(4) and Article 116(2) of the LPI,[6] which correspond, in EU law, to Article 8(2) of Directive 92/100[7] and to Article 8(2) of Directive 2006/115.[8]

In particular, the Spanish Supreme Court stated that it was competent to determine whether the performers and phonogram producers concerned might claim a single equitable remuneration from the moment that a phonogram published for commercial purposes (or a reproduction of that phonogram) had been incorporated or 'synchronised' in an audiovisual recording containing the fixation of an audiovisual work.[9]

The referring court added that since AGEDI and AIE were claiming compensation from Atresmedia for the communication to the public of audiovisual works carried out between 1 June 2003 and 31 December 2009, both Directive 92/100 and Directive 2006/115 were applicable *ratione temporis* to the main proceedings.[10]

In those circumstances, the Spanish Supreme Court decided to stay the proceedings and to refer the following questions to the Court of Justice for a preliminary ruling:

> '1) *Does the concept of the "reproduction of a phonogram published for commercial purposes" referred to in Article 8(2) of Directives 92/100 and 2006/115 include the reproduction of a phonogram published for commercial purposes in an audiovisual recording containing the fixation of an audiovisual work?*
>
> 2) *In the event that the answer to the previous question is in the affirmative, is a television broadcasting organisation which, for any type of communication to the public, uses an audiovisual recording containing the fixation of a cinematographic or audiovisual work*

---

5 Tribunal Supremo.

6 Real Decreto Legislativo 1/1996, de 12 de abril, por el que se aprueba el texto refundido de la Ley de Propiedad Intelectual, regularizando, aclarando y armonizando las disposiciones legales vigentes sobre la materia ('LPI').

7 Council Directive 92/100/EEC of 19 November 1992 on rental right and lending right and on certain rights related to copyright in the field of intellectual property ('Directive 92/100 ECC').

8 Directive 2006/115/EC of the European Parliament and of the Council of 12 December 2006 on rental right and lending right and on certain rights related to copyright in the field of intellectual property ('Directive 2006/115').

9 Para. 21 of the annotated judgment.

10 Para. 22 of the annotated judgment.

in which a phonogram published for commercial purposes has been reproduced, under an obligation to pay the single equitable remuneration provided for in Article 8(2) of the aforementioned directives?'

2. Decision

Article 8(2) of Council Directive 92/100/EEC of 19 November 1992 on rental right and lending right and on certain rights related to copyright in the field of intellectual property and Article 8(2) of Directive 2006/115/EC of the European Parliament and of the Council of 12 December 2006 on rental right and lending right and on certain rights related to copyright in the field of intellectual property must be interpreted as meaning that the single equitable remuneration referred to in those provisions must not be paid by the user where he or she makes a communication to the public of an audiovisual recording containing the fixation of an audiovisual work in which a phonogram or a reproduction of that phonogram has been incorporated.

3. Motivation and Analysis

Article 8[11] of Directive 92/100 and Article 8(2) of Directive 2006/115 oblige all Member states to provide a right in order to ensure that a single equitable remuneration is paid by the user when a phonogram published for commercial purposes, or a reproduction of such a phonogram, is used for broadcasting by wireless means or for any communication to the public, and to ensure that this remuneration is shared between the relevant performers and phonogram producers.[12]

---

11 Art. 8 Dir. 92/100 states:
'*1. Member States shall provide for performers the exclusive right to authorize or prohibit the broadcasting by wireless means and the communication to the public of their performances, except where the performance is itself already a broadcast performance or is made from a fixation.*
2. Member States shall provide a right in order to ensure that a single equitable remuneration is paid by the user, if a phonogram published for commercial purposes, or a reproduction of such phonogram, is used for broadcasting by wireless means or for any communication to the public, and to ensure that this remuneration is shared between the relevant performers and phonogram producers. Member States may, in the absence of agreement between the performers and phonogram producers, lay down the conditions as to the sharing of this remuneration between them.
3. Member States shall provide for broadcasting organizations the exclusive right to authorize or prohibit the rebroadcasting of their broadcasts by wireless means, as well as the communication to the public of their broadcasts if such communication is made in places accessible to the public against payment of an entrance fee.'

12 Para. 28 of the annotated judgment.

As stated in the preamble to Directive 92/100[13] and Directive 2006/115,[14] the aim of this provision is twofold:

(i) to guarantee an adequate income as a basis for further creative and artistic work; and

(ii) to allow for the amortisation of the investments made in the production of phonograms, which are particularly high and risky.

Such remuneration was included in the LPI, approving the amended text of the Intellectual Property Law[15] in Article 108, stating in this regard that:

> *'Users of a phonogram published for commercial purposes or of a reproduction of that phonogram that is used for any form of communication to the public shall have an obligation to pay a single equitable remuneration to the performers and phonogram producers, between whom that remuneration shall be shared. In the absence of agreement between them as to how that remuneration is to be shared, this shall be in equal parts.'*

As mentioned above, Atresmedia had been authorised by the rightholders to incorporate the phonograms in the audiovisual recordings, in return for payment of an agreed sum[16], but it had not been authorised to communicate or subsequently reproduce the phonograms. When the company decided to broadcast this content on its TV channels, the entities that managed the intellectual property rights of the phonogram producers and the rights of the performers demanded payment of the compensation provided for in Article 108 LPI.

The questions raised in this scenario were clear[17]:

Does the concept of the '*reproduction of a phonogram published for commercial purposes*' referred to in Article 8(2) of Directives 92/100 and 2006/115 include the reproduction of a phonogram published for commercial purposes in an audiovisual recording containing the fixation of an audiovisual work?

---

13 Rec. 7 states: '*Whereas the creative and artistic work of authors and performers necessitates an adequate income as a basis for further creative and artistic work, and the investments required particularly for the production of phonograms and films are especially high and risky; whereas the possibility for securing that income and recouping that investment can only effectively be guaranteed through adequate legal protection of the rightholders concerned.*'

14 Rec. 5 states: '*Whereas the creative and artistic work of authors and performers necessitates an adequate income as a basis for further creative and artistic work, and the investments required particularly for the production of phonograms and films are especially high and risky; whereas the possibility for securing that income and recouping that investment can only effectively be guaranteed through adequate legal protection of the rightholders concerned.*'

15 Real Decreto Legislativo 1/1996, de 12 de abril, por el que se aprueba el texto refundido de la Ley de Propiedad Intelectual.

16 Para. 25 of the annotated judgment.

17 Para. 23 and 31 of the annotated judgment.

If so, was Atresmedia obliged to pay the single equitable remuneration provided for in Article 8(2) of the aforementioned directives?

In order to clarify these questions, the Court of Justice first recalled the applicable legislation and some of the main definitions and principles. In particular, the Court referred to:

(i) The Vienna Convention on the Law of Treaties, according to which the context for the purpose of the interpretation of a treaty includes not only the text of the treaty but also any agreement relating to the treaty which has been concluded between all the parties in connection with the conclusion of the treaty.

(ii) The Rome Convention for the Protection of Performers, Producers of Phonograms and Broadcasting Organisations, which, although not ratified by the EU, has indirect effect in the EU by virtue of the fact that the Member States[18] are parties to it.[19]
According to Article 3 of this Convention:
'(b) "phonogram" means any exclusively aural fixation of sounds of a performance or of other sounds;
[...]
(e) "reproduction" means the making of a copy or copies of a fixation.'

(iii) The WIPO Copyright Treaty and the WIPO Performances and Phonograms Treaty ('WPPT').[20]
According to the WPPT '*phonogram*' means '*the fixation of the sounds of a performance or of other sounds, or of a representation of sounds, other than in the form of a fixation incorporated in a cinematographic or other audiovisual work.*'[21]
In this respect, the Diplomatic Conference on certain copyright and neighbouring rights questions of 20 December 1996 adopted the following relevant statement[22]:

'the definition of phonogram provided in Article 2(b) does not suggest that rights in the phonogram are in any way affected through their incorporation into a cinematographic or other audiovisual work.'

---

18 With the exception of Malta.

19 Para. 36 of the annotated judgment.

20 Approved on behalf of the European Community by Council Decision 2000/278/EC of 16 March 2000 on the approval, on behalf of the European Community, of the WIPO Copyright Treaty and the WIPO Performances and Phonograms Treaty (OJ 2000 L 89, p. 6), which entered into force in the EU on 14 March 2010.

21 Art. 2(b), quoted in para. 39 of the annotated judgment.

22 Para. 42 of the annotated judgment.

(iv) The aforementioned Directive 92/100 and Directive 2006/115, which refer to:

a. the reasons why it is necessary to establish compensation for artistic works; and
b. the obligation of the Member States to implement a remuneration for performers and phonogram producers.

This remuneration, which is regulated within the Spanish LPI (Art. 108, as cited above) and is compensatory in nature, constitutes the consideration for the use of a commercial phonogram during a broadcast or communication to the public. The act that triggers this remuneration[23] is the broadcasting or communication to the public of the performance of the work fixed on a phonogram published for commercial purposes, or on a reproduction of such a phonogram.[24]

However, is an audiovisual recording containing the fixation of an audiovisual work a 'phonogram' or a 'reproduction of that phonogram'?[25]

As the Advocate General[26] rightly pointed out, under the Vienna Convention on the Law of Treaties, the answer to this question must take account of the international regulations that directly (such as the WPPT) or indirectly (such as the Rome Convention) apply.

In fact, both the WPPT and the Rome Convention are clear in this regard: the concept of 'phonogram' is defined as any 'exclusively aural' fixation of sounds of a performance or of other sounds. The Court of Justice interpreted this as meaning that the fixation of images and sounds cannot fall within that concept, since such a fixation cannot be described as 'exclusively aural'.[27]

AGEDI, AIE and the Spanish Government claimed that the definition in the Guide to the Copyright and Related Rights Treaties Administered by WIPO[28] does not suggest that the rights in the phonogram are affected by its incorporation in a cinematographic or other audiovisual work; the Court accepted this but found that it had not effect on its previous considerations.[29] It could be

---

23 Para. 30 of the annotated judgment.

24 See, to that effect, case C-245/00, 6 February 2003, *SENA*, para. 37, case C-192/04, 14 July 2005, *Lagardère Active Broadcast*, para. 50, case C-265/19, 8 September 2020, *Recorded Artists Actors Performers*, para. 54.

25 Para. 31 of the annotated judgment.

26 Opinion of Advocate General E. Tanchev of 16 July 2020, para. 36.

27 Para. 37 of the annotated judgment.

28 An interpretative document drawn up by WIPO which, without being legally binding, assists in interpreting the WPPT. Accessible at www.wipo.int/edocs/pubdocs/es/copyright/891/wipo_pub_891.pdf

29 Para. 42 of the annotated judgment.

inferred from the WPPT itself that a phonogram incorporated in a cinematographic or other audiovisual work loses its status as a 'phonogram' in so far as it forms part of such a work, without that fact having any effect on the rights in that phonogram if it were to be used independently of the work in question.[30]

Since the content communicated to the public and reproduced by Atresmedia included audiovisual elements, the work in question was not a phonogram and could give rise to the payment of a single equitable remuneration specifically aimed at (aural) phonograms.[31]

The Court concluded its judgment by stating that when the phonograms or reproductions of those phonograms are incorporated into the audiovisual works concerned, any remuneration sought by the authors, performers and phonogram producers must be fixed in specific agreements.[32]

* *
*

Following the CJEU's judgment, the Supreme Court finally resolved the main dispute in a resolution issued on 9 February 2021.[33] In this judgment, the Supreme Court held, firstly, that the transposition of Article 8.2 of Directives 92/100 and 2006/115 into Articles 108.4 and 116.2 of the TRLPI had not increased the protection of holders of related rights, since it had merely transposed the provisions of Directives 92/100 and 2006/115 into the provisions of national law, without making any relevant additions.

For this reason, the Supreme Court held that, in order to resolve the appeal, the interpretation of Article 8.2 of Directives 92/100 and 2006/115 given by the CJEU in the annotated judgment must be followed. Next, after summarising the judgment, the Supreme Court concluded that, in view of the CJEU's answer to the questions referred for a preliminary ruling, the appeal brought by Atresmedia should be set aside and the judgment of the Court of First Instance should be confirmed.

This judgment, which clearly benefits broadcasters such as Atresmedia or Netflix and was certainly not anticipated by the complainants, will undoubtedly bring about a profound change in the exploitation and management of intellectual property rights in the EU.

In this respect, although it is common practice to reach an agreement on the incorporation of phonograms, the fact that subsequent communication to the

30 Para. 44 of the annotated judgment.
31 Paras. 51 to 53 of the annotated judgment.
32 Para. 55 of the annotated judgment.
33 STS 67/2021, 9 February 2021, procedure 10534/2020.

public or reproduction does not generate a separate remuneration will definitely be taken into account by the rightholders in order to increase the amounts requested for the incorporation of phonograms and will lead to a significant reduction in the revenues of collecting societies, which will have to adjust their rates.[34]

Moreover, this judgment reveals the different positions of the European Parliament (with its highly protective attitude when it comes to the adjudication of intellectual property rights) and the CJEU (which seems to advocate a more open and permissive perspective).

---

[34] For more information on the judgment and its effects, see the article 'Efectos de la doctrina sentada por el Tribunal de Justicia de la Unión Europea en materia de sincronización audiovisual de fonogramas' by Rafael Sánchez Aristi at https://indret.com/wp-content/uploads/2023/07/1804-numerat.pdf.

COURT OF JUSTICE 25 NOVEMBER 2020

ON ROYALTY CALCULATION METHODS OF COLLECTING SOCIETIES: POTENTIAL ABUSE OF A DOMINANT POSITION UNDER COMPETITION LAW

Case C-372/19

Summary and Analysis by Marion Nuytten[1]

Parties:

Belgische Vereniging van Auteurs, Componisten en Uitgevers CVBA (SABAM)

v

Weareone.World BVBA
Wecandance NV

1. Background and History

The Belgian Association of Authors, Composers and Publishers ('SABAM') is a Belgian copyright management society that collects and distributes copyright royalties for the reproduction and communication to the public of musical works. This includes the collection of royalties from music festivals for the use of protected works belonging to its repertoire. SABAM has a *de facto* monopoly on the Belgian market.

Weareone.World and Wecandance ('the festival organisers') organise the annual festivals Tomorrowland and Wecandance. Following various editions of these events between 2013 and 2016, SABAM sought orders of payment against both festival organisers before the Antwerp Court of Enterprise for unpaid copyright royalties relating to the use of copyrighted works from its repertoire.

The level of royalties claimed by SABAM was calculated according to the so-called 'Tariff 211'.[2] Under this tariff, the basic amount of royalties to be paid was based on the gross receipts from ticket sales, after deduction of VAT and certain costs, or on the artistic budget allocated to the artists (whichever was the

1 Marion Nuytten is an IP/IT and competition lawyer specialised in new technologies in the law firm & DE BANDT in Brussels, Belgium.

2 Tariff 211 is the applicable tariffs scheme for festivals.

higher).[3] In the case at hand, the levies were calculated on the gross receipts from ticket sales. This basic tariff included eight separate revenue tranches, to which a degressive royalty rate was applied.

Festival organisers can also benefit from discounts on this rate, depending on the proportion of musical works part of SABAM's repertoire that are actually performed at the event. This tranche-based system aims to reflect the actual use of SABAM's music catalogue: when the proportion of musical works of SABAM's repertoire performed is less than 1/3 or 2/3, SABAM only invoices 1/3 or 2/3 of the basic amount of fees, whereas when it represents 2/3 or more, the total basic amount of fees is charged ('1/3-2/3 rule').

Both festival organisers challenged the legality of Tariff 211 before the national court on the grounds that royalties calculated on the basis of that tariff did not correspond to the economic value of the services provided by SABAM.

In particular, the organisers first argued that the 1/3-2/3 rule was not sufficiently precise, as it did not identify the musical works from SABAM's repertoire that were actually performed at their events, whereas this is possible using means of modern technology.

Secondly, the festival organisers criticised SABAM for calculating the basic tariff on the basis of the gross receipts from ticket sales without allowing the deduction of all the expenses unrelated to the musical works performed that were incurred by the organisation of those festivals.

The organisers pointed out that SABAM could consequently demand higher remuneration for the use of the same works in the case of events with a higher admission fee, whereas this higher level was solely due to the organisers' efforts to make a festival a 'total experience', to the infrastructure provided or to the quality of the performers, but not to the services provided by SABAM.

In that context, the question arose whether SABAM was abusing its dominant position by charging excessive licence fees, in breach of Article 102 of the Treaty on the Functioning of the European Union ('TFEU') and Article 16 of the Directive 2014/26 of the European Parliament and of the Council of 26 February 2014 on collective management of copyright and related rights

---

3 Under Belgian law, and in particular Art. XI.249 of the Belgian Code of Economic Law ('WER/CDE'), collecting societies lay down rules on pricing, collection and distribution for all the forms of exploitation for which they manage the rights of rightholders. In practice, these parameters are negotiated with the relevant professional organisations. According to Art. XI.262 of the WER/CDE, the tariffs applied must be reasonable, taking into account *inter alia* the economic value of the use of the rights and the nature and extent of the use of the works and performances. In addition, it explicitly mentions the need to consider the economic value of the service provided by the collecting society.

and multi-territorial licensing of rights in musical works for online use in the internal market ('Directive 2014/26').[4]

Against this background, the Ondernemingsrechtbank Antwerpen (Enterprise Court, Antwerp, Belgium) decided to stay the proceedings and to refer the following question to the European Court of Justice ('CJEU') for a preliminary ruling:

> *'Must Article 102 TFEU, whether or not read in conjunction with Article 16 of Directive 2014/26 [...], be interpreted as meaning that there is abuse of a dominant position if a copyright management company which has a de facto monopoly in a Member State applies a remuneration model to organisers of musical events, for the right to communicate musical works to the public, based among other things on turnover:*
> 1. *which uses a flat-rate tariff in tranches, instead of a tariff that takes into account the precise share (making use of advanced technical tools) of the music repertoire protected by the management company played during the event?*
> 2. *which makes licence fees dependent on external elements such as, inter alia, the admission price, the price of refreshments, the artistic budget for the performers and the budget for other elements, such as decor?'*

2. Decision

Article 102 TFEU must be interpreted as meaning that it does not constitute an abuse of a dominant position, within the meaning of that article, for a collective management company which has a de facto monopoly in a Member State to impose on organisers of musical events, in respect of the right to communicate musical works to the public, a charging scheme in which:

- **the copyright royalties due are calculated on the basis of a tariff applied to the gross receipts from ticket sales, without it being possible to deduct from those receipts all the costs pertaining to the organisation of the festival which are not related to the musical works which are performed at it, provided that, in the light of all the relevant circumstances of the case, the royalties actually imposed by the management company pursuant to that charging scheme are not excessive in relation, inter alia, to the nature and scope of**

---

[4] OJ 2014 L, p. 72. Art. 16, para. 2, second indent provides that: '*Rightholders shall receive appropriate remuneration for the use of their rights. Tariffs for exclusive rights and rights to remuneration shall be reasonable in relation to, inter alia, the economic value of the use of the rights in trade, taking into account the nature and scope of the use of the work and other subject-matter, as well as in relation to the economic value of the service provided by the collective management organisation. Collective management organisations shall inform the user concerned of the criteria used for the setting of those tariffs.*'

the use of the works, the economic value generated by that use and the economic value of the services of that management company, which it is for the national court to ascertain, and

- a flat-rate system in tranches is used in order to determine the share of the musical works performed which is taken from that management company's repertoire, provided that no other method exists which enables the use of those works to be identified and to be quantified more precisely and which is capable of achieving the same legitimate aim, which is the protection of the interests of composers and music editors, without, however, leading to a disproportionate increase in the costs incurred for the purposes of the management of contracts and the supervision of the use of musical works protected by copyright; it is for the national court to ascertain that, in the light of the actual case before it and taking account of all the relevant circumstances, including the availability and reliability of the data provided and the technological tools in existence.

3. Motivation and analysis

At the outset, the Court recalled its previous case-law according to which a collective management company, such as SABAM, is an undertaking to which Article 102 TFEU applies.[5]

Since SABAM held a monopoly in the territory of a Member State – *Belgium* – over the management of copyright relating to a category of protected works – *musical works* –, it must be regarded as holding a dominant position in a substantial part of the internal market, within the meaning of that Article.[6] This position was not disputed by SABAM itself.

With regard to the royalties demanded by collective management organisations ('CMOs'), the CJEU has repeatedly held that the conduct of such undertakings may constitute an abuse, and thus fall within the scope of the prohibition of Article 102 TFEU if, when setting the royalty level, they impose a price which is excessive *in relation to the economic value of the service* that they provide, which consists in managing the repertoire of music protected by copyright and making it available to users.[7]

In the context of that assessment, it is important to take into consideration the *particular nature of copyright* and to seek an appropriate balance between the interests of rightholders and those of their users. The Court recalled that

---

5 See judgment of 27 February 2014, *OSA*, C-351/12, para. 80.

6 See judgment of 27 February 2014, *OSA*, C-351/12, para. 86 and the case-law cited.

7 See judgments of 11 December 2008, *Kanal 5 and TV 4*, C-52/07, para. 28 and the case-law cited; of 27 February 2014, *OSA*, C-351/12, para. 88; and of 14 September 2017, *Autortiesību un komunicēšanās konsultāciju aģentūra – Latvijas Autoru apvienība*, C-177/16, para. 35.

in order to ascertain whether the level of the tariffs imposed by CMOs was fair from both perspectives, it was necessary to take account not only of the economic value of the service, but also of the nature and scope of the use of the protected works and the economic value generated by this use.[8]

In order to do so, the Court once again took as its starting point its *United Brands* test, which is usually applied in unfair pricing cases, and recalled that its own case-law and the Commission's practice had also recognised other stand-alone analysis methods.[9]

In the light of these well-established principles, the CJEU answered the two sub-questions referred to it by the national court.

<u>i) Calculation of royalties based on the gross receipts from ticket sales without deduction of organisational costs is not abusive per se</u>

Regarding the impossibility of deducting organisational costs unrelated to the musical works from the gross receipts, the CJEU did not appear to be very receptive to the arguments put forward by the festival organisers according to which the receipts from ticketing bear no relation to the economic value of the service provided by SABAM.[10]

In this context, the CJEU recalled that it had already found that the collection by CMOs of royalties calculated on a percentage of the gross turnover of discotheques for the public performance of recorded musical works (*Basset*[11]) and

---

8 See para. 30 of the annotated judgment.

9 See para. 31 in which the Court recalled the principles of the two-part *United Brands* test and para. 32 outlining alternative methods: '*With regard [...] to the royalties imposed by collective management companies, those methods may, inter alia, [...] be based on a comparison between the price whose fairness is disputed and benchmarks such as prices previously charged by the dominant undertaking for the same services in the same relevant market, prices charged by such an undertaking for other services or for different types of customers, or prices charged by other undertakings for the same or comparable services in other national markets, provided, however, that that comparison is made on a consistent basis.*' In this regard, see also Opinion of Advocate General Pitruzzella, 16 July 2020, paras. 29 to 38. In the judgment *AKKA/LAA*, mentioned by the Court, the Court confirmed that comparing the rates charged in other Members States constitutes a legitimate alternative method to assess tariffs of CMOs, provided that the comparison is made on a consistent basis using objective, appropriate and verifiable criteria also taking into account the national purchasing parity index. See judgment of 14 September 2017, *Autortiesību un komunicēšanās konsultāciju aģentūra – Latvijas Autoru apvienība* ('AKKA/LAA'), C-177/16, paras. 36 and 37.

10 See paras. 35 and 36 of the annotated judgment.

11 See judgment of 9 April 1987, *Basset*, C-402/85. In this case, the Court considered that the application by the French copyright management organisation, SACEM, of an additional mechanical reproduction levy on top of a fee for public performance of musical works in discotheques did not in itself constitute an abuse of a dominant position.

of the revenue of television broadcasting companies for television broadcasting to the general public (*Kanal 5 and TV 4*[12]) must be regarded as constituting a normal exploitation of copyright which does not in itself constitute abusive conduct.[13]

According to the CJEU, this case-law is applicable to a charging scheme for royalties, such as that imposed by SABAM, which must be regarded as being a normal exploitation of copyright and, in principle, as reasonable in relation to the economic value of the service provided.[14]

By imposing such a scheme, SABAM does pursue a legitimate aim under competition law, namely safeguarding the rights and interests of its members.[15] Moreover, the royalties resulting from such a scheme represent the consideration paid for the communication to the public of those musical works.

As regards the investments made by the festival organisers, the Court stated that the above-mentioned case-law is applicable even though the gross turnover could depend, to a significant extent, on elements unrelated to the use of musical works.[16] This is especially the case as it may be particularly difficult to determine objectively the specific elements that are unrelated to the musical works performed or to quantify the economic value of those elements and their impact on the receipts from the sale of festival tickets.[17] Moreover, imposing such an obligation on CMOs would be likely to result in a disproportionate increase in the costs of managing and monitoring their repertoire.[18]

It follows that, according to the Court, the imposition by a CMO such as SABAM of royalties based on the gross receipts from festival ticket sales without deduction of the organisational costs does not in itself constitute abusive conduct within the meaning of Article 102 TFEU.[19]

The only concession made by the Court, although it was a not new one, was that the imposition of such a charging scheme by a collecting society may constitute an abuse of dominant position if it can be considered that the royalty level actually set is unreasonable in relation to the economic value of the service

---

[12] See judgment of 11 December 2008, *Kanal 5 and TV 4*, C-52/07. In this case, the Court considered that the royalties levied by the Swedish collective management organisation, STIM, for the television broadcast of musical works protected by copyright did not in themselves constitute an abuse of a dominant position.

[13] See paras. 37 and 38 of the annotated judgment.

[14] See para. 39 of the annotated judgment.

[15] See para. 40 of the annotated judgment.

[16] See para. 44 of the annotated judgment.

[17] See para. 45 of the annotated judgment.

[18] See para. 46 of the annotated judgment.

[19] See paras. 39 and 47 of the annotated judgment.

provided by the CMO.[20] This is for the national court to determine, in light of all the circumstances of the case, including the level of the royalty rate set and the receipts on which that rate is based.[21]

ii) Application of an imprecise flat-rate system in tranches may amount to an abuse of dominant position if three conditions are met

Regarding the application of a flat-rate system in tranches, such as that provided for by the 1/3-2/3 rule, the Court pointed out that, although Tariff 211 takes account to some extent of the proportion of performed musical works which come from SABAM's repertoire (since it allows a proportionate reduction of 1/3 or 2/3 of the full rate)[22], it does so in a very imprecise manner, suggesting that SABAM almost systematically collects considerably higher revenue than that corresponding to the precise quantity of works performed.[23]

Relying on its previous case-law (*Kanal 5 and TV4*), the Court pointed out that the application of a charging scheme for royalties which takes account of the number of musical works actually performed may in any case amount to an abuse of dominant position if three conditions are met: (i) when there is an alternative method of identifying and quantifying more accurately the use of those works, provided that this method is (ii) capable of achieving the same legitimate aim, namely the protection of composers and music editors, (iii) without leading to a disproportionate increase in the costs of managing the supervising of the musical repertoire.[24]

As usual, it is for the national court to ascertain this, in light of the specific and relevant circumstances of the case, including the availability and the reliability of the data provided and the existing technological tools.[25]

* *
*

Competition authorities and national courts are in principle reluctant to deal with excessive or unfair price practices due to difficulties in determining the

---

20 See para. 48 of the annotated judgment.

21 See para. 48 of the annotated judgment.

22 See para. 51 of the annotated judgment.

23 See para. 53 of the annotated judgment.

24 See judgment of 11 December 2008, *Kanal 5 and TV 4*, C-52/07, para. 40 and para. 52 of the annotated judgment.

25 See para. 53 of the annotated judgment.

appropriate price level[26] and the fear of being perceived as price regulators. However, there has been renewed interest recently in 'unfair pricing' or 'excessive pricing' conducts in the pharmaceutical sector and, to a lesser extent, in the copyright management sector.[27]

In the case at hand, in essence, the judgment leaves the door open to a finding of abuse of a dominant position where a CMO imposes unfair prices and/or where a technological tool could allow more precise determination of the musical works performed at an event without incurring unreasonable administrative costs. Although the Court appears to be rather permissive at first glance and therefore reluctant to find abusive conduct on the part of SABAM, it does not hesitate to provide the referring court with insightful factual guidance in this respect, actually supporting the position of the festival organisers.[28]

First of all, it observes that the application of the 1/3-2/3 rule requires the festival organisers to provide SABAM with a list of the works actually performed at the event in question. In principle, such a list makes it possible to determine more precisely the proportion of works performed.[29] Secondly, the Court refers to the development of musical recognition software which may be capable of identifying and quantifying the proportion of the works performed with greater precision.[30] Finally, it appears that SABAM has already applied alternative methods, such as the use of authorised monitoring companies or a new scheme of tranches, allowing for more precision in the determination of the performed works in SABAM's repertoire.[31]

Ultimately, the referring court never had the opportunity to apply the guidance of the CJEU in the SABAM case, as the dispute eventually led to an amicable settlement between the festival organisers and the Belgian collecting management

---

[26] Advocate General Pitruzzella referred in this respect to the *Procrustean dilemma* that national competition authorities and national courts are faced with when applying the concept of excessive prices. On the hand, there is the risk that antitrust over-enforcement leads to false positives, ultimately eroding efficiency and consumer welfare. On the other hand, under-enforcement leads to false negatives, which could affect the fundamental values of our societies, such as social equality through the consumption of culture. See Opinion of Advocate General Pitruzzella, 16 July 2020, paras. 21 to 27.

[27] For an overview and discussion of the decisions adopted by national antitrust authorities in the copyright management sector, see A. Zablocka-Abi Yaghi, 'Collecting societies and competition law: An overview of EU and national case law', 2 April 2020, *Concurrences*, n° 92517. For an overview and discussion of the decisions adopted at the European level, see Opinion of Advocate General Pitruzzella, 16 July 2020, paras. 39 to 48.

[28] See para. 56 of the annotated judgment.

[29] See para. 57 of the annotated judgment.

[30] See para. 58 of the annotated judgment.

[31] See para. 59 of the annotated judgment.

society.[32] Fingerprinting technology[33] is now being used jointly by SABAM and festival organisers to identify automatically the musical works performed and to create complete playlists, allowing for a more accurate collection and distribution of royalties.[34] With the proliferation of new digital technologies that allow greater precision with reduced monitoring costs, it is a safe bet that it will become increasingly difficult for CMOs to hide behind an alleged lack of available technology to impose royalty rates that are largely unrelated to the works performed.

However, it is worth mentioning that the findings of the CJEU were applied in September 2022 by the Brussels Court of Appeal,[35] in another legal dispute in which the royalty rates set by SABAM were once again the subject of allegations of abuse of dominant position by festival organisers.[36] The Brussels Court stayed the proceedings pending the CJEU's preliminary ruling in the case under discussion. The Brussels Court of Appeal, largely referring to the principles of the Court, found that some elements of the calculation of the level of royalties, such as the calculation of fees on the gross receipt with no cost deduction, were unproblematic under competition law. However, the Court found that, by increasing royalty rates by 37% in 2017 without proper justification or any reasonable link to the value of its services, SABAM had abused its dominant position. In particular, the Brussels Court of Appeal reached this conclusion on the basis of the alternative method referred to by the Court of Justice, which consisted in comparing the increased prices whose fairness was disputed with the prices previously charged by SABAM for the same services on the same relevant market.[37]

---

32 See SABAM press release, '*Le partenariat entre Tomorrowland et la Sabam : véritable valeur ajoutée pour le secteur de la musique*', 8 September 2022, https://www.sabam.be/en/node/1583.

33 Audio fingerprinting technology can be used to identify songs playing or performed, even if they have been remixed, edited or covered by another artist.

34 See Sabam press release, '*Le partenariat entre Tomorrowland et la Sabam : véritable valeur ajoutée pour le secteur de la musique*', 8 September 2022 www.sabam.be/en/node/1583. The press release also stated that the parties had reached an agreement on the remuneration due to authors and composers.

35 See Brussels, 7 September 2022, 2018/AR/1046, *Competitio*, 2022/4, p. 301. See also first instance judgment of Commercial Court (Pres.) Brussels, 12 April 2018, *Auteurs & Media*, 2nd edition, p. 44. For a detailed analysis of the judgment in appeal, see B. LAGASSE and A. DECROO, 'Het arrest van het hof van beroep te Brussel van 7 september 2022: einde van de saga Sabam?', *Competitio*, 2022/4, p. 337.

36 The price increases referred to in this case are as high as 37% for the higher tranches. At first sight, this is extremely limited compared to the increases observed in the pharmaceutical sector.

37 In particular, on the basis of para. 32 of the annotated judgment, see footnote 9 above.

Finally, it is interesting to note that SABAM subsequently adapted the general conditions of its Tariff 211 with effect from 1 January 2020.[38] First, the controversial 1/3-2/3 rule – concretely amounting to three tranches of 33.33% – was replaced by a new scheme of 10% incremental tranches in order to better reflect the actual use of its repertoire. In addition, the special conditions of Tariff 211 now explicitly stipulate that a number of limited costs may be deducted from the gross receipts from ticket sales, provided that these costs can be clearly substantiated by the organisers.[39]

The legality of this new regime has never been scrutinised by European or national jurisdictions under the prism of competition law, but these adaptations, combined with the use of technological tools, are probably sufficient to address the Court's concerns. Striking the right balance between the interests of artists and those of users is in any case never an easy task for the national judges as the economic value of music is a divisive concept.[40] Like musical performances, it is subject to a wide range of interpretations.

---

[38] See Tariff 211 applicable to festivals since 1 January 2020: www.unisono.be/sites/default/files/t211_festivals.pdf.

[39] By way of illustration, one of the cost items concerns 50% of the invoice expenses for professional security services and public assistance (such as fire, police and civil protection).

[40] As rightly pointed out by Advocate General Pitruzzella, it is in any case not for the national courts or competition authorities to determine which method of calculation should be used, but only to assess whether the applied method infringes (or not) Art. 102 TFEU and, in particular, whether it leads to the imposition of unfair or excessive prices.

COURT OF JUSTICE 17 DECEMBER 2020

ON THE PROTECTION OF GEOGRAPHICAL INDICATIONS AND DESIGNATIONS OF ORIGIN FOR AGRICULTURAL PRODUCTS AND FOODSTUFFS

Case C-490/19

Summary and Analysis by Margarida Castillo Silva and Maria Rubina Silva[1]

Parties:

Syndicat interprofessionnel de défense du fromage Morbier

v

Société Fromagère du Livradois SAS

1. Background and History

With the intent of '*[…] securing a fair return for farmers and producers […], providing clear information on products with specific characteristics linked to geographical origin, thereby enabling consumers to make more informed purchasing choices*'[2] (emphasis added), and preventing '*[…] practices liable to mislead consumers […]*'[3] (emphasis added), Regulation (EU) No 1151/2012 of the European Parliament and of the Council of 21 November 2012 on quality schemes for agricultural products and foodstuffs (hereinafter 'Regulation No 1151/2012')[4] sets out the legal framework applicable to protected designation(s) of origin (hereinafter 'PDO'), understood as identifying '*[…] a product: (a) originating in a specific place, region or, in exceptional cases, a country; (b) whose quality or characteristics are essentially or exclusively due to a particular geographical environment […]*'[5] (emphasis added).

1 Margarida Castillo Silva is an IP/IT associate and Maria Rubina Silva is an IP/IT trainee at the Portuguese law firm Abreu & Associados – Sociedade de Advogados, SP, RL, and both are members of the Portuguese Bar.

2 Rec. 18 of Reg. No 1151/2012.

3 Rec. 19 of Reg. No 1151/2012.

4 Reg. No 1151/2012 currently sets out the applicable legal scheme in the context of PDOs, having repealed Council Regulation (EC) No 510/2006 of 20 March 2006 on the protection of geographical indications and designations of origin for agricultural products and foodstuffs (hereinafter 'Reg. No 510/2006'), which, in turn, repealed Council Regulation (EEC) No 2081/92 on the protection of geographical indications and designations of origin for agricultural products and foodstuffs (hereinafter 'Reg. No 2081/92').

5 Art. 5(1) of Reg. No 1151/2012.

Against this backdrop, the name 'Morbier'[6] was entered, in 2002[7], into the Register of protected designation of origin and protected geographical indications as a PDO.[8] It had likewise '*[...] enjoyed appellation d'origine contrôlée (AOC) (registered designation of origin) status since the adoption of the decree of 22 December 2000 relating to the registered designation of origin 'Morbier' [...] which defined a geographical reference area, and the conditions necessary to claim that designation of origin, and laid down [...] a transitional period [...] to enable [undertakings outside that geographical area which had previously and continuously produced and marketed cheeses under the protected name 'Morbier'] to continue to use that name without the 'AOC' reference, until the expiry of a period of five years [...].*'[9] (emphasis added).

Owing to this classification, 'Morbier' became protected against: '*(a) [...] commercial use [...] in respect of products not covered by the registration in so far as those products are comparable to the products registered under that [...]; (b) any misuse, imitation or evocation [...]; (c) any other false or misleading indication as to the provenance, origin, nature or essential qualities of the product [...]; (d) any other practice liable to mislead the consumer as to the true origin of the product.*'[10] (emphasis added).

As it so happens, Société Fromagère du Livradois (hereinafter 'SFL'), a producer of Morbier cheese since 1979, had been authorised to use the name 'Morbier' without the 'AOC' indication, pursuant to the rules laid out above, until 11 July 2007. After that date, and in compliance with the decree of 22 December 2000, SFL substituted the use of the name 'Montboissié du Haut Livradois' for 'Morbier' for its cheeses which, by all accounts and despite not complying with the specifications for the PDO 'Morbier', maintained the visual appearance of the

---

6 Referring to '*a cheese made from raw cow's milk, with an uncooked pressed paste, in the shape of a flat cylinder 30 to 40 centimetres in diameter, 5 to 8 centimetres high, weighing 5 to 8 kg, with flat sides and a slightly convex heel. Throughout each slice the cheese has a continuous, joined, horizontal, central black mark.*' (emphasis added), as provided for in Commission Implementing Reg. (EU) No 1128/2013 of 7 November 2013 approving minor amendments to the specification for a name entered in the register of protected designations of origin and protected geographical indications (Morbier (PDO)) (hereinafter 'Reg. No 1128/2013').

7 Through Commission Reg. (EC) No 1241/2002 of 10 July 2002 supplementing the Annex to Regulation (EC) No 2400/96 on the entry of certain names in the 'Register of protected designations of origin and protected geographical indications' provided for in Council Reg. (EEC) No 2081/92 on the protection of geographical indications and designations of origin for agricultural products and foodstuffs (Gailtaler Speck, Morbier, Queso Palmero or Queso de la Palma, Thrapsano extra virgin olive oil, Turrón de Agramunt or Torró d'Agramunt) (hereinafter 'Reg. No 1241/2002').

8 In accordance with Commission Reg. (EC) No 2400/96 of 17 December 1996 on the entry of certain names in the 'Register of protected designation of origin and protected geographical indications' provided for in Reg. No 2081/92 (hereinafter 'Reg. No 2400/96').

9 Para. 9 of the annotated judgment.

10 Art. 13(1) of both Reg. No 1151/2012 and Reg. No 510/2006.

product covered by said PDO (namely the central dark line running along the cheese, as exemplified in Figure 1).

Figure 1: Appearance of typical 'Morbier' cheese

Considering this to constitute an infringement of the PDO 'Morbier' and an act of unfair and parasitic competition susceptible of creating confusion with and profiting from the reputation of the 'original' product, the Syndicat interprofessionnel de défense du fromage Morbier (hereinafter 'Syndicat') brought proceedings against SFL before the Tribunal de grande instance de Paris (Regional Court, Paris, France) on the grounds of Article 13(1) of both Regulation No 1151/2012 and Regulation No 510/2006 (hereinafter 'Article 13(1)'). Based on the traditional understanding that PDOs aim '*[...] to protect not the appearance or features of a product as described in its specification, but its name [...]*,'[11] both the Tribunal de grande instance de Paris and, later on, the Cour d'appel de Paris (Court of Appeal, Paris), dismissed the Syndicat's claim without special regard as to whether SFL's practices were susceptible of '*[...] mislead[ing] the consumer as to the true origin of the product [...]*.'[12] In short, it was argued that the mere use of similar techniques and the reproduction of the appearance of a product, provided no exclusive right exists, falls within the scope of the freedom of trade and industry (which the Syndicat was looking to curtail for commercial interests). It was further noted – considering the features an average European consumer would consider distinctive – that the contested cheeses were different (i.e. the dark-coloured central line was due to different ingredients in the two cheeses, which likewise used distinct forms of milk – pasteurized vs. raw – in their composition) and, as such, no particular investments made by the Syndicat or its members were being unduly exploited.

Materially dissenting from the Cour d'appel's decision and believing it to have misinterpreted Article 13(1), namely where it refers to any practice liable to

11 CJEU decision *sub judice*.

12 *Ibid.*

mislead the consumer as to the true origin of the product, the Syndicat referred the issue to the Cour de cassation (Court of Cassation, France). Before this court, SFL maintained that PDOs do not prevent the production and marketing of similar products, provided they do not induce confusion in the consumer or misuse/evoke said PDOs, and that the practices liable to mislead the consumer provided for in Regulation No 1151/2012 and 510/2006 must still '*[...] necessarily focus on the origin of the product.*'[13]

In light of the described situation, the Cour de cassation, seeking clarification on the scope of Article 13(1)(d) of Regulation No 1151/2012 and 510/2006, namely on whether it extends the protection afforded by PDOs beyond the use of their name to encompass the reproduction of physical characteristics of the 'original' product that might mislead consumers about its true origin, stayed proceedings to refer the following questions to the CJEU:

> *'Must Article 13(1) of Regulation No 510/2006 [of 20 March 2006 on the protection of geographical indications and designations of origin for agricultural products and foodstuffs] and Article 13(1) of Regulation No 1151/2012 [of the European Parliament and of the Council of 21 November 2012 on quality schemes for agricultural products and foodstuffs] be interpreted as prohibiting solely the use by a third party of the registered name, or must they be interpreted as prohibiting the presentation of a product protected by a designation of origin, in particular the reproduction of the shape or the appearance which are characteristic of it, which is liable to mislead the consumer as to the true origin of the product, even if the registered name is not used?'*

2. Decision

1. Article 13(1) of Council Regulation (EC) No 510/2006 of 20 March 2006 on the protection of geographical indications and designations of origin for agricultural products and foodstuffs and Article 13(1) of Regulation (EU) No 1151/2012 of the European Parliament and of the Council of 21 November 2012 on quality schemes for agricultural products and foodstuffs must be interpreted as meaning that they do not prohibit solely the use by a third party of a registered name.

2. Article 13(1)(d) of Regulation No 510/2006 and Article 13(1)(d) of Regulation No 1151/2012 must be interpreted as prohibiting the reproduction of the shape or appearance characterising a product covered by a registered name where that reproduction is liable to lead the consumer to believe that the product in question is covered by that registered name. It is necessary to assess whether such reproduction may mislead the European consumer, who

---

13 CJEU decision *sub judice.*

is normally informed and reasonably observant and circumspect, taking into account all relevant factors in the case.

3. Motivation and analysis

In the first part of its question, the referring court asked whether Article 13(1) of regulation No 510/2006 and the same article of Regulation No 1151/2012 must be interpreted as prohibiting solely the use by a third party of the registered name.

According to Article 13(1) of Regulation No 510/2006 and the same Article of Regulation No 1151/2012, registered names are protected against:

> '*(a) any direct or indirect commercial use of a registered name in respect of products not covered by the registration where those products are comparable to the products registered under that name or where using the name exploits the reputation of the protected name, including when those products are used as an ingredient;*
>
> *(b) any misuse, imitation or evocation, even if the true origin of the products or services is indicated or if the protected name is translated or accompanied by an expression such as "style", "type", "method", "as produced in", "imitation" or similar, including when those products are used as an ingredient;*
>
> *(c) any other false or misleading indication as to the provenance, origin, nature or essential qualities of the product that is used on the inner or outer packaging, advertising material or documents relating to the product concerned, and the packing of the product in a container liable to convey a false impression as to its origin;*
>
> *(d) any other practice liable to mislead the consumer as to the true origin of the product.*'

The CJEU therefore took the view that it is clear from the wording of those provisions that registered names are protected against various acts, namely, first, direct or indirect commercial use of a registered name, secondly, misuse, imitation or evocation, thirdly, false or misleading indications as to provenance, origin, nature, or essential qualities of the product on the inner or outer packaging, advertising material or documents relating to the product concerned and the packing, advertising material or documents relating to the product concerned and the packing of the product in a container liable to convey a false impression as to its origin and, fourthly, any other practice liable to mislead the consumer as to the true origin of the products.[14]

---

[14] Para. 23 of the annotated judgment.

In fact, with reference to previous case-law,[15] the CJEU stated that those provisions contain a graduated list of prohibited conduct, since whilst Article 13(1)(1) of Regulation No 510/2006 and the same Article of Regulation No 1151/2012 prohibit direct and indirect use of a registered name for products not covered by the registration, in an identical form or a form that is phonetically and/or visually highly similar, Articles 13(1)(b) to (d) of those regulations also prohibit other types of conduct against which registered names are protected and for products which do not use the names themselves either directly or indirectly.[16]

As regards more specifically Article 13(1)(d) of Regulation No 510/2006 and the same Article of Regulation No 1151/2012, the CJEU – taking into account the opinion of the Advocate General[17] – considered it clear from the words 'any other practice' used in those provisions that they are intended to cover any conduct not already covered by the other provisions of those Articles (subparas (a) to (c)) and thus to tighten the system of protection for registered names.

In light of the above, the CJEU concluded and answered negatively to the first part of question posed by the referring court, i.e., that Article 13(1) of Regulation No 510/2006 and the same Article of Regulation No 1151/2012 are not limited to prohibiting the use of the registered name itself, but a wider scope of conduct.[18]

By the second part of its question, the referring court asked, in essence, whether Article 13(1)(d) of Regulation No 510/2006 and Article 13(1)(d) of Regulation No 1151/2012 must be interpreted as prohibiting the reproduction of the shape or appearance characteristic of a product covered by a registered name where that reproduction is liable to mislead the consumer as to the true origin of the product.

In this regard, the CJEU began by taking into consideration the arguments of SFL and of the European Commission, namely that the protection provided by those provisions concerns the registered name and not the product covered by that name. Furthermore, the purpose of protection of registered names is not to prohibit, *inter alia*, the use of manufacturing techniques or the reproduction of one or more characteristics indicated in the specification of a product covered by a registered name, on the ground that they appear in that specification, in the making of another product not covered by that registration.[19]

---

15 Case C-614/17, f 2 May 2019, *Fundación Consejo Regulador de la Denominación de Origen Protegida Queso Manchego*, para. 27.

16 Para. 24 of the annotated judgment.

17 Opinion of Advocate General Pitruzzella for Case C-490/19 17 September 2020, para. 49.

18 Paras. 30 and 31 of the annotated judgment.

19 Para. 36 of the annotated judgment.

However, with reference to the Opinion of the Advocate General, the CJEU acknowledged that the PDO and the product covered by it are closely linked, as the PDO designates a product that has certain qualities or characteristics.[20]

In this sense, and having regard to, as the CJEU stated '*the open-ended nature of the expression "any other practice"*' in Article 13(1)(d) of Regulation No 510/2006 and the same Article of Regulation No 1151/2012, the CJEU answered the second part of the question by ruling that the reproduction of the shape or appearance of a product covered by a registered name may fall within the scope of those provisions without that name appearing either on the product in question or on its packaging, as long as that reproduction is liable to mislead the consumer as to the true origin of the product in question.

In order to assess whether such reproduction misleads the consumer, the CJEU followed, once again, the Opinion of the Advocate General.[21] According to the latter, first, it is necessary to refer to the perception of the average European consumer, who is reasonably well informed and reasonably observant and circumspect, and, secondly, to take into account all the relevant factors in the case, including the way in which the products in question are presented to the public and marketed.[22]

In particular, in the case at issue, it was ruled that as regards an element of the appearance of the product covered by the registered name, it is necessary to assess whether that element constitutes a baseline characteristic which is particularly distinctive of that product so that its reproduction may, in conjunction with all the relevant factors in the case, lead the consumer to believe that the product containing that reproduction is a product covered by that registered name.

* *
*

20 Para. 37 of the annotated judgment and Opinion of the Advocate General Pitruzzella for case C-490/19, 17 September 2020, para. 27.: '*In the second place, and further to what I have stated above, I would note that, in the actual words of Article 5(1)(a) and (b) of Regulation No 1151/2012, "designation of origin" is "a name which identifies a product originating in a specific place, region or, in exceptional cases, a country", "whose quality or characteristics are essentially or exclusively due to a particular geographical environment with its inherent natural and human factors". (20) PDOs are therefore protected if they designate a product which has certain "qualities" or "characteristics", namely physical attributes such as its own flavour, aroma and appearance, that are linked to its geographical origin.*'

21 Para. 39 of the annotated judgment.

22 Opinion of the Advocate General Pitruzzella for Case C-490/19, 17 September 2020, paras. 55, 57-59.

This CJEU ruling strengthens (to a considerable degree) the scope of protection granted by PDOs, with major practical implications since it allows producers of products covered by PDOs to take action against imitations of products that mislead the consumer to believe that they are covered by certain PDOs. This protection, however, as follows from the annotated judgment, must depend on a case-by-case analysis, that is, the entire factual context must be taken into account, including the presentation of the product and how it is marketed, as well as whether the characteristic or shape that is reproduced is distinctive enough to allow the consumer to be led to think, erroneously, that it is a product protected or covered by a particular PDO.

Nevertheless, some practical difficulties arise when it comes to fulfilling the criterion of whether the consumer, when faced with a certain appearance, shape or characteristic of a product that is similar or identical to one present in a product covered by a PDO, will associate it with the latter. This is a task that must be carried out by the national courts, and that will therefore be uncertain and difficult to harmonise.

COURT OF JUSTICE 17 JUNE 2021

ON THE ACT OF MAKING AVAILABLE A PROTECTED WORK TO THE PUBLIC BY USERS OF PEER-TO-PEER NETWORKS AND THE BALANCE BETWEEN THE PROTECTION OF INTELLECTUAL PROPERTY RIGHTS AND THE RIGHT TO PRIVACY

Case C-597/19

Summary and Analysis by Ina Donvil[1]

Parties:

Mircom International Content Management & Consulting (M.I.C.M.) Limited

v

Telenet BVBA

1. Background and History

Mircom International Content Management & Consulting (M.I.C.M) Limited ('Mircom'), established under Cypriot law, was the owner of certain intellectual property rights to a number of pornographic films created by American and Canadian production companies. As the rightholder of this content, Mircom's source of profit consisted of identifying infringements of its intellectual property and seeking compensation for the alleged breaches, which was then divided between Mircom and the production companies.[2] In order to identify the infringements, Mircom used software, created by a German company, to record IP addresses of users who, through the use of various peer-to-peer networks such as BitTorrent in this case specifically, had illegally downloaded the content.

After recording the IP addresses, Mircom approached Telenet BVBA ('Telenet') to request the user information connected to them. Telenet refused this request, leading Mircom to bring an action before the Ondernemingsrechtbank Antwerpen (Enterprise Court in Antwerp, Belgium) in June 2019 seeking that Telenet be ordered to provide the requested information. Telenet, supported by two other Belgian Internet service providers, opposed this action.

The referring court identified three main issues in the proceedings. Firstly, it considered the working mechanism of peer-to-peer networks, such as BitTorrent, whereby the users download a fragment of the original file, and that fragment then automatically becomes available for downloading by other users. In the end all users have access to the complete file. In this context the referring

---

1 Summer intern at & DE BANDT in Brussels, Belgium.

2 Opinion of Advocate General M. Szpunar of 17 December 2020, para. 26.

court considered whether such automatic[3] uploading of the digital file containing a copyrighted work to the network constitutes an '*act of communication to the public*.'[4] Secondly, the *modus operandi* of Mircom was considered, whether Mircom fell into the category of so-called 'copyright trolls', and if so, whether it was eligible for the protections provided by Directive 2004/48. [5] The Advocate General defined a 'copyright troll' as follows:

> '*[...] a person who, having acquired limited exploitation rights in respect of protected works, does not in fact exploit them, but merely seeks compensation from individuals who infringe those rights, in particular on the internet, in most cases on file-sharing networks such as peer-to-peer networks. Moreover, a copyright troll brings legal proceedings with the sole aim of obtaining the names and addresses of infringers in order to then offer them an amicable settlement in return for the payment of a certain sum, in most cases without pursuing those court proceedings. The copyright troll's income therefore comes mainly from sums that are paid "voluntarily" by infringers, which it shares with the holders of the copyright and related rights in respect of the works in question.*'[6]

Lastly, the referring court also considered whether the data recording software used by Mircom to register the infringing IP addresses was lawful within the meaning of Article 6(1) point (f) of Regulation 2016/679.[7]

In these circumstances, the Enterprise Court decided to stay the proceedings and refer the following questions to the Court of Justice for a preliminary ruling:

'(1)

(a) Can the downloading of a file via a peer-to-peer network and the simultaneous provision for uploading of parts thereof ... (which may be very fragmentary as compared to the whole) ('seeding') be regarded as a communication to the public within the meaning of Article 3(1) of Directive 2001/29, even if the individual pieces as such are unusable?

---

3 The referring court stated, first, that the pieces were not mere fragments of the original file, but autonomous encrypted files which were unusable in themselves, and, second, that, because of the way in which BitTorrent technology functions, the uploading of the pieces of a file, known as 'seeding', was, in principle, automatic, as that characteristic could be eliminated only by certain programs.

4 See also Case C-610/15, 14 June 2017, *Stichting Brein* and Opinion of Advocate General M. Szpunar, para. 2.

5 Dir. 2004/48/EC of the European Parliament and of the Council of 29 April 2004 on the enforcement of intellectual property rights.

6 Opinion of Advocate General M. Szpunar, para. 73.

7 Reg. (EU) 2016/679 of the European Parliament and of the Council of 27 April 2016 on the protection of natural persons with regard to the processing of personal data and on the free movement of such data, and repealing Dir. 95/46/EC (OJ L 119, p. 1), (General Data Protection Regulation). Art. 6(1)(f) of Reg. 2016/679 states: '*Processing is necessary for the purposes of the legitimate interests pursued by the controller or by a third party, except where such interests are overridden by the interests or fundamental rights and freedoms of the data subject which require protection of personal data, in particular where the data subject is a child.*'

If so,

(b) is there a de minimis threshold above which the seeding of those pieces would constitute a communication to the public?

(c) is the fact that seeding can take place automatically (as a result of the BitTorrent client settings), and thus without the user's knowledge, relevant?

(2)

(a) Can a person who is the contractual holder of the copyright (or related rights), but does not himself exploit those rights and merely claims damages from alleged infringers – and whose economic business model thus depends on the existence of piracy, not on combating it – enjoy the same rights as those conferred by Chapter II of Directive 2004/48 on authors or licence holders who exploit copyright in the normal way?

(b) How can the licence holder in that case have suffered "prejudice" (within the meaning of Article 13 of Directive 2004/48) as a result of the infringement?

(3) Are the specific circumstances set out in Questions 1 and 2 relevant when assessing the correct balance to be struck between, on the one hand, the enforcement of intellectual property rights and, on the other, the rights and freedoms safeguarded by the [Charter of Fundamental Rights of the European Union], such as respect for private life and protection of personal data, in particular in the context of the assessment of proportionality?

(4) Is, in all those circumstances, the systematic registration and general further processing of the IP-addresses of a "swarm" of "seeders" (by the licence holder himself or herself, and by a third party on his or her behalf) legitimate under Regulation [2016/679], and specifically under Article 6(1) [first subparagraph] (f) thereof?'

2. Decision

1. Article 3(1) and (2) of Directive 2001/29/EC of the European Parliament and of the Council of 22 May 2001 on the harmonisation of certain aspects of copyright and related rights in the information society must be interpreted as meaning that the uploading, from the terminal equipment of a user of a peer-to-peer network to such equipment of other users of that network, of pieces, previously downloaded by that user, of a media file containing a protected work, even though those pieces are usable in themselves only as from a certain download rate, constitutes making available to the public within the meaning of that provision. It is irrelevant that, due to the configurations of the BitTorrent client sharing software, that uploading is automatically generated by it, when the user, from whose terminal equipment that uploading takes place, has subscribed to that software by giving his or her consent to its application after having been duly informed of its characteristics.

2. Directive 2004/48/EC of the European Parliament and of the Council of 29 April 2004 on the enforcement of intellectual property rights must be interpreted as meaning that a person who is the contractual holder of certain intellectual property rights, who does not however use them himself or herself, but merely claims damages for alleged infringers, may benefit, in principle, from the measures, procedures and remedies provided for in Chapter II of that directive, unless it is established, in accordance with the general obligation laid down in Article 3(2) of that directive and on the basis of an overall and detailed assessment, that his or her request is abusive. In particular, as regards a request for information based on Article 8 of that directive, it must also be rejected if it is unjustified or disproportionate, which is for the referring court to determine.

3. Point (f) of subparagraph 1 of Article 6(1) of Regulation (EU) 2016/679 of the European Parliament and of the Council of 27 April 2016 on the protection of natural persons with regard to the processing of personal data and on the free movement of such data, and repealing Directive 95/46/EC (General Data Protection Regulation), read in conjunction with Article 15(1) of Directive 2002/58/EC of the European Parliament and of the Council of 12 July 2002 concerning the processing of personal data and the protection of privacy in the electronic communications sector (Directive on privacy and electronic communications), as amended by Directive 2009/136/EC of the European Parliament and of the Council of 25 November 2009, must be interpreted as meaning that it precludes in principle, neither the systematic recording, by the holder of intellectual property rights as well as by a third party on his or her behalf, of IP addresses of users of peer-to-peer networks whose Internet connections have allegedly been used in infringing activities, nor the communication of the names and of the postal addresses of those users to that rightholder or to a third party in order to enable it to bring a claim for damages before a civil court for prejudice allegedly caused by those users, provided, however, that the initiatives and requests to that effect of that rightholder or of such a third party are justified, proportionate and not abusive and have their legal basis in a national legislative measure, within the meaning of Article 15(1) of Directive 2002/58, which limits the scope of the rules laid down in Articles 5 and 6 of that directive, as amended.

3. Motivation and analysis

i) First preliminary question – 'seeding' as communication to the public[8]

The CJEU reformulated the question, in essence to mean whether the automatic uploading of pieces of media file containing a protected work by the user of

---

[8] *'A Bit-torrent protocol relies on a network of users ("the swarm") which connect with each other through a tracking server to share files in a decentralised manner, meaning that each downloader ("leecher") also becomes an uploader ("seeder") as soon as it acquires the downloaded content. This is made possible by the segmentation of the originally seeded file into small fragments that seeders keep sharing, without requiring a link between the original seeder and new leechers. Such segments are useless when individually downloaded, and can only lead to fragmented and qualitatively bad file previews after a certain download percentage has been reached.'* in G. Bouchè, 'Belgian court asks CJEU whether seeding is communicating to the public', *Kluwer Copyright Blog*, 30 March 2020.

a peer-to-peer network constitutes '*an act of making available to the public*' within the meaning of Article 3(1) and (2) of Directive 2001/29.[9]

The Court began by noting that, as stated in the Opinion of the Advocate General, it is irrelevant that the transmitted files are unusable on their own, since they contain the complete work divided between fragmented files rather than each file containing only part of the work.[10] Additionally, the fact that the user himself or herself is not able to download the entire original file does not prevent him or her from uploading parts of that same file to the network, leading in the end to a situation where all participants of the peer-to-peer network have access to the entire file. The Court also stated that for the purpose of establishing that an act of 'making available' within the meaning of Article 3(1) and (2) of Directive 2001/29 has taken place, it is unnecessary to prove that the user in question has already downloaded a number of parts of the file which constitute a minimum threshold.[11]

In its case law, the CJEU has established that for an *act of communication* to take place it is sufficient that a work is made available to a public and may be accessed at any time and in any place. Whether the work is actually accessed is irrelevant in this regard.[12] For the purpose of an 'act of communication' it is also irrelevant what technical means or processes are used to achieve the

---

9 Dir. 2001/29/EC of the European Parliament and of the Council of 22 May 2001 on the harmonisation of certain aspects of copyright and related rights in the information society.

10 See para. 43 of the annotated judgment and Opinion of Advocate General M. Szpunar, para 48. In para. 49, the Advocate General goes on to compare the working of peer-to-peer networks to the working of the internet in general, where information is divided between multiple data packages and distributed to the client in random order and using various channels.

11 Art. 3 of Dir. 2001/29:
'*Right of communication to the public of works and right of making available to the public other subject-matter*
1. Member States shall provide authors with the exclusive right to authorise or prohibit any communication to the public of their works, by wire or wireless means, including the making available to the public of their works in such a way that members of the public may access them from a place and at a time individually chosen by them.
2. Member States shall provide for the exclusive right to authorise or prohibit the making available to the public, by wire or wireless means, in such a way that members of the public may access them from a place and at a time individually chosen by them: (a) for performers, of fixations of their performances; (b) for phonogram producers, of their phonograms; (c) for the producers of the first fixations of films, of the original and copies of their films; (d) for broadcasting organisations, of fixations of their broadcasts, whether these broadcasts are transmitted by wire or over the air, including by cable or satellite.'

12 Para. 47 of the annotated judgment; see also Cases C-161/17, 7 August 2018, *Renckhoff*, para. 20 and C-392/19, 9 March 2021, *Bild-Kunst*, para. 30.

transmission. [13] Therefore, any act whereby a user, in full knowledge of the consequences of what he or she is doing, gives access to a protected work is liable to constitute an act of communication for the purposes of Article 3(1) and (2) of Directive 2001/29.

Furthermore, the Court added that a user who has deactivated the upload function must be distinguished from a user who has not only not done so but has additionally consented to the application of a network such as BitTorrent (after being informed of its characteristics). It is on this point that the Court departed from the opinion expressed in this case by the Advocate General, who was not convinced that such a distinction can be made.[14] Setting a 'full knowledge requirement' of the kind described by the CJEU may as a result have a negative impact on rightholders' claims in the context of infringements, as they will now have to prove that the user was aware that an act of 'making available to the public' had taken place for every individual breach.[15]

If these requirements are fulfilled, the users concerned must be regarded as acting in full knowledge of their conduct and of the consequences that it may have.[16] The Court stated that if the conduct of the users concerned was capable on these grounds of constituting *an act of making available a work*, it was then necessary to examine whether such conduct constituted making available to '*the public*' within the meaning of Article 3(1) and (2) of Directive 2001/29.

In that regard, the Court noted that, in order to fall within the concept of 'making available to the public', works must in fact be made available to *a public*, referring to an indeterminate number of potential recipients and involving a fairly large number of persons. As regards peer-to-peer networks, the Court had already held that the making available and management, on the Internet, of a sharing platform which, by means of indexation of metadata referring to protected works and the provision of a search engine, allowed users of that platform to locate those works and to share them in the context of such a network constituted a communication to the public.[17]

In the present case, the BitTorrent users network was widely used, as evidenced by the large number of IP addresses logged by Mircom. Users on this network

---

[13] See also Cases C-265/16, 29 November 2017, *VCAST*, para. 42; C-117/15, 31 May 2016, *Reha Training*, para. 38 and C-392/19, 9 March 2021, *Bild-Kunst*, para. 32.

[14] Opinion of Advocate General M. Szpunar, para. 57.

[15] K. T. O'Sullivan, 'Online copyright and the GDPR: assessing the European regulatory landscape for enforcing copyright at the user level', *European Intellectual Property Review*, 2022, 44(11), 688-696.

[16] Once it is established that they have actively subscribed to such software, the deliberate nature of their conduct is in no way negated by the fact that the uploading is automatically generated by that software.

[17] Case C-610/15, 14 June 2017, *Stichting Brein*, para. 48.

could access protected works at any time, meaning that the works were made available to an indeterminate and potentially large audience. This sharing, particularly when it involved works published without the authorisation of the rightholders, resulted in these works being made available to a *new* audience that had not initially been envisaged by the rightholders. Moreover, even if a work had been previously posted online with the consent of the copyright holder, the subsequent sharing of parts of that work through a peer-to-peer network introduced the work to a new public, which the original rightholder might not have accounted for.

The CJEU concluded that such uploading constituted making the work available to the public, regardless of whether the action was automatically triggered by the software, provided the user had consented to the software's use after being informed of its features.[18]

ii) Second preliminary question – can 'copyright trolls' enjoy the protection of Chapter II of Directive 2004/48?

With this question, the Court was essentially examining three issues:

1. Whether an entity such as Mircom has legal standing in the context of Chapter II of Directive 2004/48.
2. Whether such an entity could have possibly suffered prejudice within the meaning of Article 13 of Directive 2004/48.
3. Whether the request for information was admissible according to Article 8 and Article 3(2) of Directive 2004/48.

The Court began by stating that in order to enjoy the protection of Chapter II of the Directive, one must have legal standing under Article 4, which lists four categories of actors.[19] Since Mircom did not seem to fall under the categories listed in (b) to (d) and the referring Court classified Mircom as being the

---

[18] Concerning the right of information, the Court accepted Mircom's argument that it was sufficient that the possibility existed for the users to have acted with knowledge and consent in order to gain access to their information. Ondernemingsrechtbank Antwerpen, 19 July 2022, *Computerrecht*, 2023/8, p. 51-57.

[19] Art. 4 of Dir. 2004/48: '*Persons entitled to apply for the application of the measures, procedures and remedies Member States shall recognise as persons entitled to seek application of the measures, procedures and remedies referred to in this chapter:*
(a) the holders of intellectual property rights, in accordance with the provisions of the applicable law;
(b) all other persons authorised to use those rights, in particular licensees, in so far as permitted by and in accordance with the provisions of the applicable law;
(c) intellectual property collective rights-management bodies which are regularly recognised as having a right to represent holders of intellectual property rights, in so far as permitted by and in accordance with the provisions of the applicable law;
(d) professional defence bodies which are regularly recognised as having a right to represent holders of intellectual property rights, in so far as permitted by and in accordance with the provisions of the applicable law.'

contractual holder of intellectual property rights, the Court found that Mircom fell under (a). As this provision does not contain any requirement as to the use of the protected rights, an entity such as Mircom could enjoy the full protections of this provision and Chapter II of Directive 2004/48.

As to the second issue, the Court noted that Article 13 of that Directive should not prevent Mircom from enjoying access to the aforementioned measures for two reasons. Firstly, to claim otherwise would not be coherent with the objective of the Directive, which is to provide a high level of protection to holders of intellectual property rights.[20] Secondly, it would lead to a situation where a rightholder who chooses to outsource the recovery of compensation for infringements to a specialised company would be put in an unfavourable position in comparison to rightholders who chose to recover the compensation themselves.

Lastly, the question of the admissibility of such a request for information arose. The referring court questioned whether the request for information made by Mircom, based on Article 8 of the Directive, constituted an abuse of rights, since Mircom was not actually using the rights which it had obtained from the production companies. It was noted that there was strong evidence that Mircom had no intention of actually starting legal proceedings against the persons infringing their rights, but would instead most likely try to reach an out of court settlement.[21] The Court pointed out, however, in line with the opinion of the Advocate General, that attempts at reaching a settlement are often a prerequisite in order to be able to bring an action for damages.[22]

The essence of the issue at hand was to find a balance between the protection of rights of rightholders, such as the right to an effective remedy (Art. 47 Charter) and the right to property (including intellectual property, Art. 17(2) Charter), and the rights of the users, such as most notably the right to privacy (Art. 8 Charter), which was further addressed in the answer to the third and fourth preliminary questions.[23] Although the Court held that a request for information such as that made by Mircom in the pre-litigation phase of the proceedings should be regarded as admissible, it added that such a request must be justified and proportionate as per Article 8(1) of Directive 2004/48.[24]

---

20 Rec. 10 of Dir. 2004/48; Cases C-427/15, 18 January 2017, *NEW WAVE*, para. 23 and C-681/13, 16 July 2015, *Diageo Brands*, para. 71.

21 This point also came up in the 2019 Mircom & Golden Eye v Virgin Media case in the UK, where the High Court Judge considered the genuineness of Mircom's intention to use the information for future legal proceedings and not just to profit from fast settlements (paras. 58 and 59).

22 Para. 80 of the annotated judgment and Opinion of Advocate General M. Szpunar, para. 113.

23 Charter of Fundamental Rights of the European Union; see also Cases C-264/19, 9 July 2020, *Constantin Film Verleih*, para. 35 and C-580/13, 16 July 2015, *Coty Germany*, para. 29-33.

24 Para. 85 of the annotated judgment.

Furthermore, the Court noted, Article 3 of Directive 2004/48 contains an obligation to ensure that the measures, provisions, and remedies developed in the directive are fair and equitable and applied in a manner which will prevent their possible abuse. The specific consideration as to whether such an abuse had taken place, it added, lay entirely within the purview of the referring court. The Court offered guidance on how to establish a possible abuse of rights, focusing on the operating methods of Mircom and whether the company followed through with legal proceedings or was merely seeking to extract economic revenue rather than to combat copyright infringement.[25]

iii) Third and fourth preliminary questions

According to the Court, there were two data streams in the situation under consideration: the upstream data processing, whereby the holder of the intellectual property rights recorded the IP addresses used to commit infringements, and the downstream processing by which the user information behind the IP addresses was disclosed to the rightholder by the Internet service provider.

In essence, the third and fourth questions were about whether the registration of the IP addresses and the communication of the user information connected to the IP addresses with the purpose of bringing infringement proceedings were in line with EU legislation on data protection.[26]

Since the IP addresses could be classified as both personal and traffic data, falling under the scope of Regulation 2016/679 ('GDPR') and Directive 2002/58, the Court found that the conditions set out in relevant provisions of both these instruments should be taken into account when assessing the lawfulness of Mircom's request for information.[27]

In terms of GDPR, the data recording performed by Mircom, or more specifically by Media Protector GmbH, with the intention of using the information to bring legal proceedings against the identified users, qualified as '*processing*'

---

[25] Para. 95 of the annotated judgment.

[26] Art. 6(1)(f) of the Reg. (EU) 2016/679 of the European Parliament and of the Council of 27 April 2016 on the protection of natural persons with regard to the processing of personal data and on the free movement of such data, and repealing Dir. 95/46/EC (General Data Protection Regulation).

[27] Joined cases C-511/18, C-512/18 and C-520/18, 6 October 2020, *La Quadrature du Net and Others*, para. 152.

within the meaning of Article 4(2).[28] Article 6(1)(f) of the same Regulation establishes three cumulative conditions in order to establish whether data processing is lawful:

1. A legitimate interest must be pursued by the data controller or a third party;
2. There must be a need to process the personal data for the purpose of the legitimate interest pursued;
3. The interest or freedoms and fundamental rights of the person concerned by the data protection do not take precedence.[29]

With regard to the first condition, both the Advocate General and the Court stated that obtaining data in order to bring legal proceedings for infringements of intellectual property rights qualified as a legitimate interest, with the Court adding that this conclusion was in line with Article 9(2)(e) and (f) of the GDPR.[30] Concerning the second condition, it was noted that it would be impossible for the rightholder to bring legal proceedings in this context without identifying the users infringing its intellectual property rights, something that could only be done based on the IP address data; this made the requested information necessary for the purpose of obtaining the pursued objective. With regard to the last condition, as its assessment required a thorough analysis of the specific facts of the case, it was left up to the referring court to rule on this point.

As for Directive 2002/58, the Court established that from a joined reading of Article 15(1) of the Directive and Article 23(1)(j) of GDPR, in principle both the EU and national legislators can limit the scope of obligations relating to the confidentiality of personal data if (i) the restriction respects the fundamental freedoms, and (ii) it is a necessary and proportionate measure in a democratic society to ensure the protection of the rights and freedoms of others and the enforcement of civil law claims.[31]

The Court noted that a request such as the one made by Mircom concerned the processing of traffic data, which forms a part of personal data, with respect to which every individual enjoys the right of protection based on both Article 8 of Directive 2004/48 as well as GDPR and Article 8 of the Charter.

---

[28] Art. 4(2) of the GDPR states that '*"Processing" means any operation or set of operations which is performed on personal data or on sets of personal data, whether or not by automated means, such as collection, recording, organisation, structuring, storage, adaptation or alteration, retrieval, consultation, use, disclosure by transmission, dissemination or otherwise making available, alignment or combination, restriction, erasure or destruction*'; see also para. 103 and 104 of the annotated judgment.

[29] Para. 106 of the annotated judgment; see also Case C-13/16, 4 May 2017, *Rīgas satiksme*, para. 28.

[30] Para. 108 of the annotated judgment and Opinion of Advocate General M. Szpunar, para. 131.

[31] Para. 116 of the annotated judgment.

In this context, the Court had previously held, based on a joined reading of Article 8(3) of Directive 2004/48, Article 15(1) Directive 2001/58 and Article 6(1)(f) of GDPR, that Member States may, but are in no way required to, create an obligation for third parties, such as Telenet in the current proceedings, to disclose personal data to private persons with the aim of bringing civil proceedings. Additionally, the Court pointed out that no such obligation for third parties can be found in Article 6(1)(f) GDPR.

The Court concluded that if the referring court were to establish that (i) national legislative measures of the kind referred to in Article 15(1) of Directive 2002/58 were present and could apply to the case, (ii) Mircom had the required legal standing to bring proceedings, and (iii) the request for information was justified, proportionate and not abusive, the data processing must be regarded as lawful under GDPR.[32]

* *
*

This judgment comes at a time when more and more questions are being asked on the exact relationship and balance to be struck between the protection of intellectual property rights on the one hand and the user's right to privacy on the other. Although it offers useful guidance in the area of individual user liability for infringements of intellectual property rights, it does so in the rather narrow context of peer-to-peer networks.

In the broader context of so-called 'copyright trolls' or 'intellectual property trolls', the Court takes a nuanced approach by not excluding a priori companies such as Mircom from the protections of EU legislation. It takes the view that the mere form of a company is not enough to determine whether it is abusing its rights and leaves it to the national courts to determine if a specific request for information can be qualified as abusive.

In 2024 the Court had another opportunity to clarify when it is allowed to share user information based on recorded and retained IP addresses, in this case in response to a request by a public authority. It established three criteria for a public authority to be allowed access to user information. Firstly, the purpose of the request of information must align with the purpose of the original data retention. Secondly, it cannot lead to any serious interference with fundamental rights, and lastly a proportionality test needs to be applied,

---

32 In the case at hand, the Belgian referring court decided that the first condition was not fulfilled, as Belgium had no national legislation that could serve as a basis for such a request. Therefore, Mircom's request for information was not granted. This was as a result of the Belgian decision during the transposing of Dir. 2004/48 not to include any specific provision for this type of request in the Belgian Judicial Code.

in which the strict necessity of the request for information to obtain the objective needs to be proven.[33]

In the fast-developing world of the Internet more and more questions will be asked about the balance to be struck between data protection and the right of privacy of individual users and the right to property and protection of intellectual property rights of rightholders. The Court has already started to provide much-needed clarification on where on the scale the EU legislation can be placed and hopefully will continue to do so.

[33] Case C-470/21, 30 April 2024, *La Quadrature du Net II*, para. 95 and further.

COURT OF JUSTICE 14 OCTOBER 2021

ON THE PRESCRIPTION OF ACTIONS FOR INFRINGEMENT OF COMMUNITY PLANT VARIETY RIGHTS

Case C-186/18

Summary and Analysis by Marta Gimeno[1]

Parties:

José Cánovas Pardo SL

v

Club de Variedades Vegetales Protegidas (CVVP)

1. Background and History

i) The obtaining of legal protection for the Community plant variety concerned

In this case, in order to correctly analyse the possible prescription of the right-holders´ infringement actions, it is necessary to take account the timeline for the obtaining of legal protection for the Community plant variety to which the infringement action related.

In this regard, reference should be made to the fact that on 22 August 1995 the commercial company Nadorcott Protection S.A.R.L. filed an application with the Community Plant Variety Office ('CPVO') for the right to protect the Nadorcott variety of mandarin; a decision to grant this right was made over nine years later, on 4 October 2004.

An appeal against this decision was submitted to the CPVO, suspending its effects until the decision was final, which happened on 8 November 2005, when the Board of Appeal of the Office dismissed the appeal,[2] definitively granting protection to the Nadorcott mandarin.

ii) The alleged infringement actions and the prejudicial steps followed by the rightholder

Since 2006 (i.e. after the final granting of the Community plant variety right), Pardo had been cultivating a grove of 4,457 mandarin trees. On 30 October

---

[1] Partner and Head of the Litigation Department of Herrero & Asociados, S.L.

[2] Decision published in the Official Gazette of the CPVO on 15 February 2006.

2007 Geslive (the company in charge of defending rights over this variety at the time) sent Pardo formal notice demanding that, in the absence of the appropriate licence, it cease the cultivation of that plant variety.

Club de Variedades Vegetales Protegidas ('CVVP'), which took over the management of the rights in December 2008, sent Pardo new a letter on 30 March 2011 (that is to say, over three years after the first communication requesting Pardo to cease the infringement actions) requesting cessation of cultivation if it was the case that Pardo was cultivating approximately 5,000 mandarin trees of the Nadorcott variety.

The infringement action against Pardo was finally filed in March 2012.

iii) The judicial actions filed

In the absence of cessation of cultivation, CVVP decided to bring the case before the court.

Specifically, in November 2011 (i.e. four years after the first cease-and-desist letter was sent), CVVP filed a *request for preliminary measures* for a declaration of infringement before the Spanish Commercial Court[3], bringing two actions:

- First, for 'provisional protection' in respect of Pardo's acts prior to the grant of those rights, that is to say, acts performed before 15 February 2006;
- Second, for a declaration of infringement of the exclusive rights over the Nadorcott variety from 15 February 2006 until the cessation of cultivation.

Together with the declaration request, CVVP applied for an injunction ordering Pardo to (i) cease its unlawful cultivation, (ii) remove, if necessary, and destroy all plant material of that variety in Pardo's possession and (iii) pay compensation for such cultivation.

The Court of First Instance dismissed the action based on the prescription of the infringement action in Regulation No 2100/94 of 27 July 1994 on Community plant variety rights ('Regulation No 2100/94'[4]), on the ground that more than three years had elapsed:

- from the date on which the rightholder had identified Pardo as an unlawful cultivator (at the latest on 30 October 2007, when the first communication was sent);

---

3 Juzgado Mercantil.

4 According to Art. 96 of Council Reg. (EC) No 2100/94 of 27 July 1994 on Community plant variety rights, '*[c]laims pursuant to Articles 94 [infringement] and 95 [acts prior to grant of Community plant variety rights – provisional protection] shall be time barred after three years from the time at which the Community plant variety right has finally been granted and the holder has knowledge of the act and of the identity of the party liable or, in the absence of such knowledge, after 30 years from the termination of the act concerned.*'

– until the date on which the judicial action was brought before the court (i.e. November 2011).

CVVP appealed this decision before the Superior Court[5] in Murcia, which noted that Pardo had disputed neither its cultivation of the trees, nor its lack of permission to do so.

As the cultivation was still ongoing, the Superior Court decided to:

1. Uphold the infringement action only in respect of those acts of infringement which had taken place less than three years before the judicial action was filed (i.e. from November 2008 until November 2011); and

2. Dismiss the action with respect to the acts that had taken place more than three years prior to the filing of the claim (i.e. from 2006 until November 2008), on the grounds that the action was time-barred in respect of those specific acts.

In this regard, the Judgment stated the following:

> *'The Chamber understands that the repetition of acts infringing the exclusive exploitation rights of a plant variety is a relevant datum for the determination of the dies a quo in the computation of the limitation period established by Article 96 of Council Regulation 2100/94.*
>
> *The aforementioned article states: "The right to bring the actions referred to in Articles 94 and 95 shall lapse after three years from the date on which the Community plant variety right has been finally known and the owner has had knowledge of the act and of the identity of the infringer or, in the absence of such knowledge, after thirty years from the date of the last performance of the act".*
>
> *Certainly, the provision makes no reference to the case of repeated acts of infringement, but there is no doubt that we are dealing with a period of prescription, not of expiration of the action, so that the date of the infringement must be taken into account as the dies a quo. If the infringement is repeated, a new period for claiming against the infringer is started for each infringement, so that, in the present case, the actions prior to three years before the filing of the preliminary proceedings (which exceed the statute of limitations) could be time-barred, but not the subsequent infringements (those that have taken place since November 2009). Moreover, the defendant has not denied that during that time it has continued to exploit the said plant varieties, so that the action brought is not time-barred, without the need to resort to the jurisprudential doctrine of continuous acts, a doctrine that this Chamber considers applicable*

5 Audiencia Provincial.

and according to which the computation of the limitation period does not begin for "any" of the acts carried out until the infringement has ceased; this doctrine has been reiterated by case law (amply reflected in the brief filing the appeal) for similar cases, such as those relating to the infringement of industrial property rights or for damages arising from contractual or non-contractual negligence.

In view of the foregoing, this ground of appeal must be upheld and it must be declared that the action brought is not time-barred, which means that the merits of the case must be examined.'[6] (emphasis added)

Pardo decided to appeal on a point of law and the Supreme Court decided to stay the proceedings and refer three preliminary questions to the CJEU, based on the doubts raised by national intellectual property jurisprudence.

Specifically, in Spain, as recalled by the appellant and the Superior Court, occasional acts of infringement must be distinguished from ongoing acts, and ongoing acts cannot be time-barred.[7]

In words of the Chamber, if the infringement is repeated, a new period for claiming against the infringer is started for each infringement, so that the actions prior to three years before the filing of the preliminary proceedings (which exceed the statute of limitations) could be time-barred, but not the subsequent infringements.

That interpretation would imply that, while Pardo continued cultivating the protected plant variety, the infringement action could not be time-barred, but the Supreme Court wondered if this case-law could be applied to Article 96 of Regulation No 2100/94.

With this reasonable doubt in mind, the Spanish Supreme Court referred the following questions to the Court of Justice for a preliminary ruling:

'1) *Is an interpretation according to which, provided that the period of three years has elapsed since the holder, once Community protection of the plant variety right was granted, became aware of the infringing act and the identity of the party liable, the actions provided for under Articles 94 and 95 [Regulation No 2100/94] would be time barred, although the infringing acts were continuing until the time the action was brought, contrary to Article 96 of [that regulation]?*

---

6 Free translation of the original Spanish judgment.

7 In this regard, the Spanish Supreme Court established in its Judgment no. 871/2009 of 21 January 2010 that if the infringement actions go on, the extinctive prescription with respect to the actions (actions constituting unfair competition in the case in question) '*does not begin to run until the end of the unlawful conduct*'.

2) If the first question is answered in the negative, is it to be considered that, in accordance with Article 96 of [the regulation], the limitation period operates only in respect of infringing acts committed outside the three-year period, but not in respect of those taking place within the last three years?

3) If the answer to the second question is in the affirmative, in such a situation could the action for an injunction and also for damages succeed only in relation to those latter acts taking place within the last three years?'

2. Decision

1. Article 96 of Council Regulation (EC) No 2100/94 of 27 July 1994 on Community plant variety rights must be interpreted as meaning that, irrespective of the ongoing nature of an act of infringement of a protected variety or of the date on which that act ended, the three-year period of prescription set out in that provision in respect of claims pursuant to Articles 94 and 95 of that regulation starts to run from the date on which, first, the Community plant variety right was finally granted and, second, the holder of the right had knowledge of the act and of the identity of the party liable.

2. Article 96 of Regulation No 2100/94 must be interpreted as meaning that claims pursuant to Articles 94 and 95 of that regulation in respect of a set of acts of infringement of a protected variety brought after more than three years have elapsed are time barred only from when, first, the Community plant variety right was finally granted and, second, the right holder had knowledge of each individual act forming part of that set of acts and of the identity of the party liable for them.

3. Motivation and Analysis

i) First question on the start of the three-year period of prescription

By its first question, the referring court asks, in essence, whether Article 96 of Regulation No 2100/94 is to be interpreted as meaning that the three-year period of prescription set for infringement actions starts to run, after the Community plant variety right has been finally granted, from the date on which the holder becomes aware of the act and of the identity of the party liable, *irrespective of whether the act of infringement continues until the date on which an action is brought.*

Article 96 of Regulation No 2100/94 sets out two requirements for determining the moment from which the three-year period of prescription of claims pursuant to Article 94 and 95 of that Regulation starts to run. On the one hand, there is an objective event, namely the final grant of the Community plant variety right (in this case, 30 March 2011), and on the other hand, there is a subjective event, namely the holder's knowledge of the act of infringement and of the identity of the person responsible for it.

The commencement of the prescription period is determined by the occurrence of the later of these two events. This implies that the prescription period begins either on the date of the grant of the Community plant variety right or when the act and the identity of the party responsible are discovered.[8]

Both the CJEU and the Advocate General[9] agreed that Article 96 of Regulation No 2100/94 cannot be interpreted as meaning that the end of the act of infringement is to be regarded as the event from which the period of prescription for claims starts to run. Such an interpretation would be inconsistent with the wording of the regulation and would imply a condition in addition to those expressly laid down in its Article 96.

The CJEU emphasised that this provision does not specify whether the duration of the acts of infringement of the holder's rights or the ongoing nature of such acts should be taken into account.

In this regard, the Court highlighted that, since the wording contains no reference or even allusion to the notions of the duration of the infringement or of the continuing nature of the act of infringement, the three-year period of prescription laid down does not begin to run from the time when the acts of infringement cease, but from the time when the holder of the Community plant variety right becomes aware of those acts and of the identity of the party liable.

This interpretation is consistent with the context of the Regulation and with the purpose of the prescription period, which is to ensure legal certainty.[10] Time limits must be fixed in advance and any application 'by analogy' of a limitation period must be sufficiently foreseeable.[11]

The CJEU pointed out that interpreting the prescription period as not starting to run until the infringement had ceased would allow the rightholder to bring an action as long as the infringement continued and up to three years after the offender had ceased to act, which would create constant uncertainty for the liable party if the holder of the plant variety had tolerated such acts.

---

8 Para. 27 of the annotated judgment. See, by analogy, Case C-584/15, 2 March 2017, *Glencore Céréales France*, para. 47.

9 Opinion of Advocate General H. Saugmandsgaard Øe of 22 April 2021, paras. 33-54.

10 Case C-627/18, 30 April 2020, *Nelson Antunes da Cunha*, para. 44.

11 Case C-387/17, 23 January 2019, *Fallimento Traghetti del Mediterraneo*, para. 71 and case-law cited.

In the light of the foregoing, the CJEU concluded that, irrespective of whether an act of infringement of a protected variety is ongoing or has ended, the three-year period of prescription provided for in Article 96 of Regulation 2100/94 starts to run from the date on which, first, the Community plant variety right was finally granted and, second, the holder of the right was aware of the act and of the identity of the party liable.

ii) Second and third questions

The CJEU analysed and answered the referring court's second and third questions together.

The purpose of those questions was essentially to ascertain whether Article 96 of Regulation No 2100/94 must be interpreted as meaning that all claims relating to a set of acts of infringement of a protected variety, which are brought *after* the expiry of a period of three years from the date when (i) first, the Community plant variety right was finally granted and (ii) second, the holder had knowledge of that set of acts and of the identity of the person responsible for them, are time-barred, irrespective of the date of each of the individual acts forming part of that series of acts, or whether only claims relating to acts which occurred more than three years before such claims were brought are time-barred.

In this regard, it should be noted that Article 13(2) of Regulation No 2100/94 contains a list of individual acts of infringement, stating that:

> '2. *[…], the following acts in respect of variety constituents, or harvested material of the protected variety, both referred to hereinafter as "material", shall require the authorisation of the holder:*
> *(a) production or reproduction (multiplication);*
> *(b) conditioning for the purpose of propagation;*
> *(c) offering for sale;*
> *(d) selling or other marketing;*
> *(e) exporting from the Community;*
> *(f) importing to the Community;*
> *(g) stocking for any of the purposes mentioned in (a) to (f).*'

These are therefore the individually identified acts which may not be carried out without the rightholder's consent.

Article 96 of the EU Regulation refers to acts individually identified which, in the opinion of both the CJEU and the Advocate General,[12] must be examined individually, irrespective of whether they are repeated, ongoing or form part of a set of acts.

---

[12] Opinion of Advocate General H. Saugmandsgaard Øe of 22 April 2021, paras. 58-80.

In this regard, the CJEU considered that the date on which the holder of the Community plant variety right became aware of an individual act of infringement and of the identity of the party liable is decisive for determining whether claims are time-barred, by virtue of the three-year period laid down in Article 96 of the Regulation.

Accordingly, in this case, the Supreme Court would have to analyse each individual act (i.e. production or reproduction, conditioning for the purpose of propagation, offer, sale, import, export and storage) to determine whether CVVP had been aware of each of them for more than three years at the time of filing the infringement action. Any other interpretation would leave the rightholder without any remedy against separate (though possibly linked) acts of infringement and would be contrary to the purpose of the Regulation (i.e. the protection of plant varieties).

The Court therefore concluded that the answer to the second and third questions must be that Article 96 of Regulation No 2100/94 is to be interpreted as meaning that infringement claims pursuant to Articles 94 and 95 of that Regulation in respect of a set of acts of infringement of a protected variety, brought after more than three years have elapsed, are time-barred only from the date on which, first, the Community plant variety right was finally granted and, second, the right holder had knowledge of each of the acts forming part of that set of acts and of the identity of the party liable for them.

* *
*

On 26 January 2022 the Supreme Court upheld Pardo´s cassation appeal and dismissed the infringement action filed by CVVP, on the basis that the action was time-barred.[13]

This judgment is particularly relevant given that the CJEU took the view (as the Spanish Supreme Court had also assumed in this case) that the theory of 'continuing acts', which is regularly applied in Spain in intellectual property matters, is not applicable to plant varieties or, at least, not as it was conceived.

Under this theory, the limitation period would begin to run anew each time a new act of infringement was committed, giving the rightholders the possibility of delaying the filing of legal actions for up to three years after the offender had ceased to infringe. Now each act will have to be analysed separately, and this could lead to difficult decisions for rightholders.

---

[13] STS 239/2022 - ECLI:ES:TS:2022:239.

In my opinion, this ruling will require holders of plant varieties to take a more active role and will undoubtedly prevent them from delaying the filing of legal actions against acts of infringement, on the grounds that they will become time-barred.

Moreover, the ruling may have an impact in other areas of intellectual property, meaning that it will have to be taken into account in infringement actions in those areas in Spain.

COURT OF JUSTICE 3 MARCH 2022

ON THE APPLICABLE LAW CONCERNING CLAIMS SUPPLEMENTARY TO AN ACTION FOR INFRINGEMENT

Case C-421/20

Summary and Analysis by Dilan Mienert[1]

Parties:

Acacia Srl

v

Bayerische Motoren Werke AG

1. Background and History

Acacia is a company incorporated under Italian law which produces wheel rims for motor vehicles In Italy and distributes them in a number of Member States. The rims are imported to Germany (among other countries) and marketed there. Taking the view that Acacia's distribution of certain wheel rims in Germany constituted an infringement of a registered Community design of which it was the holder, BMW brought an action for infringement before a Community design court designated by the Federal Republic of Germany (the Düsseldorf Regional Court). Düsseldorf Regional Court, which declared that it had jurisdiction pursuant to Article 82(5) of Council Regulation (EC) No 6/2002 of 12 December 2021 on Community Designs,[2] found that Acacia had committed the acts of Community design infringement alleged by BMW. Acacia brought an appeal before the referring Oberlandesgericht Düsseldorf (Higher Regional Court, Düsseldorf, Germany), which stated that the jurisdiction of the Community design courts designated by the Federal Republic of Germany arose in the present case from Article 82(5) of Regulation No 6/2002 and that Acacia had committed the acts of infringement alleged by BMW.[3] However, the Court had doubts as to which national law applied to BMW's supplementary claims (for damages, information, issue of documents, rendering of accounts and surrender for the purpose of destruction). It considered that it could follow from Article 8(2) of Regulation (EC) No 864/2007 of the European Parliament and of the Council of 11 July 2007 on the law applicable to non-contractual obligations

---

[1] Dilan Mienert is an IP/IT/commercial lawyer at the German law firm GÖRG Partnerschaft von Rechtsanwälten mbB and is a member of the Berlin Bar.

[2] Art. 82(5) of Reg. No 6/2002 states: '*Proceedings in respect of the actions and claims referred to in Article 81(a) and (d) may also be brought in the courts of the Member State in which the act of infringement has been committed or threatened.*'

[3] Oberlandesgericht Düsseldorf, 31 August 2020 – 20 U 73/15, GRUR-RR 2020, 28034.

(Rome II)[4], as interpreted by the Court in the judgment of 27 September 2017, Nintendo (C-24/16 and C-25/16, EU:C:2017:724),[5] that Italian law applied in the present case. The referring court determined that the event causing the damage occurred in Italy, as the products in question were shipped to Germany from that Member State. However, the infringing products at the centre of the main proceedings were sold in Germany, where they were also advertised online to consumers.

In light of this, the Higher Regional Court of Düsseldorf decided to stay the proceedings and to refer the following questions to the Court of Justice for a preliminary ruling on the basis of Article 267 TFEU:

> '1. *In proceedings for an infringement of Community designs, can the national court dealing with the infringement proceedings having international jurisdiction pursuant to Article 82(5) of [Regulation No 6/2002] apply the national law of the Member State in which the court dealing with the infringement proceedings is situated (lex fori) to [supplementary] claims in relation to the territory of its Member State?*
>
> 2. *If Question 1 is answered in the negative: Can the "initial place of infringement" for the purposes of the [Court in judgment of [27 September 2017, Nintendo (C-24/16 and C-25/16, EU:C:2017:724)] regarding the determination of the law applicable to [supplementary] claims under Article 8(2) of [Regulation No 864/2007] also lie in the Member State where the consumers to whom internet advertising is addressed are located and where goods infringing designs are put on the market within the meaning of Article 19 of [Regulation No 6/2002], in so far as only the offering and the putting on the market in that Member State are challenged, even if the internet offers on which the offering and the putting on the market are based were launched in another Member State?*'

2. Decision

Article 88(2) and Article 89(1)(d) of Regulation No 6/2002, and Article 8(2) of Regulation No 864/2007 must be interpreted as meaning that the Community design courts before which an action for infringement pursuant to Article 82(5) of Regulation No 6/2002 is brought concerning acts of infringement committed or threatened within a single Member State must examine

---

4 Art. 8(2) of Reg. No 864/2007 states: 'In *the case of a non-contractual obligation arising from an infringement of a unitary Community intellectual property right, the law applicable shall, for any question that is not governed by the relevant Community instrument, be the law of the country in which the act of infringement was committed.*'

5 Case C-24/16 and C-25/16, 27 September 2017, *Nintendo Co.Ltd / BigBen Interactive GmbH*, GRUR Int. 2018, para. 62.

the claims supplementary to that action, seeking the award of damages, the submission of information, documents and accounts and the handing over of the infringing products with a view to their being destroyed, on the basis of the law of the Member State in which the acts allegedly infringing the Community design relied upon are committed or are threatened, which is the same, in the circumstances of an action brought pursuant to that Article 82(5) of Regulation No 6/2002, as the law of the Member State in which those courts are situated.

3. Motivation and Analysis

In the case at hand, the focus was on conflict of laws The Court needed to determine the applicable law for subsequent claims in a Community design infringement case when the action is brought in the Member State where the infringement occurred. This case illustrates that uniform protection rights do not necessarily entail uniform legal protection. While EU law recognises designated Community design courts, these are national courts of Member States applying the procedural rules of the *lex fori* in the absence of other regulations in Regulation No 6/2002.

Significant attention was given to determining international jurisdiction. Both the court's jurisdiction according to Article 82(5) of Regulation No 6/2002 and the determination of applicable law under Article 88(2) and Article 89(1)(d) of the same regulation, which refers to Article 8(2) of the Rome II Regulation, hinge on identifying the Member State '*where the infringement occurred.*' This raises a classic, doctrinal dispute in international intellectual property law: whether 'where the infringement occurred' refers to the location of the factual infringement action under Article 19(1) of Regulation No 6/2002 or to a naturalistic action, and if the latter, how this location is determined.

In the 'Nintendo' case, the Court had previously addressed conflict of laws. However, as observed in the current case,[6] the 'Nintendo' scenario had peculiarities: the defendants were accused of various, similar infringement actions located in different Member States. Focusing on the place of the factual infringement action under Article 8(2) of the Rome II Regulation would have required a mosaic-like approach. Therefore, the Court chose to use as its criterion the place of the *original infringement action*, which is the action that triggers all subsequent violations under Article 19(1) of Regulation No 6/2002. In such cases, the law of the home state of the infringer typically applies. This overall consideration prevents the assessment of subsequent applications based on different legal systems in cases of multiple infringements in different Member States.

6 See paras. 47-49 of the annotated judgment; agreeing: BeckOK MarkenR/Grüger, 35th ed. 1 October 2023, UMV 2017 Art. 129 para. 38-40.

In the present case, the Court's interpretation suggests that such an overall consideration of similar infringement actions is not applicable, as the court at the place of infringement, under Article 83(2) of Regulation No 6/2002, is only empowered to recognise infringements committed in Germany. Thus, the Court did not follow the opinion of the Advocate General[7] and the Higher Regional Court of Düsseldorf,[8] which argued for applying the principles of the 'Nintendo' case.

The Court's rationale was that there was only one infringement action in a single Member State (Germany), so the principles of the 'Nintendo' case did not apply.[9] These were developed for scenarios involving multiple infringements in different Member States.[10] Therefore, the relevant location was not the original infringement action but the place of the factual infringement action. The Court strengthened this doctrinal argument with evaluative considerations: there is no conflict between the 'Nintendo' and 'Acacia/BMW' decisions, as the jurisdiction of German courts in the 'Acacia/BMW' case was initially limited to Germany under Article 82(5) in conjunction with Article 83(2) of Regulation No 6/2002.[11]

The Court's perspective is persuasive. The principles established in the 'Nintendo' case cannot be applied to the circumstances of the initial proceedings. It is logical for a national court with jurisdiction across the European Union to adjudicate multiple infringements occurring in different Member States concurrently. This approach prevents the need to compare each infringement against another national legal system. However, when a court's jurisdiction is confined to a single Member State, as in the case at hand, adopting a comprehensive approach that requires pinpointing an original infringement and potentially conjecturing about actions in various Member States is not required.

The judgment of the Court is compelling. It aligns closely with the objectives of the Rome II Regulation.[12] By localising the infringement action in Germany, it improves the predictability of the applicable law.[13] This approach simplifies the process by eliminating the need to identify an '*original infringement action*'.[14]

---

7 Opinion of Advocate General Maciej Szpunar, 28 October 2021, paras. 61-72.

8 Opinion of Oberlandesgericht Düsseldorf, 31 August 2020 – 20 U 73/15, *GRUR-RR*, 2020, 2803415, paras. 15-16.

9 See para 47 of the annotated judgment.

10 See paras. 48-49 of the annotated judgment.

11 See paras. 48-49 of the annotated judgment.

12 See R. Janal/J. L. Müller, 'Acacia' for the fourth time – The ECJ on subsequent applications for infringement of a Community design, *GRUR*, 2022, p. 541-543.

13 See R. Janal/J. L. Müller, 'Acacia' for the fourth time – The ECJ on subsequent applications for infringement of a Community design, *GRUR*, 2022, p. 541-543.

14 See G. Würtenberger/S. Freischem, Opinion of the GRUR Committee of Experts for Design Law on the reference for a preliminary ruling from the Düsseldorf Higher Regional Court submitted on 8 September 2020 'Acacia/BMW' (C-421/20), *GRUR*, 2021, p. 935-538.

Additionally, legal certainty is enhanced as it allows the court in the jurisdiction where the act occurred to apply its own law.[15] This effectively reduces the need for time-intensive and expensive expert analyses of foreign law.[16]

[15] See G. Würtenberger/S. Freischem, Opinion of the GRUR Committee of Experts for Design Law on the reference for a preliminary ruling from the Düsseldorf Higher Regional Court submitted on 8 September 2020 'Acacia/BMW' (C-421/20), *GRUR*, 2021, p. 935-538.

[16] See R. Janal/J. L. Müller, 'Acacia' for the fourth time – The ECJ on subsequent applications for infringement of a Community design, *GRUR*, 2022, p. 541-543.

COURT OF JUSTICE 26 APRIL 2022

ON THE FREEDOM OF EXPRESSION AND INFORMATION, THE PROTECTION OF INTELLECTUAL PROPERTY AND THE OBLIGATIONS IMPOSED ON ONLINE CONTENT-SHARING SERVICE PROVIDERS

Case C-401/19

Summary and Analysis by Patrycja Gierdal[1]

Parties:

Republic of Poland

v

European Parliament
Council of the European Union

1. Background and History

This case concerned the mechanism of the Directive on copyright and related rights in the digital single market. Adopted on 17 April 2019, the Directive introduces new regulations concerning copyright in the digital realm. Article 17 provides for the '*use of protected content by online content-sharing service providers*,' stipulating that providers are directly liable where works and other protected subject matter are unlawfully uploaded by users of their services. However, the providers concerned may be exempt from this liability. To be exempt, they are required to monitor actively the content uploaded by users, in order to prevent the placing online of protected subject matter that right holders do not wish to make available on those services. In determining whether the service provider has complied with its obligations, and in light of the principle of proportionality, the CJEU indicated that account should be taken of (a) the type, (b) the audience, (c) the size of the service and the type of works or other subject matter uploaded by the users of the service, and (d) the availability of suitable and effective means and their cost for service providers.

In cases where authorisation is lacking, providers bear primary liability for the content, unless they can prove that they (a) have made their best efforts to obtain authorisation, (b) have made their best efforts to prevent the availability of content flagged by rightholders (a point contested by the Republic of Poland), and (c) have promptly responded to takedown notices while actively ensuring that such content remains inaccessible (a point disputed by Poland).

---

1 Patrycja Gierdal is a lawyer at Wardyński & Partners law firm, Poland.

The application of the proportionality principle is essential to evaluate whether a provider meets the legal requirements in a given situation.

The requirement for platforms to actively filter and block user communications, with the potential for direct liability in cases of user-committed copyright infringement, raises substantial concerns. Given that copyright infringement assessments often depend on context, there is a considerable risk of user-generated content being blocked excessively. This outcome could negatively impact the exercise of freedom of expression, hinder access to information, and impede other fundamental rights of users. The use of upload filters is notably problematic, as it tends to create a chilling effect on platform users, significantly undermining their basic freedom to share information.

Despite the Directive's implementation deadline passing on 7 June 2021, only a few Member States have incorporated it into their legal frameworks so far.

In the present case, by an application dated 24 May 2019, the Republic of Poland (applicant) brought an action asking the CJEU to annul Article 17(4)(b) and (c) of the Directive, in so far as the wording '*and made best efforts to prevent their future uploads in accordance with point (b)*' is concerned. The applicant alleged an infringement of the right to freedom of expression and information guaranteed by Article 11(1) of the Charter of Fundamental Rights of the European Union (the Charter). According to Article 11(1) of the Charter, '*everyone has the right to freedom of expression*', which includes '*freedom to hold opinions and to receive and impart information and ideas without interference by public authority and regardless of frontiers.*'

The applicant argued that the provisions of the Directive requiring the providers to perform preventive monitoring by using automated filtering tools did not provide adequate safeguards to ensure that the right to freedom of expression and information was respected. The risk being that platforms would use automated filtering which could potentially undermine lawful online speech. Alternatively, it requested the CJEU to consider that the aforementioned provisions (i.e. Art. 17(4)(b) and (c)) of the Directive could not be separated from the other provisions of Article 17 without changing them. It therefore asked the CJEU to annul the Article entirely. The European Parliament, on the other hand, sought to have the application dismissed as unfounded.

2. Decision

The CJEU dismissed the action brought by Poland against Article 17 of the Directive on copyright and related rights in the Digital Single Market. The main result of the judgment is that Article 17 contains sufficient guarantees to ensure a good balance between the protection of intellectual property rights and the right to freedom of expression and information. In particular, the judgment

acknowledged that online content-sharing service providers are required to use automatic recognition and upload filtering tools. At the same time, the CJEU recognised that the freedom of expression and information are not absolute and may be subject to limitations. Moreover, any such restrictions must comply with the principle of proportionality, i.e. they must be necessary and genuinely meet the objectives of general interest recognised by the Union or the need to protect the rights and freedoms of others.

3. Motivation and Analysis

The CJEU addressed the very admissibility of the action at the outset. CJEU largely aligned with the Advocate General's stance in his Opinion. Like the Advocate General, the CJEU emphasised that the assessment of Article 17 should be comprehensive, meaning that the elements in Article 17(4)(b) and (c), *in fine*, should not be evaluated separately. Article 17 constitutes a comprehensive liability regime with interconnected components. As a result, the CJEU emphasised the indivisibility of Article 17, indicating that it could only be annulled in its entirety or not at all. Importantly, any potential annulment of Article 17 would not impact the other provisions of the Directive.[2]

The key question revolved around whether Article 17 of the Directive violated Article 11(1) of the Charter by failing to establish adequate safeguards ensuring respect for the right to freedom of expression and information.

The applicant's argument was centred on the contention that online content service providers are obliged to conduct preventive monitoring of all potential content in order to be exempt from any liability for providing public access to copyright-protected works or other safeguarded materials uploaded by their users in violation of copyright. To achieve this, service providers must employ IT tools allowing prior automatic filtering of such content. The applicant contested that imposing such measures adversely affects the right to freedom of expression and information and is therefore unjustified.[3]

The CJEU, in assessing the validity of the liability regime introduced by Article 17 of the new Copyright Directive, clarified that a service operator hosting illegally posted content is not actively engaging in '*communication to the public of that content*' unless the platform provides access to such content in violation of copyright. Additionally, to be exempt, the platform must not play an active role that gives it knowledge of or control over the content uploaded by users. The European legislature believed that a specific liability mechanism

2 Paras. 20 and 21 of the annotated judgment.

3 Para. 24 of the annotated judgment.

was necessary to ensure a fair licensing market between rightholders and service providers due to the vast amount of online content.[4]

Article 17(4) introduces a specific liability requiring authorisation. A service provider can only be exempted from liability under certain conditions, including making best efforts to obtain authorisation, ensuring the unavailability of specific works based on rightholders' information, and acting promptly on receipt of substantiated notices from rightholders to disable or remove notified works. The applicant argued that these conditions limit the right to freedom of expression and information guaranteed by Article 11 of the Charter, especially in terms of preventive review and the risk of blocking lawful content through algorithms.[5]

The CJEU noted that the rights guaranteed in Article 11 have the same meaning and scope as those guaranteed in Article 10 of the European Convention on Human Rights (ECHR), emphasising that sharing of information on online content-sharing platforms falls within the scope of Article 10 ECHR and Article 11 of the Charter. The CJEU acknowledged that the liability regime under the Directive inherently imposes a limitation on the right to freedom of expression and information of users.[6]

The CJEU further held that the Directive reflects ECHR case-law, emphasising the need for strictly targeted measures to protect copyright without unduly affecting law-abiding users of service providers.[7] Despite the limitation, the CJEU justified the specific liability regime under Article 17, considering it appropriate and necessary to meet the objective of ensuring a high level of protection for rightholders.[8]

The CJEU then put forth six arguments justifying the limitation imposed by Article 17(4) on freedom of expression, asserting that it does not disproportionately hinder the right to freedom of expression and information for users of these services.

First, the EU legislature, established clear and precise limits for preventive measures, excluding measures that filter and block lawful content during uploading. Such a filtering system, which is unable to distinguish between lawful and unlawful content, would contradict the requirements of Article 17 and the fair balance between competing rights and interests.[9]

---

4 Paras. 28 and 29 of the annotated judgment.

5 Paras. 40 and 41 of the annotated judgment.

6 Paras. 44 and 45 of the annotated judgment.

7 Para. 81 of the annotated judgment.

8 Para. 83 of the annotated judgment.

9 Paras. 85 and 86 of the annotated judgment.

Secondly, Article 17 grants users authorisation, under national law, to upload self-generated content for purposes like parody or pastiche (para. 7) and states that online content sharing service providers (OCSSPs) must inform users of their right to use works under exceptions or limitations (para. 9). Notably, the CJEU explicitly describes these exceptions as 'user rights'.

Thirdly, the liability regime requires rightholders to provide '*relevant and necessary information*' (para. 4(b)) or a '*sufficiently substantiated notification*' (para. 4(c) *in fine*). The CJEU believes that this precondition safeguards the right to freedom of expression and information for users who lawfully use these services.[10]

Fourthly, Article 17(8) clarifies that its application should not result in any general monitoring obligation. This serves as an additional safeguard to ensure the protection of the right to freedom of expression and information for users of OCSSPs. These providers cannot be compelled to prevent the uploading and public availability of content that, to be deemed unlawful, would require an independent assessment by them in light of the information provided by rightholders and any exceptions and limitations to copyright.[11]

Fifthly, the various procedural safeguards introduced by Article 17(9) are deemed sufficient to address situations of over-blocking.[12]

Sixthly, in accordance with Article 17(10), the Commission conducted stakeholder dialogues and produced guidance to supplement the system of safeguards outlined in Article 17(7) to (9). This included considerations for balancing fundamental rights and the use of exceptions and limitations. Additionally, it provided user organisations with access to adequate information from OCSSPs on the functioning of their practices related to Article 17(4).[13]

In light of these considerations, the CJEU concluded that the structure of Article 17 incorporates appropriate safeguards to ensure the right to freedom of expression and information for users of these services (Art. 11 of the Charter) and a fair balance between this right and the right to intellectual property (Art. 17(2) of the Charter).[14]

Finally, the CJEU drew the attention of Member States to the need when transposing Article 17 of the Directive into their national law to act on the basis of an interpretation of that provision which allows a fair balance to be struck between the various fundamental rights protected by the Charter. It is

10 Para. 89 of the annotated judgment.

11 Paras. 90 – 92 of the annotated judgment.

12 Para. 93 of the annotated judgment.

13 Para. 96 of the annotated judgment.

14 Para. 98 of the annotated judgment.

crucial, it noted, to avoid interpretations that may conflict with fundamental rights or other overarching principles of EU law, such as the principle of proportionality.[15]

* *
*

The judgment will definitely have a big impact on the future obligations of service providers. The main result of the judgment is that Article 17 contains sufficient guarantees to ensure a good balance between the protection of intellectual property rights and the right to freedom of expression and information.

The judgment serves as a definitive interpretation of the Directive, imposing several obligations on Member States for its integration into their national legal frameworks. EU directives are binding on Member States in terms of achieving a specific objective, leaving the means of achieving this goal to the discretion of national legislators. While some states may opt for a straightforward transposition of a directive's text into national laws, the judgment makes it clear that such a mechanical approach will not be adequate in the case of this Directive.

In light of the judgment, it is now evident that a more nuanced and specific legal approach is required during the implementation of Article 17. National legislators must propose legal solutions and adopt an interpretation of the provision that ensures a fair balance between the various fundamental rights protected by the Charter. Moreover, the authorities and courts of Member States must not only align their national laws with the provision but also ensure that their actions are in harmony with fundamental rights and other general principles of EU law.

---

[15] Para. 99 of the annotated judgment.

COURT OF JUSTICE 28 APRIL 2022

ON THE CONCEPT OF THE COMPENSATION OF REASONABLE AND PROPORTIONATE LEGAL COSTS

Case C-531/20

Summary and Analysis by Kerim Uzman[1]

Parties:

NovaText GmbH

v

Ruprecht-Karls-Universität Heidelberg

1. Background and History

NovaText GmbH (hereinafter: 'NovaText') is a company incorporated under German law. The Ruprecht-Karls-Universität Heidelberg (hereinafter: 'University of Heidelberg') brought an action for a cease-and-desist order against NovaText in 2017 on the grounds of infringement of its EU trade marks and lodged subsequent claims under trade mark law before the Regional Court Mannheim (Germany) as an EU trade mark court of first instance. The proceedings concluded when the parties reached a judicial settlement and NovaText was subsequently ordered to pay the legal costs of the proceedings. The Regional Court Mannheim set the value of the dispute at EUR 50,000. In the following application for cost reimbursement the University of Heidelberg's lawyer referred to the assistance of a patent lawyer, which the patent lawyer confirmed that he had provided. The University's lawyer also claimed that the essential steps of the proceedings had been coordinated with the patent lawyer. The settlement talks, however, had taken place without his participation. The Regional Court Mannheim later fixed the costs for reimbursement and included EUR 325.46 for the participation of the patent lawyer in the first instance.

NovaText's appeal against the setting of costs for the patent lawyer's confirmed participation in the proceedings was dismissed by the Higher Regional Court Karlsruhe. It held that in the dispute before it in relation to trade marks and distinctive signs within the meaning of Paragraph 140(4) of the Gesetz über den Schutz von Marken und sonstigen Kennzeichen (German Trade Mark Act, henceforth: 'MarkenG'), it was unnecessary to consider whether the involvement of the patent lawyer was '*necessary for the purpose of obtaining the*

[1] Kerim Uzman is an IP/Commercial Litigation lawyer at the German law firm GÖRG Partnerschaft von Rechtsanwälten mbB and is a member of the Berlin Bar.

legal remedy sought,' or whether that involvement amounted to '*added value*' in relation to the service provided by the lawyer instructed by the University of Heidelberg. In the opinion of the Higher Regional Court of Karlsruhe, the wording of paragraph 140 (4) of MarkenG[2] was to be regarded as compliant with Directive 2004/48 (henceforth 'the Directive') and an interpretation of this provision to the effect that it was necessary to examine whether recourse to the patent attorney was required would clearly run counter to the objective of the national legislators, which would rule out an interpretation of paragraph 140 (4) MarkenG in conformity with EU law.

A discrepancy between the principles of German civil procedure and MarkenG had thus provided the basis for the phenomenon of cooperation between lawyers and patent lawyers in trade mark proceedings. As the provision of paragraph 140 (4) MarkenG in principle provided for an automatic additional claim for reimbursement of the costs of patent lawyers, this had been taken advantage of by lawyers and patent lawyers alike, who could work on various matters and with varying workloads. The motivation for this cooperation could also be seen in the rigid and very non-specific scale of fees in Germany, which some might argue to be unfit for economically accurate cost reimbursement, specifically in the field of intellectual property rights and their enforcement.[3]

Following a further appeal by NovaText the German Federal Court of Justice (BGH) had to then consider the question of the conformity of the previous interpretation and implementation of paragraph 140 (4) MarkenG with Article 3(1)[4] and Article 14 of the Directive. Having regard to the judgment *United Video Properties* (C-57/15, EU:C:2016:611)[5] the BGH expressed doubt as to the consistency of paragraph 140(4) MarkenG with Article 3(1) and Article 14 of Directive 2004/48. The BGH – as the referring court – posed various questions as to the consistency between the national and European regulations involved. The court held that a more or less 'automatic' reimbursement of patent lawyer costs might be '*unnecessarily costly*' if an adequately qualified layer had already been mandated.

---

2 Para. 140 (4) MarkenG: Of the costs incurred as a result of the involvement of a patent attorney in a trademark dispute, the fees pursuant to Sec. 13 of the Lawyers' Fees Act and, in addition, the necessary expenses of the patent attorney shall be reimbursed.

3 Some courts operate on dispute value structures so as to be able to assess the basis for the necessary cost reimbursement. The dispute value is often set at EUR 50,000 by the courts.

4 According to Art. 3 Dir., measures, procedures, and remedies to ensure the enforcement of IP rights should *inter alia* not be unnecessarily complicated or costly. At the same time such measures should be dissuasive according to Art. 3 (2).

5 The Court of Justice of the European Union ruled in this judgment that Art. 14 Dir. 2004/48 must be interpreted as precluding national legislation which provides for reimbursement of the costs of a technical adviser only in the event of misconduct on the part of the unsuccessful party, provided that those costs are directly and closely connected with an action for enforcement of an intellectual property right.

In light of this, the BGH decided to stay the proceedings and to refer to the Court of Justice (CJEU) for a preliminary ruling on the basis of Article 267 TFEU:

> *'Must Articles 3 and 14 of Directive 2004/48 be interpreted as precluding national legislation or an interpretation thereof which does not allow the court before which a procedure falling within that directive has been brought to take due account, in each case brought before it, of the specific characteristics of that case for the purpose of assessing whether the legal costs incurred by the successful party are reasonable and proportionate?'*

2. Decision

Articles 3 and 14 of Directive 2004/48/EC of the European Parliament and of the Council of 29 April 2004 on the enforcement of intellectual property rights must be interpreted as precluding national legislation or an interpretation thereof which does not allow the court before which an action is brought under that directive to take due account, in each case brought before it, of its specific characteristics for the purposes of assessing whether the legal costs incurred by the successful party are reasonable and proportionate.

3. Motivation and Analysis

The CJEU answered the question referred to it by the BGH in its adjusted form in the affirmative, thereby ruling out any interpretation of paragraph 140 (4) MarkenG that would prevent the possibility of the competent court evaluating whether reimbursable costs are reasonable and proportionate.[6]

For its judgment, the CJEU firstly referred to Article 3 of the Directive and its requirement for the costs of the proceedings to be, *inter alia*, fair and equitable as well as not unnecessarily costly.[7] The Court first established that the matter of costs is not be viewed as isolated, but linked to the general provision of the Directive and its purpose of ensuring the enforcement of intellectual property rights.[8] Against this background, the CJEU pointed out that within the meaning of Article 14 of the Directive, the distribution of legal costs must, *inter alia*, be reasonable and proportionate.[9] The CJEU also clarified in that regard that in view of the requirements of the Directive these requirements must normally be given an autonomous and uniform interpretation throughout the European

---

[6] Para. 55 of the annotated judgment.

[7] Para. 24 of the annotated judgment.

[8] Para. 23 of the annotated judgment.

[9] Para. 25 of the annotated judgment.

Union, irrespective of their treatment in the Member States, having regard to their wording, their context and the objectives pursued by the rules of which they form part.[10] Although the CJEU also held that the Directive itself does not state in so many words that the reimbursable legal costs must be *necessary per se* for the purpose of obtaining the legal remedy sought, the further provisions of the Directive require that the competent court must – at least in individual cases – be able to verify that costs incurred by the party defeated in the proceedings are not excessive.[11] In accordance with the purpose of the Directive, the CJEU also indicated that the infringed party should not be deterred by unreasonably high costs of the proceedings.[12] While the court also touched on the principles of cost allocation and the scale of fees, it specifically established that the fact that cost reimbursement could – according to the previous application of paragraph 140 (4) MarkenG – simply be granted if the involvement of another legal expert is confirmed is not compatible with the requirement of the Directive.

The CJEU in this respect seems to have attached particular importance to a differentiated and more general decision in the matter. This is clear from its reformulation in accordance with Article 267 TFEU of the BGH's question, which was originally worded as follows:

> *'Are Article 3(1) and Article 14 of Directive [2004/48] to be interpreted as precluding national legislation imposing an obligation on the unsuccessful party to reimburse the costs incurred by the successful party for assistance by a patent lawyer in proceedings brought under trade mark law, whether or not the patent lawyer's assistance was necessary for the purpose of appropriate legal action?'*[13]

As is apparent from the judgment, the CJEU wanted neither to restrict itself to the matter of patent lawyer costs, nor to deviate from the terms of the underlying directive. Its judgment *Constantin Film Verleih*, C-264/19, EU:C:2020:542 was therefore cited in relation to the provision for '*minimum harmonisation*' by the EU legislature.[14]

The CJEU also touched on the decision *United Video Properties*, C-57/15, EU:C:2016:611 in relation to the general eligibility for reimbursement of costs of technical advisers. Against this background the CJEU further established that the reimbursement of similar flat rates also required that such rates be reasonable – that is, neither unreasonably high nor unreasonably low.[15]

---

[10] Para. 26 of the annotated judgment.

[11] Para. 25 of the annotated judgment.

[12] Case C-681/13, 16 July 2015, *Diageo Brands*, para. 77.

[13] Para. 20 of the annotated judgment.

[14] Para. 34 of the annotated judgment.

[15] Paras. 43 and 45 of the annotated judgment.

The practical impact of the judgment naturally goes beyond ending the unintentionally encouraged practice of collaboration between lawyers and patent lawyers in trade mark proceedings before German courts. In a welcome move, the CJEU provided the competent courts of the Member States with the explicit possibility of correcting possible inequities in the reimbursement of costs – something that the courts were previously unable to do. In light of the Directive, the margin of judgment has thus been expanded considerably.

On the other hand, lawyers in Germany and in other Member States with similar provisions to paragraph 140 (4) MarkenG may fear that the national courts could overestimate the scope of the decision or possibly misinterpret it. This could in the future be relevant for proceedings that might be deemed overly simple by the competent court or cases in which the involvement of a patent lawyer is objectively necessary. The latter can – according to German law – be the case if, for example, technical implications are relevant for the assessment of the protectability[16] of a trademark (para. 3 [2] No. 2).

16 Cf. B. Hauck, C-205/13; Lego Juris, C-48/09.

Court of Justice 2 June 2022

On the issue whether the proprietor of a trade mark may prevent a third party from using, in the course of trade, an earlier right applying in a particular locality

Case C-112/21

Summary and Analysis by Roderick Chalmers Hoynck van Papendrecht[1]

Parties:

X BV

v

Classic Coach Company vof ('CCC')
Y
Z

1. Background and History

A family feud over the question of who owned the earliest right to use the family name for the purpose of distinguishing coach companies and their passenger transport services resulted in a judgment of the Court of Justice.

The timeline as established in the national proceedings is as follows:
- From 1935, the father provided occasional coach transport services;
- Between 1968 and 1977, two brothers (sons of the father) were partners in a general partnership engaged in passenger transport by coach;
- In 1975, Brother 1 created a limited liability company (*besloten vennootschap*, commonly abbreviated as BV) called [M] Touringcars BV. In 1975 or 1978, this BV started using a trade name with the family surname [M] in it to distinguish the coach company;
- In 1977, Brother 2 created a limited liability company called Reis- en Touringcarbedrijf Amersfoort's Bloei BV, which also engaged in passenger transport services by coach. The family surname was displayed on the coaches;
- In 1991, Brother 2 formed a general partnership (*vennootschap onder firma*, commonly abbreviated as VOF) which also traded under the family surname;
- In 1995, the two sons of Brother 2 (by now deceased) continued the activities of their father's BV and VOF, creating for that purpose a new VOF called

[1] Roderick Chalmers Hoynck van Papendrecht is a member of the Dutch Bar who has an LL.M. degree from Leiden University and holds a PhD from Erasmus University in Rotterdam. He is a partner and attorney-at-law at AKD in Rotterdam, the Netherlands. A commentary by Roderick on this case was also published in *Berichten Industriële Eigendom* 2022/5, no. 10, p. 236-246.

Classic Coach Company VOF, which also traded under part of the family surname ('CCC').
- The BV of Brother 1 was the proprietor of a Benelux word mark registered on 15 January 2008 and corresponding to the surname common to the two brothers.

In the fact-finding proceedings, the Hague Court of Appeal[2] judged that the BV of Brother 1 ('[M] Touringcars') was the proprietor of the earliest trade name incorporating the family surname (from 1978). It was followed by the CCC trade name (from 1991), and [M] Touringcars obtained subsequently a Benelux trade mark (in 2008).

[M] Touringcars based its action on the fact that CCC had infringed its trade mark rights, as referred to in (former) Article 2.20(1)(b) and (d) of the Benelux Convention on Intellectual Property (Trade Marks and Designs) ('BCIP'),[3] and its trade name rights, as referred to in Article 5 of the Dutch Trade Names Act (*Handelsnaamwet* – 'Hnw'). CCC defended the action by arguing that [M] Touringcars had forfeited its rights to invoke the trade name against CCC (through acquiescence), that CCC's right to the trade name was of an earlier date than the trade mark right relied upon by [M] Touringcars, and that for this reason – pursuant to Article 2.23(2) BCIP – [M] Touringcars was estopped from enforcing its trade mark.

The District Court had upheld the action brought by [M] Touringcars,[4] but the Court of Appeal set aside that judgment. The Hoge Raad der Nederlanden (Supreme Court of the Netherlands) had doubts about the outcome.[5] The doubts concerned the question of what constitutes an 'earlier right' within the meaning of Article 2.23(2) BCIP and Article 6(2) of Directive 2008/95 ('Trade Marks Directive (old)'),[6] and whether the assumption of that earlier right would require the right to be capable of prohibiting the use of the (later) mark.

The doubts were aggravated by the legislative history of Article 6(2) Trade Marks Directive (old), to which history Advocate-General of the Supreme Court Van Peursum referred in his Opinion. The legislative history makes clear that an initial proposal by the Italian delegation was formulated in such a way that the scope of the limitation extended to earlier rights of local significance '*which can no longer be relied upon against the later registered mark*.' This wording was

---

[2] The Hague Court of Appeal 12 February 2019, ECLI:NL:GHDHA:2019:1530.

[3] Now Art. 2.20(2)(b) and (d) BCIP. The matter was settled in accordance with the old legislation. In this annotation, I will make a single reference to each provision applicable to this matter, and all subsequent references will be to the current legislation.

[4] The Hague District Court judgment of 10 May 2017, ECLI:NL:RBDHA:2017:4772.

[5] Supreme Court judgment of 15 January 2021, ECLI:NL:HR:2021:42 and of 19 February 2021, ECLI:NL:HR:2021:271.

[6] Currently Art. 15(3) Dir. 2015/2436 ('TMD').

ultimately not adopted. The question is whether this should be understood to mean that there is in fact a requirement that only an earlier right that is capable of prohibiting the use of a later mark constitutes an earlier right within the meaning of Article 14(3) TMD.

Against that background, the Supreme Court of the Netherlands decided to stay[7] the proceedings and to refer the following questions to the Court of Justice for a preliminary ruling:

> *'(1) For the purposes of determining whether there is an 'earlier right' of a third party as referred to in Article 6(2) of [Directive 2008/95],*
> - *(a) is it sufficient that, prior to the filing of the trade mark, that third party had made use in the course of trade of a right which is recognised by the laws of the Member State in question; or*
> - *(b) is there a requirement that that third party, on the basis of that earlier right, under the applicable national legislation, is entitled to prohibit the use of the trade mark by the trade mark holder?*
>
> *(2) In answering Question 1, is it also relevant whether the trade mark holder has an even earlier right (recognised by the laws of the Member State in question) in relation to the sign registered as a trade mark and, if so, is it relevant whether the trade mark holder may, on the basis of that even earlier recognised right, prohibit the use by the third party of the alleged "earlier right"?'*

2. Decision

1. Article 6(2) of Directive 2008/95/EC of the European Parliament and of the Council of 22 October 2008 to approximate the laws of the Member States relating to trade marks must be interpreted as meaning that, for the purposes of establishing the existence of an 'earlier right' within the meaning of that provision, there is no requirement that the proprietor of that right must be able to prohibit the use of the later mark by the proprietor of that mark.

2. Article 6(2) of Directive 2008/95 must be interpreted as meaning that an 'earlier right' within the meaning of that provision may be granted to a third party in a situation in which the proprietor of the later trade mark has an even earlier right recognised by the laws of the Member State in question over the sign registered as a trade mark to the extent that, under those laws, the proprietor of the trade mark and of the even earlier right may no longer, on the basis of its even earlier right, prohibit the use by the third party of its more recent right.

---

[7] Supreme Court decision of 15 January 2021, ECLI:NL:HR:2021:42 and of 19 February 2021, ECLI:NL:HR:2021:271.

3. Motivation and Analysis

This analysis focuses primarily on the first question raised by the Supreme Court of the Netherlands.[8] The dispute revolves around the principle of priority of earlier rights. Earlier case law of the Court of Justice established that the principle of the primacy of the prior exclusive right is one of the basic principles of trade mark law and, more generally, of all industrial-property law.[9] The principle was laid down in applicable provisions of international law, such as Article 16 of the TRIPs Agreement, but also in the law of the European Union, such as Article 14(3) TMD.

The Court of Justice considered that the concept of priority means '*that the basis for the right concerned must have arisen at a time prior to the grant of the trade mark with which it is alleged to conflict*,'[10] and that the earlier right '*must [...] still be protected at the time when it is relied on by its proprietor in order to counter the claims of the proprietor of the trade mark with which it is alleged to conflict.*'[11]

In Anheuser-Busch, the Court of Justice ruled that the right to the trade name is an industrial-property right that may be regarded as an existing prior right if the proprietor of the trade name has a right falling within the substantive and temporal scope of the TRIPs Agreement which arose prior to the trade mark with which it is alleged to conflict and which entitles him to use a sign identical or similar to that trade mark.

In the case before us, the Court of Justice held that the concept of 'earlier right' used in Article 14(3) TMD must have the same meaning as the concept of 'existing prior right' as used in the TRIPs Agreement, which would mean that the right to the trade name (subject to the conditions stated) may constitute an earlier right for the purposes of the application of Art. 14(3) TMD.[12]

As regards the conditions for the application of Article 14(3) TMD, the Court of Justice noted that the terms of a provision of EU law which makes no express reference to the law of the Member States for the purpose of determining

---

[8] With regard to the second question, it suffices to note that the Court of Justice held that the fact that the proprietor of the later trade mark has an even earlier right recognised by the local laws over the sign registered as a trade mark may have a bearing on the existence of an 'earlier right' within the meaning of that provision to the extent that, by relying on that even earlier right, the proprietor of the trade mark is actually able to counter the claim of an earlier right or limit it. That is for the referring court to determine, in accordance with the applicable national law.

[9] Para. 40 of the annotated judgment, with reference to the Court of Justice's judgment of 16 November 2004, *Anheuser-Busch*, para. 98.

[10] Para. 40 of the annotated judgment.

[11] Para. 38 of the annotated judgment.

[12] Para. 43 of the annotated judgment.

its meaning and scope must normally be given an autonomous and uniform interpretation throughout the European Union, having regard to its wording, its context and the objectives pursued by the legislation of which it forms part. Article 14(3) TMD makes no reference to the law of the Member States.

According to the Court of Justice, it is not borne out by the terms of the provision or by its context and the general scheme of the Directive that the rights to a prior mark must confer on its proprietor the right to prohibit the use of the later trade mark.[13]

The context and general scheme of the Directive was considered in the light of Article 4(4)(b) and (c) of the Trade Marks Directive (old),[14] which offers the Member States the non-mandatory option to provide in their domestic law that a trade mark is not to be registered or, if registered, is liable to be declared invalid where (i) rights to a sign used in the course of trade were acquired prior to the date of application for registration of the subsequent trade mark, and (ii) this non-registered trade mark or other sign confers on its proprietor the right to prohibit the use of a subsequent trade mark. Contrary to Article 14(3) TMD, Article 5(4) does provide in explicit terms that the earlier sign must be capable of prohibiting the use of the subsequent trade mark.

According to the Court of Justice, the conditions for the application of Article 14(3) TMD are more flexible than those that apply to Article 5(4) TMD. This is correct if one considers the question whether the prior right should be capable of prohibiting the use of the subsequent trade mark. The Court of Justice considered this to be consistent with the objectives of the TMD, which generally seeks to strike a balance between the interest of the proprietor in safeguarding its essential function on the one hand, and the interests of other economic operators in having signs capable of denoting their goods and services on the other hand. If Article 14(3) TMD were subject to the condition that its scope was limited to earlier rights capable of prohibiting the use of subsequent marks, such a condition would – according to the Court of Justice – deprive that provision of all practical effect, as it would treat the conditions for the application of Article 5(4) TMD in the same way as the conditions for the application of Article 14(3) TMD.[15]

The Court concluded that Article 14(3) TMD must be interpreted as meaning that, for the purposes of establishing the existence of an 'earlier right' within the meaning of that provision, there is no requirement that the proprietor of that right must be able to prohibit the use of the later mark by the proprietor of that mark.

* *
*

[13] Paras. 45-46 of the annotated judgment.

[14] Now Art. 5(4) TMD.

[15] Para. 51 of the annotated judgment.

I wonder whether the Court's reasoning is entirely waterproof. First of all, Article 5(4) TMD is an optional provision. This means that there are Member States – such as the Benelux countries – which have not transposed this provision into their national legal order. As a result, it is not possible in the Benelux countries to file opposition proceedings with the Benelux Office for Intellectual Property ('BOIP') seeking the refusal of registration of a Benelux trade mark or, if registered, a declaration of invalidity of that trade mark by relying on the trade name as an existing prior right.[16] It follows that in Member States such as the Benelux countries, the practical effect of Article 14(3) TMD is not removed by a provision of national law implementing Article 5(4) TMD, even in the situation where the requirements that must be met in order for Article 14(3) and Article 5(4) TMD to be applicable are the same.

Given the balance of interests involved, it is fair for the threshold of Article 14(3) TMD to be lower than that for successful reliance on the provision of Article 5(4) TMD. After all, successful reliance on one provision has an essentially different consequence than successful reliance on the other. In the one case, the proprietor's right is extinguished, while in the other case the right will continue to exist, but a situation of co-existence will arise between the parties because the proprietor of the trade mark cannot prohibit the use of the senior trade name.

i) A particular locality must actually be local

In addition, Article 14(3) TMD includes another key condition, which is that the challenge of a trade mark right by the proprietor of an earlier right will only be successful if the latter applies '*only in a particular locality*.' There is no Court of Justice case law on the meaning of this concept yet.

The wording suggests that a party using a prior trade name with more than just local significance cannot rely on this provision. Paragraph 48 of the judgment is important for determining the meaning of the phrase 'only in a particular locality'. The Court of Justice removes any doubt there may have been that these words must indeed be interpreted literally. According to the Court of Justice, they mean:

> '*that, from a geographical point of view, they cannot cover a territory as large as that covered by a registered trade mark, since that mark normally covers the whole of the territory for which it was registered.*'

---

16 In the Benelux countries, therefore, the proprietor of a prior trade name will still need to apply to the civil courts. If he does so, he can only rely on the invalidity of the registered trade mark if the registered trade mark deceives the public (Art. 2.4(b) BCIP) or the registration of that trade mark was filed in bad faith (Art. 2.4(f) BCIP).

Previously the majority of Dutch authors[17] argued that the user of the senior local trade name was not the only one who could rely on the limitation of the proprietor's exclusive right as a defence against the latter's enforcement action, in that the party using a senior trade name with national significance could rely on it as well. That same conclusion was arrived at by the Court of Appeal of the Hague in the dispute before us.[18] International authors have argued that a narrow interpretation of the text was called for. This was advocated, for example, by Edinborough, Elias and Von Bomhard commenting on Article 111 of the (old version of the) Community Trade Mark Regulation ('CTMR'), which is similar to Article 2.23(2) BCIP.[19]

> *'[I]t is clear that it [a senior right only applying in a particular locality] cannot refer to a right that extends throughout the whole of the territory of a Member State, such as an earlier registered trade mark. This is because in such a case, the senior right could be used to invalidate the junior CTM right. If this occurred, the junior CTM could be converted to a number of national trade marks, excluding the Member State in which the senior right exists, pursuant to art. 112. Once conversion has been effected, there would be no need to invoke these provisions.'*

This substantiation has (some) validity with regard to the European Union trade mark. After all, Article 8(4) in conjunction with Articles 46 and 60 EUTMR allows for the option for proprietors of senior trade names of initiating opposition and invalidity actions with *more than mere local significance* and the option for the proprietor to convert the trade mark to national marks in such a situation.

Although the meaning of the phrase '*earlier right only applying in a particular locality*' has not previously been interpreted by the Court of Justice, case law can be found on the interpretation of the phrase '*senior right of more than mere local significance*' within the meaning of Article 8(4) EUTMR. The trade name must actually and in a sufficiently significant manner be used in the course of trade and its geographical extent must not be *merely local*. Factors to be taken into consideration are the duration and intensity of the use of the sign.[20] Thus, the test has two dimensions: an economic one and a geographical one.[21]

---

[17] P.G.F.A. Geerts, T&C IE 2021, note 1.e. to Art. 2.23 BVIE; T. Cohen Jehoram, C.J.J.C. van Nispen & J.L.R.A. Huydecoper, Industriële Eigendom Deel 2 – Merkenrecht, Kluwer: Deventer, 2008, p. 409; R. Chalmers Hoynck van Papendrecht, 'De Handelsnaamwet onder de loep', diss. EUR, Delex: Amsterdam, 2020, p. 356.

[18] The Hague Court of Appeal 12 February 2019, ECLI:NL:GHDHA:2019:1530, para. 7.

[19] M. Edinborough, T. Elias & V. von Bomhard, in Gielen/Von Bomhard (red.), *Concise European Trade Mark and Design Law*, 2011, note 3 to Art. 111 CTMR (old). Now Art. 138 EUTMR. The most recent edition of this publication does not include this same substantiation.

[20] Case C-96/09 P, 29 March 2011, *Anheuser-Busch/Budějovický Budvar*, paras. 159-160.

[21] R. Chalmers Hoynck van Papendrecht, 'De handelsnaamwet onder de loep', diss. EUR, Delex: Amsterdam, 2020, p. 364.

In *Peek & Cloppenburg*, the Court of Justice added that for the purpose of the application of Article 8(4) EUTMR it is not required that the use of the junior trade mark can be prohibited throughout the country by virtue of the senior trade name as long as a prohibition can be obtained for *a substantial part of the territory*.[22]

Legal authors have argued that '*the senior right only applying in a particular locality*' and '*the senior right of more than mere local significance*' are each other's logical counterparts. If the conditions of sufficient geographical and economic significance are not met, the senior right automatically becomes a right only applying in a particular locality.[23] The Court of Justice's consideration in paragraph 48 of the judgment before us seems to fit this approach,[24] which makes sense given the necessity of harmonious interaction between the Community and the national trade mark systems.

The rationale behind the condition that only a sign with *more* than mere local significance can be relied upon to counter the validity of the registration of a Union trade mark is the objective of limiting the number of conflicts between signs by preventing older signs of insufficient importance or significance from being used to challenge the registration or validity of a Union trade mark. If this bar were not set, the obstacles to registering a Union trade mark would be insurmountable, given the number of economic operators using earlier similar signs with a merely local significance.[25] The proprietor of this insufficiently important or insufficiently significant trade name does have the option of relying on the defence offered by Article 138(3) EUTMR or deciding to bring infringement proceedings by virtue of the senior trade name in the region or the country where the senior trade name and the junior trade mark are in conflict.

Nevertheless, I am not fully convinced by the arguments used by Edinborough et al., as their approach implies that the user of the senior trade name with more than mere local significance will be compelled to bring opposition, invalidity or injunction proceedings against the junior trade mark proprietor, because sitting back and raising the defence of Article 138 EUTMR is not an option. That will not be welcome to any user of a senior trade name.

What needs to be made clear in any case is that this substantiation for the system with European Union trade marks does not justify the limitation of the defence

---

22 Case C-325/13 P and C-326/13 P, 10 July 2014, *Peek & Cloppenburg*, with reference to Case C-96/09 P, 29 March 2011, *Anheuser-Busch/Budějovický Budvar*.

23 K. Hughes, in von Bomhard/von Mühlendahl (red.), *Concise EU Trade Mark Law*, 2018, Art. 138 EUTMR, note 2.

24 Although para. 48 of the annotated judgment refers exclusively to the geographical component and not to the economic one as meant in Case C-96/09 P, 29 March 2011, *Anheuser-Busch/Budějovický Budvar*, paras. 159-160.

25 Case C-96/09 P, 29 March 2011, *Anheuser-Busch/Budějovický Budvar*, paras. 156 *ff*.

options for senior trade names with *more than mere local significance* in the Benelux countries (through Art. 2.23(2) BCIP), since proprietors of the latter trade names are not offered the options of bringing opposition or invalidity proceedings on the basis of a senior trade name by the relevant Benelux legislation.[26]

For the Benelux situation the question arises whether a trade name with national extent must be considered a sign of local significance, even though the trade name enjoying protection throughout the Netherlands (or Belgium or Luxembourg) *does not, in geographical terms, relate to a territory as large as a registered Benelux trade mark does* (which automatically covers the entire territory of Benelux). After this matter was referred back to the Supreme Court of the Netherlands, the Advocate-General in his opinion[27] argued that the trade name enjoying protection throughout the Netherlands does not cover the whole of the territory for which a Benelux trademark is registered, and hence its proprietor can invoke the defence option for senior trade names with *mere local significance* (through Art. 2.23(2) BCIP). The Supreme Court of the Netherlands is less explicit in its judgment, but it seems to agree with the Advocate-General.[28] I doubt whether that is a correct ruling. In any case it is clear that the geographical Benelux situation is rather unusual, and that other Member States do have to deal with the wording of paragraph 48 of the judgment of the Court of Justice.

<u>ii) The options for national trade names</u>

The question can be raised whether the strict interpretation of Article 2.23(2) BCIP and Article 14(3) TMD – essentially meaning that only the user of a locally used trade name can defend enforcement action taken by a subsequent trade mark – actually meets the requirements of international law, since it follows from the third full sentence of Article 16(1) of the TRIPs Agreement that the owner of the prior trade name is allowed to use a sign that is identical or similar to the registered trade mark of a later date. It is my opinion that the Court of Justice's interpretation is not in line with the purport of Article 16(1) of the TRIPs Agreement, or indeed with the principle of the primacy of the prior right as a fundamental principle within the law on distinguishing marks.

In order to arrive at a result that can be reconciled with reason, with the principle of priority, and with the obligations conferred by international law, it is important to circumvent the literal wording of paragraph 48 in order to safeguard the position of the senior trade name against a junior trademark registration.

---

[26] Incidentally, the optional provision of Art. 5(4) TMD, by virtue of which proprietors of prior trade names may bring opposition or invalidity proceedings against subsequent trade marks, does not include a limitation to the effect that the registration may be contested only on the basis of a prior right with *more* than mere local significance.

[27] Opinion of 26 May 2023, ECLI:NL:PHR:2023:530. It must be noted that the Advocate-General in his opinion explicitly took into consideration the concerns expressed by me in this contribution.

[28] Supreme Court of the Netherlands 8 September 2023, ECLI:NL:HR:2023:1161.

Luckily, there are various ways to argue that the interests of the owner of the prior trade name can be sufficiently safeguarded in another way.

First of all, following the entry into effect of the EUTMR and the TMD, users of prior trade names used throughout a whole nation may have been given access to another possible defence. The entry into effect and transposition of this legislation caused the opening words of Article 9(2) EUTMR and Article 10(2) TMD to be altered. They now read: '*Without prejudice to the rights of proprietors acquired before the filing date or the priority date of the registered trade mark [...].*' Although I am inclined to think that the legislators intended the amendment to the opening words of Article 10(2) TMD to firmly embed in particular the order of precedence between registered trade marks in the law, I think that accepting a broad interpretation is reasonable in order to safeguard compliance with Article 16(1) of the TRIPs Agreement.

Second, one could argue that for the application of Article 9(2) EUTMR and Article 10(2) TMD it is a prerequisite that the prior trade name *causes* the likelihood of confusion with the registered trademark,[29] and that this is impossible in the situation where the trade name with national extent predates the registered trademark.

Finally, one could argue that exercising a junior registered trademark against a senior trade name with national extent qualifies as abuse of right in the context of private law under applicable national laws. The exercise of the trademark right would violate good faith and elementary fairness.

[29] The requirement that the later sign causes the likelihood of confusion is explicitly mentioned in the Dutch version of the Art. 9(2) EUTMR and Art. 10(2) TMD, but not in e.g. the English and French versions of the EUTMR and the TMD.

COURT OF JUSTICE 8 SEPTEMBER 2022

ON THE LEGALITY OF:

(I) THE SYSTEM IMPLEMENTED IN SPAIN IN ORDER TO CONTROL AND MANAGE THE PAYMENT OF COMPENSATION FOR PRIVATE COPYING, THE EXEMPTIONS FROM PAYMENT AND REIMBURSEMENTS BY A PRIVATE LAW ENTITY CONTROLLED SOLELY BY COPYRIGHT MANAGEMENT SOCIETIES

(II) THE FACULTY CONFERRED TO SAID ENTITIES TO REQUEST ACCESS TO THE INFORMATION NECESSARY FOR THE EXERCISE OF THE POWERS OF REVIEW, WITHOUT IT BEING POSSIBLE, IN PARTICULAR, FOR THE PERSON UNDER REVIEW TO RELY ON THE CONFIDENTIALITY OF BUSINESS ACCOUNTS

Case C-263/21

Summary and Analysis by Marta Gimeno[1]

Parties:

Asociación Multisectorial de Empresas de la Electrónica, las Tecnologías de la Información y la Comunicación, de las Telecomunicaciones y de los Contenidos Digitales (Ametic)

v

Administración del Estado,
Entidad de Gestión de Derechos de los Productores Audiovisuales (EGEDA)
Asociación para el Desarrollo de la Propiedad Intelectual (ADEPI)
Artistas Intérpretes o Ejecutantes, Sociedad de Gestión de España (AIE)
Artistas Intérpretes, Entidad de Gestión de Derechos de Propiedad Intelectual (AISGE)
Ventanilla Única Digital
Derechos de Autor de Medios Audiovisuales (DAMA)
Centro Español de Derechos Reprográficos (CEDRO)
Asociación de Gestión de Derechos Intelectuales (AGEDI)
Sociedad General de Autores y Editores (SGAE)

1. Background and History

i) The regulation challenged

In this case, the Spanish company Asociación Multisectorial de Empresas de la Electrónica, las Tecnologías de la Información y la Comunicación, de las Telecomunicaciones y de los Contenidos Digitales ('**Ametic**') requested before the

---

[1] *Partner and Head of the Litigation Department of Herrero & Asociados, S.L.*

Tribunal Supremo (Spanish Supreme Court) the invalidation of several articles set forth in Spanish Royal Decree 1398/2018 of 23 November 1996 implementing Article 25 of the consolidated text of the Law on Intellectual Property, approved by Royal Legislative Decree 1/1996 of 12 April 1996, as regards the system of fair compensation for private copying, including Articles 3 and 10.

Ametic is an association of manufacturers, traders and distributors in the information technology and communications technology sector whose activities include trading in reproduction equipment, devices and media subject to compensation for private copying. Ametic believed that the new system of fair compensation for private copying precluded the old system, which was to be charged to the general State budget.

ii) The system implemented by Spanish Royal Decree 1398/2018: fair compensation payable to rightholders, exception and possible reimbursement

The challenged system of compensation for private copying, payable to copyright holders, for the reproduction of protected works, exclusively for private use, by means of non-typographical technical devices or instruments, was introduced by Article 25 of the Law on Intellectual Property, approved by Royal Legislative Decree 1/1996 of 12 April 1996 ('LPI').

In essence, Article 25(3) of the LPI provides that persons who manufacture or distribute, on Spanish territory, equipment capable of being used for the purpose of reproducing protected works are *required to pay fair compensation for private copying*. These manufacturers and distributors may pass on the amount of that compensation to their customers, wholesalers or retailers, who may in turn pass it on to the final consumers.

Nevertheless, purchases of reproduction equipment, devices and media by legal or natural persons acting as final consumers who can prove that the equipment, devices or media purchased will be used exclusively for professional purposes are *automatically exempted* from payment of compensation for private copying, provided that such equipment, devices or media have not been made available, in law or in fact, to private users and that they are clearly reserved for uses other than the making of private copies.

Such evidence must be furnished by means of a certificate issued by a legal person which, in accordance with the LPI, is to be set up by intellectual property management organisations and engaged by them to manage (i) exemptions from payment compensation for private copying; and (ii) reimbursements in respect of such compensation.

Persons who do not hold such a certificate must bear the burden of compensation for private copying at the time of purchase. However, if they can prove the exclusively professional use of the reproduction equipment, devices, or media purchased, and provided that these (i) have not been made available to private users and (ii) are clearly reserved for uses other than private copying, they may apply to this legal person for *reimbursement* of the compensation which they have previously paid.

Moreover, the distributors, wholesalers and retailers who subsequently purchase the goods in question may apply to the management organisations for reimbursement of the compensation for private copying which they have previously paid on the sales which they have made to holders of an exemption certificate.

In this regard, the now challenged Royal Decree 1398/2018 describes an '*exemption certificate*' as a certificate that may be held by, *inter alia*, the aforementioned persons and establishes the procedure for obtaining and using it.

Finally, Royal Decree 1398/2018 allows the entity responsible for granting or refusing these certificates the possibility to request accounting information from the applicants, in order to verify and control the application of the exceptions and to manage any reimbursements. It is expressly stated that economic operators may not rely on the confidentiality of business accounts, as provided for by national law, to deny access to such information.

iii) The issue raised by Ametic and the referring court: the composition of the entities which manage and control the payment of compensation, exemptions and reimbursements

The key issue raised concerned the nature of the entity in charge of managing, granting or refusing these certificates and controlling the reimbursements. Specifically, *the system is controlled by intellectual property rights management organisations, i.e.*, by entities *which exclusively represent the interests of* potential recipients of compensation for private copying, and which, according to the claimant and the Supreme Court, *could be influenced when deciding on these requests*.

Moreover, according to the referring court, that 'imbalance or asymmetry'[2] in the system is liable to infringe the principle of equality before the law, especially since it is on that legal person that the possibility of simplifying the steps to be taken when purchasing reproduction equipment, devices and media depends.

The referring court explained that its doubts were intensified by the extraordinary powers conferred on the legal person in question as regards review, under which it may require information relating to the activities of the persons concerned, since the scope of those powers extends so far as to deprive the

2 Para. 23 of the annotated judgment.

economic operator concerned of the possibility of relying on the confidentiality of business accounts.[3]

The fact that decisions of that legal person may be the subject of a complaint brought before the Ministry of Culture and Sport, whose decisions may themselves be the subject of judicial proceedings, did not appear to the referring court to be sufficient to remove the difficulties which seemed, in its view, to result from the form of composition of that legal person.

In those circumstances, the Spanish Supreme Court decided to stay the proceedings and to refer the following questions to the Court of Justice for a preliminary ruling:

> *'1) Is the form of composition of the legal person provided for in paragraph 10 of the new Article 25 of the [Law on Intellectual Property] compatible with Directive [2001/29] or, more generally, with the general principles of EU law?*
>
> *2) Is it compatible with Directive [2001/29] or with the general principles of EU law for national legislation to confer on the aforementioned legal person powers to request information, including accounting information, from those applying for a certificate of exemption from the obligation to pay compensation for private copying?'*

2. Decision

1. Both Article 5(2)(b) of Directive 2001/29/EC of the European Parliament and of the Council of 22 May 2001 on the harmonisation of certain aspects of copyright and related rights in the information society and the principle of equal treatment must be interpreted as not precluding national legislation under which a legal person established and controlled by intellectual property rights management organisations is entrusted with the management of (i) exemptions from payment in respect of compensation for private copying and (ii) reimbursements in respect of such compensation, where that national legislation provides that exemption certificates and reimbursements must be granted in good time and in accordance with objective criteria which do not allow that legal person to refuse an application for the granting of such a certificate or of reimbursement on the basis of considerations involving the exercise of discretion and that the decisions of that legal person refusing such an application may be challenged before an independent body.

2. Article 5(2)(b) of Directive 2001/29 and the principle of equal treatment must be interpreted as not precluding national legislation which empowers a

---

3 Para. 23 of the annotated judgment.

legal person, which is established and controlled by intellectual property rights management organisations and which is entrusted with the management of (i) exemptions from payment in respect of compensation for private copying and (ii) reimbursements in respect of such compensation, to request access to the information necessary for the exercise of the powers of review conferred on it in that regard, without it being possible, in particular, for the person under review to rely on the confidentiality of business accounts provided for by national law, that legal person being obliged to safeguard the confidential nature of the information obtained.

3. Motivation and Analysis

i) Admissibility of the first question

The entities ADEPI, Ventanilla Única Digital and DAMA first challenged the admissibility of the first question on the ground that the referring court did not specify (i) either the provisions of Directive 2001/29[4] or (ii) the general principles of EU law in respect of which interpretation was sought.

On this point, the CJEU first acknowledged[5] that the Supreme Court was seeking a ruling on the compatibility of a provision of national law with EU law without specifying the provisions and principles at issue, and that it is not for the Court of Justice to rule on the compatibility of provisions of national law with EU law.[6]

Nevertheless, the Court reminded the parties that it is its duty to provide the national court with an answer which will be of use to it.[7] Moreover, the CJEU emphasised its duty to interpret all provisions of EU law which national courts require in order to rule on the cases pending before them, even if those provisions are not expressly indicated in the questions referred to the Court by those courts.[8]

To that extent, the Court concluded that, having regard to the information provided by the Spanish Supreme Court and in view of the subject matter of the dispute in the main proceedings, it could extract the points of EU law

---

4 Dir. 2001/29/EC of the European Parliament and of the Council of 22 May 2001 on the harmonisation of certain aspects of copyright and related rights in the information society *OJ L* 167, 22.6.2001, p. 10-19.

5 Para. 26 of the annotated judgment.

6 Case C-203/14, 6 October 2015, *Consorci Sanitari del Maresme*, para. 43.

7 Para. 27 of the annotated judgment.

8 Case C-263/18, 19 December 2019, *Nederlands Uitgeversverbond and Groep Algemene Uitgevers*, para. 31.

which required interpretation,[9] concluding that in this case it was clear that the request for a preliminary ruling concerned the Spanish system for collecting compensation for private copying.[10]

Additionally, the CJEU highlighted that the Spanish Supreme Court expressly referred to the principle of equality between debtors and creditors of the compensation in question.

Consequently, the Court considered the question to be admissible.

ii) Substance – first question

In essence, with its first question the Supreme Court was asking whether Article 5(2)(b) of Directive 2001/29 and the principle of equal treatment are to be interpreted as precluding national legislation under which *a legal person established and controlled by intellectual property rights management organisations* is entrusted with the management of (i) exemptions from payment in respect of compensation for private copying and (ii) reimbursements in respect of such compensation.

On the one hand, and focusing on the EU regulations, it should be noted that the reason for the obligation to pay a compensation to rightholders (in principle and as a general rule) is the harm caused by private copying.[11] Nevertheless, Directive 2001/29 does not provide details on how the payment of fair compensation should be implemented, thus giving Member States broad discretion to set up an appropriate system, determining who should pay, and the form, arrangements for and amount of the payment.[12]

On the other hand, Directive 2001/29 gives Member States the possibility of providing for exceptions in respect of reproductions on any medium made by a natural person for private use and for ends that are neither directly nor indirectly commercial, on condition that rightholders receive fair compensation which takes into account the application or non-application of technological measures referred to in Article 6 of that Directive to the work or subject matter concerned.

The challenge of identifying the private users who should pay the compensation and managing its payment is enormous, so Member States are allowed to

---

[9] See in this context case Case C-263/18, 19 December 2019, *Nederlands Uitgeversverbond and Groep Algemene Uitgevers*, para. 32.

[10] Paras. 28-29 of the annotated judgment.

[11] Case C-470/14, 9 June 2016, *EGEDA and Others*, para. 19 and the case-law cited, and case C-110/15, 22 September 2016, *Microsoft Mobile Sales International and Others*, para 26

[12] Case C-463/12, 5 March 2015, *Copydan Båndkopi*, para. 20 and the case-law cited, and case C-470/14, 9 June 2016, *EGEDA and Others*, paras. 22 and 23 and the case-law cited.

establish an *indiscriminate 'private copying levy'* to finance fair compensation, which is not levied on the private persons concerned, but on those who own reproduction equipment, devices and media and who make them available to private users on that basis, in law or in fact.

Since such a system allows those liable to pay the levy to pass on the amount of the private copying levy in the price charged for the supply of such reproduction equipment, devices and media available, the burden of the levy will ultimately be borne by the private user who pays that price, in a manner consistent with the 'fair balance' between the interests of the holders of the exclusive right of reproduction and those of the users of protected subject matter.[13]

Additionally, in order to maintain such a fair balance, the system to be implemented by the Member States must also exempt from payment of the levy the supply of reproduction equipment, devices and media to persons other than natural persons for purposes clearly unrelated to the making of copies for private use.[14] This means that *the system imposing such a private copying levy must ensure that final users who purchase reproduction equipment, devices and media for purposes clearly unrelated to the making of copies for private use can still be exempted.*

Focusing *on Spain*, the system correctly implemented implies that, initially, the final users will have to bear the compensation for private copying, but that they may be able to request an exemption certificate or to request reimbursement when the necessary requirements are met.[15]

Nevertheless, the Supreme Court wondered whether the fact that the entities deciding on the application of the exception and managing the reimbursement were controlled by intellectual property rights management organisations could lead to an 'imbalance' or 'asymmetry' in the interests pursued, and if this could lead to a breach of the equal treatment principle.

In this regard, the CJEU[16] set out the requirements that the compensation system must meet:

1. The right to a reimbursement of the private copying levy for persons other than natural persons who purchase reproduction equipment for purposes clearly unrelated to the making of copies for private use, *must be effective* and must not make it *excessively difficult* to obtain a refund of the levy paid.

---

13 Case C-110/15, 22 September 2016, *Microsoft Mobile Sales International and Others*, para. 33.

14 C-463/12, 5 March 2015, *Copydan Båndkopi*, paras. 45 to 47, and C-110/15, 22 September 2016, *Microsoft Mobile Sales International and Others*, paras. 34-36.

15 Para. 44 of the annotated judgment.

16 Para. 45 of the annotated judgment.

2. The procedure established for the granting of exception certificates and administration of any refunds must be *effective, easily available, adequately publicised and simple* in order to ensure the correction of any imbalance that might derive from the automatic private copying levy system.

At this stage, the CJEU did not disregard the fact that the income of the collective management organisations is copyright revenue whose collection, management and distribution depends on the very same organisations that represent the rightholders, being among their tasks.[17]

It is commonly known in the EU that the existence of management organisations allows rightholders to enforce their rights efficiently, and the CJEU pointed out[18] that Recital 14 of Directive 2014/26 expressly allows these organisations to be formed by holders of copyright or related rights and other collective management organisations.

In analysing the system implemented, the CJEU considered that the mere fact that rightholders might participate in or control the collective management entities does not automatically create a disadvantage for the debtors or users.[19]

According to the CJEU[20] ruling, the Spanish legislation:

i. had implemented a system that enabled exemption certificates to be issued, and reimbursements made, in a timely manner and on the basis of objective criteria these criteria did not entail any discretion on the part of the person competent to examine applications submitted for that purpose, and allowed for the correction of any imbalances that might be created by the private copying levy system;

ii. provided for the possibility of appealing to an independent body against decisions of that legal person refusing to grant such a certificate or reimbursement, thereby avoiding any risk of bias on the part of the legal person in the granting of (i) exemption certificates and (ii) reimbursements, and thus preventing any distortion of the fair balance.

The CJEU concluded that *the Spanish system appeared to be capable of correcting any imbalances created by the private copying levy system*, but that it was nevertheless for the national court to verify this.

Finally, the Court considered that the position of the creditors and debtors was not the same, since they held different rights and obligations and that there

---

17 Para. 48 of the annotated judgment.

18 Para. 47 of the annotated judgment.

19 Para. 49 of the annotated judgment.

20 Paras. 55 and 58 of the annotated judgment.

could therefore be no breach of the equal treatment principle, which requires that comparable situations must not be treated differently, and different situations must not be treated in the same way unless such treatment is objectively justified.[21]

According to this reasoning, the CJEU concluded that both Article 5(2)(b) of Directive 2001/29 and the principle of equal treatment must be interpreted as not precluding national legislation under which a legal person established and controlled by intellectual property rights management organisations is entrusted with the management of (i) exemption certificates in respect of private copying levies and (ii) reimbursements in respect of such levies, where that national legislation provides that exemption certificates and reimbursements must be granted in good time and in accordance with objective criteria which do not allow that legal person to refuse an application for the granting of such a certificate or of reimbursement on the basis of considerations involving the exercise of discretion and that the decisions of that legal person refusing such an application may be challenged before an independent body.[22]

iii) Admissibility of the second question

DAMA also disputed the admissibility of the second question on the ground that the referring court had not specified either the provision of Directive 2001/29 or the general principles of EU law in respect of which interpretation was sought.

Based on the arguments given when analysing the first question, the CJEU declared the admissibility of this question.[23]

Additionally, ADEPY and Ventanilla Única Digital claimed that the obligation to release accounting information cannot be derived from the Spanish regulations and that the question therefore relates to a hypothetical situation that should not be analysed by the CJEU.

In this regard, it should be noted that it is solely for the national court before which a dispute has been brought to determine, in the light of the particular circumstances of the case (i) the need for a preliminary ruling in order to enable it to deliver judgment and (ii) the relevance of the questions which it submits to the Court.

Thus, where the questions submitted concern the interpretation of EU law, the CJEU is, in principle, bound to give a ruling.

---

21 Case C-110/15, 22 September 2016, *Microsoft Mobile Sales International and Others*, para. 44.

22 Para. 58 of the annotated judgment.

23 Paras. 60-66 of the annotated judgment.

Additionally, the CJEU recalled[24] that questions concerning EU law enjoy a presumption of relevance and that it may only decline to give a ruling on them:

- where it is manifestly clear that the interpretation of EU law that is sought bears no relation to the actual facts of the main proceedings or its purpose;
- where the problem is hypothetical; or
- where the Court does not have before it the factual or legal material necessary to give a useful answer to the questions submitted to it.[25]

The CJEU stated that the interpretation of national law put forward by ADEPI and Ventanilla Única Digital with regard to the information to which the legal person is entitled were not sufficient to overturn the presumption of relevance previously referred to, and that the question must therefore be considered admissible.[26]

iv) Substance – second question

In its second question, the Spanish Supreme Court was asking, in essence, whether Article 5(2)(b) of Directive 2001/29 and the principle of equal treatment must be interpreted as precluding national legislation which empowers a legal person which is established and controlled by intellectual property rights management organisations and which is entrusted with the management of (i) exemptions from payment in respect of compensation for private copying and (ii) reimbursements in respect of such compensation, to request access to the information necessary for the exercise of the powers of review conferred on it in that regard, without it being possible, in particular, for the person under review to rely on the confidentiality of business accounts provided for by national law.

In this regard, the CJEU[27] reminded the parties that having access to certain information is essential for the effective recovery of the amount intended to compensate the authors concerned for the harm suffered. Moreover, this information is also necessary in order to evaluate the relevance of a certificate of exemption and the right to request a reimburse.

Without access to this kind of information, the management organisations cannot verify that the conditions for granting an exemption certificate are met, nor can they ensure the effective collection of the compensation for private copying when these conditions are not met.

Specifically, access to this information will allow these entities to calculate and collect the amounts due by way of compensation when the conditions for granting an exemption certificate are or are no longer satisfied.

---

24 Para. 63 of the annotated judgment.

25 Case C-572/13,12 November 2015, *Hewlett-Packard Belgium*, para. 25 and the case law cited.

26 Para. 65 of the annotated judgment.

27 Para. 68 of the annotated judgment.

In analysing the possible breach of the equal treatment principle, the CJEU referred to its previous reasoning (first question) and the fact that debtors and creditors are not in equal positions and therefore cannot be treated equally.

Finally, having regard to the foregoing and to the fact that the receiving entities have the obligation to safeguard the confidential nature of the information concerned, the CJEU[28] concluded that Article 5(2)(b) of Directive 2001/29 and the principle of equal treatment must be interpreted as not precluding national legislation which empowers a legal person, established and controlled by intellectual property rights management organisations and entrusted with the management of (i) exemptions from payment in respect of compensation for private copying and (ii) reimbursements in respect of such compensation, to request access to the information necessary for the exercise of the powers of review conferred on it in that regard, without in particular allowing the person to be inspected to rely on the confidentiality of business accounts provided for by national law, that legal person being under an obligation to preserve the confidential nature of the information obtained.

* *
*

In my view, this decision is controversial to say the least, since the CJEU bases a relevant part of its decision on the idea that debtors and creditors hold different rights and obligations and, consequently, there can be no equal treatment.

It hardly makes sense to judge the problem raised through the prism of the difference inherent in the opposing roles of creditor and debtor. The parties have obvious conflicting interests with regard to the burden represented by the private copying levy and that ought to imply that the legal entity in charge of managing the exemption certificates and refunds should not be exclusively formed by the representatives of the creditors of the compensation.

The fact that the decisions taken by these entities can be challenged before the Ministry of Culture and the courts is, in my opinion, not a sufficient guarantee either.

[28] Para. 73 of the annotated judgment.

Court of Justice 8 September 2022

On the concept of 'broadcast retransmission' for the purpose of related rights infringement

Case C-716/20

Summary and Analysis by Manuel Durães Rocha and Leonor Sá e Frade[1]

Parties:

RTL Television GmbH

v

Grupo Pestana S.G.P.S. SA
SALVOR – Sociedade de Investimento Hoteleiro SA

1. Background and history

RTL v Grupo Pestana is a judgment issued by the Court of Justice of the European Union[2] following a preliminary ruling request from the Portuguese Supreme Court of Justice on the interpretation of Article 1(3) of Council Directive 93/83/EEC of 27 September 1993 on copyright and rights related to copyright applicable to satellite broadcasting and cable retransmission.[3] The main proceedings opposed RTL Television GmbH ('RTL'), as applicant, and Grupo Pestana, S.G.P.S. SA ('Grupo Pestana'), the direct holder of 98.98% of SALVOR – Sociedade de Investimento Hoteleiro SA ('Salvor'), as defendant. They related to the fact that the defendants were making RTL channel programmes available in the hotel rooms they operated, without RTL's authorisation.

The case seemed straightforward, but RTL lost at all three court instances in Portugal it appealed each time and finally took the case to the Court of Justice of the European Union.

RTL is a well-known German-language television channel, whose programmes offer a very wide range of television formats (films, series, shows, documentaries, sporting events, news, and current affairs programmes). As a German-language-based

---

1 Manuel Durães Rocha and Leonor Sá e Frade are lawyers at the Portuguese law firm Abrue Abogados.

2 Available at OJ 1993, L 248, p. 15 ('the Decision').

3 That provision, under the title 'Definitions', reads as follows: '*for the purposes of this Directive, "cable retransmission" means the simultaneous, unaltered and unabridged retransmission by a cable or microwave system for reception by the public of an initial transmission from another Member State, by wire or over the air, including that by satellite, of television or radio programmes intended for reception by the public.*'

free-to-air channel (free-access channel)[4] which is naturally mostly watched by the German-speaking public in the European Union, RTL's funding stems solely from advertising revenues in German-speaking countries (specifically, Germany, Austria, and Switzerland).

The dispute arose, because the (unencrypted) broadband of RTL's satellite signal (ASTRA 19.2 Satellite), despite being directed at German-speaking countries, can be received much further away (including in Portugal), via a satellite dish positioned towards ASTRA 19.2. Portugal, where the alleged infringing act took place, is a common tourist and holiday destination for German nationals,[5] and RTL came to learn that Grupo Pestana, a holding company whose subsidiaries (including Salvor) operate hotels, was granting access to RTL channel programmes at no extra charge to its hotel guests on televisions placed in each room of at least two of its hotels (the Pestana D. João II and Pestana Alvor Praia).

In the summer of 2012, RTL's parent company asked Grupo Pestana to pay a fixed fee for making RTL channel programmes available in its hotel rooms;[6] Grupo Pestana replied that in accordance with Portuguese law, hotels were not required to pay related rights and other fees to broadcasters for the mere reception of a television signal.[7] RTL then brought a suit against Grupo Pestana, claiming: (i) recognition of its entitlement to authorise or prohibit the retransmission of its shows; (ii) compensation for the prior unauthorised retransmission both at Salvor's hotels, and at hotels of other group companies; (iii) that Grupo Pestana should be required to adopt intra-group measures to ensure that

---

4 Meaning that the general public is not expected to pay a fee or a licence to access its contents on private (as opposed to commercial) devices.

5 According to the Lisbon's Court of Appeal's Decision (Acórdão do Tribunal da Relação de Lisboa, nº 196/14.4YHLSB.L1-8, full text available at dgsi.pt, 'the Appeal Decision'), around a tenth (10%) of guests in the Pestana Alvor Praia and Pestana D. João II hotels in the years preceding the dispute were of German nationality (para. 24 of the facts).

6 RTL based this demand on Art. 2(e) of EU Dir. 2001/29, entitled 'Reproduction right', which provides that '*Member States (MSs) shall provide*' '*broadcasting organisations*' with '*the exclusive right to authorise or prohibit direct or indirect, temporary or permanent reproduction by any means and in any form, in whole or in part*' '*of fixations of their broadcasts, whether those broadcasts are transmitted by wire or over the air, including by cable or satellite*' and on Art. 3(2)(d), which imposes on MSs the requirement to provide to '*broadcasting organisations*' of '*the exclusive right to authorise or prohibit the making available to the public, by wire or wireless means, in such a way that members of the public may access them from a place and at a time individually chosen by them*' '*of fixations of their broadcasts, whether these broadcasts are transmitted by wire or over the air, including by cable or satellite.*'

7 Its argument was based, as mentioned in the Appeal Decision, among other elements, on a legal opinion issued by PHA in 2004 to the effect that there would be no applicable fees to be paid by hotels to broadcasters in cases such as the one described (paras. 27-33 of the Appeal Decision). As such, Grupo Pestana concluded in its letter that it was only under an obligation to pay an individual fee for copyright and related licensing rights related to 'video on demand' systems.

the companies in its ownership did not make the RTL channel available in the hotels they operated.

The Portuguese Intellectual Property Court, where the case was first examined, found that while making the RTL channel's broadcasts available in the hotel rooms in question constituted an act of communication to the public within the meaning of Article 187(1)(e) of the CDADC[8] and in accordance with Recital 23 of Directive 2001/29/EC of the European Parliament and of the Council of 22 May 2001,[9] the distribution of that channel could not be regarded as 'retransmission of broadcasts' (under Art. 187(1)(a) of the CDADC), since neither the defendant nor the hotels identified in the action were broadcasting organisations,[10] defined in Article 176(10) of the CDADC as an '*organisation which makes audio or visual broadcasts, where broadcast means the transmission of sounds or images, or the representation thereof, separately or cumulatively, whether by wire or wireless means, in particular by radio waves, optical fibres, cable or satellite, intended for reception by the public.*' It thus considered the classification of the parties (as broadcasting organisations) an essential requirement of the concept of 'broadcast retransmission'.

RTL brought an appeal against that judgment before Lisbon's Court of Appeal. In the grounds of appeal, RTL considered there were faults as to the assessment of both the evidence produced and the applicable law: first, RTL argued that the judgment had omitted important facts resulting from the evidence produced (specifically, the technical description of how the distribution of the signal to the rooms took place[11] and the fact that the defendant had benefitted economically from the distribution of RTL's signal[12]); second, RTL argued that the Court had misapplied the law. Specifically, it was argued that Article 187(1)(a) CDADC defining the concept of 'retransmission' did not require it be carried out by a broadcasting organisation,[13] and that technical retransmission, of which the

---

[8] Código do Direito de Autor e dos Direitos Conexos (Portuguese Code of Copyright and Related Rights; 'the CDADC'), which reads '*broadcasters shall have the right to authorise or prohibit the communication to the public of their broadcasts if such communication is made in places accessible to the public against payment of an entrance fee.*'

[9] Which states that '*the author's right of communication to the public [...] should be understood in a broad sense covering all communication to the public not present at the place where the communication originates*' including '*transmission or retransmission of a work to the public by wire or wireless means, including broadcasting.*'

[10] Paras. 9-10 of the Appeal Court Decision's description of the grounds of appeal.

[11] Namely, the fact that the material (*de facto*) distribution of a broadcast transmission *was possible* through reception of a signal via a satellite dish and the use of a head-end device to further distribute the received broadcast transmission to multiple television devices across several hundred hotel rooms, through an operation that is '*not essentially different from that of cable operators.*' See paras. 35-39 of the Appeal Court Decision's description of the grounds of appeal.

[12] Paras. 11-13 of the Appeal Court Decision's description of the grounds of appeal.

[13] See also the summary of the Appeal by the CJEU in para. 44 of the annotated decision.

hotels were capable, was sufficient to constitute (cable) 'retransmission of broadcast'[14] under the broad language used in Articles 3 and 8 of Decree-Law 333/97 of 27 November 1997,[15] implementing Directive 93/83/EEC. Confidence in this argument was so strong that the appellant even suggested that the Appeal Court should stay the proceedings and refer a preliminary inquiry to the CJEU.[16]

In its judgment the Lisbon Court of Appeal entirely upheld the first-instance judgment. Upon examination, it concluded that the evidence that was allegedly lacking was either merely complementary (and thus not essential)[17] or simply untrue,[18] and would not, in any case, affect the judgment, as '*distribution by coaxial cable of the broadcasts of the RTL channel to numerous television sets installed in the rooms of the hotel establishments operated by the defendants in the main proceedings does not constitute a retransmission of broadcasts*' (in violation of Art. 187)[19], because, again '*in the light of the definition contained in Article 176(10) of the CDADC, neither the hotels nor the legal persons operating it can be considered "retransmitting broadcasting organisations"*.'[20]

The applicants again appealed, this time to the Portuguese Supreme Court of Justice, which stayed the proceedings to request a preliminary ruling on the matter by the CJEU. In short, the Supreme Court was uncertain whether the interpretation by the two lower courts was compatible with Directive 93/83, or if, instead, the use of a coaxial cable to broadcast the RTL channel in the rooms of Grupo Pestana's hotels constituted a retransmission of those broadcasts, subject to authorisation by the broadcasting organisation, in this case RTL, under Article 187(1)(a) of the CDADC. It hence referred the following questions:

> '*(1) Must the concept of "cable retransmission", as provided for in Article 1(3) of [Directive 93/83] be interpreted as meaning that it covers,*

---

14 Paras. 24-32 of the Appeal Court Decision's description of the grounds of appeal.

15 Art. 3 defines retransmission without consideration of who is performing it, and Article 8 extends the related rights granted in Art. 178, 184, and 187 of CDADC to broadcasts originally communicated or retransmitted to the public via satellite or cable.

16 Para. 40 of the Appeal Court Decision's description of the grounds of appeal.

17 Such as the description of the technical process by which RTL was made available to hotel guests: see the judgment on the facts of the Appeal Decision.

18 As the evidence had not shown the hotels had effectively benefitted from the retransmission of RTL broadcasts, but only that it might have done so, as any benefit was merely *potential*. See the judgment on the facts of the Appeal Decision.

19 See, para. 3 of the Appeal Decision.

20 Since that article states: '*"broadcasting organisation" means any organisation which makes audio or visual broadcasts, where broadcast means the transmission of sounds or images, or the representation thereof, separately or cumulatively, whether by wire or wireless means, in particular by radio waves, optical fibres, cable or satellite, intended for reception by the public' and '"retransmission" means "the simultaneous transmission by a broadcasting organisation of a broadcast by another broadcasting organisation"*.'

in addition to the simultaneous transmission by one broadcasting organisation of a broadcast by another broadcasting organisation, the distribution to the public, on a simultaneous basis and entirely by cable, of a primary transmission of television or radio programmes intended for reception by the public (whether or not the person performing that distribution to the public is a broadcasting organisation)?

(2) Does the simultaneous distribution of the satellite broadcasts of a television channel, through television sets installed in hotel rooms, and by means of coaxial cable, constitute a "retransmission" of such broadcasts within the meaning of the concept provided for in Article 1(3) of [Directive 93/83]?'

2. Decision

Article 1(3) of Council Directive 93/83/EEC of 27 September 1993 on the coordination of certain rules concerning copyright and rights related to copyright applicable to satellite broadcasting and cable retransmission, read in conjunction with Article 8(1) thereof, must be interpreted as meaning:
- **that it does not provide for an exclusive right for broadcasting organisations to authorise or prohibit cable retransmission, within the meaning of that provision, and**
- **that the simultaneous, unaltered and unabridged distribution of television or radio programmes broadcast by satellite and intended for reception by the public, where that retransmission is carried out by a person other than a cable operator, within the meaning of that directive, such as a hotel, does not constitute cable retransmission.**

3. Motivation and analysis

To address the questions referred by the Portuguese Supreme Court, the CJEU started by observing that '*cable retransmission*,' within the meaning of Article 1(3) of Council Directive 93/83/EEC of 27 September 1993, does not imply that the entity carrying out the retransmission must be a broadcasting organisation. '*Admittedly*,' as the CJEU puts it, the adoption of Directive 93/83/EEC was intended to broaden the concept of 'retransmission', so as to include, for example, *cable operators*.[21] This expansion in the subjective scope of the obligations arising out of copyright related rights was, however, according to the CJEU, '*limited to the scope of that directive*,' meaning that the concept of 'cable retransmission' in Article 1(3) of Directive 93/83 was expressly provided (only)

---

21 See Rec. 8 and 10 of Dir. 93/83 and para. 67 of the annotated decision.

'for the purposes of' that Directive.[22] And the purpose of that Directive was not to '*require MSs to introduce a specific cable retransmission right nor [to] define the scope of any such right*,' but merely to impose on MSs a requirement to ensure that the applicable copyright and related rights were observed in cases of broadcast retransmission across their territories[23] to '*facilitate [...] satellite broadcasting and [...] cable retransmission, by promoting the granting of authorisations [...] through collecting societies.*'[24,25]

As such, concluded the Court, '*Directive 93/83 governs only the exercise of the cable retransmission right in the relationship [...] holders of related rights, on the one hand, and "cable operators" or "cable distributors", on the other.*'[26] Cable distributors and operators are, in this context, the operators of traditional cable networks *only*.[27] Any other interpretation would, in the opinion of the Court, '*extend the scope of the related right provided for in Article 8(3) of Directive 2006/115, treating it in the same way as the exclusive right of communication to the public, as provided for in Article 3(1) of Directive 2001/29 in favour of authors.*'[28]

This judgment is in line with the Opinion of the Advocate General ('the AG's Opinion'). To the AG, the applicant appeared to have assumed that Portuguese domestic law extended copyright-related rights beyond what was required by the Directives by introducing a concept of 'cable distributor' different from the one that could be construed from EU law.[29] The AG argued, however, that such interpretation of national law put forward by the applicant (according to which broadcasting organisations enjoyed specific rights not recognised by the Directive in respect of entities such as hotels, which were therefore regarded as 'cable

---

22 See paras. 67 and 68 of the annotated decision.

23 Judgment of 3 February 2000, Egeda, C-293/98, EU:C:2000:66, para. 24.

24 See Stamatoudi, I.A., and Torremans, P., *EU Copyright Law: A Commentary*, Edward Elgar Publishing, 2014, p. 408, paras. 69 to 73 of the Decision, Rec. 28 of Dir. 93/83 and para. 38 of Advocate General Pitruzzella´s Opinion ('the AG's Opinion'), delivered on 10 March 2022, reference ECLI:EU:C:2022:187.

25 Therefore, its objective was not to confer rights, but to enable full use to be made of the new communications technology (satellite and cable) introduced at the time, and in particular, to address certain shortcomings in the contractual system within the market for the granting of cross-border licences in the case of cable retransmission. See Kur, A., Dreier, T., and Luginbuehl, S., *European Intellectual Property Law*, Elgar, 2019, pp. 304-305.

26 See para. 76 of the annotated decision.

27 See para. 77 of the annotated decision and para. 73 of the AG's Opinion.

28 See para. 78 of the annotated decision.

29 Namely, anyone who carries out the activity of broadcast retransmission on a professional basis is placed on the same footing as entities such as hotels, which, by picking up the free-to-air signal via a satellite dish, reproduce the signal by coaxial cable in their hotel rooms. See para. 26 of the Opinion.

distributors' themselves), was simply '*not in conformity with EU law.*'[30] And, although the *Verwertungsgesellschaft Rundfunk* judgment should be interpreted broadly, encouraging MSs to introduce additional rights to remunerate situations such as the one at issue, and although in principle EU law did not preclude national legislatures from introducing additional rights, '*what national law certainly cannot do is to give a different meaning to concepts defined by EU law.*'[31]

The AG concluded that these terms did have definitions, even though they did not appear in Directive 93/83. In particular, since, when interpreting the law, '*the [same] concepts [...] must have the same meaning, unless the EU legislature has expressed a different intention in a specific legislative context,*'[32] the AG resorted to CJEU case-law – specifically, the *ITV Broadcasting and Others* judgment[33] – where the concept of cable had already been defined as '*a sub-category of the wider concept of wired transmission.*'[34] It could thus be presumed that '*if the EU legislature had intended to give the concept of "cable" [...] a technologically neutral meaning, [...] it would have chosen a more general concept, or that it would at least have made clear that the concept of "cable" included other technologies.*'[35] *Thus, 'the concept of "cable" [...] is restricted to traditional cable networks operated by conventional cable service providers.*'

Additionally, the AG highlighted that '*the concept of "act of communication to the public" [...] [would have been] better suited to the present case than the concept of "cable retransmission",*'[36] following CJEU case law in *Egeda,*[37] which stated that the fact that a hotel receives satellite or terrestrial television signals and distributes them by cable to the various rooms of that hotel is an act of communication to the public. In the opinion of the AG, in short, the applicant in the main proceedings was mistaken in its interpretation that the conduct of the hotel was both a communication to the public and a cable retransmission. This observation was relevant because it led to the conclusion that the acts that constituted retransmission did not overlap with the ones that constituted communication to the public. The latter framing, however, would be disadvantageous for the applicant, because '*with regard to the broadcasters,*' the exercise of the right of '*communication to the public*' (under Art. 187(1)(e) CDADC) was

---

30 See para. 75 of the AG's Opinion.

31 Para. 80 of the AG's Opinion.

32 See Opinion in *ITV Broadcasting and Others* (C-275/15, EU:C:2016:649, point 70).

33 C-275/15, EU:C:2016:649, where the referring court asked, in essence, whether the concept of 'cable' in Art. 9 of Dir. 2001/29 was linked to a particular technology, restricted to traditional cable networks operated by conventional cable service providers, or alternatively whether it had a technologically neutral meaning which could include functionally similar services transmitted via the internet.

34 See para. 54 of the AG's Opinion.

35 See para. 55 of the AG's Opinion.

36 See para. 62 of the AG's Opinion.

37 See the judgment of 3 February 2000 (C-293/98, EU:C:2000:66, para. 29).

essentially '*likened to the specific economic advantage enjoyed by the person retransmitting the [free-to-air] broadcast*'[38] (e.g. the payment of an entrance fee), which, as demonstrated, was lacking in this case.[39]

In conclusion, there are interesting points in the judgment. First, it is essentially based on the formal argument that, as the defendant could not be considered either a 'broadcasting organisation' or a 'cable operator', it was not subject to the related legal regimes.

Although RTL framed the alleged infringement of its IP rights as an act of retransmission, the Appeal Court of Lisbon, the AG's Opinion and previous CJEU case-law[40] all categorised the distribution of television signals to televisions in hotel rooms as an act of communication to the public, and not a retransmission.

Importantly, the judgment concludes that acts of transmission do not overlap with acts of communication to the public. The one is not simply a form of the other, nor do they share requirements – they are entirely different acts, infringing entirely different rights.

Lastly, it is worth noting that despite the AG's Opinion which emphasises fairly strongly[41] that the rights arising from the retransmission of television programmes vary considerably depending on the chosen business model of the broadcaster,[42] and that '*it would be a mistake to confuse them*' (since retransmission of free-to-air broadcasts is only subject to the payment of a fee whenever there is the prior payment of a fee to access the retransmission, because, precisely, it is not a pay

---

38 See judgment of 16 February 2017, *Verwertungsgesellschaft Rundfunk* (C-641/15, EU:C:2017:131).

39 As the Appeal Court observed, one of the requirements for the application of Art. 187(1) was the payment of an entrance fee specifically to the place where the broadcast was being retransmitted, and this requirement was not considered to be met in cases where the broadcasting service was a mere complement to a central service for no additional charge. See the judgment on the facts of the Appeal Decision. This was also the opinion of the CJEU, based on Art. 8(3) of Dir. 2006/115 and confirmed in the judgment of 16 February 2017, *Verwertungsgesellschaft Rundfunk*, C-641/15, EU:C:2017:131, paras. 23 to 26, from which it was clear that the communication of television and radio programmes by means of television sets installed in hotel rooms did not constitute a communication made in a place accessible to the public in return for payment of an entrance fee, because the price of a hotel room constituted consideration for the accommodation service, to which, according to the hotel category, certain additional services were added, such as the communication of TV and radio broadcasts by means of receiving equipment in the rooms.

40 CJEU judgment of 7 December 2006, *SGAE* (C-306/05, EU:C:2006:764, paras. 47 and 54).

41 Para. 86 of the AG's Opinion.

42 'Pay TV' systems involve a specific type of remuneration by private and commercial consumers (although normally to a different extent), whereas in free-to-air retransmission, the broadcaster is remunerated through advertising revenues.

TV system), the judgment in this case observed that no specific fee was being paid by Grupo Pestana to RTL for the reception of RTL's TV signal, but did not explore how the business model of the broadcaster might impact its copyright-related rights. We suppose that this and other remaining points of interest must be left for another CJEU judgment.

In conclusion, all the courts involved in this case considered and decided that:

1) Making programmes available in the hotel rooms did not constitute a '*communication to the public in a place open to the public with paid entry*' in the sense of EU Directive 2006/115 and Portuguese IP law, based on the view that the interpretation of the legal provisions arising from the transposition of a EU Directive must be consistent with European Union law and take account of the sense of the interpretation of those provisions adopted by the CJEU.

2) The service of retransmission of a primary transmission by the hotel to the rooms was not a communication to the public in an open place in return for an entrance fee, since it was only a supplementary service of the hotel to its guests that was included in the price of the room.

3) There was no retransmission by the hotels of the signal of RTL because the hotels were not broadcasting entities and therefore did not meet the technical conditions for retransmission.

4) The hotels were not cable distributors or cable operators as defined in EU Directive 93/83, as the concept of cable retransmission was only applicable to the relations between the owners of copyright and neighbouring rights and cable distributors or operators in the traditional interpretation of these concepts; in particular the exercise of such retransmission as a main economic activity differed from the economic activity of a hotel.

5) The Portuguese Supreme Court held that the broadcasters' right to authorise or prohibit was only applicable to the cases in which the entity performing the retransmission was itself a broadcasting entity, which was not the case with the hotels.

COURT OF JUSTICE 27 OCTOBER 2022

ON THE CONCEPT OF GROUNDS FOR OPPOSING FURTHER COMMERCIALISATION OF THE GOODS BEARING THE TRADE MARK

Case C-197/21

Summary and Analysis by Åsa Krook and Jonna Rask[1]

Parties:

Soda-Club (CO2) SA,
SodaStream International BV

v

MySoda Oy

1. Background and History

SodaStream is a multinational entity, founded in 1903, that manufactures and sells carbonating machines, which allow consumers to prepare sparkling water and flavoured non-alcoholic beverages from tap water. In Finland, SodaStream markets its machines with a carbon dioxide refillable cylinder, which it also offers for sale separately. The companies forming SodaStream are the proprietors of the EU trade marks and the national trade marks SODASTREAM and Soda-Club. Those marks appear on the labelling of, and are engraved on, the aluminium body of the refillable cylinders.

MySoda, a company whose registered office is in Finland, markets carbonating machines for beverages under the MySoda trade mark in packaging that does not normally include a carbon dioxide cylinder. Since June 2016, MySoda has been offering for sale in Finland carbon dioxide cylinders that are filled and are compatible with both its own carbonating machines and those of SodaStream. Some of those cylinders were originally placed on the market by SodaStream.

It is common practice in the industry for the consumer to bring an empty carbon dioxide cylinder to a retailer and receive a full cylinder for the sole price of the carbon dioxide. The cylinders are then returned to operators for refilling. The filling of cylinders is in Finland a regulated activity. When refilled, the cylinders are relabelled in such a way that the trade mark and information engraved on the surface by the original carbon dioxide cylinder manufacturer remains visible.

---

1 Åsa Krook is an IP partner at the Finnish law firm Waselius & Wist and is a member of the Finnish Bar. Jonna Rask is an Associate Lawyer at the Finnish law firm Waselius & Wist.

Some of the cylinders that MySoda refilled were originally put on the market by SodaStream. When refilling the cylinders MySoda used two different labels. The pink-coloured label displayed in a large font the MySoda logo and the text '*Finnish carbon dioxide for carbonating machines*', and, in a small font, MySoda as the company that had filled the cylinder. In addition to the pink label, MySoda also used a white-coloured label. The white-coloured label displayed the words 'carbon dioxide' in capital letters in five languages, and included in the product information, written in small font, the name MySoda as the company that had filled the cylinder together with a statement that that company had no connection with the original supplier of the cylinder or with its company or registered trade mark which appeared on the cylinder. Both labels also included a reference to the MySoda website for further information.

In 2017, SodaStream brought an action before the Finnish Market Court claiming that MySoda had infringed the trade marks SODASTREAM and SODACLUB by putting on the market and selling refilled carbon dioxide cylinders bearing the aforementioned trade marks without the authorisation of their proprietors. SodaStream claimed that MySoda's conduct adversely affected the rights conferred by those marks and created a significant likelihood of confusion for the public concerned as to the origin of carbon dioxide cylinders by creating the false impression that there was a commercial or financial connection between SodaStream and MySoda.[2]

MySoda responded that changing the label did not adversely affect the function of the trade mark, which was to indicate the origin of the cylinder, since the relevant public understood that the labelling indicated solely the origin of the carbon dioxide and the identity of the reseller who had refilled the cylinder, the origin of which was engraved on the body of that cylinder.[3] The Market Court considered that it had not been shown that MySoda's conduct changed or impaired the carbon dioxide cylinder or its contents, or damaged SodaStream's reputation due to risks to the safety of its goods, or that that conduct caused harm such as to give SodaStream a legitimate reason to oppose that conduct.

As regards the white labels, the Market Court took the view that they had not created a false impression as to an economic connection between MySoda and SodaStream. In contrast, it held that the use of pink labels was liable to create the impression in the mind of the average consumer, who was reasonably

---

2 Paras. 17-18 of the annotated judgment: SodaStream argued that the so-called *Bristol-Myers Squibb* conditions, as defined in the case law of the CJEU, should be applied when considering the case. In particular, SodaStream relied on the condition of necessity. However, the Market Court held in its interim judgment that the conditions were not applicable since the present case did not involve parallel imports but a practice within a single Member State.

3 Para. 19 of the annotated judgment.

well-informed and reasonably observant, that there was such a connection.[4] Accordingly, the Market Court held in its interlocutory judgment that the use of these pink labels justified SodaStream's opposition to MySoda's conduct and hence allowed SodaStream's claims.[5] Both parties filed an appeal to the Supreme Court of Finland.

The Supreme Court of Finland decided to stay the proceedings and to refer the following question to the Court of Justice for a preliminary ruling:

> '1. *Do the so-called Bristol-Myers Squibb criteria developed in the Court of Justice's case-law on repackaging and relabelling in cases of parallel imports, and in particular the condition of "necessity" also apply in the case of repackaging or relabelling of goods, which have been put on the market in a Member State by the trade mark proprietor or with its consent, for the purposes of resale in the same Member State?*
>
> 2. *Where the trade mark proprietor has affixed its trade mark to the cylinder, both on the label and engraved on the neck of the cylinder, when putting a cylinder containing carbon dioxide on the market, do the Bristol-Myers Squibb criteria referred to above, and in particular the condition of "necessity" apply when a third party refills the cylinder with carbon dioxide for the purposes of resale, removes the original label and replaces it with a label bearing its own logo, while, at the same time, the trade mark of the person that put the cylinder on the market continues to be visible in the engraving on the neck of the cylinder?*
>
> 3. *In the situation described above, can the view be taken that the removal and replacement of the label bearing the trade mark undermines, in principle, the function of the trade mark as an indication of the origin of the cylinder, or is it of significance, with regard to the applicability of the conditions for repackaging and relabelling, that:*
> - *it is to be assumed that the relevant public should perceive the label as referring exclusively to the origin of the carbon dioxide contained in the cylinder (and thus to the person who has refilled the cylinder); or*
> - *it is to be assumed that the relevant public should perceive the label as also referring, at least in part, to the origin of the cylinder?*
>
> 4. *If the removal and replacement of the label affixed on carbon dioxide cylinders is to be assessed on the basis of the condition of necessity, can the fact that the labels affixed to the cylinders put on the market by the trade mark proprietor have been accidentally damaged or become detached or have been removed and replaced by a person's previous refilling constitute a circumstance on the basis of which the regular replacement*

4 The Market Court based its assessment on the judgment of the CJEU in the Case C-46/10, 14 July 2011, *Viking Gas*.

5 The Finnish Market Court, 5 September 2019, MAO:388/19.

of the labels by the label of the person who refilled the cylinders is to be regarded as being necessary for putting the refilled cylinders on the market?'

2. Decision

Article 15(2) of Regulation (EU) 2017/1001 of the European Parliament and of the Council of 14 June 2017 on the European Union trade mark and Article 15(2) of Directive (EU) 2015/2436 of the European Parliament and of the Council of 16 December 2015 to approximate the laws of the Member States relating to trade marks must be interpreted as meaning that the proprietor of a trade mark who has put on the market, in a Member State, goods bearing that mark and intended to be reused and refilled numerous times, is not entitled, under those provisions, to oppose subsequent commercialisation of those goods, in that Member State, by a reseller who has refilled them and has replaced the label on which the original mark appeared by another label, while leaving visible the original mark on those goods, unless that new labelling creates a false impression, in the minds of consumers, that there is an economic connection between the reseller and the trade mark proprietor. That likelihood of confusion must be assessed globally in the light of the information appearing on the product and its new labelling and having regard to the distribution practices of the sector concerned and the level of knowledge that consumers have of those practices.

3. Motivation and Analysis

In accordance with Article 9 of Regulation 2017/1001, the proprietor of an EU trade mark and a national trade mark has an exclusive right that enables the proprietor to prohibit any third party from offering, placing on the market or stocking goods bearing the holder's trade mark for such purposes. However, under Article 15(1) of Regulation 2017/1001 and Article 15(1) of Directive 2015/2436, the trade mark proprietor cannot, in principle, oppose use of that trade mark once it has been put on the market in the EEA by the trade mark proprietor or with its consent.[6]

As previously stated, it was common ground between the parties that the carbon dioxide cylinders in question had initially been placed on the market in Finland by SodaStream, i.e. the trade mark proprietor. In the light of the foregoing, the trade mark proprietor would not be entitled to oppose the conduct at issue in the main proceedings. However, according to Article 15(2) of Regulation 2017/1001 and Article 15(2) of Directive 2015/2436, the trade mark proprietor may oppose the subsequent marketing of goods bearing its trade mark, in particular

[6] Case C-46/10, 14 July 2011, *Viking Gas*, para. 26.

where the goods are subject to alterations or deterioration after they have been placed on the market. The sole purpose of that possibility of opposition, which derogates from the fundamental principle of the free movement of goods, is to safeguard the rights which are based on the essential character of the trade mark, understood in the light of its essential function.[7]

The CJEU has ruled on numerous occasions that the specific purpose of trade mark rights is to guarantee to the proprietor of a trade mark that it has the right to use that trade mark for the purpose of putting a product into circulation for the first time and thus to protect it against competitors wishing to take advantage of the status and reputation of the trade mark by illegally selling goods bearing that same mark.[8] Therefore, the question whether the proprietor may oppose further commercialisation must be examined in the light of the legitimate interests of the proprietor, and in particular that of safeguarding the essential function of the trade mark, which is to guarantee the identity of the origin of the marked product to the consumer or end user.[9]

According to the case law of the CJEU, the sale of a refillable gas bottle by the proprietor of the marks affixed to it exhausts the rights which the proprietor has from the registration of those marks and transfers to the purchaser the right to use that bottle freely, which includes the right to exchange it or have it refilled. This also applies to the competitors of the proprietor. Consequently, MySoda's conduct was capable of falling within the scope of Article 15(2) of Regulation 2017/1001 and Article 15(2) of Directive 2015/2436.[10]

Notwithstanding the above-mentioned Article 15(2) of Regulation 2017/1001 and Article 15(2) of Directive 2015/2436, the proprietor is entitled, despite the placing on the market of goods bearing the proprietor's mark, to oppose further commercialisation of those goods where legitimate reasons justify such opposition. A legitimate reason may be, for example, alteration or impairment of the condition of the goods, as the CJEU has stated in its previous judgments.[11] The situation relating to the alteration or impairment of the condition of goods, which is expressly mentioned in those provisions, is given only as an example, since those provisions do not provide an exhaustive list of legitimate reasons which may exclude the application of the principle of exhaustion.[12] Such legitimate reason can also exist when the use by a third party of a sign identical with or similar to a trade mark seriously damages the reputation of that mark or when that use is carried out in such a way as to give the impression that

---

7 Case C-143/00, 24 April 2022, *Boehringer Ingelheim*, para. 28.

8 Case C-291/16, 20 December 2017, *Schweppes*, para. 37.

9 Para. 36. of the annotated judgment.

10 Case C-46/10, 14 July 2011, *Viking Gas*, paras. 39-40.

11 Case C-558/08, 8 July 2010, *Portakabin*, paras. 79-80; Case C-46/10, 14 July 2011, *Viking Gas*, para. 37.

12 Case C-46/10, 14 July 2011, *Viking Gas*, para. 41.

there is a commercial link or other special relationship between the trade mark proprietor and that third party.

The CJEU noted that the kind of situation set out above involving the likelihood of confusion may occur when the reseller removes the label on which the original mark appears and affixes its own label to that product, while leaving visible the original mark engraved on the product. To evaluate whether such a false impression may exist, account must be taken of all the circumstances relating to the reseller's activity, such as the way in which the refillable cylinders are presented and sold to consumers following the new labelling, and in particular the practices of refilling those cylinders which prevail in the sector concerned.[13]

The CJEU drew attention to a few particular details that should be taken into account when assessing whether the trade mark proprietor has the right to oppose such use of its trade mark. First, the extent of information appearing on the new labels is significant. The overall impression created by the new label must be assessed in order to determine whether the information relating to the trade mark proprietor and that relating to the reseller is clear and unambiguous to a consumer who is reasonably well-informed and reasonably observant.[14] The information must not give the impression that there is a financial connection between the parties. Secondly, account must also be taken of the practices in the sector concerned and the question whether consumers are accustomed to the cylinders being refilled by operators other than the original operator and trade mark proprietor. Therefore, it is of utmost significance whether there exists such a false impression among consumers.[15]

The CJEU further noted that in this case, where neither the proprietor of the original trade marks nor the reseller offered their carbon dioxide cylinders directly to consumers, since those cylinders were available for sale only in the distributors' stores, there was an absence of direct contact with the reseller, which might give rise to a likelihood of confusion among consumers as to the relationship between the reseller and the proprietors of the original trade marks. Such a situation was therefore liable to prevent the essential function of the trade mark and, therefore, to justify the application of Article 15(2) of Directive 2015/2436 and Article 15(2) of Regulation 2017/1001.[16]

Thirdly, the CJEU stated that it follows from its own case law that the fact that the original mark on the cylinder remained visible in spite of the additional labelling affixed by the reseller constituted a relevant factor in so far as it seemed

---

[13] Paras. 44-45 of the annotated judgment; Case C-46/10, 14 July 2011, *Viking Gas*, paras. 39-40.

[14] Opinion of Advocate General Pitruzzella, 12 May 2021, *Sodaclub*, para. 51.

[15] Paras. 47-49 of the annotated judgment.

[16] Para. 52 of the annotated judgment.

to rule out that the labelling changed the condition of the cylinders by masking their origin.[17]

In its ruling, the CJEU did not focus on the requirements established in case law concerning parallel imports of repackaged medicinal products, but noted that it had drawn up a list of exemptions to frame the existence of such reasons in that specific context.[18] The main focus in the CJEU's preliminary ruling at hand was on a trade mark's essential function to guarantee the origin of a product bearing the trade mark as a legitimate reason to oppose further commercialisation of the goods put on the market.

Even though the CJEU's evaluation is context-specific and relies on factors such as the design of the respective labels and common practice in the business sector in question, it further clarifies the interpretation of Article 15(2) of Regulation 2017/1001 and Article 15(2) of Directive 2015/2436 in a way that is welcome.

The question what extent the proprietor of a trade mark has the right to oppose further commercialisation of its products in the specific case was left to the national courts to assess in accordance with the rules of interpretation expressed by the CJEU. In the matter at hand, the Finnish Supreme Court came to the same conclusion as the Market Court and upheld the Market Court's interlocutory judgment.[19] The matter has now been referred back to the Market Court, where the proceedings will continue with regard to the damage claim and claim for compensation based upon the infringement of SodaStream's trade mark right by the use of the pink label, which was considered to mislead the public by creating the impression in the mind of the average consumer that there was an economic connection between SodaStream and MySoda.

---

17 Case C-46/10, 14 July 2011, *Viking Gas*, para. 41.

18 Para. 42 of the annotated judgment.

19 The Finnish Supreme Court judgment KKO:2023:87.

Court of Justice 17 November 2022

On the parallel import of a generic medicinal product under the trade mark of the reference (originator) medicinal product

Joined cases C-253/20 and C-254/20

Summary and Analysis by Karel Janssens and Victoria Heinen[1]

Parties:

Impexeco NV

v

Novartis AG (C-253/20)

and

PI Pharma NV

v

Novartis AG,
Novartis Pharma NV (C-254/20)

1. Background and history

Requests for a preliminary ruling were made in two sets of proceedings brought, first, by Impexeco NV against Novartis AG and, second, by PI Pharma NV against Novartis and Novartis Pharma NV.

Novartis is the parent company of the Novartis group, which is active in the production of medicinal products. The group also includes the Pharmaceuticals and Sandoz divisions which are responsible, respectively, for the development of originator medicinal products and for generic medicinal products.

Impexeco and PI Pharma are two Belgian companies active in the parallel trade in medicinal products.

Novartis markets a medicinal product with the active substance letrozole in Belgium and in the Netherlands under the EU trade mark 'Femara'. Sandoz markets the generic medicinal product 'Letrozol Sandoz 2.5 mg' in Belgium and

---

[1] Karel Janssens specialises in IP and IT law and is a partner at the Belgian law firm & DE BANDT. Victoria Heinen is also an attorney-at-law at & DE BANDT and specialises in Belgian and European regulatory law.

in the Netherlands. The 'Femara' and 'Letrozol Sandoz' medicinal products are identical.

In 2016, Impexeco marketed in Belgium the medicinal product Letrozol Sandoz 2.5 mg, imported from the Netherlands and repackaged in new packaging bearing the trade mark 'Femara'. Novartis claimed that the marking of that product with the trade mark of the reference (originator) medicinal product, i.e. 'Femara', infringed its trade mark rights and brought an action against Impexeco before the Brussels Court of Cessations (the President of the Brussels Enterprise Court).

Novartis also markets a medicinal product with the active substance methylphenidate in Belgium under the Benelux word mark 'Rilatine'. In the Netherlands, this medicinal product is marketed under the trade mark 'Ritalin'. Sandoz markets in the Netherlands the generic medicinal product 'Methylphenidate HC1 Sandoz 10 mg', which is identical to the product 'Ritalin 10 mg tablet'.

In 2016, PI Pharma imported from the Netherlands and placed on the Belgian market the medicinal product Methylphenidate HC1 Sandoz 10 mg in new outer packaging on which it affixed the trade mark 'Rilatine'. Again, Novartis opposed the parallel import by PI Pharma on the grounds of trade mark infringement and brought an action before the Brussels Court of Cessations.

In both cases, the Brussels Court of Cessations held that the practice of affixing the trade marks 'Femara' and 'Rilatine' to the repackaged generic medicinal products 'Letrozol Sandoz 2.5 mg' and 'Methylphenidate HC1 Sandoz 10 mg' respectively, imported from the Netherlands, infringed Novartis' trade mark rights within the meaning of Article 9(2)(a) of Regulation No 207/2009 and Article 2.20(1)(a) of the Benelux Convention respectively.

Impexeco and PI Pharma appealed against these two judgments before the Brussels Court of Appeal, arguing that the practices of using different packaging and different trade marks for the same product both contributed to the partitioning of Member States' markets.

The Court of Appeal decided to stay the proceedings and to refer the following questions to the Court of Justice of the European Union (CJEU) for a preliminary ruling:

> *'(1) Must Articles 34 to 36 TFEU be interpreted as meaning that, where a branded medicine (reference medicine) and a generic medicine have been put on the market in the EEA by economically linked undertakings, a trade mark proprietor's opposition to the further commercialisation of the generic medicine by a parallel importer after the repackaging of that generic medicine by the affixing to it of the trade mark of the branded medicine (reference medicine) in the country of importation may lead to an artificial partitioning of the markets of the Member States?*

(2) If the answer to that question is in the affirmative, must the trade mark proprietor's opposition to that [new marking] be assessed by reference to the [...] conditions [set out in paragraph 79 of the judgment of 11 July 1996, Bristol-Myers Squibb and Others (C-427/93, C-429/93 and C-436/93, EU:C:1996:282)]?

(3) Is it relevant to the answer to those questions that the generic medicine and the branded medicine (reference medicine) are identical or have the same therapeutic effect as referred to in Article 3(2) of the [...] Royal Decree of 19 April 2001 on parallel imports [of medicinal products for human use and the parallel distribution of medicinal products for human and veterinary use, as amended by the Royal Decree of 21 January 2011]?'

2. Decision

Article 9(2) and Article 13 of Council Regulation (EC) No 207/2009 of 26 February 2009 on the European Union trade mark, as amended by Regulation (EU) 2015/2424 of the European Parliament and of the Council of 16 December 2015, and Article 5(1) and Article 7 of Directive 2008/95/EC of the European Parliament and of the Council of 22 October 2008 to approximate the laws of the Member States relating to trade marks, read in the light of Articles 34 and 36 TFEU,

must be interpreted as meaning that the proprietor of the trade mark of a reference medicinal product and the trade mark of a generic medicinal product may oppose the placing on the market of a Member State, by a parallel importer, of that generic medicinal product imported from another Member State, where that medicinal product has been repackaged in new outer packaging to which the trade mark of the corresponding reference medicinal product has been affixed, unless, first, the two medicinal products are identical in all respects and, second, the replacement of the trade mark satisfies the conditions laid down in paragraph 79 of the judgment of 11 July 1996, *Bristol-Myers Squibb and Others* (C-427/93, C-429/93 and C-436/93, EU:C:1996:282); in paragraph 32 of the judgment of 26 April 2007, *Boehringer Ingelheim and Others* (C-348/04, EU:C:2007:249); and in paragraph 28 of the judgment of 17 May 2018, *Junek Europ-Vertrieb* (C-642/16, EU:C:2018:322).

3. Motivation and Analysis

According to the CJEU, the referring court had asked, in essence, whether the proprietor of the trade mark of a reference (originator) medicinal product and of the trade mark of a generic medicinal product may oppose the placing on the market of a Member State, by a parallel importer, of that generic medicinal product, imported from another Member State, where that medicinal product has been repackaged in new outer packaging to which the trade mark of the corresponding reference medicinal product has been affixed.

In this regard, the CJEU first recalled its previous case law,[2] according to which the proprietor of a trade mark may oppose the further commercialisation in one Member State of a pharmaceutical product bearing its trade mark and imported from another Member State, where the importer of that product has repackaged it and reaffixed that trade mark to it, unless the following conditions (the 'BMS conditions') are fulfilled, i.e.:

1. it is established that the use of the trade mark rights by their proprietor to oppose the marketing of the relabelled products under that trade mark would contribute to the artificial partitioning of the markets between Member States;
2. it is shown that the repackaging cannot affect the original condition of the product inside the packaging;
3. the new packaging states clearly who repackaged the product and the name of the manufacturer;
4. the presentation of the repackaged product is not such as to be liable to damage the reputation of the trade mark and of its proprietor; and
5. the importer gives notice to the trade mark proprietor before the repackaged product is put on sale, and, on demand, supplies it with a specimen of the repackaged product.

The CJEU then focused its analysis on the application of the first condition. The CJEU recalled that, as held in *Upjohn*, a trade mark owner which markets in different Member States *an identical medicinal product* under different trade marks contributes to artificial partitioning of the markets between Member States if it opposes the replacement of the trade mark used in the exporting Member State with that used by that proprietor in the importing Member State, where that replacement is *objectively necessary* to market the product in the importing Member State by the parallel importer.[3]

In the case at hand, however, the disputes were characterised by the fact that the medicinal products being traded in parallel were generic medicinal products, whereas the trade marks affixed to the new outer packaging of those medicinal products were the trade marks of the corresponding reference (originator) medicinal products. The Court therefore had to examine:

1. whether the generic medicinal products and their corresponding reference products might be regarded as identical for the purposes of the case law relating to the exhaustion of trade mark rights, and

---

2 See *inter alia* CJEU, 11 July 1996, Joined Cases C-427/93, C-429/93 and C-436/93, *Bristol-Myers Squibb and Others v Paranova*, ECLI:EU:C:1996:282; CJEU, 26 April 2007, C-348/04, *Boehringer Ingelheim and Others*, ECLI:EU:C:2007:249; CJEU, 17 May 2018, C-642/16, *Junek Europ-Vertrieb*, ECLI:EU:C:2018:322.

3 CJEU, 12 October 1999, Case C-379/97, *Upjohn*, EU:C:1999:494, paras. 19 and 38 to 40.

2. whether the opposition of the trade mark proprietor to the replacement of the trade mark of a generic medicinal product by that of the corresponding reference medicinal product constituted an obstacle to the effective access of the product to the market of the importing Member State.

With regard to the first question, the CJEU held that, to treat a reference medicinal product and its therapeutically equivalent generic counterpart as identical products for the purposes of *Upjohn* could mislead health professionals and patients as regards the exact composition of the products concerned, with potentially serious consequences for the health of those patients. The composition of the generic medicinal product may differ from that of the reference medicinal product as regards the pharmaceutical form, the chemical form of the active substance and its excipients. It may also be contraindicated to replace, during treatment, a medicinal product with an equivalent medicinal product, whether it is a reference medicinal product or a generic medicinal product.

For these reasons, the CJEU concluded that only a medicinal product which is identical *in all respects* to another medicinal product can be repackaged in new outer packaging bearing the trade mark of the other medicinal product. The CJEU held that this may be the case, in particular, when the reference medicinal product and a generic medicinal product are manufactured by the same entity or by economically linked entities and, in fact, constitute one and the same product marketed under two different sets of rules, as was the case in the main proceedings.

As regards the second question, the CJEU reiterated that a trade mark proprietor cannot oppose the replacement of that trade mark by a parallel importer if the latter is able to establish that it is objectively necessary to replace the trade mark of origin by that of the importing Member State for the purpose of placing that product on the market in that Member State and if, moreover, that replacement is carried out under the BMS conditions.[4] Conversely, where the parallel importer is able to market the generic product under its trade mark of origin by adapting, where appropriate, the packaging in order to satisfy the market requirements of the importing Member State, the condition of necessity is not satisfied.

Then, in paragraph 72 of the judgment, the CJEU referred to its finding in *Delfarma* that a Member State cannot, in principle, refuse to grant a parallel import licence for a generic medicinal product where the corresponding reference medicinal product has a marketing authorisation in that Member State, unless such a refusal is justified by considerations relating to the protection of health and life of humans.[5] From this, the Court inferred that the condition of necessity

[4] CJEU, 12 October 1999, C-379/97, *Upjohn*, ECLI:EU:C:1999:494, paras. 42 and 43; CJEU, 28 July 2011, C-400/09 and C-207/10, *Orifarm and Others*, ECLI:EU:C:2011:519, para. 24.

[5] CJEU, 3 July 2019, Case C-387/18, *Delfarma*, ECLI:EU:C:2019:556.

cannot be satisfied where a generic medicinal product corresponds in every respect to the reference medicinal product covered by that authorisation given that, in such a situation, the parallel importer must be regarded as being able to market the generic medicinal product under its mark of origin.

Finally, the CJEU held that a trade mark proprietor is entitled to oppose the marketing, under that trade mark, of products repackaged by a parallel importer where the replacement of the trade mark of origin by another trade mark of the proprietor is exclusively motivated by the pursuit of an economic advantage, as is the case, in particular, where an economic operator seeks to take advantage of the reputation of the trade mark of a reference medicinal product or to place a product in a more profitable category.

In the light of these considerations, the CJEU concluded that the proprietor of the trade mark of a reference medicinal product and the trade mark of a generic medicinal product may oppose the affixing by a parallel importer on that generic medicinal product of the trade mark of the corresponding reference medicinal product, unless (i) the two medicinal products are identical in all respects, and (ii) the replacement of the trade mark satisfies the BMS conditions.

* *
*

Although the Court provided a useful reminder here of its previous case law regarding parallel import, several considerations raise concerns.

For example, if rebranding of medicinal products by a parallel importer is only possible where the products are '*identical in all respects*' and even '*slight differences*' are now excluded,[6] this may have unintended consequences for the free movement of medicinal products within the EEA. In theory, this would allow a trade mark proprietor to prevent rebranding (and parallel import as such) by, for example, changing the colour or another non-essential excipient of an otherwise completely identical medicinal product, even though a parallel import licence could in principle be validly obtained (since this does not require strict

---

6 In *Centrafarm*, the CJEU appeared to tolerate 'slight' differences: '*The therapeutic effects of the Seresta and Serenid tablets are identical. Nevertheless the composition of the two is not quite the same. As far as the consumer is concerned the most obvious difference lies in the taste. […] According to their wording the questions submitted <u>concern one and the same product, despite certain slight differences which may exist between the product as marketed under one or other mark</u>, so that the Court of Justice is not required to give a ruling on the basis that the two marks were used for two products each of which has its own characteristics.*' (CJEU, Case 3/78, 10 October 1978, *Centrafarm*, ECLI:EU:C:1978:174, para. 1 and 5; emphasis added).

identity[7]) and rebranding is objectively necessary to access the market of the importing Member State.

In our view, the condition of identity may or should still be fulfilled if (a) there are only slight differences (such as, e.g. colour) between two medicinal products which are otherwise identical and (b) the substitution of one product for another does not have any adverse effect on patient safety. Another interpretation may leave room for a partitioning of the markets and seems difficult to reconcile with Articles 34 and 36 TFEU.

Also, the conclusions drawn by the CJEU from its *Delfarma*[8] judgment are surprising. The rebranding of a generic medicinal product as a reference medicinal product would *de facto* not be possible if the CJEU's observation in paragraph 72 must be interpreted as meaning that the condition of objective necessity can *never* be fulfilled when the reference product has a marketing authorisation in the importing Member State. The reason for this is that the status of a 'reference product' (almost always) implies a marketing authorisation in the importing Member State. However, even though it may (in theory) be possible to obtain a parallel import licence under the trade mark of the generic product, other circumstances may exist in the importing Member State which make the rebranding of the product as a reference (originator) product objectively necessary. In accordance with the CJEU's case law, the 'objective necessity' can take various forms, including national provisions, (prescriptive) practices and/or consumer protection rules that prevent the use, in the importing Member State, of the trade mark used in the exporting Member State.[9] A restrictive interpretation of paragraph 72 is also difficult to reconcile with both paragraphs 69 to 71 and 73 and the operative part of the judgment, which indicate that national courts must still verify whether the five BMS conditions have been satisfied.

In the *Novartis v Impexeco* case, the Brussels Court of Appeal issued a ruling on 10 June 2024[10]. With reference to the *Impexeco* judgment, the Court decided that Impexeco was not able to prove an objective necessity to rebrand the imported product with the trade mark of the reference (originator) product. The Court did not come to this conclusion on the basis of a mere finding that the reference product had a marketing authorisation in Belgium (cf. para. 72)

---

7 CJEU, Case C-201/94, 12 November 1996, *The Queen v The Medicines Control Agency*, ECLI:EU:C:1996:432, para. 26.

8 CJEU, Case C-387/18, 3 July 2019, *Delfarma*, ECLI:EU:2019:556.

9 Cf. e.g. CJEU, 12 October 1999, C-379/97, *Upjohn*, ECLI:EU:C:1999:494, para. 43.

10 Other judgments in a similar factual context are the decisions of the Brussels Court of Cessations of 23 May 2023 (A/21/00684) and of 23 May 2024 (A/23/03788).

but assessed whether other circumstances existed on the Belgian market which made the rebranding of the product objectively necessary.[11]

[11] Under current Belgian legislation, for example, advertising by the holder of a parallel import licence must be limited to '*the economic aspects of the medicinal product concerned or to advertising whose sole purpose is to recall the name of the medicinal product*.' Both the Belgian Supreme Court (Cour de Cassation) and the Brussels Court of Appeal have found that, if the name of the parallel imported product is not known on the Belgian market, a parallel importer is *de facto* prevented from carrying out any promotion for that product under its original name (since reminder advertising is not possible or at least not useful when the name is not known on the Belgian market). Consequently, it is objectively necessary for the parallel importer to use the name of the reference product in order to gain effective access to the Belgian market (Cass. 7 November 2016, C.14.0507.N/1; Court of Appeal Brussels, 18 March 2014, *IEFbe* 843, nr. 2013/AR/164). In the *Novartis v Impexeco* case, however, the Court of Appeal decided that, in view of the specific circumstances of the case (and *inter alia* the fact that the generic name 'Letrozol Sandoz' was known on the Belgian market), this argument could not be accepted.

Court of Justice 17 November 2022

On striking a balance between free movement of goods in the European internal market, the essential function of trade marks and the safety of medical products

Case C-224/20

Summary and analysis by Louise Thorning Ahle[1]

Parties:

Merck Sharp & Dohme BV
Merck Sharp & Dohme Corp.
MSD Danmark ApS

v

Abacus Medicine A/S

and

Novartis AG

v

Abacus Medicine A/S

and

Novartis AG

v

Abacus Medicine A/S

and

Novartis AG

v

Paranova Danmark A/S

and

H. Lundbeck A/S

v

Paranova Danmark A/S

and

MSD Danmark ApS

---

1 Louise Thorning Ahle a Senior Attorney at the IP firm Zacco in Denmark.

MSD Sharp & Dohme GmbH
Merck Sharp & Dohme Corp.

v

2CARE4 ApS

and

Ferring Lægemidler A/S

v

Paranova Danmark A/S

1. Background and History

In recitals 2, 3, 11, 12, 29 and 33 of Directive 2011/62/EU of the European Parliament and of the Council of 8 June 2011 amending Directive 2001/83 (OJ 2011 L 174, p. 74), it is stated that:

> *'There is an alarming increase of medicinal products detected in the Union which are falsified in relation to their identity, history or source. Those products usually contain sub-standard or falsified ingredients, or no ingredients or ingredients, including active substances, in the wrong dosage thus posing an important threat to public health.*
>
> *Past experience shows that such falsified medicinal products do not reach patients only through illegal means, but via the legal supply chain as well. This poses a particular threat to human health and may lead to a lack of trust of the patient also in the legal supply chain. Directive [2001/83] should be amended in order to respond to this increasing threat.'*

The Maritime and Commercial Court, Denmark (in Danish: Sø- og Handelsretten) requested a preliminary ruling under Article 267 TFEU. The request stemmed from seven cases between, on the one hand, manufacturers of medicinal products, namely Merck Sharp & Dohme BV, Merck Sharp & Dohme Corp., MSD Danmark ApS, Novartis AG, H. Lundbeck A/S, MSD Sharp & Dohme GmbH and Ferring Lægemidler A/S, proprietors of trade marks under which the medicinal products they produced were sold, and, on the other hand, parallel importers of pharmaceutical products, namely Abacus Medicine A/S, Paranova Danmark A/S and 2CARE4 ApS, concerning the importation into Denmark of medicinal products placed on the market in other Member States by those manufacturers.

The disputes in the main proceedings concerned parallel imported pharmaceuticals, repackaged in new outer packaging and made available to the market in Denmark. Some of the disputes in the main proceedings were related to the manufacturer's registered trade marks being affixed to the new packaging. In other disputes the mark had been replaced by a new product name, although it was still indicated on the packaging that the medicinal product within corresponded to that marketed by the trade mark proprietor under its trade mark and contained blister packs which bore that mark. The new leaflet accompanying the medicinal product in question also indicated that that product corresponded to that sold by the proprietor under its trade mark.[2]

The medical companies claimed that under trade mark law the trade mark proprietors had the right to oppose the repackaging of the medicinal products in new packaging. The parallel importers disagreed and argued that repackaging was necessary and therefore lawful.

Thus, the central question was whether the pharmaceutical companies could oppose repackaging by the parallel importers. This would compel the parallel importers to market the products in Denmark using relabelled original outer packaging, replacing the package leaflet accompanying the medicinal products and affixing a new unique identifier and a replacement anti-tampering device.[3]

Taking the view, in these circumstances, that the disputes in the main proceedings raised questions of interpretation of EU law, the Sø- og Handelsretten (Maritime and Commercial Court, Denmark) decided to stay the proceedings and to refer the following questions to the Court of Justice for a preliminary ruling:

> *'(1) Must Article 15(2) of [Directive 2015/2436] and Article 15(2) of [Regulation 2017/1001] be interpreted as meaning that a trade mark proprietor may oppose further commercialisation of a medicinal product which a parallel importer has repackaged in new external packaging to which the trade mark has been reaffixed, where:*
>
> *(a) the importer is able to achieve packaging which may be marketed [in,] and gain effective access to[,] the market of the Member State of importation by breaking the original external packaging in order to affix new labels to the inner packaging and/or replace the package leaflet and then reseal the original external packaging with a new device to verify whether the packaging has been tampered with, in accordance with Article 47a of [Directive 2001/83] and Article 16 of [Delegated Regulation 2016/161]?*
>
> *(b) the importer is not able to achieve packaging which may be marketed [in,] and gain effective access to[,] the market of the Member State of importation by breaking the original external packaging in order to affix new labels to the inner packaging and/or replace the package leaflet and then reseal the original external packaging with a new device to verify whether the packaging has*

---

[2] Para. 36 of the annotated judgment.

[3] Para. 39 of the annotated judgment.

been tampered with, in accordance with Article 47a of [Directive 2001/83] and Article 16 of [Delegated Regulation 2016/161]?

(2) Must [Directive 2001/83], including, in particular, Article 47a and point (o) of Article 54, be interpreted as meaning that a new device to verify whether the packaging has been tampered with ("anti-tampering device"), affixed to the original packaging of the medicinal products (in connection with additional labelling after the packaging has been opened in such a way that the original anti-tampering device has been fully or partially covered and/or removed), within the meaning of Article 47a(1)(b), is "equivalent as regards the possibility to verify the authenticity, identification and to provide evidence of tampering [with] the medicinal product" and, within the meaning of Article 47a(1)(b)(ii), "is equally effective in enabling the verification of authenticity and identification of medicinal products and in providing evidence of tampering with medicinal products", where the packaging of the medicinal products [...] displays visible signs that the original anti-tampering device has been tampered with, or [...] that can be established by touching the product, including:

- *(a) through mandatory verification of the integrity of the anti-tampering device carried out by the manufacturers, wholesalers, pharmacists and persons authorised or entitled to supply medicinal products to the public (see Article 54a(2)(d) of [Directive 2001/83] and Article 10(b) and Articles 25 and 30 of [Delegated Regulation 2016/161]), or*
- *(b) after the packaging of the medicinal products has been opened, for example by a patient?*

(3) If the answer to Question 2 is in the negative:

Must Article 15 of [Directive 2015/2436], Article 15 of [Regulation 2017/1001] and Articles 36 and 34 TFEU, then be interpreted as meaning that repackaging in new external packaging is objectively necessary for effective access to the market of the State of importation, where it is not possible for the parallel importer to affix additional labelling and reseal the original packaging in accordance with Article 47a of [Directive 2001/83], that is to say without the packaging of the medicinal products [...] displaying visible signs that the original anti-tampering device has been tampered with, or [...] that can be established by touching the product, as described in Question 2, in a manner which is not in accordance with Article 47a?

(4) Must [Directive 2001/83] and [Delegated Regulation 2016/161] in conjunction with Articles 34 and 36 TFEU and Article 15(2) of [Directive 2015/2436 and Article 15(2) of Regulation 2017/1001], be interpreted as meaning that a Member State (in Denmark [the Medicines Agency]) is entitled to lay down guidelines, in accordance with which, in general, repackaging in new external packaging is to be carried out and it is only on application, in exceptional cases (for example where there is a risk to the supply of the medicinal product), that additional labelling and resealing may be

permitted to be carried out by attaching new security features to the original external packaging, or is the Member State's issuing and observance of such guidelines incompatible with Articles 34 and 36 TFEU and/or Article 47a of [Directive 2001/83] and Article 16 of [Delegated Regulation 2016/161]?

(5) Must Article 15(2) of [Directive 2015/2436] and Article 15(2) of [Regulation 2017/1001], in conjunction with Articles 34 and 36 TFEU, be interpreted as meaning that repackaging in new external packaging carried out by a parallel importer in accordance with the guidelines laid down by a Member State, as referred to in Question 4, must be regarded as necessary for the purposes of the case-law of the Court of Justice of the European Union,

(a) where such guidelines are compatible with Articles 34 and 36 TFEU and the case-law of the [Court of Justice] on parallel imports of medicinal products?

(b) where such guidelines are incompatible with Articles 34 and 36 TFEU and the case-law of the [Court of Justice] on parallel imports of medicinal products?

(6) Must Articles 34 and 36 TFEU be interpreted as meaning that the repackaging of a medicinal product in new external packaging must be objectively necessary for effective access to the market of the importing State, even if the parallel importer has not reaffixed the original trade mark (product name), but instead given the new external packaging a product name which does not contain the trade mark proprietor's product trade mark (de-branding)?

(7) Must Article 15(2) of [Directive 2015/2436] and Article 15(2) of [Regulation 2017/1001] be interpreted as meaning that a trade mark proprietor may oppose further commercialisation of a medicinal product which a parallel importer has repackaged in a new external packaging, in so far as the parallel importer has reaffixed only the trade mark proprietor's product-specific trade mark, but has not reaffixed the other trade marks and/or commercial indications which the trade mark proprietor had affixed to the original external packaging?'

2. Decision

1. Article 9(2) and Article 15 of Regulation (EU) 2017/1001 of the European Parliament and of the Council of 14 June 2017 on the European Union trade mark, and Article 10(2) and Article 15 of Directive (EU) 2015/2436 of the European Parliament and of the Council of 16 December 2015 to approximate the laws of the Member States relating to trade marks, read in conjunction with Articles 34 and 36 TFEU, must be interpreted as meaning that the proprietor of a trade mark is entitled to oppose the marketing, by a parallel importer, of a medicinal product repackaged in new outer packaging to which

that trade mark is affixed where the replacement of the anti-tampering device of the original outer packaging, carried out in accordance with Article 47a(1) of Directive 2001/83/EC of the European Parliament and of the Council of 6 November 2001 on the Community code relating to medicinal products for human use, as amended by Directive 2012/26/EU of the European Parliament and of the Council of 25 October 2012, would leave visible or tangible traces of that original outer packaging having been opened, provided that:

- there is no doubt that those traces of opening are attributable to the repackaging of that medicinal product by that parallel importer; and
- those traces do not cause, on the market of the Member State of importation or on a substantial part of it, such strong resistance from a significant proportion of consumers to the medicinal products repackaged in that way that it would constitute a barrier to effective access to that market.

2. Directive 2001/83, as amended by Directive 2012/26, and Commission Delegated Regulation (EU) 2016/161 of 2 October 2015 supplementing Directive 2001/83, must be interpreted as precluding a Member State from requiring that medicinal products imported in parallel must, in principle, be repackaged in new packaging and that recourse may be had to relabelling and to the affixing of new safety features to the original outer packaging of those medicinal products only on application and in exceptional circumstances, such as, inter alia, a risk of disruption to the supply of the medicinal product concerned.

3. Article 9(2) and Article 15 of Regulation 2017/1001 and Article 10(2) and Article 15 of Directive 2015/2436, read in conjunction with Articles 34 and 36 TFEU, must be interpreted as meaning that a Member State rule which requires that medicinal products imported in parallel must, in principle, be repackaged in new packaging and that recourse may be had to relabelling and to the affixing of new safety features to the original outer packaging of those medicinal products only on application and in exceptional circumstances does not impede the exercise by a trade mark proprietor of his or her right to oppose the marketing by a parallel importer of a medicinal product repackaged in new outer packaging to which that mark is affixed.

4. Article 9(2) and Article 15(2) of Regulation 2017/1001 and Article 10(2) and Article 15(2) of Directive 2015/2436, read in conjunction with Articles 34 and 36 TFEU, must be interpreted as meaning that the first of the five conditions set out in paragraph 79 of the judgment of 11 July 1996, Bristol-Myers Squibb and Others (C-427/93, C-429/93 and C-436/93, EU:C:1996:282) – according to which the proprietor of a trade mark may legitimately oppose the further marketing in a Member State of a medicinal product bearing that mark and imported from another Member State, where the importer of that medicinal product has repackaged that product and reaffixed that trade mark to the packaging and where such repackaging of that medicinal product in new outer packaging is not objectively necessary for the purposes of its being marketed in the Member State of importation – must be satisfied where the trade mark which

appeared on the original outer packaging of the medicinal product concerned has been replaced by a different product name on the new outer packaging of that medicinal product, provided that the immediate packaging of that product bears that trade mark and/or that new outer packaging refers to that mark.

5. Article 9(2) and Article 15(2) of Regulation 2017/1001 and Article 10(2) and Article 15(2) of Directive 2015/2436 must be interpreted as meaning that the proprietor of a trade mark may oppose the marketing in a Member State by a parallel importer of a medicinal product imported from another Member State which that importer has repackaged in new outer packaging to which he or she has reaffixed the trade mark of the proprietor specific to that product, but not the other trade marks and/or other distinctive signs which appeared on the original outer packaging of that medicinal product, where the presentation of that new outer packaging is in fact liable to damage the reputation of the trade mark or where that presentation does not enable normally informed and reasonably attentive consumers, or enables them only with difficulty, to ascertain whether that medicinal product originates from the proprietor of the trade mark or an undertaking economically linked to him or her or, on the contrary, originates from a third party, thus adversely affecting the function of indicating the origin of the mark.

3. Motivation and Analysis

To provide guidance on the topic, on 18 December 2018 and later in an updated version dated 20 January 2020, the Lægemiddelstyrelsen (Medicines Agency, Denmark) published a document containing questions and answers about safety features on the packaging of medicinal products. These documents included, in the section entitled 'Parallel imports', the following question: '*Would it be against the regulation for a parallel importer to replace the anti-tampering device with another device?*'

The Danish Medicines Agency answered this question as follows:[4]

> '*Yes. The Medicines Agency considers that it is a general rule that parallel importers must repackage the products in new packaging according to the new rules of the regulation. That also follows from the purpose of the new rules of the regulation, including the requirement for an anti-tampering device to be designed in such a way that any opening of, or tampering with, the package can be identified. Parallel importers which open the packaging of medicinal products and break the anti-tampering device for the purpose of placing a Danish package leaflet etc. in the packaging must therefore, in accordance with the new rules of the regulation, repackage the products in new packaging and attach*

4 Para. 41 of the annotated judgment.

> *a new unique identifier and anti-tampering device on the packaging, as well as upload information etc.'*

The European Commission stated in the document titled 'Safety features for medicinal products for human use – Questions and answers version 18' that, *under certain specific conditions*, it is possible for parallel importers 'lawfully' to open the packaging of medicinal products with a view, *inter alia*, to placing a new package leaflet in the packaging and then replacing the original anti-tampering device with a new anti-tampering device, provided this is carried out under the supervision of the competent authorities and provided the new anti-tampering device seals the packaging completely and covers all visible signs of the lawful opening. In addition, the replacement of the anti-tampering device must be carried out in accordance with [good manufacturing practice] for medicinal products and a parallel importer who lawfully opens the packaging of medicinal products and attaches a new anti-tampering device must verify beforehand the authenticity of the unique identifier and the integrity of the anti-tampering device on the original packaging in accordance with Article 47a(1)(a) of Directive 2001/83.

Taking the view that the disputes in the main proceedings raised questions of interpretation of EU law, as already described, the Maritime and Commercial Court decided to stay the proceedings and to refer seven questions to the Court of Justice for a preliminary ruling.

The fourth to seventh questions primarily concern the Regulation on Safety Features, and will not be discussed further here.

First to third preliminary questions

The CJEU pointed out that the proprietor of a trade mark is entitled to oppose the marketing by a parallel importer of a medicinal product repackaged in new outer packaging to which that trade mark is affixed, where the replacement of the anti-tampering device of the original outer packaging would leave visible or tangible traces of the original outer packaging having been opened, provided that:

- there is no doubt that those traces of opening are attributable to the repackaging of that medicinal product by that parallel importer; and
- those traces do not cause, on the market of the Member State of importation or on a substantial part of it, such strong resistance from a significant proportion of consumers to the medicinal products repackaged in that way that it would constitute a barrier to effective access to that market.[5]

---

[5] Para. 79 of the annotated judgment.

The Court took the opportunity to refer to previous trade mark-related case-law for the understanding of Article 9(2) and Article 15(2) of Regulation 2017/1001[6] and Article 10(2) and Article 15(2) of Directive 2015/2436[7], read in conjunction with Articles 34 and 36 TFEU.[8] The previous decision which the Court referred to was the old judgment from 1996, Bristol-Myers Squibb and Others,[9] and in particular the first of the five conditions set out there. The Court stated that the referring court was in essence asking whether the cited articles of EU legislation must be interpreted as meaning that the first of the five conditions set out in paragraph 79, '*proprietor of a trade mark may legitimately oppose the further marketing in a Member State of a medicinal product bearing that trade mark and imported from another Member State, where the importer of that medicinal product has repackaged that product and reaffixed that trade mark to the packaging and where such repackaging of that medicinal product in new outer packaging is not objectively necessary for the purposes of its being marketed in the Member State of importation – must be satisfied where the trade mark which appeared on the original outer packaging of the medicinal product concerned has been replaced by a different product name on the new outer packaging of that medicinal product, provided that the immediate packaging of that product bears that trade mark and/ or that new outer packaging refers to that mark.*' (emphasis added)

In other words, even though the rights of the trade mark proprietor are exhausted when they have brought the medical products into the Internal Market, they do not have to tolerate the product being repackaged without the original trade mark affixed to the new package.

The Court went on to explain the considerations behind the right bestowed on the trade mark proprietor, emphasising that European trade mark legislation should not be (mis)used to hinder the free movement of goods in the internal market:[10] '*The trade mark proprietor's opposition to repackaging, in that it constitutes a derogation from free movement of goods, cannot be accepted if the proprietor's exercise of the rights conferred by a trade mark constitutes a disguised restriction on trade between Member States within the meaning of the second sentence of Article 36 TFEU (see, by analogy, judgment of 17 May 2018, Junek Europ-Vertrieb (C-642/16, EU:C:2018:322, paragraph 25 and the case-law cited). Trade mark rights are not intended to allow their owners to partition national markets and thus promote the retention of price differences which may exist between Member States.*'

---

6 Regulation (EU) 2017/1001 of the European Parliament and of the Council of 14 June 2017 on the European Union trade mark *OJ L* 154, p. 1-99.

7 Directive (EU) 2015/2436 of the European Parliament and of the Council of 16 December 2015 to approximate the laws of the Member States relating to trade marks (recast) (Text with EEA relevance) *OJ L* 336, p. 1-26.

8 Consolidated version of the Treaty on the Functioning of the European Union *OJ C* 326, p. 47-390.

9 Joined cases C-427/93, C-429/93 and C-436/93, 11 July 1996, Bristol-Myers Squibb and Others.

10 Paras. 47-49 of the annotated judgment.

The Court found in paragraph 57 that '*the trade mark proprietor may oppose replacement packaging where the parallel importer is able to reuse the original packaging for the purpose of marketing in the Member State of importation by affixing labels to that packaging.*'[11] However, the trade mark proprietor is entitled to oppose the parallel importer's use of that replacement packaging only on condition that the relabelled medicinal product is able to have effective access to the market concerned.[12]

To address the third consideration, namely the need to prevent the introduction of falsified medicine to the European market, the Court provided guidelines on what visible traces of re-labelling – instead of repackaging – should be acceptable. Here the Court took an opposite point of view to the Danish Medicines Agency, which allowed the safety features to bear traces of the package having been opened (to insert a new pamphlet in the national language into the original package). The Court found that safety features, which are intended to guarantee the authenticity of the medicinal product and the absence of any tampering, may be removed or covered only under strict conditions:[13]
- the safety features in question must be replaced by 'equivalent' safety features,
- the safety features must be equally effective as a verification of the authenticity of the medicinal products,
- the parallel importer must verify – before opening – that the medicinal product concerned is authentic and that it has not been tampered with.

To sum up, professionals must be able to identify that '*those traces of opening are attributable to the repackaging of that medicinal product by a parallel importer. In that regard, the reference on that outer packaging to the repackager provides information to downstream actors in the supply chain as to the possible origin of those traces of opening. That reference, combined with the anti-tampering device and the replacement unique identifier, enables those persons to ensure that the presence of such traces is due to lawful tampering.*'[14]

Repackaging in new packaging must be regarded as objectively necessary where the existing anti-tampering device cannot objectively be replaced by an equivalent device, but the presence of traces of opening is, in itself, insufficient to support the inference that the condition of equivalence has not been satisfied.[15]

The Court then addressed the question of whether a Member State is entitled to set guidelines similar to those laid down by the Danish Medicines Agency,

---

11 Case C-143/00, 23 April 2002, *Boehringer Ingelheim and Others*, para. 49 and the case-law cited.

12 See, to that effect, Case C-143/00, 23 April 2002, *Boehringer Ingelheim and Others*, para. 50.

13 Para. 63 of the annotated judgment.

14 Para. 68 of the annotated judgment.

15 Paras. 68, 70 and 71 of the annotated judgment.

according to which a parallel importer must, as a general rule, repackage imported medicinal products if the original packaging has been damaged. The CJEU concluded that the relevant authority within a Member State cannot require that medicinal products imported in parallel must, in principle, be repackaged in new packaging. Neither the repackaging nor the relabelling of medicinal products imported in parallel should have priority, but should be considered as equivalent ways of meeting the obligations of the parallel importer. Which method to use should therefore be decided on a case-by-case basis.[16]

In other words, the CJEU found that repackaging is not an obligation. Placing an equivalent anti-tampering device must ensure the pack is perfectly resealed and no signs of the original, broken anti-tampering device are visible. This therefore leaves room for relabelling instead of repackaging – a measure that will tend to be regarded by the trade mark proprietor as less intrusive and drastic measure. It was also pointed out that the trade mark proprietor may oppose repackaging if the parallel importer is able to reuse the original packaging for the purpose of marketing in the Member State of importation, by affixing labels to that packaging and on condition that the medicinal product is able to have effective access to the market. Effective market access for the parallel importer can also be obtained by re-labelling.

* *
*

The decision in Case C 224/20 Merck Sharp & Dohme etc. is a perfect example of how the CJEU manages to balance the objectives of free movement of goods in the European internal market, the essential function of trade marks and the safety of medical products. Each of the objectives is taken into account with none prevailing, and all the parties concerned – the parallel importer, the trade mark proprietor and the consumer – must show some flexibility to achieve the balance represented by relabelled medicine products.

A practical impact of the decision on trade mark holders in the pharmaceutical industry is that it provides clarity regarding the extent of their rights when dealing with parallel imports. While they retain the right to object to repackaging in certain cases, they must accept that some modifications are necessary to meet public health and safety standards in the importing country.

Further, trade mark holders will have an opportunity to review repackaging practices and ensure that their products are not being altered in a way that could damage their reputation or cause confusion among consumers.

At the same time the decision strengthens the position of parallel importers by confirming that they can modify packaging to comply with national regulations

---

[16] Para. 78 of the annotated judgment.

without necessarily infringing trade mark rights. However, they must meet stringent conditions to justify such modifications, particularly in ensuring that any changes are limited to what is necessary for regulatory compliance.

However, clearer guidelines on when and how parallel importers can modify packaging to comply with local health and safety laws while respecting trade mark rights are desirable.

Court of Justice 17 November 2022

On enforcement proceedings in trade mark cases, identifying the goods covered by the judicial decision, fair trial, rights of defence and equality of arms

Case C-175/21

Summary and Analysis by Barbara Załęcka-Wysocka[1]

Parties:

Harman International Industries Inc.

v

AB S.A.

1. Background and History

The subject in dispute in the main proceedings was the infringement by the Polish company AB S.A. ('AB') of several EU trade marks registered to Harman International Industries Inc. ('Harman').

Harman, an American producer of products bearing EU trade marks, initiated infringement proceedings against AB, which had been distributing Harman products in Poland that it had purchased from a supplier other than the distributor authorised by Harman.

Harman argued that it had not previously consented to marketing within the EEA.

AB contended that trade mark rights had been exhausted because Harman had marketed or had consented to the products being marketed in the EEA. AB relied on a declaration from its supplier, but did not have any other evidence in support of its position.

The referring court observed that the marking systems used by Harman were insufficient to identify the destination market for each of the products. To ascertain whether a product was destined for the EEA market it would be necessary to review Harman's database.

The referring court reasoned that AB could theoretically seek to obtain from its supplier information as to the identity of the sellers involved upstream in the

1 Barbara Załęcka-Wysocka is an associate at Wardyński & Partners law firm, Poland.

distribution chain. The court acknowledged, however, that suppliers were not usually disposed to disclose sources of supplies so not to lose sales, and that it was unlikely that AB would be able to obtain that type of information.

Against this background, the referring court was in doubt as to the compliance with EU law of a judicial practice by which the operative part of a decision upholding an action for the infringement of an EU trade mark was drafted in general terms which left it to the enforcement authority to determine to which products the decision applied. In this regard the referring court considered that in the context of national enforcement procedures, the defendant was confronted with a number of obstacles in law to the possibility of successfully contesting the measures ordered and had only limited procedural guarantees.

The question that was referred to the CJEU was:

> *'Must the second sentence of Article 36 TFEU, read in conjunction with Article 15(1) of Regulation (EU) 2017/1001 of the European Parliament and of the Council of 14 June 2017 on the European Union trade mark, and in conjunction with the second sentence of Article 19(1) of the Treaty on European Union, be interpreted as precluding the practice of the national courts of the Member States, which is that the courts:*
>
> – *when upholding claims by a proprietor of an EU trade mark to prohibit the importation, putting on the market, offering, advertising of goods bearing the EU trade mark, to order their withdrawal from the market or to order their destruction;*
> – *when ruling, in protective proceedings relating to the seizure of products bearing an EU trade mark, refer in their rulings to "goods which have not been put on the market within the [EEA] by the right holder or with its consent", with the result that it is left to the enforcement authority, in view of the general wording of the ruling, to determine which items bearing the EU trade mark are subject to the injunctions and prohibitions granted (that is to say, which items have not been put on the market within the European Economic Area by the right holder or with its consent) which basis that determination on the statement of the right holder or tools provided by it (including its IT tools and databases), while the possibility of challenging the aforementioned findings of the enforcement authority before a court in declaratory proceedings is excluded or limited by the nature of the legal remedies available to the defendant in protective proceedings and in enforcement proceedings?'*

2. Decision

Article 15(1) of Regulation (EU) 2017/1001 of the European Parliament and of the Council of 14 June 2017 on the European Union trade mark, read in combination with the second sentence of Article 36 TFEU, Article 47 of the Charter of Fundamental Rights of the European Union and Directive 2004/48/EC of the European Parliament and of the Council of 29 April 2004 on the enforcement of intellectual property rights, must be interpreted as not precluding a judicial practice by which the operative part of the decision upholding an action for infringement of an EU trade mark is drafted in terms which, owing to their general nature, leaves it to the authority with competence to enforce that decision to determine the products to which that decision applies, provided that, in the context of the enforcement procedure, the defendant is permitted to contest the determination of the products covered by that procedure and that a court may examine and decide, in compliance with the provisions of Directive 2004/48, which products have in fact been placed on the market in the EEA by the proprietor or with its consent.

3. Motivation and Analysis

At the outset, the CJEU clarified that the question comprised three parts, namely:

1. the exhaustion of rights conferred by a trade mark and the requirements flowing from the protection of the free movement of goods;
2. the requirements that must be satisfied, in accordance with Directive 2004/48, by the measures, procedures, and remedies necessary to ensure the enforcement of intellectual property rights;
3. the obligation, for the Member States, to establish the remedies in law necessary to ensure effective judicial protection in an area to which EU law applies, and to guarantee a fair hearing, in accordance with Article 47 of the Charter.

With respect to the first part – exhaustion of rights to a trade mark – the CJEU recalled the principles relating to this issue, in particular, that:
- the seller alleging exhaustion of trade mark rights against whom an infringement action is brought by the proprietor of an EU trade mark, bears, in principle, the burden of proving that the applicable conditions have been satisfied, i.e. that the products bearing the mark were marketed in the EEA by that proprietor or with the consent of the proprietor[2], lies with the proprietor;
- the burden of proof in that regard is reversed in the seller's favour where it is liable to permit the proprietor to partition national markets and, thus, help

[2] Para. 50 of the annotated decision.

to maintain price differences between Member States; in particular, this is the case where there is an exclusive distribution system[3];

- the proprietor of a trade mark is not, however, required to adopt a marking system for products that permits it to be established, for each product, whether it was destined for the EEA market.[4]

As to the second part, the CJEU pointed out that:

- the procedural aspects of compliance with intellectual property rights, are governed, in principle, by national law[5];
- any national procedure relating to an action for the infringement of an EU trade mark must, however, comply with Directive 2004/48.[6]

The CJEU found that the procedural aspect referred to in the question of the national court was not governed by Directive 2004/48, as that Directive did not contain any provision on the formulation of the operative part of judicial decisions relating to an infringement action. That question, therefore, raised the principle of procedural autonomy.[7]

In that regard, and referring to the third part of the question, the CJEU observed that the difficulties with which the defendant could be confronted at the stage of enforcement result from enforcement proceedings brought after the infringement action, and not from the formulation of the operative part of the decision terminating the main proceedings.[8]

Therefore, the CJEU deemed it necessary to examine whether, at the enforcement stage, the limited remedies in law and procedural guarantees that are available to a defendant, under national law, fail to meet the requirements of effective judicial protection imposed by EU law.[9]

In that regard the CJEU referred to the right to an effective remedy provided in Article 47 of the Charter of Fundamental Rights of the European Union, the essence of which is the possibility for the person having that right of accessing a court or tribunal that has authority to ensure respect for the rights guaranteed to that person by EU law and, to that end, to consider all the issues of fact and of law that are relevant for resolving the case before it.[10]

---

[3] Paras. 50 and 51 of the annotated decision.

[4] Paras. 44-49 and 53 of the annotated decision.

[5] Para. 56 of the annotated decision.

[6] Para. 56 of the annotated decision.

[7] Para. 57 of the annotated decision.

[8] Para. 58 of the annotated decision.

[9] Para. 59 of the annotated decision.

[10] Paras. 60 and 61 of the annotated decision.

The CJEU also emphasised that the principle of equality of arms was an integral part of the principle of effective judicial protection and that it implied that each party must be afforded a reasonable opportunity to present its case, which includes evidence, under conditions that do not place it at a substantial disadvantage *vis-à-vis* an opponent, even in the absence of a specific law to that effect.[11]

The CJEU pointed out that it is for the national legal order of each Member State to establish procedural rules for the remedies (principle of procedural autonomy) on condition, however, that those rules are not – in situations governed by EU law – less favourable than in similar domestic situations (principle of equivalence) and that they do not make it impossible in practice or excessively difficult to exercise the rights conferred by EU law (principle of effectiveness).[12]

The CJEU concluded that having regard to the principle of procedural autonomy, EU law could not preclude the judicial practice in the case at issue according to which the operative part of a decision upholding an action for infringement of an EU trade mark is drafted in general terms, provided, however, that the defendant enjoyed the effective judicial protection of the rights that it derived from Articles 34 and 36 TFEU and Article 15(1) of Regulation 2017/1001.[13]

In such a situation, therefore, the defendant should benefit, at the enforcement stage, from all the guarantees of a fair hearing so as to be able effectively to contest the existence of an infringement or threat of an infringement of the exclusive rights of the proprietor of a trade mark and to challenge the seizure of products in respect of which the exclusive rights of the trade mark proprietor have been exhausted and which can therefore freely circulate within the EEA.[14]

Specifically, as to the circumstances mentioned by the referring court that, without access to Harman's database, it was not objectively possible for AB to demonstrate that the products it purchased had been marketed in the EEA by Harman, or with its consent, the CJEU considered that it may be necessary, even when no exclusive distribution is established, for a competent enforcement authority (or the court adjudicating appeals brought against the acts of that authority), to reverse the burden of proof, to the extent that the rule on the burden of proof is liable to permit the proprietor of a trade mark to partition national markets and thus assist the maintenance of price differences between Member States.[15]

* *
*

---

[11] Para. 62 of the annotated decision.

[12] Para. 65 of the annotated decision.

[13] Para. 69 of the annotated decision.

[14] Para. 71 of the annotated decision.

[15] Para. 72 of the annotated decision.

The CJEU permitted a judicial practice by which the operative part of a decision in a matter concerning the exhaustion of trade mark rights was formulated in general terms. As a result, the CJEU accepted that the enforcement authority (a bailiff) was entitled to determine the specific goods to which that decision applied. What is crucial in this regard, however, is the condition set by the CJEU: namely, that a party must be afforded the right during enforcement proceedings effectively to challenge in court a bailiff's decision as to which items are to be seized.

The CJEU did not comment, however, on whether particular provisions of national law cited in the case fulfilled that condition.

National enforcement procedures can provide various solutions in the area discussed. It will therefore be for the national courts to establish whether in particular circumstances the mentioned condition is to be satisfied. If not, a court will need to aim for precision to leave no doubt for the bailiff as to which specific goods a judgment applies.

As an additional issue, it is disappointing that the CJEU did not delve deeper into the subject of an owner of a trade mark partitioning national markets, justifying the reversal of the burden of proof in a case involving exhaustion of trade mark rights.

The CJEU decision is likely to give rise to discussions on these important topics.

COURT OF JUSTICE 22 DECEMBER 2022

ON THE LIABILITY OF AN OPERATOR OF AN ONLINE MARKETPLACE WHERE THIRD PARTIES ADVERTISE COUNTERFEIT GOODS

Joined Cases C-148/21 and C-184/21

Summary and Analysis by Isaline d'Hoop de Synghem and Marie Manhaeve[1]

Parties:

Christian Louboutin

v

Amazon Europe Core Sàrl
Amazon EU Sàrl
Amazon Services Europe Sàrl
Amazon.com Inc.
Amazon Services LLC

1. Background and History

Mr Louboutin, a French designer of luxury footwear and handbags, is famous for his red-soled shoes. He registered the colour red, applied to the outer sole of a high-heeled shoe, as a Benelux and EU trade mark.

Amazon is an operator of an online marketplace where products are sold both directly by Amazon, in its own name and on its own behalf, and indirectly by third-party sellers, to whom Amazon provides an online sales platform. Once sold, the products are shipped either by these third-party sellers or by Amazon, which stores the goods in its distribution centres and dispatches them to customers from its own warehouses.

Amazon's websites showcased advertisements for red-soled shoes, which Mr Louboutin claimed related to goods that had been placed on the market without his authorisation.

In 2019, Louboutin brought two trade mark infringement proceedings against Amazon before the Luxembourg District Court (C-148/21) and the Brussels Companies Court (C-184/21) for the advertising and sale of counterfeit goods, in particular shoes with red soles, by third parties on its websites.

---

1 Marie Manhaeve and Isaline d'Hoop de Synghem are IP/IT lawyers at the Brussels Bar, Belgium.

These actions were based on Article 9(2)(a) of Regulation 2017/1001 of the European Parliament and of the Council of 14 June 2017 on the European Union trade mark.[2]

i) Case C-148/21

In the case before the Luxembourg District Court, Mr Louboutin accused Amazon of playing an active role in the use of a sign identical to his trade mark for goods identical to those for which the Louboutin trade mark was registered, by displaying advertisements relating to goods bearing that identical sign and by stocking, shipping and delivering those goods. Moreover, since the advertisements relating to the infringing goods formed part of Amazon's own commercial communication and Amazon provided assistance to the sellers, in particular regarding how best to present their offers, Louboutin argued that Amazon could not be regarded as a mere website host or neutral intermediary.

Referring to earlier case-law of the Court of Justice,[3] Amazon argued that, as the mere operator of an online marketplace, it could not be held liable for the use of a sign identical to the trade mark at issue by third-party sellers using its online marketplace. Amazon asserted that the inclusion of its logo in third-party advertisements does not imply any endorsement of those advertisements. It further claimed that the ancillary services it provides to third-party sellers cannot justify their offers being considered part of its own commercial communication.

---

2 Reg. (EU) 2017/1001 of the European Parliament and of the Council of 14 June 2017 on the European Union trade mark, (OJ 2017 L 154, p. 1-99). Art. 9(2)(a) Reg. 2017/1001 on the European Union trade mark states: '*Without prejudice to the rights of proprietors acquired before the filing date or the priority date of the EU trade mark, the proprietor of that EU trade mark shall be entitled to prevent all third parties not having his consent from using in the course of trade, in relation to goods or services, any sign where: (a) the sign is identical with the EU trade mark and is used in relation to goods or services which are identical with those for which the EU trade mark is registered; […].*'

3 Amazon referred in particular to several judgments of the Court involving online marketplace operators, such as the eBay/L'Oréal case. In its judgment in this case, the Court ruled that: '*If a sign identical with, or similar to, the proprietor's trade mark is to be "used", within the meaning of Article 5 of Directive 89/104 and Article 9 of Regulation No 40/94, by a third party, that implies, at the very least, that that third party uses the sign in its own commercial communication. In so far as that third party provides a service consisting in enabling its customers to display on its website, in the course of their commercial activities such as their offers for sale, signs corresponding to trade marks, it does not itself use those signs within the meaning of that EU legislation […] the operator of an online marketplace does not "use" – for the purposes of Article 5 of Directive 89/104 or Article 9 of Regulation No 40/94 – signs identical with or similar to trade marks which appear in offers for sale displayed on its site.*' (Case C-324/09, 12 July 2011, *L'Oréal and Others*, paras. 102 and 105).

The Luxembourg District Court noted that Amazon's operating method involves a 'hybrid' business model, grouping its own advertisements with those of third-party sellers on its online sales websites, thereby distinguishing it from companies like eBay or Rakuten, which operate solely as online marketplaces without engaging in sales activities themselves. Accordingly, the referring court held that it was necessary to determine:

- In the light of the L'Oréal and Others (C-324/09) judgment, whether this 'hybrid' business model '*may lead to the use, by the operator of those sites, of a sign which is identical with the trade mark at issue owing to the incorporation of third-party sellers' advertisements by displaying that sign in its own commercial communication*';[4]
- If the public's perception may be significant as regards the more or less active role played by the operator of online sales websites incorporating an online marketplace in the publication of advertisements; and
- If '*such an operator should be regarded as using a sign which is identical with a protected trade mark if it undertakes to ship the goods bearing that sign.*'[5]

Given these questions, the Luxembourg District Court decided to stay the proceedings and to refer the following questions to the Court of Justice for a preliminary ruling:

> '*(1) Is Article 9(2) of [Regulation 2017/1001] to be interpreted as meaning that the use of a sign identical with a trade mark in an advertisement displayed on a website is attributable to the website operator or to entities economically linked with it owing to the combination on that website of the operator or its economically linked entities' own offers and those of third-party sellers, by the incorporation of those advertisements in the operator's or its economically linked entities' own commercial communication?*
>
> *Is such incorporation strengthened by the fact that:*
> - *the advertisements are presented uniformly on the website?*
> - *the operator's own advertisements and those of economically linked entities and the advertisements of third-party sellers are displayed without distinction as to their origin, but clearly display the logo of the operator or of economically linked entities, in the advertising categories of third-party websites in the form of "pop-ups"?*
> - *the operator or economically linked entities offer a comprehensive service to third-party sellers, including providing assistance in preparing the advertisements and setting selling prices, stocking the goods and shipping them?*
> - *the website of the operator and economically linked entities is designed in such a way as to be presented in the form of shops*

[4] Para. 14 of the annotated judgment.

[5] Para. 16 of the annotated judgment.

> *and labels such as "best sellers", "most sought after" or "most popular", without apparent distinction, at first sight, between the operator's and economically linked entities' own goods and third-party sellers' goods?*

(2) Is Article 9(2) of [Regulation 2017/1001] to be interpreted as meaning that the use of a sign identical with a trade mark in an advertisement displayed on an online store is, in principle, attributable to its operator or to economically linked entities if, in the perception of a reasonably well-informed and reasonably observant internet user, that operator or an economically linked entity has played an active role in the preparation of that advertisement or if that advertisement is perceived as forming part of that operator's own commercial communication?

Is such a perception influenced by:

- *the fact that that operator and/or economically linked entities is a well-known distributor of a vast range of goods, including goods in the category of those featured in the advertisement; or*
- *the fact that the advertisement thus displayed shows a heading in which the service mark of that operator or economically linked entities is reproduced, that mark being well known as a distributor's mark; or*
- *the fact that that operator or economically linked entities offer, together with that display, services traditionally offered by distributors of goods in the same category as that to which the goods featured in the advertisement belongs?*

(3) Must Article 9(2) of [Regulation 2017/1001] be interpreted as meaning that the shipment, in the course of trade and without the consent of the proprietor of a trade mark, to the final consumer of goods bearing a sign identical with the mark, constitutes use attributable to the shipper only if the shipper has actual knowledge that the sign has been affixed to the goods?

Is such a shipper the user of the sign concerned if the shipper itself or an economically linked entity has informed the final consumer that it will undertake the shipment after it or an economically linked entity has stocked the goods for that purpose?

Is such a shipper the user of the sign concerned if the shipper itself or an economically linked entity has previously made an active contribution to the display, in the course of trade, of an advertisement for the goods bearing that sign or has taken the final consumer's order on the basis of that advertisement?'[6]

---

[6] Para. 17 of the annotated judgment.

ii) Case C-184/21

In the case before the Brussels Companies Court, the same arguments as in Case C-148/21 were put forward by Mr Louboutin. Amazon claimed that its publications of the commercial offers of third-party sellers of shoes alleged to be counterfeit on the online marketplaces incorporated in its online sales websites and its handling of the shipment of these goods did not constitute use of the trade mark at issue.

The Brussels Companies Court considered that it was necessary to determine:

- '*in what circumstances the use of an infringing sign in a commercial offer from a third-party seller may be attributed to the operator of an online sales website incorporating an online marketplace*';
- '*whether, and in what circumstances, the perception of the public in relation to that offer must be taken into account in order to determine the attributability of such use*'; and
- '*whether and, if appropriate, in what circumstances the fact that Amazon ships goods bearing a sign which is identical with a trade mark constitutes, in itself, use of that trade mark, which may be attributed to that company, under Article 9(2)(a) of Regulation 2017/1001*'.

In this case as well, given these circumstances, the Brussels Companies Court decided to stay the proceedings and to refer the following questions to the Court of Justice for a preliminary ruling:

> '*(1) Must Article 9(2) of [Regulation 2017/1001] be interpreted as meaning that the use of a sign identical with a trade mark in an advertisement displayed on a website is, in principle, attributable to its operator if, in the perception of a reasonably well-informed and reasonably observant internet user, that operator has played an active part in the preparation of that advertisement or if that advertisement may be perceived by such an internet user as forming part of that operator's own commercial communication?*
>
> *Will such perception be influenced:*
>
> - *by the fact that that operator is a well-known distributor of a wide range of goods, including goods in the category of those featured in the advertisement; or*
> - *by the fact that the advertisement thus displayed presents a heading in which the service mark of that operator is reproduced, that mark being well known as a distributor's trade mark; or*
> - *furthermore, by the fact that, as well as displaying that advertisement, that operator offers services traditionally offered by distributors of goods in the same category as that to which the goods featured in the advertisement belong?*
>
> *(2) Must Article 9(2) of [Regulation 2017/1001] be interpreted as meaning that the shipment, in the course of trade and without the consent of*

the proprietor of a trade mark, to the final consumer of goods bearing a sign identical with the mark constitutes a use attributable to the shipper only if the shipper has actual knowledge that that sign has been affixed to those goods?

Is such a shipper the user of the sign concerned if the shipper itself or an economically linked entity has informed the final consumer that it will undertake the shipment after it or an economically linked entity has stocked the goods for that purpose?

Is such a shipper the user of the sign concerned if the shipper itself or an economically linked entity has previously made an active contribution to the display, in the course of trade, of an advertisement for the goods bearing that sign or has taken the final consumer's order on the basis of that advertisement?'[7]

2. Decision

Article 9(2)(a) of Regulation (EU) 2017/1001 of the European Parliament and of the Council of 14 June 2017 on the European Union trade mark must be interpreted as meaning that the operator of an online sales website incorporating, as well as that operator's own sales offerings, an online marketplace may be regarded as itself using a sign which is identical with an EU trade mark of another person for goods which are identical with those for which that trade mark is registered, where third-party sellers offer for sale, on that marketplace, without the consent of the proprietor of that trade mark, such goods bearing that sign, if a well-informed and reasonably observant user of that site establishes a link between the services of that operator and the sign at issue, which is in particular the case where, in view of all the circumstances of the situation in question, such a user may have the impression that that operator itself is marketing, in its own name and on its own account, the goods bearing that sign. In that regard, the following are relevant: the fact that that operator uses a uniform method of presenting the offers published on its website, displaying both the advertisements relating to the goods which it sells in its own name and on its own behalf and those relating to goods offered by third-party sellers on that marketplace; the fact that it places its own logo as a renowned distributor on all those advertisements; and the fact that it offers third-party sellers, in connection with the marketing of goods bearing the sign at issue, additional services consisting *inter alia* in the storing and shipping of those goods.

7 Para. 21 of the annotated judgment.

3. Motivation and Analysis

i) 'Use' and 'commercial communication' as trade mark law concepts

The Court started by explaining that, according to Article 9(2)(a) of Regulation 2017/1001, an EU trade mark proprietor has the authority to prohibit any third party from using, within the course of trade, any sign which is identical with the registered trade mark, if that use is made for goods or services which are identical with those for which the trade mark is registered.[8]

In this regard, the expression '*using*' is not explicitly defined in the Regulation but the Court specified that, in accordance with its settled case-law, and more particularly the Coty Germany[9] and L'Oréal and Others[10] judgments, the term involves both (i) *active behaviour* and (ii) *direct or indirect control* of the act constituting the use, which include offering the infringing goods, putting them on the market or stocking them for those purposes.[11]

Article 9 of Regulation 2017/1001 is intended to provide the proprietor with a legal mechanism to prevent any unauthorised use of its trade mark by a third party, but only a third party who directly or indirectly controls the act of use and can actually put an end to that use and thus comply with the prohibition.[12] In addition, the use of a sign which is identical or similar to the proprietor's trade mark by a third party implies, at the very least, that that third-party uses the sign in its *own* commercial communication.[13]

As such, the Court held that, with regard to the operator of an online marketplace, *the use* of signs which are identical with or similar to trade marks in sales offers displayed on that marketplace *is made only by the sellers* who are customers of that operator and *not by the operator itself, if* the latter does not use that sign in its own commercial communication. Simply facilitating the technical requirements for the use of a sign and receiving compensation for such services does not imply a use of the sign by the service provider, even if it aligns with its own financial interests.[14] As such, when an online marketplace operator

---

[8] This concerns the essential function of the trade mark, which is to guarantee in particular to the consumers the provenance of the good or service. See to that effect case C-179/15, 3 March 2016, *Daimler*, para. 26.

[9] Case C-567/18, 2 April 2020, *Coty Germany*, para. 40.

[10] Case C-324/09, 12 July 2011, *L'Oréal and Others*, paras. 102 and 103.

[11] Art. 9(3) of Reg. 2017/1001 enumerates in a non-exhaustive manner the types of use that the trade mark proprietor can prohibit and refers only to *active* conduct by the third party.

[12] Case C-567/18, 2 April 2020, *Coty Germany*, para. 38.

[13] Para. 29 of the annotated judgment. A person may thus allow its customers to use signs which are identical or similar to trade marks without itself using those signs. See in that regard Case C-567/18, 2 April 2020, *Coty Germany*, para. 39.

[14] Paras. 30-31 of the annotated judgment.

offers a storage service to the third-party sellers active on its marketplace, only the third-party sellers will be considered to make use of a sign if the operator is unaware of the trademark infringement and if it stores the goods without pursuing the aim of marketing or offering those goods itself.[15]

Although the Court referred to this earlier case-law, a clear distinction was made between the earlier cases and the facts in the annotated judgment. Prior to the annotated judgment, the Court had not been asked about the effect of the fact that the online sales website in question incorporates, in addition to the online marketplace, sales offers from the operator of that site itself.

It was precisely in light of this context that the referring courts had raised the issue of that effect and the significance of the perception of the users of the website in question and of other circumstances, such as (i) the fact that the operator presents the sales offers published on its website in a uniform manner, displaying at the same time its own advertisements and those of third-party sellers, (ii) the fact that the operator attaches its own logo as a renowned distributor to all those advertisements, and (iii) the fact that the operator offers additional services to third-party sellers, such as support in the presentation of their advertisements and the storing and shipping of their goods.[16]

The Court then addressed the definition of the '*commercial communication*'[17] of an undertaking, explaining that it encompasses any communication directed towards third parties aimed at promoting its business activities, goods or services or indicating the exercise of such activities. Furthermore, the use of a sign in the undertaking's own commercial communication implies that that sign is perceived by third parties as an integral part of the communication and, consequently, a part of that undertaking's activity.[18]

The Court referred to cases C-324/09, *L'Oréal and Others* and Case C-119/10, *Frisdranken Industrie Winters*, where it ruled that, when the service provider uses a sign which is identical or similar to the trade mark of another person in order to endorse products marketed by one of its customers through said service, that provider itself makes use of that sign if it uses it in such a way that

---

[15] Para. 32 of the annotated judgment. See to that effect Case C-567/18, 2 April 2020, *Coty Germany*, paras. 45 and 53. It should be noted that in the Coty case, (i) the operator was unaware of the fact that the goods at issue infringed a trade mark right, (ii) the operator had not itself offered the goods concerned for sale or put them on the market, (iii) the operator did not intend to do so itself and (iv) the goods were dispatched by external service providers.

[16] Para. 35 of the annotated judgment.

[17] Although the Court largely differs from the Advocate General in the judgment, they agree on the interpretation as far as this definition is concerned: see Opinion of Advocate General M. Szpunar of 2 June 2022, paras. 55-56.

[18] Para. 39 of the annotated judgment.

it establishes *a link* between the sign and the services it offers.[19] As such, the Court had ruled that a service provider cannot be considered as using a sign identical or similar to another person's trade mark if the service it offers is not comparable to one aimed at promoting goods bearing that sign. Furthermore, if the service does not establish a link between the sign and the service provided, particularly because the service provider is not readily apparent to consumers, any association between the services and the sign in question is excluded.[20]

On the other hand, the Court affirmed that such a link does exist when the operator of an online marketplace employs an Internet referencing service using a keyword identical to another person's trade mark to advertise goods bearing that trade mark, which are offered for sale by its customers on the online marketplace. This form of advertising establishes a clear association in the minds of Internet users between the trade-marked goods and the option to purchase them through the marketplace. Consequently, the proprietor of the trade mark has the right to prohibit that operator from such use if the advertising infringes the trade mark rights, if it fails to make it sufficiently clear to well-informed and reasonably observant Internet users or makes it difficult for them to discern whether the goods originate from the trade mark proprietor, an economically affiliated entity of that proprietor, or a third party.[21]

ii) The impact and significance of the perception of the users of the website in question

From the above, the Court stated that to ascertain whether the operator of an online sales website incorporating an online marketplace itself makes use of a sign identical to another person's trade mark, as seen in advertisements for products sold by third-party sellers on the platform, it is essential to determine if a well-informed and reasonably observant user of the website perceives a link between the services provided by the operator and the sign in question[22] and might believe that the operator is marketing, in its own name and on its own account, the goods for which the sign in question is being used.[23]

The Court pointed out, firstly, that the above can be established by examining the *manner in which the advertisements are presented*, both individually and as

---

[19] Case C-324/09, 12 July 2011, *L'Oréal and Others*, para. 92 and Case C-119/10, 15 December 2011, *Frisdranken Industrie Winters*, para. 32.

[20] Case C-119/10, 15 December 2011, *Frisdranken Industrie Winters*, para. 33.

[21] Case C-324/09, 12 July 2011, *L'Oréal and Others*, paras. 93 and 97.

[22] Para. 43 of the annotated judgment.

[23] Specifically, if the operator of an online sales platform categorises various offerings, whether from itself or a third party, under labels like 'bestsellers', 'most sought after', or 'most popular', especially with the intention of promoting certain products, it is likely to reinforce the perception of the informed and attentive user that these promoted goods are being sold by the operator itself. Paras. 43 and 48 of the annotated judgment.

a whole, on the website in question. When an operator of an online sales website incorporating an online marketplace uses a uniform method of presenting both its own advertisements and those of third-party sellers, it is difficult for a well-informed and reasonably observant user to make a distinction between those offers. This distinction is made even more difficult when such an operator places its own logo as a renowned distributor on its own website and on all those advertisements. These methods of presentation may establish a link, in the eyes of the user, between that sign and the services provided by that same operator.[24]

Secondly, the Court stated that the *nature and scope of the services* provided by the operator of an online sales website incorporating an online marketplace are also important in assessing whether a well-informed and reasonably observant user could establish a link between that operator's services and the signs placed on goods and in advertisements of third-party sellers. In particular, when an operator provides services such as dealing with users' questions relating to the goods or to the storage, shipping and management of returns of the goods, a website user may, according to the Court, have the impression that those goods are being marketed by the operator, in its own name and on its own behalf.[25]

This led the Court to the conclusion that an operator of a 'hybrid' website, i.e. a website that incorporates both its own sales offerings as an online marketplace and those of third-party sellers, can be held directly liable for the promotion and distribution of counterfeit goods, when a well-informed and reasonably observant Internet user establishes a link between the services of that operator and the sign at issue. This is in particular the case where, in view of all the circumstances of the situation in question, such a user may have the impression that that operator itself is marketing, in its own name and on its own account, the goods bearing that sign.[26]

* *
*

In this dispute between Louboutin and Amazon, the Court clarified the interpretation of the concept of 'use' in trade mark law. According to the Court, for trade mark law to refer to 'use', active behaviour is required, and this concept implies at least that the sign is used in the context of the operator's own commercial communication. Signs displayed on online marketplaces are in principle only used by the third-party sellers of the operator of the marketplace, as the operator does not use this sign in the context of its own commercial communication. What is new in this judgment is that the Court introduces '*the perception of the users of the online marketplace*' as a relevant factor for determining whether the sign in question is used in the marketplace operator's own commercial communication.

---

[24] Paras. 49-52 of the annotated judgment.

[25] Para. 53 of the annotated judgment.

[26] Para. 54 of the annotated judgment.

In its defence, Amazon cited previous rulings on this question. However, the crucial difference between previous case-law and the annotated judgment lies in the fact that, in those rulings, the operator of the online marketplace did not also offer products in its own name.[27] In other words, in those previous cases, it was clear to website users that a party other than the operator of the online marketplace was actually selling the products. Conversely, in the annotated judgment, Amazon was not only offering an online marketplace but simultaneously and on the same website presenting its own sales offers. Additionally, Amazon's logo was used in both third-party sales offers and its own offers, and the company did not merely act as a facilitator by offering its platform as a sales venue. Consumers could ask Amazon questions about third-party products and Amazon offered the option of handling shipping and managing returns of third-party products.

The above mode of presentation of advertisements and the nature and scope of the services gave consumers the impression that Amazon itself was offering the products offered by third parties, leading to the assumption of a link between Amazon and the infringing sign.

The CJEU did not issue a judgment on Amazon's liability but clarified the factors to be considered by the national courts when determining liability. Thus, the existence or non-existence and concurrence of these elements provides guidance. These factors include (i) whether the online marketplace uses a uniform method of presenting the offers published on its website, displaying both the advertisements relating to goods it sells in its own name and on its own behalf and those relating to goods offered by third-party sellers on that marketplace, (ii) whether it places its own logo as a renowned distributor on all those advertisements and (iii) whether it offers third-party sellers, in connection with the marketing of goods bearing the trade mark at issue, additional services such as the storing and shipping of the infringing goods.

This judgment confirms the tendency to attribute more extensive liability to intermediaries and represents an important new instrument for trade mark owners to protect their trade marks against product counterfeiting. It clears the way not only to compel platform operators to delete the corresponding advertisements but also to claim damages directly from the platform operator for trade mark infringements. The ruling may contribute to a more active role being played by online marketplaces in the fight against counterfeiting and platforms will certainly need to adapt the way they present their advertisements to ensure that consumers are clearly able to distinguish between products sold by the platform itself and those offered by third-party sellers.

---

27 This means that, prior the annotated judgment, the court had not been asked about the effect of an online sales site incorporating, in addition to the online marketplace, sales offers from the operator of that site itself.

Court of Justice 16 February 2023

On conditions for the protection of a component part of a complex product, the concepts of 'visibility' and 'normal use', and the novelty, individual character and visibility of a component part of a complex product during normal use

Case C-472/21

Summary and analysis by Huib Berendschot[1]

Parties:

Monz Handelsgesellschaft International mbH & Co. KG

v

Büchel GmbH & Co. Fahrzeugtechnik KG

1. Background and History

This case relates to a request of the Bundesgerichtshof for a preliminary ruling concerning the interpretation of Article 3(3) and (4) of Directive 98/71/EC of the European Parliament and of the Council of 13 October 1998 on the legal protection of designs, in particular requirements relating to visibility of design ('the Directive').[2]

The request was made in proceedings between Monz Handelsgesellschaft International mbH & Co. KG ('Monz') and Büchel GmbH & Co. Fahrzeugtechnik KG ('Büchel') concerning an application for a declaration of invalidity of a registered national design filed by Büchel.

From 3 November 2011 Monz was the holder of a design registered at the Deutsches Patent- und Markenamt (German Patent and Trade Mark Office, Germany; 'the DPMA') relating to 'saddles for bicycles or motorcycles'. The design was registered with a single representation showing the underside of a saddle as follows:

[1] Huib Berendschot is an attorney at law at AKD, the Netherlands, and works within the Intellectual Property & Technology practice group.

[2] Dir. 98/71/EC of the European Parliament and of the Council of 13 October 1998 on the legal protection of designs *OJ L* 289, 28.10.1998, p. 28-35.

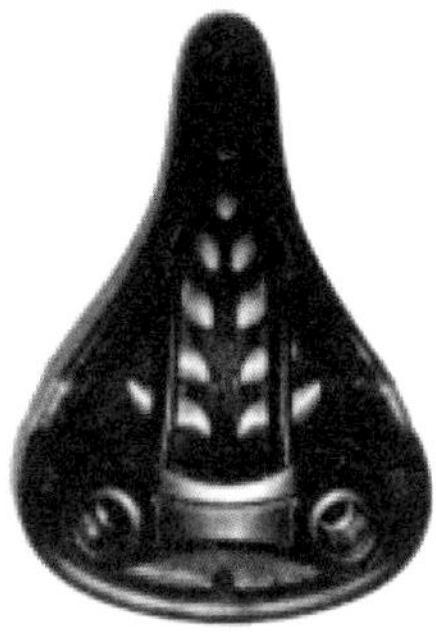

On 27 July 2016, the German company Büchel filed an application with the DPMA for a declaration of invalidity of the design of Monz. Büchel claimed that the registered design of Monz did not meet the requirements for legal protection as a design under paragraph 4 of the DesignsGesetz ('DesignsG').

Paragraph 4 of DesignsG states that a design applied to or incorporated in a product which constitutes a component part of a complex product is to be considered to be new and to have individual character only if the component part, once it has been incorporated into the complex product, remains visible during normal use of the product and to the extent that those visible features of the component part fulfil in themselves the requirements as to novelty and individual character.

Büchel argued that the design applied to a saddle, which is a component part of a complex product such as a bicycle, was not visible during normal use of the product.[3]

On 10 August 2018, the DPMA rejected Büchel's application for a declaration of invalidity, holding that there were no grounds for excluding the design at issue from protection under paragraph 4 of DesignsG. The DPMA considered that, although the bicycle saddle to which the design was applied was indeed a '*component part of a complex product*,' the component part nevertheless remained visible during normal use of the complex product.

The DPMA took the view that normal use of such a product also covered '*the disassembly and reassembly of the saddle for purposes other than maintenance, servicing or repair work*,' although the latter was included in an exhaustive list of uses excluded from that concept, within the meaning of paragraph 1(4) of DesignsG.

Following an appeal by Büchel, on 27 February 2020 the Bundespatentgericht (Federal Patent Court, Germany; 'BPG') declared the design of Monz which was

3 Para. 13 of the annotated judgment.

at issue in the proceedings invalid on the ground that it did not meet the requirements of novelty and individual character.[4]

The BPG stated (in accordance with para. 4 of DesignsG) that only component parts which remain '*visible, as component parts of the complex product, after they have been incorporated in it*' are automatically eligible for the legal protection of designs. On the contrary, a component part which is visible only as a result of or at the time of its separation from a complex product cannot be regarded as satisfying the condition of visibility and cannot, therefore, benefit from that protection.

In addition, the BPG took the view that only riding and getting on and off a bicycle are normal use within the meaning of paragraph 1(4) of DesignsG. According to the BPG, during such use, the underside of the saddle is not visible either to the end user or to a third party.

Monz then brought a further appeal – on a point of law and against the decision of the BPG – before the Bundesgerichtshof (Federal Court of Justice, Germany; 'BGH' – the referring court). The BGH considered that the outcome of the dispute in the main proceedings depended on how the concepts of 'visibility' and 'normal use', within the meaning of Article 3(3) and (4) of the Directive, were to be interpreted.

The BGH stated, first of all, that it shared the view of the BPG that, in accordance with the case law of the CJEU, resulting in particular from the judgment of 20 December 2017, *Acacia and D'Amato*,[5] a bicycle is a complex product and the saddle is a component part of that product.

The BGH considered that, for the purpose of resolving the dispute before it, it was necessary to determine, in the first place, whether the requirement of 'visibility' of a component part, once it has been incorporated into the complex product, during 'normal use' of that product must be assessed by taking into account certain conditions of use of that product or certain observer perspectives or, to the contrary, only the objective possibility of recognising the design applied to the component part integrated in the complex product.[6]

Against that background the BGH noted that, on the one hand, the BPG had concluded that it would be necessary for the component part to remain visible to the end user or to a third party during normal use by the end user of the complex product in which that component part is incorporated. On the other hand, the applicant in the main proceedings had claimed that it is sufficient, in order for a design to be protected, that it can be identified when the component part

---

[4] Para. 15 of the annotated judgment.

[5] Cases C-397/16 and C 435/16, 20 December 2017, *Acacia and D'Amato*, para. 64.

[6] Para. 18 of the annotated judgment.

to which it is applied is integrated in the complex product. It is therefore irrelevant whether the design can easily be observed from a particular 'perspective'.

The BGH then decided to raise the question of the interpretation of Article 3(3) and (4) of the Directive, taking the view that the purpose of those provisions cannot be clearly deduced from the Directive.

Article 3(3) and 3(4) of the Directive, entitled 'Protection requirements', provide as follows:

> '*(3) A design applied to or incorporated in a product which constitutes a component part of a complex product shall only be considered to be new and to have individual character:*
>
> *(a) if the component part, once it has been incorporated into the complex product, remains visible during normal use of the latter, and*
>
> *(b) to the extent that those visible features of the component part fulfil in themselves the requirements as to novelty and individual character.*
>
> *(4) "Normal use" within the meaning of paragraph 3(a) shall mean use by the end user, excluding maintenance, servicing or repair work.*'

The BGH took the view that the contention that a manufacturer who sees no benefit in visibly presenting a design has no interest in invoking the protection of that design is too simplistic, given that the design holder, the manufacturer of the component part and the manufacturer of the complex product are not necessarily one and the same.

It also observed that that contention runs counter to the principle that a design's eligibility for legal protection must already be established at the time of registration of the design concerned. The BGH considered that that supports a strict interpretation of Article 3(3) and (4) of the Directive.

The BGH pointed out that, although the meaning in everyday language of the word 'visible' suggests an objective comprehension referring to the possibility of identifying something, it cannot be inferred from the words 'normal use' that particular forms of observation of the complex product are excluded.

Furthermore, it stated that it is necessary to determine the criteria which are relevant for the purpose of assessing the 'normal use' of a complex product by the end user, within the meaning of Article 3(4) of the Directive.

In that regard, the question arose, in particular, whether, in the context of such an assessment, account should be taken of the use desired by the manufacturer of the component part or of the complex product or only of the customary use of the complex product by the end user.

The BGH considered that the definition of 'normal use' in Article 3(4) of the Directive may be understood as meaning that, in the view of the EU legislature, any use by the end user of the complex product is, as a matter of principle, normal use, subject to the exceptions set out in that provision.

In this context, the BGH stayed the proceedings and referred the following questions to the Court of Justice for a preliminary ruling:

> '*(1) 'is a component part incorporating a design a "visible" component within the meaning of Article 3(3) of the Directive if it is objectively possible to recognise the design when the component is mounted, or should visibility be assessed under certain conditions of use or from a certain observer perspective?*
>
> *(2) if the answer to Question 1 is that visibility under certain conditions of use or from a certain observer perspective is the decisive factor:*
> *(a) when assessing the "normal use" of a complex product by the end user within the meaning of Article 3(3) and (4) of the Directive, is it the use intended by the manufacturer of the component part or complex product that is relevant, or the customary use of the complex product by the end user?*
> *(b) what are the criteria for assessing whether the use of a complex product by the end user constitutes a "normal use" within the meaning of Article 3(3) and (4) of the Directive?'*

2. Decision

Article 3(3) and (4) of Directive 98/71/EC of the European Parliament and of the Council of 13 October 1998 on the legal protection of designs must be interpreted as meaning that the requirement of 'visibility', laid down in that provision, that is to be met in order for a design applied to or incorporated in a product which constitutes a component part of a complex product to be eligible to benefit from the legal protection of designs, must be assessed in the light of a situation of normal use of that complex product, so that the component part concerned, once it has been incorporated into that product, remains visible during such use.

To that end, the visibility of a component part of a complex product during its 'normal use' by the end user must be assessed from the perspective of that user as well as from the perspective of an external observer, and that normal use must cover acts performed during the principal use of a complex product as well as acts which must customarily be carried out by the end user in connection with such use, with the exception of maintenance, servicing and repair work.

3. Motivation and Analysis

As it often does, the CJEU rephrased the question of the referring court, the BGH. It took the view that the BGH was asking, in essence[7]:

- first, whether Article 3(3) and (4) of the Directive must be interpreted as meaning that the requirement of 'visibility', laid down in that provision, that is to be met in order for a design applied to or incorporated in a product which constitutes a component part of a complex product to be eligible to benefit from the legal protection of designs, must be assessed on the basis of certain conditions of use of that complex product or only the objective possibility of recognising the design applied to the component part as integrated in the complex product; and
- second, what the relevant criteria are for determining the 'normal use' of a complex product by the end user.

The CJEU then noted that the questions had been raised in proceedings arising from the application made by Büchel for a declaration that the design at issue in the main proceedings was invalid on the ground that it could not benefit from legal protection as a design since the bicycle saddle, as a component part of a complex product such as a 'bicycle' or 'motorcycle', is not visible during normal use of that complex product.

In the present case, the saddle of a bicycle or motorcycle constituted a component part of a complex product, within the meaning of Article 3(3) of the Directive. A bicycle or motorcycle constituted, in itself, a complex product within the meaning of Article 1(c) of that Directive. A saddle may be replaced permitting disassembly and re-assembly of the bicycle or motorcycle. Without a bicycle or motorcycle, the saddle cannot be subject to normal use.[8]

<u>i) In the first place</u>

The Court stated that it must be borne in mind that, under Article 3(3) of the Directive, read in the light of recital 12 thereof,[9] a design applied to or incorporated in a product which constitutes a component part of a complex product is to be considered to be new and to have individual character only if the component part, once it has been incorporated into the complex product, remains

[7] Para. 32 of the annotated judgment.

[8] See, by analogy, cases C-397/16 and C 435/16, 20 December 2017, *Acacia and D'Amato*, paras. 64-66.

[9] *'[...] protection should not be extended to those component parts which are not visible during normal use of a product, or to those features of such part which are not visible when the part is mounted, or which would not, in themselves, fulfil the requirements as to novelty and individual character; whereas features of design which are excluded from protection for these reasons should not be taken into consideration for the purpose of assessing whether other features of the design fulfil the requirements for protection'.*

visible during normal use of that product (point (a)) and the visible features of the component part fulfil in themselves the requirements as to novelty and individual character (point (b)).[10]

Secondly, it pointed out that it is the appearance of the whole or part of a product which is the subject matter of the legal protection for designs under the Directive.[11]

The CJEU reiterated that prior to the request for a preliminary ruling it had already held that appearance is the decisive element of a design and that the fact that a characteristic of a design is visible constitutes an essential feature of that protection.[12]

In relation to component parts of a complex product the Court had previously stated that, in order for the appearance of the component part of a complex product to be protected as a design, it must, by definition, be visible and defined by features which constitute its particular appearance, namely by particular lines, contours, colours, shapes and texture. That presupposes that the appearance of that component part cannot be completely lost in the product as a whole.[13]

In an interim conclusion the CJEU – referring back to recital 12 of the Directive – then (in para. 41) considered that for a component part incorporated into a complex product to be eligible for protection as a design, that component part must remain visible during normal use of that product. Protection may not be extended to component parts which are not visible during normal use of a product, or to those features of such a part which are not visible when that part is mounted, or which would not, in themselves, fulfil the requirements as to novelty and individual character.[14]

It stated that the limitation of the legal protection of designs to the visible features of the component part concerned is explained by the fact that the appearance of that component part derives exclusively from those features. The protection of designs under the Directive applies only to the characteristics which

---

[10] Para. 35 of the annotated judgment.

[11] Para. 37 of the annotated judgment.

[12] See, to that effect, cases C-361/15 P and C-405/15 P, 21 September 2017, *Easy Sanitary Solutions and EUIPO v Group Nivelles*, paras. 62 and 63, and case C-123/20, 28 October 2021, *Ferrari*, para. 30.

[13] Para. 39 of the annotated judgment. See, to that effect, case C-123/20, 28 October 2021, *Ferrari*, paras. 49 and 50.

[14] Para. 41 of the annotated judgment.

determine the appearance of the whole or part of a product. A visible component part necessarily contributes to the appearance of the complex product.[15]

The Court considered that it is clear from the wording of the Directive that, in order to benefit from the legal protection of designs, the component part, once it has been incorporated into the complex product, must remain visible 'during normal use' of that product.

It therefore concluded that an assessment *in abstracto* of the visibility of the component part incorporated into a complex product, unconnected to any practical use of the product, is not sufficient to allow a component part to benefit from protection as a design under the Directive. The Directive nevertheless does not require a component part that is incorporated into a complex product to remain fully visible the whole time that the complex product is being used.[16]

ii) In the second place

Under Article 3(4) of the Directive, the concept of 'normal use' of a complex product is defined as '*use by the end user, excluding maintenance, servicing or repair work*.' It follows that 'normal use' corresponds to use by the end user. Uses by the end user which form part of the maintenance, servicing or repair of the complex product are expressly excluded.[17]

The Court took the view that it was therefore necessary to determine whether the concept of 'normal use' of a product by the end user, within the meaning of Article 3(4) of the Directive, corresponds to (i) the use intended by the manufacturer or designer of the component part, or to (ii) that intended by the manufacturer or designer of the complex product or to (iii) the customary use of the complex product by the end user.

As regards the first question of the BGH, namely whether the 'normal use' of a complex product corresponds to the use intended by the manufacturer of the component part, to that intended by the manufacturer of the complex product or to the customary use of that product by the end user, the CJEU stated at the outset that, in accordance with Article 3(4) of the Directive, that provision covers the 'normal use' of the complex product by the end user.[18]

---

15 Para. 42 of the annotated judgment. See, by analogy, Cases C-397/16 and C 435/16, 20 December 2017, *Acacia and D'Amato*, para. 73.

16 The Advocate General stated in paras. 33 and 34 of his Opinion of 8 September 2022 that the visibility of a component part incorporated into a complex product, within the meaning of Art. 3(3) of the Directive, read in conjunction with Art. 3(4) thereof, cannot be assessed solely from the perspective of the end user of that product. In that regard, the visibility of such a component part to an external observer must also be taken into consideration.

17 Para. 47 of the annotated judgment.

18 Para. 49 of the annotated judgment.

The CJEU considered that the different language versions of Article 3(3) and (4) of the Directive all indicate that the component part incorporated in a complex product must remain visible during the 'normal' or 'customary' use of that product.

The Court noted the European Commission's observation[19], with regard to the concept of 'normal use', that the EU legislature intended to refer to the customary use of the complex product by the end user, in order to exclude the use of that product at other stages of trade and thus to prevent circumvention of the visibility condition. The assessment of the 'normal use' of a complex product thus cannot be based solely on the intention of the manufacturer of the component part or of the complex product.

As regards the second question of the BGH, i.e. what use of a complex product by the end user constitutes 'normal use' within the meaning of the Directive, the CJEU noted that the fact that that provision does not specify what type of use of such a product is covered by that concept but makes a general reference to the use of such a product by the end user supports a broad interpretation of that concept.

In that regard, in practice, use of a product in its principal function often requires various acts which may be performed before or after the product has fulfilled that principal function, such as storage and transportation.[20] As a result, it must be held that 'normal use' of a complex product, within the meaning of Article 3(4) of the Directive, covers all those acts, with the exception of those expressly excluded by paragraph 4, namely acts relating to maintenance, servicing and repair work.

Accordingly, the CJEU held that 'normal use', within the meaning of Article 3(4) of the Directive, must cover acts relating to the customary use of a product as well as other acts which may reasonably be carried out during such use and which are customary from the perspective of the end user, including those which may be performed before or after the product has fulfilled its principal function, such as storage and transportation.

* *
*

This case concerned a national design and thus dealt with the interpretation of provisions in the Directive. However, terms in the Directive and in the Community Design Regulation ('CDR') must be interpreted in the same way. For a component part of a complex product, an additional requirement for

---

19 Para. 51 of the annotated judgment.

20 See the Advocate General in para. 38 of his Opinion.

protection is that it remains visible during normal use of the complex product (Art. 4(2)(a) CDR; Art. 3(3)(a) Directive). In this ruling about the underside of a bicycle saddle, the CJEU explained what is to be understood by 'normal use' and 'remaining visible'.

i) Part of a product

Before considering the effects in Germany of this decision of the CJEU, we should recall that a part of a product, to qualify for protection, must also be delimited by lines, an outline, colours, shapes or a specific texture. That presupposes that the appearance of that part of the product or that component part of a complex product is capable, in itself, of producing an overall impression and cannot be completely lost in the product as a whole.[21]

ii) End user, external observer and main function

The judgment teaches us two relevant things about the protection of component parts. Their visibility must be judged from the perspective of the end user and an external observer. As to the function, normal use is not limited to the principal function. It includes acts which may be performed before or after the product has fulfilled its principal function, such as storage and transportation.

iii) Referral back to the German courts

Following the judgment of the CJEU, the BGH rendered a decision on 15 June 2023,[22] setting aside the decision of the BPG and requiring the case to be heard and decided on again.

The BGH stated that the visibility of the component and the features of the design embodied in it can also be fulfilled by acts associated with the transport or storage of a bicycle. It found that the BPG had so far only assumed the visibility of the design in such acts in favour of the design owner and would have to make findings in this regard. If necessary, it would also have to examine other acts presented by the parties.

Since the Design Act presumes in favour of the design owner that the requirements for the legal validity of its registered design are met, the applicant must, as a prerequisite for the success of its application, demonstrate and prove the negative fact that the design does not remain visible after the component has been incorporated into the complex object in its normal use. As the party not bearing the burden of proof, it is incumbent on the design owner to substantiate this negative fact as far as it can reasonably be expected to do so by presenting the circumstances in favour of the opposing positive fact. The party with the

---

21 *Case C-123/20, 28 October 2021, Ferrari*, para 50.

22 *ECLI:DE:BGH:2023:150623BIZB31.20.0*

burden of proof must then disprove the circumstances in favour of the positive fact (on the previously recognised set of shapes).[23]

The BPG had so far limited its assessment to what it considered to be the obvious appearance of the design on the underside of a bicycle saddle, without going into a possible use on the underside of a motorbike saddle. Since the design owner had indicated 'motorbike saddles' as a further product, the BPG should also extend its examination to this product if necessary.

To the extent that the BPG affirmed the visibility of the design, it was instructed by the BGH to decide on the second question to be examined, namely whether the visible features of the component itself fulfilled the requirements of novelty and individual character. So far, the BPG had assumed this without examining the support for such a claim.

To date the BPG has not yet rendered a decision, so it is unclear what effect the judgment of the CJEU has on the final outcome.

iv) Reference to the annotated judgment in proceedings in the Netherlands

The CJEU's judgment in Monz v Büchel has been taken into account in a case in the Netherland.

On 11 September 2024, the court of The Hague rendered judgment in a case between Knaap Bikes B.V. and Euro Cycle Company B.V.. The case related to the design of a so-called fat bike, a particular kind of electric bike. Knaap held a Registered Community Design under number 008408629-002, relating to the frame of a bike. Issues as to the visibility of the design were raised in the case.

The court – fully in line with the annotated judgment – considered that normal use includes acts that are performed in the main use of a complex product as well as acts that must usually be performed by the end-user in the context of such use. In the case of a fat bike, the main use is cycling, and acts performed in the context of the main use are – among others – parking the bicycle or walking with the bicycle. The court considered that especially in the latter cases, the frame is (clearly) visible to the end user, but also to an external observer. It held that the design in question met the visibility requirement of Article 4(2) of the CDR.

Before arriving at this conclusion, the court, referring to the *Monz v Büchel* judgment, considered that 'normal use' by the end-user must be assessed from the perspective of that user as well as from the perspective of an external observer, and that normal use must cover acts performed during the principal use of a

---

23 BGH, judgment of 11 January 2018 – I ZR 187/16, GRUR 2018, 832 [juris para. 80] = WRP 2018, 950 – *Ballerina shoe.*

complex product as well as acts which must customarily be carried out by the end user in connection with such use, with the exception of maintenance, servicing and repair work. In fact, the court copied the last sentence of paragraph 56 of the judgment of the CJEU.

To date we therefore have one known example of the application of the *Monz v Büchel* judgment of the CJEU.

Court of Justice 20 April 2023

On the notion of communication to the public in the context of broadcasting of musical works in a means of passenger transport

Joined Cases C-775/21 and C-826/21

Summary and Analysis by Marie Manhaeve[1]

Parties:

Blue Air Aviation SA

v

UCMR – ADA Asociația pentru Drepturi de Autor a Compozitorilor (C-775/21),

and

Uniunea Producătorilor de Fonograme din România (UPFR)

v

Societatea Națională de Transport Feroviar de Călători (SNTFC) 'CFR Călători' SA (C-826/21)

1. Background and History

i) Case C-775/21

Blue Air is a Romanian air transport company that operated aircrafts installed with sound systems and software for the broadcasting of musical works. The Romanian Musical Performing and Mechanical Rights Society ('UCMR') is a collective management organisation that manages music copyrights.

In 2018, the UCMR took legal action against Blue Air on the basis of Article 3(1) of Directive 2001/29.[2] The UMCR sought payment for the alleged communication to the public of musical works on Blue Air's aircrafts without obtaining the necessary licence. The Bucharest Regional Court upheld UCMR's

---

[1] Marie Manhaeve is an IP/IT lawyer at the Brussels Bar, Belgium.

[2] Dir. 2001/29/EC of the European Parliament and of the Council of 22 May 2001 on the harmonisation of certain aspects of copyright and related rights in the information society (OJ 2001 L 167, p. 10). Art. 3(1) of Dir. 2001/29 states: '*Member States shall provide authors with the exclusive right to authorise or prohibit any communication to the public of their works, by wire or wireless means, including the making available to the public of their works in such a way that members of the public may access them from a place and at a time individually chosen by them.*'

claim, finding that the equipping of aircraft with devices enabling the communication to the public of musical works as background music creates a rebuttable presumption of use thereof and constitutes a communication to the public.

Blue Air lodged an appeal with the Bucharest Court of Appeal, arguing that it had not communicated background music for which no licence had been obtained and that the mere existence of sound systems did not constitute a communication to the public. Blue Air emphasised its lack of profit motive and claimed that sound systems were essential for crew communication and passenger safety.

In those circumstances the Bucharest Court of Appeal decided to stay the proceedings and to refer the following questions to the Court of Justice ('**Court**') for a preliminary ruling:

> *'(1) Must Article 3(1) of Directive 2001/29/EC [...] be interpreted as meaning that the broadcasting, inside a commercial aircraft occupied by passengers, of a musical work or a fragment of a musical work on take-off, on landing or at any time during a flight, via the aircraft's public address system, constitutes a communication to the public within the meaning of that provision, particularly (but not exclusively) in the light of the criterion relating to the profit-making objective of the communication?*
>
> *If the answer to the first question is in the affirmative:*
>
> *(2) Does the existence on board the aircraft of an address system required by air traffic safety legislation constitute a sufficient basis for making a rebuttable presumption as to the communication to the public of musical works on board that aircraft?*
>
> *If the answer to that question is in the negative:*
>
> *(3) Does the presence on board the aircraft of an address system required by air traffic safety legislation and of software which enables the communication of phonograms (containing protected musical works) via that system constitute a sufficient basis for making a rebuttable presumption as to the communication to the public of musical works on board that aircraft?'*

ii) C-826/21

In 2013, the UPFR, a Romanian collective management organisation overseeing the related rights of phonogram producers, initiated legal action against the CFR, a rail transport company. The UPFR sought payment of outstanding remuneration and penalties for the alleged communication to the public of musical works in passenger carriages operated by the CFR. The UPFR argued that, since the applicable railway legislation mandated the installation of sound systems in the trains, the presence of these systems constituted a communication to the public within the meaning of Article 3(1) of Directive 2001/29.

The Regional Court of Bucharest dismissed the UPFR's action, stating that while the mere installation of a sound system enabling public access to musical works qualifies as a communication to the public, there was no evidence proving the presence of such systems in the trains in service.

The UPFR appealed the decision before the Bucharest Court of Appeal. The Bucharest Court of Appeal highlighted that Romanian case-law[3] generally considers the mere presence of sound systems in a train carriage as a communication to the public of musical works. Despite this majority view, the referring court expressed uncertainty on this matter and decided to stay the proceedings and to refer the following questions to the Court of Justice for a preliminary ruling:

> *'(1) Does a rail carrier which uses train carriages in which sound systems intended for the communication of information to passengers are installed thereby make a communication to the public within the meaning of Article 3 of Directive 2001/29/EC [...]?*
>
> *(2) Does Article 3 of Directive 2001/29/EC [...] preclude national legislation which establishes a rebuttable presumption of communication to the public on the basis of the existence of sound systems, where those sound systems are required by other provisions of law governing the carrier's activity?'*

2. Decision

1. Article 3(1) of Directive 2001/29/EC of the European Parliament and of the Council of 22 May 2001 on the harmonisation of certain aspects of copyright and related rights in the information society must be interpreted as meaning that the broadcasting, in a means of passenger transport, of a musical work as background music constitutes a communication to the public within the meaning of that provision.

2. Article 3(1) of Directive 2001/29 and Article 8(2) of Directive 2006/115/EC of the European Parliament and of the Council of 12 December 2006 on rental right and lending right and on certain rights related to copyright in the field of intellectual property must be interpreted as meaning that the installation, on board a means of transport, of sound equipment, and, where appropriate, of software enabling the broadcasting of background music, does not constitute a communication to the public within the meaning of those provisions.

3. Article 8(2) of Directive 2006/115 must be interpreted as precluding national legislation, as interpreted by the national courts, which establishes a rebuttable

---

3 Which specifically relies on Case C-306/05, 7 December 2006, *SGAE*.

presumption that musical works are communicated to the public because of the presence of sound systems in means of transport.

3. Motivation and Analysis

i) On the preliminary questions regarding the broadcasting of protected works as background music

Article 3(1) of Directive 2001/29 provides that authors have the exclusive right to authorise or prohibit any communication to the public of their works.

Since the concept of 'communication to the public' under Article 3(1) is not explicitly defined and Directive 2001/29 aims to establish a high level of protection for authors, the Court emphasised the need for a broad interpretation of this concept, covering all forms of communication to the public, including broadcasting and retransmission of works through wire or wireless means.[4]

In accordance with the Court's case-law, the notion of 'communication to the public' includes two cumulative criteria, namely (i) an act of transmission or retransmission of a work and (ii) the communication of that work to a public.[5]

The interpretation of this autonomous notion also requires an individual and factual assessment of the case at hand.[6] In conducting this assessment, the Court has developed a set of complementary criteria to consider.[7] The Court has firstly highlighted the indispensable role and deliberate nature of the intervention of the user, emphasising that an act of communication occurs when the user, with full awareness of the consequences of his or her actions, gives access to a protected work to his or her customers.[8] Secondly, the Court has held that the profit-making nature of the communication is relevant but not an essential condition for the existence of a communication to the public.[9]

---

4 Paras. 45-46 of the annotated judgment. See also Recs 4, 9, 10 and 23 in the preamble to Dir. 2001/29 and Case C-161/17, 7 August 2018, *Renckhoff*, para. 17.

5 The term 'a public' here refers to an indeterminate number of potential recipients and implies, moreover, a fairly large number of people (Cases C-682/18 and C-683/18, 22 June 2021, *YouTube and Cyando*, para. 69 and Case C-637/19, 28 October 2020, *BY (Photographic evidence)*, para. 25.

6 Case C-753/18, 2 April 2020, *Stim and SAMI*, para. 30, and Case C-682/18 and C-683/18, 22 June 2021, *YouTube and Cyando*, para. 66.

7 Case C-610/15, 14 June 2017, *Stichting Brein*, para. 25, and Case C-682/18 and C-683/18, *YouTube and Cyando*, para. 67.

8 Case C-610/15, 14 June 2017, *Stichting Brein*, para. 26.

9 Case C-607/11, 7 March 2013, *ITV Broadcasting and Others*, para. 42 and Case C-117/15, 31 May 2016, *Reha Training*, para. 49.

Applying these principles to the case at hand, the Court concluded that broadcasting a musical work as background music in a passenger transport vehicle constituted a communication to the public under Article 3(1) of Directive 2001/29. The operator was acting in full knowledge of the consequences of its conduct to provide customers access to the work. In addition, the public in question consisted of all the groups of passengers who, simultaneously or successively, were present in the transport vehicle, and such a number of persons could not be regarded as too small, or even as an insignificant number, within the meaning of the case-law of the Court. The fact that the profit-making nature of such a communication was highly debatable was not decisive since this is not a prerequisite for finding that there is a communication to the public.

ii) On the preliminary questions regarding the mere installation of equipment enabling the broadcasting of protected work

The examination of the second preliminary questions addressed whether Article 3(1) Directive 2001/29 and Article 8(2) of Directive 2006/115[10] must be interpreted as meaning that the mere installation of sound equipment or software on board a means of transport, enabling a subsequent and potential broadcasting of background music, constitutes a communication to the public within the meaning of those provisions.[11]

Referring to Recital 27 of Directive 2001/29,[12] which excludes the mere provision of physical facilities from constituting a communication to the public, the Court stated that the mere installation of sound equipment and software in

---

10 Dir. 2006/115/EC of the European Parliament and of the Council of 12 December 2006 on rental right and lending right and on certain rights related to copyright in the field of intellectual property (OJ 2006 L 376/28, p. 3). Art. 8(2) of Dir. 2006/115 states: '*Member States shall provide a right in order to ensure that a single equitable remuneration is paid by the user, if a phonogram published for commercial purposes, or a reproduction of such phonogram, is used for broadcasting by wireless means or for any communication to the public, and to ensure that this remuneration is shared between the relevant performers and phonogram producers. Member States may, in the absence of agreement between the performers and phonogram producers, lay down the conditions as to the sharing of this remuneration between them.*'

11 For completeness, we should note that in the context of Art. 267 TFEU, in order to facilitate cooperation between national courts and the Court of Justice, it is crucial that the CJEU provides answers that help the national court to settle the case. This allows the CJEU to reformulate the questions raised by the national court to provide complete interpretations essential to the pending dispute. In the annotated judgment, the Court stated that, reformulating the questions, the essence was whether the installation of sound equipment on transport vehicles constitutes a communication to the public.

12 Examining Rec. 27 of Dir. 2001/29, which excludes the mere provision of physical facilities from constituting communication, the Court concluded that the installation of sound equipment on transport does not qualify as an act of communication. Unlike intentional transmissions in establishments like hotels, the installation on transport is a mere provision of facilities.

means of transport enabling the broadcasting of background music does not, taken by itself, qualify as an act of communication.

The Court made a distinction between (i) the mere provision of physical facilities that enable a possible communication to the public by the installation of a sound system or software[13] and (ii) the subsequent and intentional use of these facilities to transmit protected works to the public, e.g. by operators of a public house, a hotel or a spa establishment.[14] In this context, it referred to its previous case-law confirming that the latter falls under the definition of a communication to the public while the former does not.[15]

iii) On the preliminary question regarding the rebuttable presumption in national legislation of communication to the public on the basis of the existence of sound systems

The above interpretation seamlessly brought the Court to answer the third preliminary question, related to the interpretation of Article 8(2) of Directive 2006/115. The referring court sought clarification on whether this provision prohibits national legislation, as construed by national courts, from establishing a rebuttable presumption that musical works are communicated to the public due to the presence of sound systems in means of transport.

The Court first recalled that Directive 2001/29 aims to eliminate legislative disparities and legal uncertainties in the field of copyright protection and to prevent inconsistencies between the Member States. Consequently, accepting broader interpretations of the concept of 'communication to the public' than those set out in Article 3(1) of Directive 2001/29 would lead to legal uncertainty and undermine the harmonisation objectives of the Directive. The Court emphasised the need for consistency of copyright protection across Member States to prevent fragmentation of the internal market. It reaffirmed that a Member State cannot provide greater or wider protection to copyright holders by expanding the scope of the notion of 'communication to the public' beyond the limits set by Directive 2001/29. These principles are applicable by analogy to the concept of 'communication to the public' within Directive 2006/115.[16]

In response to the specific circumstances of the case, where sound equipment was installed in means of transport for the benefit of passengers, the Court

---

13 Para. 69 of the annotated judgment.

14 Para. 71 of the annotated judgment.

15 See in this regard Case C-306/05, 7 December 2006, *SGAE*, para. 47; Case C-403/08 and C-429/08, 4 October 2011, *Football Association Premier League and Others*, para. 196 and Case C-351/12, 27 February 2014, *OSA*, para. 26 and Case C-117/15, 1 May 2016, *Reha Training*, paras. 55 and 56.

16 Case C-160/15, 8 September 2016, *GS Media*, para. 33, and Case C-597/19, 17 June 2021, *M.I.C.M.*, para. 41.

interpreted Article 8(2) of Directive 2006/115 as meaning that the installation on board a means of transport of sound equipment and, where appropriate, of software enabling the broadcasting of background music for the benefit of travellers independently of their will, does not constitute a 'communication to the public' within the meaning of that provision.

Therefore, national legislation establishing a rebuttable presumption that musical works are communicated to the public due to the presence of sound systems in means of transport is incompatible with Article 8(2) of Directive 2006/115. Such legislation may have the consequence of requiring payment of remuneration for the mere installation of those sound systems, even in the absence of any act of communication to the public, contrary to the aforementioned provision.

* *
*

This judgment again demonstrates that, on the matter of 'communication to the public', the Court is very active in adjudicating law and is required to examine very similar cases, which, however, do not always result in a similar outcome. Whereas the broadcasting of protected works in hotel rooms (C-306/05, Rafael Hoteles), rehabs (C-117/15, Reha Training) or spas (C-351/12, *OSA*) has been considered by the Court as acts of communication to the public, the Court ruled the contrary with respect to the broadcasting of protected works in dentists' waiting rooms (C-135/10, *Del Corso*). More recently, the Court found that the hiring out of motor vehicles equipped with radio receivers does not constitute a communication to the public (C-753/18, *Stim and SAMI*).

Here, the Court confirmed that examining this concept requires a case-by-case analysis, taking into account a number of criteria. The case highlighted the indispensable role played by the user and the deliberate nature of his/her intervention, where, in the absence of that intervention, customers would not have been able to enjoy the protected work. In addition, the Court confirmed that the profit-making nature of the act is not an essential criterion.

This judgment is a noteworthy addition to the rich jurisprudence on the notion of 'communication to the public'. The Court made a clear distinction between the installation of the systems, which is not an act of communication, and the subsequent playing of background music through these systems, which the Court recognised as an act of communication. This interpretation aligns with the CJEU's early clarification in C-306/05, Rafael Hoteles, emphasising that the installation requires an additional intervention on the part of the user in order for it to be considered a *communication* and not a mere installation.

The question arises as to what distinguishes this judgment from case C-135/10, *Del Corso*. In Del Corso, the Court held that (i) patients who could listen to the radio in the dentist's waiting room are not to be considered a public, since the number of people concerned would be rather limited, and (ii) that the broadcasting of background music in a dental practice could not be regarded as having a profit motive, since patients go to a dental practice only for dental care and the broadcasting of phonograms is not an aspect inherent to dental care. Although trains and aeroplanes are more crowded than dentists' waiting rooms, it could be argued that the patients who succeed each other during the course of the day may possibly represent a reasonably large number of people and could therefore also be qualified as a public. Similarly, we question whether playing background music on trains and planes has any profit motive; although the criterion of profit is not determinative, it is not irrelevant either.

In this context, it seems wise to follow the Opinion[17] of the Advocate General in C-117/15, Reha Training, where he writes that the strict approach taken by the Court in the Del Corso judgment departs from established case-law. Therefore, the scope of the Del Corso judgment should not be extended but, on the contrary, should be limited to the specific factual circumstances which gave rise to that judgment. A different reasoning would, in my view, lead to an overly restrictive conception of copyright and related rights, and go against the high level of protection envisaged by the Union legislature and applied by the Court itself in its settled case-law.

17 Opinion of Advocate General Y. Bot of 3 February 2016, paras. 54-55.

COURT OF JUSTICE 27 APRIL 2023

ON THE PREREQUISITES FOR JURISDICTION OF MEMBER STATE COURTS IN TRADE MARK INFRINGEMENT CASES

Case C-104/22

Summary and Analysis by Åsa Krook and Jonna Rask[1]

Parties:

Lännen MCE Oy

v

Berky GmbH
Senwatec GmbH & Co. KG.

1. Background and History

Lännen MCE Oy ('Lännen', the applicant company) is a company established in Finland, manufacturing, *inter alia*, amphibious dredgers which it markets under the EU trade mark WATERMASTER, registered on 12 July 2004 under number 003185758.

Lännen filed an infringement action before the Finnish Market Court against two German companies, Berky GmbH ('Berky', the defendant company) and Senwatec GmbH & Co ('Senwatec', the defendant company),[2] alleging that they had violated its trade mark rights in Finland.[3] The key issue in the case was that the defendants were domiciled in Germany.

Lännen claimed that Senwatec had infringed its trade mark by using paid advertising on a Finnish internet search engine. When the term 'Watermaster' was searched for in Finland, an advertisement for Senwatec's products appeared as the top result. Berky was accused of infringing the trade mark by using the keyword 'Watermaster' in meta tags for images on the photo-sharing website Flickr.com, which showed Berky's machines when a search was conducted using the same Watermaster term.

The key issue was whether these actions by Berky and Senwatec constituted trade mark infringement in Finland, as the defendants argued that their marketing

---

1 Åsa Krook is an IP partner at the Finnish law firm Waselius & Wist and is a member of the Finnish Bar Association. Jonna Rask is an Associate Lawyer at the Finnish law firm Waselius & Wist.

2 After some structural changes. Senwatec has been considered a sister company of Berky since the end of 2015.

3 Case number MAO:5/2022.

activities were not targeted at Finland. The referring court sought clarification on factors determining jurisdiction and whether the national top-level domain of the search engine's website is relevant in this context. The court also asked whether the geographical areas where the products were intended to be supplied should be taken into account when determining the jurisdiction in cases involving online advertising directed at consumers or traders in different EU Member States.

Ultimately, the case centred on not only whether the actions of Berky and Senwatec could be considered trade mark infringement in Finland, but also how jurisdiction should be determined in such cases involving online advertising and global product distribution. The request for a preliminary ruling focused on the conditions under which the acts of infringement alleged by the applicant could be considered to have taken place in the territory of Finland within the meaning of Article 125(5) of Regulation (EU) 2017/1001 and, consequently, on the jurisdiction of the Finnish Market Court to examine the actions. In particular, the case concerned the conditions under which the electronically published advertisements at issue in the alleged infringing acts could be considered to have been directed at a Finnish target group.

In these circumstances, the Finnish Market Court decided to stay the proceedings and to refer the following question to the Court of Justice for a preliminary ruling:

> '*Company A is established in Member State X, where it has its registered office, and has used on a website a sign identical to an [EU] trade mark belonging to Company B, in advertising or as a keyword.*
>
> 1. *In the situation described above, may it be concluded that the advertising is directed at consumers or traders in Member State Y, where Company B has its registered office, and does an [EU] trade mark court in Member State Y have jurisdiction to hear an action for infringement of an [EU] trade mark under Article 125(5) of [Regulation 2017/1001] where, in the advertising published electronically or on an advertiser's website connected to that advertising via a link, the geographical area where the goods are to be supplied is not specified, at least not expressly, or no individual Member State is expressly excluded from that area? May the nature of the goods to which the advertising relates and the fact that the market for Company A's products is allegedly global and thus covers the entire territory of the European Union, including Member State Y, be taken into account in that respect?*
> 2. *May it be concluded that the above advertising is directed at consumers or traders in Member State Y if it appears on a search engine website operated under the national top-level domain of Member State Y?*
> 3. *If Question 1 or 2 is answered in the affirmative, what other factors, if any, should be taken into account in determining whether the advertisement is directed at consumers or traders in Member State Y?*'

2. Decision

Article 125(5) of Regulation (EU) 2017/1001 of the European Parliament and of the Council of 14 June 2017 on the European Union trade mark must be interpreted as meaning that the proprietor of an EU trade mark who considers that he or she has been prejudiced by the use, without his or her consent, by a third party, of a sign identical with that mark in online advertisements and offers for sale in respect of goods identical with, or similar to, those for which that mark is registered, may bring an infringement action against that third party before an EU trade mark court of the Member State in which consumers and traders targeted by those advertisements or offers for sale are located, notwithstanding the fact that the third party does not expressly and unambiguously list that Member State among the territories to which a supply of the goods in question might be made, if that third party has made use of that sign by means of paid referencing on a search engine website which uses a national top-level domain name of that Member State. By contrast, that is not the case simply because the third party concerned has used the natural referencing of images of its goods on an online photo-sharing service under a generic top-level domain, having recourse to meta tags using the trade mark concerned as a keyword.

3. Motivation and Analysis

First, the CJEU interpreted Article 125(5) of Regulation 2017/1001, which pertains to the jurisdiction of EU trade mark courts in cases of infringement. Specifically, the article addresses whether the proprietor of an EU trade mark, which believes its intellectual property rights have been violated by a third party's use of an identical sign in online advertisements and offers for sale, can file an infringement action in a Member State not expressly listed by the third party as a geographical area where the goods are to be supplied.

Regulation 2017/1001 provides the legal framework for actions related to EU trade marks. The CJEU pointed out that certain provisions of Regulation No 1215/2012[4] do not apply in this context due to Regulation 2017/1001 having the character of *lex specialis* in relation to them.[5] Therefore, an infringement action relating to an EU trade mark brought on 28 January 2020 falls within the scope of the rules on jurisdiction laid down in Regulation 2017/1001.

The CJEU continued assessing the jurisdiction and noted that Article 126(1) of Regulation 2017/1001 provides that where an action is brought before an EU trade mark court on the basis of Article 125(1) of that regulation, the court

---

4 Art. 66(1) of Reg. No 1215/2012 states that the Reg. applies to legal proceedings instituted as from 10 January 2015 concerning an EU trade mark.

5 Case C-172/18, 5 September 2019, *AMS Neve and Others*, para. 34.

is to have jurisdiction in respect of infringements committed within the territory of any of the Member States. In comparison, Article 126(2) of Regulation 2017/1001 provides that where an action is brought before such a court on the basis of Article 125(5) of that regulation, that court is to have jurisdiction only in respect of acts committed within the territory of the Member State in which it is situated.[6] This distinction implies that the choice between Articles 125(1) and 125(5) determines the territorial scope of the court's jurisdiction. Article 125(1) potentially covers acts of infringement throughout the EU, while Article 125(5) limits the action to a single Member State.[7] Therefore, the applicant's choice between these two articles determines the territorial jurisdiction of the court, providing flexibility in bringing targeted actions related to acts of infringement within a specific Member State.

Despite this, the CJEU stated that the applicant could not, with reference to the same acts of infringement, simultaneously bring actions based on both paragraphs 125(1) and 125(5) of Regulation No 2017/1001. Article 125(5) is to be seen as an alternative to the forum indicated in the other paragraphs of that article. EU legislation therefore enables the proprietor of the EU trade mark to bring targeted actions, each of which relates to acts of infringement committed within a single Member State.[8]

The alleged acts of infringement in the present case involved the online display of content related to the products of the trade mark proprietor's competitors. These displays occurred through paid and natural referencing on the basis of a sign identical to that trade mark, specifically targeting consumers or traders located in Finland.

Concerning the questions of whether the online display in question was actually directed at consumers or traders located in Finland and which factors are relevant for determining whether the referring court has international jurisdiction under Article 125(5) of Regulation 2017/1001, the CJEU stated that it would be excessive to require the court to carry out a detailed examination of these complex matters of fact and law. Thus, a reasonable presumption that acts of infringement have been committed on the territory of a Member State is enough to establish jurisdiction under Article 125(5) of Regulation 2017/1001.[9] Additionally, the CJEU noted that the determination of the jurisdiction of the court seized of an infringement action does not amount to an examination of the substance of that action.[10]

---

6 Para. 29 of the annotated judgment.

7 Case C-172/18, 5 September 2019, *AMS Neve and Others*, para. 40.

8 Paras. 31-32 of the annotated judgment; Case C-172/18, 5 September 2019, *AMS Neve and Others*, paras. 41-42.

9 Paras. 34-39 of the annotated judgment.

10 Case C-12/15, 16 June 2016, *Universal Music International Holding*, para. 44.

When assessing Article 125(5) of Regulation 2017/1001, the CJEU pointed out that in this context it must be observed that according to the case law of the CJEU[11], the criterion for jurisdiction relates to active conduct on the part of the infringing party. Where the display of online content is, even if only potentially, directed at consumers or traders located in the territory of a Member State, the details of the geographical areas of supply of the products in question are particularly important for the purposes of the aforementioned assessment.[12] The CJEU emphasised that the national court of the geographical area of consumers or traders, to whom advertising and offers for sale are directed, is particularly suited to assessing whether the alleged infringement exists.[13] However, in the case in question it must be found, that the geographical areas of delivery of the products were not mentioned in the advertisement. The map on Senwatec's website, which according to Lännen, proved that Senwatec's market was global, could not in itself establish a connecting factor with Finland since it did not support the conclusion that Senwatec directed its activities towards the Finnish market.[14]

After considering the absence of precise information of the geographical areas of delivery of the products in question, the CJEU stated that the connecting factor with the Member State concerned must be established in the light of other factors for the applicant to be able to bring an infringement action on the basis of Article 125(5) of Regulation 2017/1001.

In connection with the above, seeking support for the interpretation of Article 17(1)(c) of Regulation 1215/2012, the CJEU held that various indicia are capable of supporting the conclusion that the trader's activities are directed to the Member State of the consumer's domicile, such as, for example, the international nature of the activity or use of a top-level domain name other than that of the Member State in which the trader is established.[15] In the present case, this last point was found relevant by the Court, but the Court also stated that the mere fact that a website is accessible from the territory covered by the trade mark is not a sufficient basis for concluding that the offers for sale displayed are targeted at consumers in that territory.[16] If a company pays the operator of a search engine website with a national top-level domain of a Member State other than that in which it is established, in order to display, for the public of that Member State, a link to that company's website, thereby enabling a specifically targeted public to access its product offering, this would be considered as active

[11] Case C-172/18, 5 September 2019, *AMS Neve and Others*, para. 44.

[12] Case C-324/09, 12 July 2011, *L'Oréal and Others*, para. 65.

[13] Case C-172/18, 5 September 2019, *AMS Neve and Others*, para. 57.

[14] Para. 43 of the annotated judgment.

[15] Para. 46 of the annotated judgment; Case C-585/08, 7 December 2010, *Pammer and Hotel Alpenhof*, para. 93.

[16] Case C-324, 12 July 2011, *L'Oréal and Others*, para. 64.

conduct on the part of the infringing party that would constitute a sufficient connection for jurisdiction.[17]

Using a trade mark as a meta tag in natural referencing differs from paid referencing and may not establish a sufficient connection factor, according to the CJEU.[18] This is because in a case of such natural referencing, the condition of active conduct is not capable of being fulfilled, since a website with a generic top-level domain is not intended for the public of any specific Member State, and because the meta tag is intended only to enable search engines to increase the website's accessibility. The CJEU therefore ruled that the referring court cannot declare that it has jurisdiction on the basis of Article 125(5) of Regulation 2017/1001, in the absence of other factors capable of proving that such natural referencing was intended for a public established in Finland.

To summarise, the CJEU stated that it is the responsibility of the court hearing the infringement action to assess various factors, including the nature of the products in question and the extent of the geographical market, in order to determine whether the referincing accessible in a given territory is directly targeted at consumers within that territory. Additionally, the CJEU emphasised that the absence of precise information about the geographical areas of delivery of the products in question may necessitate the consideration of other factors to establish jurisdiction. Consequently, it remained for the referring court to assess on a case-by-case basis the extent to which those matters were relevant in order to conclude that referencing accessible on the territory covered by the trade mark was targeted at consumers in that same territory.[19]

The Finnish Market Court issued its ruling in the case on 6 October 2023 (Case number MAO:453/2023). While the Market Court declared the action inadmissible as regards Berky, it confirmed that Senwatec had infringed EU trade mark number 003185758 WATERMASTER in Finland by using it without authorisation as a keyword or other symbol in the promotion of its own engines. Due to the infringement, the Market Court prohibited Senwatec from repeating the infringement of the trade mark under penalty of a fine of EUR 100,000.

When considering jurisdiction on Senwatec's case, the Market Court noted that the Senwatec website did not provide any information leading to the conclusion that the company was targeting the Finnish market. Therefore, the link to Finland had to be established on other grounds. The Market Court found that paid referencing on a search engine website, performed by Senwatec, could be considered as a sufficient connecting factor to the Member State. Therefore, in the case of Senwatec, the infringement act – namely, its Google advertisement – was deemed to be directed at a target audience in Finland, and the alleged

[17] Paras. 46-50 of the annotated judgment.

[18] Para. 51 of the annotated judgment.

[19] Case C-324/09, 12 July 2011, *L'Oréal and Others*, para. 61.

infringement had therefore taken place in Finland within the meaning of Article 125(5) of Regulation No 2017/1001. Therefore, it was concluded that the Market Court had jurisdiction to hear the action.[20]

The Market Court also considered whether it had jurisdiction to hear Berky's case. It stated that the Google search using the term 'watermaster amphibious dredger', resulting in a link to Flickr.com for the images of Berky machines, was a result of natural referencing and not paid. As the CJEU had stated, this kind of action alone does not indicate that the internet site is directed at consumers in a specific Member State. Therefore, the Market Court found that the alleged infringement by Berky had not occurred in Finland within the meaning of Article 125(5) of Regulation 2017/1001, and, as a result, the Market Court did not have jurisdiction in the matter.[21] However, the Market Court's decision is not yet final.

It seems that the CJEU may by its preliminary judgment in *Lännen MCE* have lowered the threshold for establishing jurisdiction from where it '*is apparent*' in *AMS Neve and Others*[22] to '*a reasonable presumption*' as stated in *Lännen MCE*. What this means in a specific case is difficult to predict. According to both thresholds, it seems clear that while buying an AdWord on a search engine website with a national top-level domain of a Member State is considered sufficient evidence to establish a connecting factor with that Member State, using a meta tag on an online photo-sharing service under a generic top-level domain is not considered sufficient to establish such a connection. There are, however, a lot of situations that are unclear.

The CJEU made clear that '*mere accessibility*' of a website in a territory covered by the EU trademark was not sufficient, but it did not specifically answer the referring court's question whether the fact that that display occurred on the website of a search engine operating under the national top-level domain of that Member State was a relevant factor. To conclude, it seems, however, that in addition to the supply of goods to a geographical territory, any other act which indicates that consumers and customers in a certain country may have been targeted is sufficient to establish a connecting factor for the purpose of Article 125(5) of Regulation 2017/1001. This means that companies have to pay sufficient attention to their advertising strategies in the light of both their key areas of supply and their freedom to operate, taking into account third parties' EU and national IP rights. The decision also provides guidance on international jurisdiction for Community design matters, since Article 82(5) of Regulation 6/2002 concerning Community designs basically corresponds to Article 125(5) of Regulation 2017/1001.

---

20 Finnish Market Court, MAO:453/2023, paras. 17-22.

21 Finnish Market Court, MAO:453/2023, paras. 29-37.

22 Case C-172/18, 5 September 2019, *AMS Neve and Others*, para. 56.

COURT OF JUSTICE 27 APRIL 2023

ON THE CONDITIONS OF MAJORITY REQUIRED BETWEEN JOINT PROPRIETORS FOR GRANTING AND TERMINATING A LICENCE OF THEIR TRADE MARK

Case C-686/21

Summary and Analysis by Ana Panão and Matilde Ortins de Bettencourt[1]

Parties:

VW
Legea Srl

v

SW
CQ
ET
VW
Legea Srl

1. Background and History

VW, SW, CQ and ET were joint proprietors in equal shares of the national and EU trade mark Legea, registered for sporting goods.[2]

In 1993, VW, SW, CQ and ET unanimously decided to grant Legea Srl an exclusive licence, free of charge and for an indefinite period, to use the national and EU trade mark LEGEA of which they were joint proprietors.

According to the parties' written observations, the company Legea Srl was formed in 1993, within the family, by VW, CQ and another brother who was a minor at the time, with each holding equal shares.[3]

At the end of 2006, VW opposed the continuation of the licence agreement. According to VW, between 1993 and 2006, as a result of a series of capital increases, his shareholding in the company Legea had fallen to 2.5%. From that minority position, he made a claim against the company for payment for use of the trade mark.

---

[1] Ana Panão is an IP/IT Associated Partner and Matilde Ortins de Bettencourt is an IP/IT Associate at the Portuguese law firm Abreu & Associados – Sociedade de Advogados, SP, RL, and both are members of the Portuguese Bar.

[2] Registration was granted on 11 May 1995 under number 650850.

[3] Joint ownership of the trade mark had already been agreed, also within the family circle, between the parents (SW and ET) and their children (CQ and VW).

On 16 November 2009, Legea brought an action against VW before the Tribunale di Napoli (District Court, Naples, Italy) seeking a declaration of invalidity of marks containing the sign 'Legea' which VW had registered. By way of counterclaim, VW requested, first, a declaration of invalidity of marks registered by Legea and, second, a declaration of unlawful use of the marks at issue by that company.[4]

By a judgment of 11 June 2014, the Tribunale di Napoli (District Court, Naples) found that Legea, acting with the consent of all the joint proprietors, had made legitimate use of the marks at issue until 31 December 2006. However, the court held that, after that date, because of VW's opposition to the continuation of the licence agreement, that use was unlawful.

By a judgment of 11 April 2016, the Corte d'appello di Napoli (Court of Appeal, Naples, Italy) varied that judgment in part. Taking the view that the unanimous consent of the joint proprietors was not required in order to grant a trade mark licence to a third party, that court held that the will of three of the four joint proprietors of the marks at issue was sufficient to continue the licence agreement after 31 December 2006, notwithstanding VW's opposition. The Court of Appeal thus considered that in the case of joint proprietorship, there would be no need for the unanimous agreement of the joint proprietors to assign the exclusive use of the trade mark to a third party.

VW appealed against the appellate judgment before the Corte suprema di cassazione (Supreme Court of Cassation, Italy).

The referring court, hearing appeals against the judgment of 11 April 2016, was uncertain as to the arrangements for the individual exercise of the exclusive right that is jointly held by the joint proprietors of a trade mark, in the light of the provisions of EU law, and referred, in that regard, to Article 10 of Directive 2015/2436[5] and to Articles 9 and 25 of Regulation 2017/1001.[6]

In summary, the Supreme Court of Cassation of Italy put forward the following arguments as the basis for its request for a preliminary ruling:

- The provisions of the Civil Code governing joint ownership of property, which are applicable to joint proprietorship of trade marks, along with the provisions governing withdrawal from a contract, must be interpreted in the light of EU trade mark legislation.

---

4 See in this regard also the opinion of Advocate General Campos Sánchez-Bordona for Case C-686/21, 8 December 2022, para. 20.

5 Directive of the European Parliament and of the Council of 16 December 2015 to approximate the laws of the Member States relating to trade marks (OJ 2015 L 336, p. 1).

6 Regulation of the European Parliament and of the Council of 14 June 2017 on the European Union trade mark (OJ 2017 L 154, p. 1).

- EU trade mark law provides that trade marks may be the subject of a licence and acknowledges the possibility of joint proprietorship of a mark. However, it does not lay down any express rules governing whether the exercise of the rights relating to joint ownership of property requires unanimous or majority agreement to assign the right of exclusive use of a mark to a third party, for an indefinite period and free of charge.
- It was also necessary to clarify whether, where such an assignment occurs by unanimous agreement, one of the joint proprietors may subsequently dissent and terminate the assignment.

In those circumstances, the Supreme Court of Cassation decided to stay the proceedings and to refer the following questions to the CJEU for a preliminary ruling:

> *'(1) Are the EU rules [provided for in Article 10 of Directive 2015/2436 and Articles 9 and 25 of Regulation 2017/1001], in so far as they provide for the exclusive rights of the proprietor of an EU trade mark and, at the same time, for the possibility of such a mark being owned by several individuals in shares, to be interpreted as meaning that the assignment to a third party of the exclusive right to use a shared trade mark, free of charge and for an indefinite period, can be decided upon by a majority of the joint proprietors, or as meaning that it requires their unanimous consent instead?*
>
> *(2) If it is the latter, in the case where an EU trade mark or a national trade mark is owned by several individuals, would it be consistent with the principles of EU law for it to be impossible for one of the joint proprietors of the mark, after the mark has been assigned to a third party by unanimous decision, free of charge and for an indefinite period, unilaterally to withdraw from that decision or, alternatively, would it, on the contrary, be consistent with the principles of EU law if the joint proprietor were not bound in perpetuity by the original intent, such that he or she could retract, with the resulting effect on the act of assignment?'*

2. Decision

First Council Directive 89/104/EEC of 21 December 1988 to approximate the laws of the Member States relating to trade marks and Council Regulation (EC) No 40/94 of 20 December 1993 on the Community trade mark must be interpreted as meaning that the question of whether the grant or the termination of a licence to use a national trade mark or an EU trade mark held in joint proprietorship requires a unanimous decision by the joint proprietors or a decision by a majority of them comes within the scope of the applicable national law.

3. Motivation and Analysis

As a preliminary point, the CJEU clarified that, in view of the date of the facts in the main proceedings (which occurred in 1993 and December 2006[7]), those proceedings were governed, as regards EU trade marks, by Regulation No 40/94[8] and, as regards national trade marks, by First Council Directive 89/104.[9] As such, the CJEU decided to examine the questions submitted in the light of these frameworks.[10] However, since the content of the two legal frameworks (Dir. 89/104 and Reg. No 40/94, on the one hand, and Dir. 2015/2436 and Reg. 2017/1001, on the other) is similar in this regard, the arguments concerning Regulation No 40/94 and First Council Directive 89/104 may be applied to Regulation 2017/1001 and Directive 2015/2436, respectively.

Firstly, the analysis had to focus on the possibility for joint proprietors of holding a trade mark in joint ownership. In accordance with Article 5 of Regulation No 40/94, natural or legal persons, including authorities established under public law, may be proprietors of EU trade marks. Although the Regulation does not expressly and directly mention that it is legitimate for a number of joint proprietors to own a trade mark, it does indirectly refer to such a possibility – as in the case of Article 16(3) where reference is made to the situation in which '*two or more persons are mentioned in the Register of Community trade marks as joint proprietors*,' as well as in the case of Article 21(2) regarding insolvency proceedings, where reference is made to '*joint proprietorship of a Community trade mark*.'

Unlike the Regulation, Directive 89/104 does not refer implicitly or explicitly to the possibility of co-ownership of a national trade mark. Notwithstanding, the CJEU considered that the fact that the Directive does not contain references to joint ownership of a trade mark only implies that this is governed by national law (from which the rules applicable to the exercise of the rights conferred by the trade mark will derive), and does not mean that the Directive excludes or prohibits joint ownership of the trade mark.[11]

---

7 See in this regard also the opinion of Advocate General Campos Sánchez-Bordona for Case C-686/21, 8 December 2022, para. 33-35.

8 Council Regulation (EC) No 40/94 of 20 December 1993 on the Community trade mark (OJ 1994 L 11, p. 1), in the version resulting from Council Regulation (EC) No 422/2004 of 19 February 2004, amending Council Regulation (EC) No 40/94 on the Community Trade Mark (OJ 2004 L.70, p. 1).

9 First Council Directive 89/104/EEC of 21 December 1988 to approximate the laws of the Member States relating to trade marks (OJ 1989 L 40, p. 1).

10 Para. 29 of the annotated decision.

11 Para. 34 of the annotated decision; see in this regard also the opinion of Advocate General Campos Sánchez-Bordona for Case C-686/21, 8 December 2022, para. 47-48.

Although Regulation No 40/94 recognises the possibility of joint ownership of a trade mark, the EU legislation is silent on the regime applicable to the conditions for the exercise of joint ownership of trade marks, in particular whether a unanimous decision by the joint proprietors is required to grant or terminate a licence to use that trade mark, or whether a majority decision is required (which corresponded to the first question referred for a preliminary ruling).

Similarly, both Regulation No 40/94 (in Art. 22(1)) and First Council Directive 89/104 (in Art. 8(1)) recognise and legislate for the possibility of a national trade mark, or an EU trade mark being licensed, either exclusively or non-exclusively, for all or part of the goods or services for which they are registered. Furthermore, neither the Regulation nor the Directive stipulate the conditions applicable to the conclusion, or termination, of licence agreements.[12]

The CJEU considered that the silence of the legislation on this subject had to be analysed within the meaning of Article 16(1) of Regulation 40/94. Article 16(1) provides that an EU trade mark as an object of property is to be dealt with as a national trade mark registered in the particular Member State. As such, the CJEU deemed that in the absence of a provision in that Regulation, it would be for the Member State concerned to regulate the issues not covered by EU law.

To apply national rules to a specific subject omitted by European legislation, it is necessary for national law to safeguard the full effectiveness of EU law.[13] In the proceedings under analysis, it was considered that the information available in the proceedings did not suggest that the rules governing joint ownership of trade marks in Italy made it impossible or excessively difficult to exercise the rights conferred by EU legislation.[14]

As a result, the CJEU ruled that the question of whether the grant or the termination of a licence to use a national trade mark or an EU trade mark held in joint proprietorship requires a unanimous decision by the joint proprietors or a decision by a majority of the joint proprietors, falls within the scope of the applicable national law.[15]

12 See in this regard also the opinion of Advocate General Campos Sánchez-Bordona for Case C-686/21, 8 December 2022, paras. 51-57.

13 Case C-425/16, 19 October 2017, *Raimund*, paras. 40 and 41.

14 See in this regard also the opinion of Advocate General Campos Sánchez-Bordona, 8 December 2022, paras. 58-59.

15 Paras. 37-38 of the annotated decision. As mentioned by the Advocate General Campos Sánchez-Bordona, in accordance with Italian legislation (Art. 6(1) of the Industrial Property Code), the rights of joint proprietors of a trade mark are to be governed, except as otherwise established by conventions with rules to the contrary, by the provisions of the Civil Code relating to joint ownership, to the extent they are compatible.

The second question concerned the right of one of the trade mark´s owner to unilaterally withdraw the decision to grant the trade mark licence to a third party where said decision had been taken unanimously by all the trade mark´s owners and for an indefinite period of time.

In this respect, the CJEU merely decided that in view of the analysis and answer to the first question, the second question did not need to be answered. However, it is important to note that the Court had already ruled in a previous decision[16] that under Directive 89/104, it is possible for the proprietor of a trade mark, who has granted a licence for its use to a third party, to withdraw that consent, and therefore from the same reasoning it can be concluded that the same applies to all the joint owners of the trade mark.[17] Nonetheless, the question remains as to how the decision to revoke or withdraw the licence should be taken in the case of jointly owned trade marks. Therefore, in this regard, considering the CJEU's reasoning regarding the answer to the first question, it can be concluded that it will be up to national law to regulate this aspect.

Therefore, the applicable laws of Member States to regulate the exercise of rights in relation to a licence to use a jointly owned trade mark. The provision currently contained inof Article 19 of the EU Trade Mark Regulation 2017/1001 can be taken into consideration, in particular with respect to joint owners residing in EU Member States where strategic options are available to choose who is mentioned as the first of the joint proprietors in the application. This for reason that his or her national law will govern the exercise of joint ownership.

Since the CJEU did not directly resolve the questions posed to it, it could have taken the opportunity to analyse the issues raised from another angle – for example, in light of Article 17(2) of the EU Charter of Fundamental Rights,[18] which provides for the protection of intellectual property. In this respect, the CJEU had previously ruled[19] that the protection conferred by this article is not aimed at mere commercial interests or opportunities (i.e. not just the 'static' protection of property),[20] but at rights that have a patrimonial value, from which arises an acquired legal position that allows the autonomous exercise of these rights by and in favour of their holder. The CJEU could therefore have taken the opportunity to adopt a harmonised or at least guiding perspective that would enable Member States to apply national law in line with European principles and rules.

---

16 Case C-661/11, 19 September 2013, *Martin Y Paz Diffusion*, para. 62.

17 See in this regard also the opinion of Advocate General Campos Sánchez-Bordona for Case C-686/21, 8 December 2022, para. 60-64.

18 Charter of Fundamental Rights of the European Union, 2012/C-326/02.

19 Case C-283/11, 22 January 2013, *Sky Österreich GmbH v Österreichischer Rundfunk*, para. 34.

20 See also E. Rosati, CJEU rules out that EU trade mark law governs regime applicable to jointly owned trade mark, *IPKat Blog*, 2023.

COURT OF JUSTICE 27 APRIL 2023

ON THE ISSUE OF THE NEED TO ESTABLISH THE EXISTENCE OF AN INTELLECTUAL PROPERTY RIGHT IN INCIDENTAL PROCEEDINGS TO ENSURE ENFORCEMENT OF INTELLECTUAL PROPERTY RIGHTS SUCH AS A REQUEST TO PROVIDE INFORMATION SUBMITTED PRIOR TO FORMULATING A STATEMENT OF CLAIMS

Case C-628/21

Summary and Analysis by Ewa Nagy[1]

Parties:

TB

v

Castorama Polska sp. z o.o.
Knor sp. z o.o.

1. Background and History

The subject of the dispute in main proceedings was an allegation that Castorama Polska z o.o. (hereinafter 'Castorama') and Knor sp. z o.o. (hereinafter 'Knor') infringed copyright to three images that TB (a natural person) claimed to have created. These images were composed of a simple graphic consisting of a limited number of colours, geometric figures and short sentences. The sentences on the images were: '*Mój dom moje zasady*' ('My house, my rules'); '*Nie ma ludzi idealnych a jednak jestem*' ('Perfect people don't exist, and yet here I am') and '*W naszym domu rano słychać tupot małych stopek. Zawsze pachnie pysznym ciastem. Mamy dużo obowiązków, mnóstwo zabawy i miłości*' ('In our house, the patter of tiny feet can be heard in the morning. It always smells like delicious cake. We have lots of chores, lots of fun and lots of love').

TB operates her own online shop in which she sells decorative articles, including reproductions of the images in question, which she makes mechanically. Reproductions of the images are also sold by Castorama in its online and bricks-and-mortar shops. They are provided by Knor. Two of the reproductions are exact copies of those sold in TB's online shop. The third one has a text identical to that sold by TB, but there are some differences in terms of graphics and fonts. Neither the reproductions nor images indicate the author or product origin. TB claims not to have consented to Castorama and Knor selling the reproductions in their channels of distribution.

---

1 Ewa Nagy is a senior associate at Wardyński & Partners law firm, Poland.

On 13 October 2020, TB sent Castorama a cease-and-desist letter claiming infringement of moral and economic copyright. On 15 December 2020, TB took action at the Regional Court in Warsaw and requested it to issue an order requiring Castorama and Knor to provide information about the reproductions at issue, particularly with regard to distribution networks and quantity of goods received or ordered by them, and a complete list of their suppliers, the dates on which the goods were placed on sale in Castorama's bricks-and-mortar shops and online shop and the quantity and proceeds from the sale of the goods broken down into physical sales and online sales.

TB stated in the request that she held an economic and moral copyright to the reproduced images and that the information was necessary for bringing an action for copyright infringement and seeking damages for unfair competition. The evidence presented by TB consisted only of the printouts of pages from her online shop displaying articles for sale, invoices for the period of 2014 and onwards, printouts from the Castorama website and invoices relating to the sale of the products in question in the Castorama online shop.

Castorama argued in defence that the request at most should proceed only with respect to information on copyright and that the images at issue were not works within the meaning of the Copyright Act. Castorama claimed that the images were neither original nor new and that accepting the request would mean granting protection to ideas and concepts. According to Castorama, both the graphic and text elements were trivial and were not original in terms of the composition, colours or fonts used in comparison with other similar products available on the market. Castorama also referred to the need to protect its business secrets and argued that TB had not proved that the copyright to the images belonged to her.

The Regional Court in Warsaw decided to stay the proceedings and refer the following questions to the Court of Justice for a preliminary ruling:

> *'(1) Should Article 8(1) read in conjunction with Article 4(1) of Directive [2004/48] be understood to refer to a measure to protect intellectual property rights only when the rightholder's intellectual property right has been confirmed in these or other proceedings?*
>
> *If Question 1 is answered in the negative:*
>
> *(2) Should Article 8(1) […], read in conjunction with Article 4(1) of Directive [2004/48] be interpreted as meaning that it is sufficient to lend credence to the fact that that measure refers to an existing intellectual property right, and not to prove that circumstance, especially in a case where a request for information about the origin and distribution networks of goods or services precedes the assertion of claims for compensation on account of an infringement of intellectual property rights?'*

In simple words, the CJEU was requested to provide an answer to a question on what is a standard of evidence that must be presented in incidental proceedings, the aim of which is to receive information needed to prepare a statement of claim against infringer of intellectual property rights. The referring court wanted to establish whether an applicant must prove that the intellectual property right underlying the request belongs to the applicant or whether it is sufficient to substantiate that fact, especially in a situation when a statement of claims has not yet been submitted.

2. Decision

Article 8(1) of Directive 2004/48/EC of the European Parliament and of the Council of 29 April 2004 on the enforcement of intellectual property right must be interpreted as meaning that, in proceedings concerning an infringement of an intellectual property right under that provision, the applicant must, for the purpose of a request for information under Article 8, provide any reasonably available evidence enabling the court seised of that request to satisfy itself with a sufficient degree of certainty that the applicant is the rightholder, by submitting evidence appropriate to the nature of that right and any special applicable formalities.

3. Motivation and analysis

The CJEU noted first that the purpose of Directive 2004/48/EC of the European Parliament and of the Council of 29 April 2004 on the enforcement of intellectual property right was to provide a high standard of protection of intellectual property rights on the internal market.[2]

According to Article 8(1)(a) of the Directive, Member States are to ensure that, in proceedings concerning infringement of an intellectual property right and in response to a justified and proportionate request from the applicant, competent judicial authorities may order that information on the origin and distribution networks of goods or services which infringe an intellectual property right be provided by the infringer and/or any other person who was found in possession of the infringing goods on a commercial scale.[3]

The CJEU further stated that the provision cited above does not require that the applicant should provide evidence of being the owner of the intellectual property right concerned.[4]

---

2 Para. 32 of the annotated decision.

3 Para. 32 of the annotated decision.

4 Para. 33 of the annotated decision.

The CJEU also noted that Article 4 of the Directive lists entities eligible to apply to the court to order the other party to provide information relating to infringement on grounds of Article 8(1)(a) of the Directive. These entities are:

> *'a) the holders of intellectual property rights, in accordance with the provisions of the applicable law;*
>
> *b) all other persons authorised to use those rights, in particular licensees, in so far as permitted by and in accordance with the provisions of the applicable law;*
>
> *c) intellectual property collective rights-management bodies which are regularly recognised as having a right to represent holders of intellectual property rights, in so far as permitted by and in accordance with the provisions of the applicable law;*
>
> *d) professional defence bodies which are regularly recognised as having a right to represent holders of intellectual property rights, in so far as permitted by and in accordance with the provisions of the applicable law.'*[5]

The CJEU acknowledged that because Article 4(a) refers to rightholders, the provision could be understood as requiring the applicant to prove actual ownership of intellectual property rights.[6]

However, the CJEU stated that such reasoning would be contrary to the context and purposes of the Directive. The CJEU noted specifically that for the purposes of:
- a request for disclosure of evidence by the opposing party (Art. 6 Dir.);
- a request for preservation of evidence (Art. 7 Dir.);
- a request for a preliminary injunction or seizure or delivery of goods suspected of infringing intellectual property rights (Art. 9(1) and (2) Dir.)[7]

an applicant must present:
- '*reasonably available evidence sufficient to support [his or her] claims*' (Art. 6 Dir.);
- '*reasonably available evidence to support his/her claims that his/her intellectual property right has been infringed*' (Art. 7 Dir.);
- '*any reasonably available evidence in order to satisfy [the authorities] with a sufficient degree of certainty that the applicant is the rightholder and that the applicant's right is being infringed*' (Art. 9(1) and (2) Dir.).[8]

As, according to a CJEU ruling of 18 January 2017 in *NEW WAVE*, C-427/15, a request to provide information can be submitted not only in the framework

[5] Para. 34 of the annotated decision.

[6] Para. 35 of the annotated decision.

[7] Para. 38 of the annotated decision.

[8] Para. 38 of the annotated decision.

of proceedings for infringement, but also separately after such proceedings conclude, such proceedings must be considered as separate proceedings.[9]

Moreover, the right to information provided in Article 8(1) of the Directive must be considered as a concretisation of the remedy provided in Article 47 of the Charter of Fundamental Rights of the European Union, which guarantees effective enforcement of the fundamental right to property.[10]

The CJEU consequently pointed out that the aim of a request to provide information on the basis of Article 8(1) of the Directive is different from the aim of proceedings to establish that an infringement has occurred. The aim of proceedings regulated in Article 8 of the Directive is to:

- identify entities that infringe an intellectual property right;
- enable necessary steps to protect an intellectual property right such as submitting requests for a preliminary injunction or seizure of goods provided in Art. 9 of the Directive;
- enable precise calculation of the amount of damages to which the applicant is entitled by reason of the infringement.[11]

If the same standard of evidence were required with respect to both the request to provide information and the statement of claim, the separate proceedings provided for in Art. 8 of the Directive would lose their practical meaning.[12]

The CJEU concluded that, in order to specify what evidence would be sufficient in the context of the procedure for requesting information provided for in Article 8 of the Directive, one must take into consideration the nature of the right in question and formalities required to have been granted that right.[13]

Because obtaining copyright does not require registration, the referring court must therefore analyse whether the evidence produced by the applicant proves that the applicant is in fact entitled to claim copyright to a work. The referring court must also consider whether a submitted request is not an abuse of the right. If the request is considered to be an abuse, the court should dismiss it.[14]

This led the CJEU to conclude that an applicant in proceedings based on Article 8 of the Directive must present any reasonably available evidence enabling the court seized of that request to satisfy itself with a sufficient degree of certainty that the

---

[9] Para. 41 of the annotated decision.

[10] Para. 43 of the annotated decision.

[11] Para. 43 of the annotated decision.

[12] Para. 45 of the annotated decision.

[13] Para. 46 of the annotated decision.

[14] Para. 52 of the annotated decision.

applicant is the rightholder; such evidence must be appropriate to the nature of that right and meet any special applicable formalities.[15]

* *
*

The CJEU confirmed the prevailing view among Polish practitioners that the standard of evidence in proceedings based on Article 8 of the Directive should be lower than in proceedings for protection of an intellectual property right and that in a request for information an applicant must only substantiate claims and not prove them. Regrettably, however, the CJEU judgment did not give practical guidelines on examples of evidence that can be considered sufficient to be granted a request for information within the meaning of Article 8(1) of the Directive. Notions such as '*a sufficient degree of certainty that the applicant is the rightholder*' are vague and subject to interpretation. Unquestionably, such a degree of satisfaction is easier to accomplish in proceedings concerning registered intellectual property rights than in proceedings relating to intellectual property rights whose existence does not require registration (such as copyright).

15 Para. 55 of the annotated decision.

COURT OF JUSTICE 8 JUNE 2023

ON THE QUESTION OF WHETHER A COUNTERCLAIM FOR A DECLARATION OF INVALIDITY OF AN EU TRADEMARK MAY RELATE TO ALL THE RIGHTS WHICH THE PROPRIETOR OF THAT MARK DERIVES FROM ITS REGISTRATION

Case C-654/21

Summary and Analysis by Patrycja Gierdal[1]

Parties:

LM

v

KP

1. Background and History

LM is the proprietor of the EU word mark Multiselect (the 'contested mark'), registered on 5 June 2018 for goods and services in Classes 9, 41, and 42 of the Nice Agreement (*inter alia* for vocational guidance, education information, publication of texts and provision of online electronic publications). Since 2009 KP had been offering a guide for prospective police officers. The guide, available in both print and digital formats, aimed to assist candidates in preparing for psychological tests (covered by the contested mark), which constituted a part of the recruitment process for police officers. KP promoted its guide across various platforms.

On 26 February 2020, LM filed a lawsuit against KP before the Regional Court in Warsaw (the 'referring court') alleging infringement of the contested mark. LM sought an order for KP to cease using the contested mark on goods and services and on all materials connected with the marketing of those goods and services.

In response, KP filed a counterclaim on 30 July 2020, seeking a declaration of invalidity of the contested mark for certain goods and services for which it had been registered, based on Article 59(1) of Regulation 2017/1001. KP argued that the contested mark should be invalidated not only for the goods and services that were the subject of the main action but also for other goods and services.

In its judgment of 7 October 2021, the referring court dismissed LM's infringement claim entirely. However, in relation to KP's counterclaim, it expressed

[1] Patrycja Gierdal is a lawyer at Wardyński & Partners law firm, Poland.

uncertainty about the scope of examination it should undertake. The counterclaim extended beyond a defence against the infringement action, raising questions about the scope of a declaration of invalidity sought in a counterclaim, specifically, whether the trade mark could be invalidated only with respect to the goods and services directly related to the infringement proceedings or more broadly.

Additionally, the referring court explained that on the date on which the action for infringement at issue in the main proceedings was brought, Polish law did not provide for the possibility of defendants in infringement proceedings brought by proprietors of trade marks registered in Poland filing a counterclaim for a declaration of invalidity, since Article 479 of the Code of Civil Procedure, inserted by the Law of 13 February 2020, had not yet entered into force on that date. It therefore had doubts as to whether, for the purposes of the case in the main proceedings, those provisions could be regarded as '*rules of procedure governing the same type of action relating to a national trade mark*' within the meaning of Article 129(3) of Regulation 2017/1001.

Consequently, the referring court decided to stay the proceedings and refer the following questions to the Court of Justice for a preliminary ruling:

> *'Must Article 124(d) of Regulation [2017/1001], in conjunction with Article 128(1) thereof, be interpreted to mean that a "counterclaim for [...] a declaration of invalidity" may only encompass claims connected with the claimant's EU trademark infringement claim, thereby permitting a national court to disregard counterclaims broader in scope than those linked to the claimant's infringement claim?'*
>
> *'Must Article 129(3) of Regulation [2017/1001] be construed as Referring to the national procedural rules applicable to specific proceedings concerning infringement of an EU trademark (and resulting from a counterclaim seeking a declaration of invalidity), or does it encompass the general national procedural rules present in a Member State's legal system, particularly relevant when the legal procedures for counterclaims for a declaration of invalidity were absent from the legal order of a Member State at the time the infringement proceedings concerning an EU trademark were initiated?'*

2. Decision

Article 124(d) of Regulation (EU) 2017/1001 of the European Parliament and of the Council of 14 June 2017 on the European Union trademark, read in conjunction with Article 128(1) thereof, must be interpreted as meaning that a counterclaim for a declaration of invalidity of an EU trademark may relate to all the rights which the proprietor of that mark derives from its registration and

that the subject matter of that counterclaim is not restricted by the scope of the dispute as defined by the action for infringement.

3. Motivation and Analysis

i) The first question

In addressing the first question raised by the referring court, the CJEU primarily examined whether Article 124(d) of Regulation 2017/1001, when read together with Article 128(1) thereof, allowed for a broad interpretation of the scope of a counterclaim for a declaration of invalidity of an EU trademark. The CJEU noted the absence of a specific definition of 'counterclaim' in the regulation and commented that it was general understood to mean a cross-action initiated by the defendant in response to proceedings initiated by the claimant before the same court.[2]

Emphasising the distinction between a counterclaim and a mere defence,[3] the CJEU underscored that a counterclaim constitutes a separate legal claim, independent of the main action, which can proceed even if the principal claim is dismissed. It serves to extend the subject matter of the dispute, aiming to secure recognition of a distinct claim, such as the invalidity of the trademark in question.[4]

The CJEU reinforced its interpretation by highlighting that the nature of a counterclaim remains independent, notwithstanding its link to the main action. It asserted that the outcome of a counterclaim is not contingent upon the resolution of the infringement action, underscoring its independent procedural treatment.[5]

Further, the CJEU examined the provisions of Regulation 2017/1001 concerning the grounds for invalidity that may be invoked in support of a counterclaim. It explained that although the Regulation distinguishes between the entities eligible to file an application for invalidity before EUIPO and those authorised to file a counterclaim in infringement proceedings, such a distinction does not curtail the subject matter of the counterclaim. The CJEU asserted that a counterclaim

2 Para. 31 of the annotated decision.

3 In answering the preliminary question, the CJEU relied on its recent judgment of 13 October 2022 in Case C-256/21 KP v TV, (Gemeinde Bodman-Ludwigshafen), in which it held that the national court must rule on a counterclaim for rescission or revocation even if the infringement action had been withdrawn.

4 Paras. 32-33 of the annotated decision.

5 Para. 34 of the annotated decision.

for invalidity, as per Article 128(1), may rely only on grounds explicitly outlined in the regulation but is not confined to the claimant's interests.[6]

The CJEU also analysed the implications of Article 59 and Article 7(1) of Regulation 2017/1001, which outline absolute grounds for invalidity, affirming that some of these grounds may relate only to all goods or services covered by the trade mark registration.[7] It contended that restricting the subject matter of a counterclaim based on these grounds would contravene the principle of procedural economy.[8]

In conclusion, the CJEU affirmed that a counterclaim for a declaration of invalidity of an EU trademark can encompass all rights derived from the trade mark's registration, without limitation by the scope of the infringement dispute.[9]

ii) The second question

In addressing the second question, the referring court sought clarification on whether general national procedural rules governing the scope of counterclaims in other legal contexts, in the absence of specific national provisions concerning counterclaims for a declaration of invalidity of national trade marks, could be considered as '*rules of procedure governing the same type of action*' under Article 129(3) of Regulation 2017/1001.

However, given its response to the first question, which affirmed the expansive scope of a counterclaim for a declaration of invalidity of an EU trademark, the CJEU deemed it unnecessary to address the second question. Since it had established that EU law does indeed govern the scope of such counterclaims, there was no need to delve into the applicability of national procedural rules in this context. Therefore, the CJEU's decision on the first question had rendered the second question superfluous.[10]

* *
*

The decision means that defendants have the choice between filing an invalidity or revocation application with EUIPO, or bringing a counterclaim in the infringement proceedings. The CJEU clarified that the two have the same scope and are equally suitable to attack the EUTM on which the infringement action is based.

---

6 Para. 36-40 of the annotated decision.

7 Paras. 41-46 of the annotated decision.

8 Para. 44 of the annotated decision.

9 Para. 55 of the annotated decision.

10 Paras. 56-57 of the annotated decision.

The CJEU emphasised that a counterclaim constitutes a distinct action separate from an infringement lawsuit. Consequently, a counterclaim should be addressed even if the infringement case is dismissed or withdrawn and is not constrained by the subject matter of the infringement claim. The CJEU confirmed that as a result of the counterclaim the entire trade mark can be declared invalid even if the main action only concerns its use for some goods or services.

COURT OF JUSTICE 11 JUNE 2023

ON THE COPYRIGHT PROTECTION OF A PRODUCT

Case C-833/18

Summary and Analysis by Eva Gostiša[1]

Parties:

SI
Brompton Bicycle Ltd

v

Chedech/Get2Get

1. Background and History

The central issue in this case was the protection arising from copyright and whether that protection can apply to a product whose shape is, at least in part, necessary to obtain a technical result.

Brompton, a company incorporated under English law whose founder is SI, markets a folding bicycle, sold in its current form since 1987 ('the Brompton bicycle'). The Brompton bicycle, which is characterised by the fact that it can have three different positions (a folded position, an unfolded position and a stand-by position enabling the bicycle to stay balanced on the ground), had been protected by a patent which had subsequently expired.[2]

[1] Eva Gostiša is a partner at the Slovenian law firm Jadek & Pensa d.o.o., specialising among other things in IP law, and is a member of the Slovenian Bar Association.

[2] Paras. 10-11 of the annotated judgment.

Get2Get marketed a bicycle ('the Chedech bicycle') which was visually very similar to the Brompton bicycle, and which could be folded into the three positions mentioned in the preceding paragraph.[3]

In 2017, SI and Brompton brought an action before the Tribunal de l'entreprise de Liège (Enterprise Court of Liège, Belgium) seeking a ruling that Chedech bicycles infringed Brompton's copyright and SI's non-pecuniary rights and, consequently, an order that Get2Get cease its activities infringing their rights and withdraw the product from all sales outlets.

In its defence, Get2Get contended that the appearance of the Chedech bicycle was dictated by the technical solution sought, which is to ensure that the bicycle can fold into three different positions. In those circumstances, such an appearance could be protected only under patent law, not under copyright law. However, the applicants in the main proceedings, Brompton and SI, claimed that the three positions of the Brompton bicycle could be obtained by shapes other than those given to the bicycle by its creator, which meant that its shape could be protected by copyright.[4]

The Enterprise Court of Liège observed that, under Belgian law, any creation is protected by copyright when it is expressed in a particular shape and is original, which means that a utilitarian object, such as a bicycle, may be protected by copyright. In that regard, although shapes necessary to obtain a technical result are excluded from copyright protection, the fact remains that doubt arises when such a result can be obtained by means of other shapes.

In the field of design law, the CJEU had already interpreted Article 8(1) of Regulation No 6/2002[5] as meaning that, in order to determine whether the features of appearance of a product are exclusively dictated by its technical function, it must be established that the technical function is the only factor which determined those features, the existence of alternative designs not being decisive in

[3] Para. 12 of the annotated judgment.

[4] Paras. 14-15 of the annotated judgment.

[5] Council Regulation (EC) No 6/2002 of 12 December 2001 on Community designs.

that regard.[6] The question therefore was whether a similar solution should be adopted in the field of copyright when the appearance of the product in respect of which copyright protection was sought under Directive 2001/29 was necessary in order to achieve a particular technical effect.

In those circumstances, the Enterprise Court of Liège decided to stay the proceedings and to refer the following questions to the Court of Justice for a preliminary ruling:

> *'1) Must EU law, in particular Directive [2001/29], which determines, inter alia, the various exclusive rights conferred on copyright holders, in Articles 2 to 5 thereof, be interpreted as excluding from copyright protection works whose shape is necessary to achieve a technical result?*
>
> *2) In order to assess whether a shape is necessary to achieve a technical result, must account be taken of the following criteria:*
> - *The existence of other possible shapes which allow the same technical result to be achieved?*
> - *The effectiveness of the shape in achieving that result?*
> - *The intention of the alleged infringer to achieve that result?*
> - *The existence of an earlier, now expired, patent on the process for achieving the technical result sought?'*

2. Decision

Articles 2 to 5 of Directive 2001/29/EC of the European Parliament and of the Council of 22 May 2001 on the harmonisation of certain aspects of copyright and related rights in the information society must be interpreted as meaning that the copyright protection provided for therein applies to a product whose shape is, at least in part, necessary to obtain a technical result, where that product is an original work resulting from intellectual creation, in that, through that shape, its author expresses his creative ability in an original manner by making free and creative choices in such a way that that shape reflects his personality, which it is for the national court to verify, bearing in mind all the relevant aspects of the dispute in the main proceedings.

3. Motivation and Analysis

A crucial point of discussion was whether Articles 2 to 5 of Directive 2001/29[7] must be interpreted as meaning that the copyright protection provided for

[6] Case C-395/16, 8 March 2018, *DOCERAM GmbH v CeramTec.*

[7] Dir. 2001/29/EC of the European Parliament and of the Council of 22 May 2001 on the harmonisation of certain aspects of copyright and related rights in the information society.

therein applies to a product whose shape is, at least in part, necessary to obtain a technical result. Under Articles 2 to 5 of Directive 2001/29, authors are protected against the reproduction, communication to the public and distribution to the public of their works without their authorisation.

The CJEU grounded its decision on the concept of 'work'.[8] It explained that the concept of 'work' has two conditions. First, it entails an original subject matter which is the author's own intellectual creation and, second, it requires the expression of that creation.[9] As to the first condition, the CJEU explained that if a subject matter is to be capable of being regarded as original, it is both necessary and sufficient that the subject matter reflects the personality of its author, as an expression of his free and creative choices.[10] In this regard the CJEU pointed out the settled case-law according to which, where the realisation of a subject matter has been dictated by technical considerations, rules or other constraints which have left no room for creative freedom, that subject matter cannot be regarded as possessing the originality required for it to constitute a work and, consequently, to be eligible for the protection conferred by copyright.[11] As to the second condition, the concept of 'work' that is the subject of Directive 2001/29 necessarily entails the existence of a subject matter that is identifiable with sufficient precision and objectivity.[12]

From the above, the CJEU deduced that a subject matter which satisfies the condition of originality may be eligible for copyright protection, even if its realisation has been dictated by technical considerations, provided that this has not prevented the author from reflecting his personality in that subject matter, as an expression of free and creative choices.[13] The CJEU also pointed out that the criterion of originality cannot be met by elements of an object which differ only in their technical function, since copyright protection does not extend to ideas.[14] The protection of ideas by copyright would amount to making it possible to monopolise ideas, to the detriment, in particular, of technical progress and industrial development.[15] Where the expression of those components is

---

8 Para. 22 of the annotated judgment.

9 See, by analogy, C-683/17, 12 September 2019, *Cofemel – Sociedade de Vestuário SA v G-Star Raw CV*, paras. 29 and 32.

10 Para. 23 of the annotated judgment, see, by analogy, C-683/17, 12 September 2019, *Cofemel – Sociedade de Vestuário SA v G-Star Raw CV*, para. 30.

11 Para. 24 of the annotated judgment, see, by analogy, C-683/17, 12 September 2019, *Cofemel – Sociedade de Vestuário SA v G-Star Raw CV*, para. 31.

12 Para 25, of the annotated judgment, see, by analogy, C-683/17, 12 September 2019, *Cofemel – Sociedade de Vestuário SA v G-Star Raw CV*, para. 32.

13 Para. 26 of the annotated judgment.

14 Article 2 of the WIPO Copyright Treaty: '*The Copyright protection extends to expressions and not to ideas, procedures, methods of operation or mathematical concepts as such.*'

15 Para. 27 of the annotated judgment, see, by analogy, C-406/10, 2 May 2012, *SAS Institute Inc. v World Programming Ltd*, paras. 33 and 40.

dictated by their technical function, the different methods of implementing an idea are so limited that the idea and the expression become indissociable.[16]

The CJEU established that the shape of the Brompton bicycle appears necessary to obtain a certain technical result, namely that the bicycle may be folded into three positions, one of which allows it to be kept balanced on the ground. However, in spite of that fact, it directed the referring court to take account of all the relevant aspects of the present case, as they existed when that subject matter was designed, irrespective of the factors external to and subsequent to the creation of the product. The CJEU therefore allowed the possibility that even if the shape of a certain product is partly necessary to obtain a certain technical result, it can still be eligible for copyright protection, i.e. that through that choice of the shape of the product, its author has expressed his creative ability in an original manner by making free and creative choices and has designed the product in such a way that it reflects his personality.

The CJEU also provided a partial answer to the second question posed by the national court concerning possible criteria to be taken into account when assessing whether a shape is necessary to obtain a technical result. As regards the point that the existence of other possible shapes capable of achieving the same technical result makes it possible to establish the existence of a choice, the CJEU followed its settled case-law[17] and pointed out that, in so far as only the originality of the product in question is to be assessed, the existence of other possible shapes capable of achieving the same technical result, although making it possible to establish the existence of a choice, is not decisive in assessing the factors which influenced the choice made by the creator.[18] Furthermore, according to the CJEU, the intention of the alleged infringer is irrelevant in such an assessment.[19] The CJEU also commented on previous patent protection and concluded that the existence of an earlier, already expired, patent and the effectiveness of the shape in achieving the same technical result should be taken into account only in so far as those factors make it possible to determine what was taken into consideration in choosing the shape of the product concerned.[20]

With this last point, the CJEU followed the approach suggested by the Advocate General M. Campos Sánchez-Bordona in his Opinion[21] on the cumulation of

---

[16] See C-393/09, 22 December 2010, *Bezpečnostní softwarová asociace – Svaz softwarové ochrany v Ministerstvo kultury*, paras. 48 and 49.

[17] See C-395/16, 8 March 2018, *DOCERAM GmbH v CeramTec*, para. 32: '*[...] the technical function is the only factor which determined those features, the existence of alternative designs not being decisive in that regard*,' representing the rejection by the CJEU of the so-called 'multiplicity of forms theory'.

[18] Para. 35 of the annotated judgment.

[19] Para. 35 of the annotated judgment.

[20] Para. 36 of the annotated judgment.

[21] Opinion of Advocate General M. Campos Sánchez-Bordona delivered on 6 February 2020.

rights, in which he considered that an earlier patent right may have a twofold effect: firstly, a registered patent may serve to determine whether there were technical constraints which dictated the shape of the product and, secondly, the choice of a patent as a means for protecting the activity of the person registering that patent makes it possible to assume that there is a close relationship between the patented shape and the result intended. The shape is that which the inventor decided was effective, achieving the desired functionality.

With this decision the CJEU clarified its approach to designs and copyright works and aspects of their protection when it comes to the appearance of a product which is determined solely by its technical function. It correctly held that even if the realisation is dictated by technical considerations, there is still room for the author's creativity, which must be adequately protected.

On the other hand, it should be noted that while in the DOCERAM[22] case the CJEU adopted the causality approach, in the present case, although following the same approach, the Court was somewhat more careful in its choice of words, emphasising '*the author's creative ability in an original manner by making free and creative choices in such a way that that shape reflects his personality, which it is for the national court to verify, bearing in mind all the relevant aspects of the dispute in the main proceedings.*'[23]

The CJEU thus reiterated the important distinction between the functionality of a design and the creativity of copyright works. As explained in the Cofemel[24] case, '*the protection of designs, on the one hand, and copyright protection, on the other, pursue fundamentally different objectives and are subject to distinct rules. The purpose of the protection of designs is to protect subject matter which, while being new and distinctive, is functional and liable to be mass-produced. Further, that protection is to apply for a limited time, but sufficient time to ensure a return on the investment necessary for the creation and production of that subject matter, without thereby excessively restricting competition. For its part, the protection attached to copyright, the duration of which is significantly greater, is reserved to subject matter that merits being classified as works.*'

---

22 See C-395/16, 8 March 2018, *DOCERAM GmbH v CeramTec.*

23 Para. 38 of the annotated judgment.

24 Case C-683/17, 12 September 2019, *Cofemel – Sociedade de Vestuário SA v G-Star Raw CV*, para. 50.

Court of Justice 13 July 2023

On the scope of the 'private copying' exception and the right to communication to the public with regard to IPTV service providers

Case C-426/21

Summary and Analysis by Marie Manhaeve[1]

Parties:

Ocilion IPTV Technologies GmbH

v

Seven.One Entertainment Group GmbH, Puls 4 TV GmbH & Co. KG

1. Background and History

Ocilion provides an Internet television service ('IPTV service') to commercial customers such as network operators, telephone companies and hotels ('network operators').

By using Ocilion's IPTV services, these network operators are able to offer their end-users a dual functionality.[2] The IPTV service consists of both (i) the retransmission of television broadcasts and (ii) the possibility for end-users to temporarily record these broadcasts via an online recording tool. The recorded material is made available to any other end-user programming the same broadcast due to a de-duplication process, which prevents multiple copies from being made.

This service is offered either (i) as an on-premises solution, in which Ocilion makes the necessary hardware and software available to the network operators with technical support, or (ii) as a cloud-hosting solution, directly managed by Ocilion.

Seven.One Entertainment Group GmbH and Puls 4 TV GmbH & Co ('Seven.One and others'), are TV broadcasting companies that hold retransmission rights over TV programs made available via Ocilion's IPTV service. They objected to two aspects of Ocilion's IPTV service.

---

1 Marie Manhaeve is an IP/IT lawyer at the Brussels Bar, Belgium.

2 Para. 42 of the annotated judgment.

Seven.One and others argued that there was (i) a violation of their exclusive right of communication to the public of their television programs,[3] as they did not consent to the retransmission of this content through Ocilion's service, and (ii) a violation of their exclusive right of reproduction,[4] since the means by which Ocilion's online recorder operates does not fall within the 'private copying' exception.

Seven.One and others filed an application for interim measures to prevent Ocilion from making their TV programs available to its customers or reproducing them without their consent. This application was granted at first instance, and the decision was upheld on appeal. Consequently, Ocilion brought the case before the Oberster Gerichtshof (Supreme Court, Austria) for further review.

The Austrian Supreme Court decided to stay the proceedings and to refer the following questions to the Court of Justice for a preliminary ruling:

> '1. *Is a national provision compatible with EU law if it permits, on the basis of Article 5(2)(b) of Directive [2001/29], the operation of an online video recorder which is [made available] by a commercial provider and which*
>
> *(a) by virtue of the de-duplication process implemented as a technical means, does not create an independent copy of the programmed broadcasting content for each recording initiated by a user, but, in so far as the content in question has already been stored on the initiative of another user who was the first user to record that content, merely makes a referencing – in order to avoid redundant data – which allows the subsequent user to access the content already stored;*
>
> *(b) has a replay function via which the entire television programme of all selected channels is recorded around the clock and made available for retrieval over a period of seven days, provided that the user makes a one-off selection to that effect in respect of the channels concerned by ticking a box in the menu of the online video recorder; and*
>
> *(c) also provides the user with access (either embedded in a cloud service of the provider or as part of the complete on-premises IPTV solution provided by the provider) to protected broadcasting content without the consent of the rightholders?*

---

[3] Para. 18a(1) of the Urheberrechtsgesetz (Law on Copyright) of 9 April 1936 provides that: '*the author shall have the exclusive right to make the work available to the public, by wire or wireless means, in such a way that allows members of the public to access it from a place and at a time chosen by them.*'

[4] Para. 15 of the Urheberrechtsgesetz (Law on Copyright) of 9 April 1936 provides that: '*the author shall have the exclusive right to reproduce the work, irrespective of the process used and the quantity reproduced, temporarily or permanently.*'

2. Is the term "communication to the public" in Article 3(1) of Directive 2001/29 to be interpreted as meaning that such communication is carried out by a commercial provider of a complete (on-premises) IPTV solution, in the context of which it provides, in addition to software and hardware for receiving TV programmes via the internet, technical support and makes adjustments to the service on an ongoing basis, but that service is operated entirely on the customer's infrastructure, if the service provides the user with access not only to broadcasting content whose online use has been authorised by the respective rightholders, but also to protected content for which rights clearance has not been obtained, and the provider

(a) can influence which TV programmes can be received by the end user via the service,

(b) is aware that its service also enables the reception of protected broadcasting content without the consent of the rightholders, but

(c) does not advertise that possibility of unauthorised use of its service, thereby creating a major incentive to purchase the product, but rather advises its customers at the time of conclusion of the contract that they must take care of the granting of rights on their own responsibility, and

(d) does not provide, through its activity, special access to broadcasting content which, in the absence of its intervention, could not be received or could be received only with difficulty?'

2. Decision

1. Article 2 and Article 5(2)(b) of Directive 2001/29/EC of the European Parliament and of the Council of 22 May 2001 on the harmonisation of certain aspects of copyright and related rights in the information society must be interpreted as meaning that the exception to the exclusive right of authors and broadcasting organisations to authorise or prohibit the reproduction of protected works does not cover a service offered by an operator of retransmission of online television broadcasts to commercial customers allowing, on the basis of a cloud-hosting solution or based on the necessary hardware and software made available on premises, a continuous or one-off recording of those broadcasts, on the initiative of the end users of that service, where the copy made by the first of those users to have selected a broadcast is made available, by the operator, to an indeterminate number of users who wish to view the same content.

2. Article 3(1) of Directive 2001/29 must be interpreted as meaning that the supply by an operator of retransmission of online television broadcasts to its commercial customer of the necessary hardware and software, including technical assistance, which enables that customer to allow its own customers to replay online television broadcasts, does not constitute a 'communication to the public' within the meaning of that provision, even if that operator is aware that

its service may be used to access protected broadcasting content without the consent of the authors.

3. Motivation and Analysis

i) First preliminary question – the 'private copying' exception

In accordance with Article 2 of Directive 2001/29 ('InfoSoc Directive'),[5] copyright holders enjoy an exclusive right to authorise or prohibit the reproduction of their works. Article 5(2), subparagraph b of the InfoSoc Directive provides for an exception to the exclusive right to reproduction, the so-called 'private copying' exception.[6] This exception allows natural persons to make copies of protected works for their private use and for non-commercial purposes without the rightsholders' consent.

In its analysis of the first preliminary question, the Court reiterated that the concept of 'reproduction' must be construed broadly to ensure a high level of protection for the rightsholders and legal certainty within the internal market. The Court also emphasised that the exceptions and limitations provided for in Article 5(2) of the InfoSoc Directive should only be applied where they do not hinder the normal exploitation of the work or unreasonably prejudice the legitimate interests of the rightsholder.[7] The underlying rationale is the need to strike a fair balance between the rights of authors and broadcasters and the rights of users.[8]

In the light of the foregoing, the Court then examined whether a service, such as that offered by Ocilion, is capable of falling within the 'private copying' exception.

---

5 Dir. 2001/29/EC of the European Parliament and of the Council of 22 May 2001 on the harmonisation of certain aspects of copyright and related rights in the information society (OJ 2001 L 167, p. 10).

6 Art. 5(2)(b) Dir. 2001/29 states: '*in respect of reproductions on any medium made by a natural person for private use and for ends that are neither directly nor indirectly commercial, on condition that the rightholders receive fair compensation which takes account of the application or non-application of technological measures referred to in Article 6 to the work or subject-matter concerned.*'

7 Rec. 44 in the preamble to Dir. 2001/29 states that: '*Such exceptions and limitations may not be applied in a way which prejudices the legitimate interests of the rightholder or which conflicts with the normal exploitation of his work or other subject-matter.*'

8 See also Case C-516/17, 29 July 2019, *Spiegel Online*, para. 54 and Case C-682/18 and C-683/18, 22 June 2021, *YouTube and Cyando*, para. 64.

The first consideration here was whether the findings in the very similar VCAST case[9] could be transposed to a service such as the one offered by Ocilion. As a reminder, VCAST offered a B2C service for the remote recording of private copies by actively involving itself in the recording and without the rightsholder's consent. In that regard, the Court held that, since legal persons are excluded from the benefit of the exception, Ocilion – offering its service in the context of its commercial activity – in any event cannot be considered as making a copy falling within the private copying exception.[10]

Ocilion argued, however, that its IPTV service was limited to the mere provision of a tool enabling an end user to replay television programs on his/her own initiative and solely for his/her private purposes. It further stated that the de-duplication technique it used did not unreasonably prejudice the legitimate interests of exclusive rightsholders.[11]

The Court rebutted Ocilion's argument on various grounds.

Firstly, the Court found that, although it was true that the end user himself or herself programmed the recordings, the content recording and the making available of these recordings to an *indeterminate number of end users* was *the main interest* of the offer provided, and the IPTV service had an underlying commercial interest that fell outside the scope of Article 5(2)(b) of the InfoSoc Directive.[12] Secondly, the system used did not satisfy the three-step test provided for in Article 5(5) of the InfoSoc Directive,[13] as access to recorded broadcasts for an indeterminate number of recipients for commercial purposes could unreasonably prejudice the legitimate interest of exclusive rightsholders and undermine the fair balance between their interests and those of end-users.

In those circumstances, the Court ruled that the service offered by Ocilion was not covered by the 'private copying' exception.[14]

ii) Second preliminary question – the communication to the public

Article 3 of the InfoSoc Directive provides that authors have the exclusive right to authorise or prohibit any communication to the public of their protected works, using wired or wireless methods, which includes offering their works to

[9] Case C-265/16, 29 November 2017, *VCAST*.

[10] Para. 39 of the annotated judgment.

[11] Para. 40 of the annotated judgment.

[12] Paras. 40-49 of the annotated judgment.

[13] Art. 5(5) of Dir. 2001/29 states that: '*The exceptions and limitations provided for in paragraphs 1, 2, 3 and 4 shall only be applied in certain special cases which do not conflict with a normal exploitation of the work or other subject-matter and do not unreasonably prejudice the legitimate interests of the rightholder.*'

[14] Para. 46 of the annotated judgment.

the public in a manner that allows individuals to access them from a place and time of their own choosing.

The Court emphasised that this concept is also to be interpreted broadly[15] and covers all forms of communication to the public beyond the location of the initial communication,[16] including broadcasting. The overall aim of the InfoSoc Directive is to establish a robust level of protection for authors, ensuring that they receive fair compensation for the use of their works, including in the context of a communication to the public.[17]

The notion of 'communication to the public' includes two cumulative criteria, namely (i) an act of transmission or retransmission of a work, irrespective of the technical means or process used,[18] and (ii) the communication of that work to a public.

The Court also required an individual assessment,[19] including an assessment of the 'indispensable role' played by the service provider.[20] In this regard, the Court had previously ruled that a service provider engages in an act of communication when it deliberately provides its customers with access to a protected work, fully aware of the implications of its actions, particularly where, without the provider's intervention, those customers would not be able to enjoy the broadcast work.[21] By contrast, Recital 27 of Directive 2001/29 states that '*the mere provision of physical facilities for enabling*

---

15 Rec. 23 in the preamble to Dir. 2001/29 states that: '*This Directive should harmonise further the author's right of communication to the public. This right should be understood in a broad sense covering all communication to the public not present at the place where the communication originates. This right should cover any such transmission or retransmission of a work to the public by wire or wireless means, including broadcasting. This right should not cover any other acts.*'

16 Para. 55 of the annotated judgment.

17 See also Case C-775/21 and C-826/21, 20 April 2003, *Blue Air Aviation*, para. 46.

18 See also Case C-265/16, 29 November 2017, *VCAST*, para. 42.

19 The interpretation of the autonomous notion of 'communication to the public' requires an individual and factual assessment of the case at hand. Whereas the broadcasting of protected works in hotel rooms (C-306/05, Rafael Hoteles), rehabs (C-117/15, Reha Training) or spas (C-351/12, OSA) has been considered by the Court as acts of communication to the public, the Court ruled the contrary with respect to the broadcasting of protected works in dentists' waiting rooms (C-135/10, Del Corso). More recently, the Court found that the hiring out of motor vehicles equipped with radio receivers does not constitute a communication to the public (C-753/18, Stim and SAMI).

20 Case C-610/15, 14 June 2017, *Stichting Brein*, para. 26 and Case C-775/21 and C-826/21, 20 April 2003, *Blue Air Aviation*, para. 49.

21 Case C-775/21 and C-826/21, 20 April 2003, *Blue Air Aviation*, para. 49 and para. 59 of the annotated judgment.

or making a communication does not in itself amount to communication within the meaning of [that] Directive.'[22]

In analysing the second question, the Court noted that Ocilion itself did not provide end users with access to protected works. While Ocilion equipped network operators with the hardware and software that end-users needed to be able to watch content broadcast on television, the network operators were the only ones who granted the end-users access to protected works. Hence, Ocilion could not be deemed to have performed an act of communication to the public.[23]

The Court added that the mere knowledge on the part of Ocilion that this IPTV service might be used to access protected broadcasting content without the rightholders' consent was not in itself sufficient for it to be regarded as engaging in an act of communication to the public.[24]

In those circumstances, the Court, in line with previous judgments,[25] ruled that the mere provision of hardware and software that enables a customer to allow its own customers to replay online television broadcasts does not constitute a communication to the public.[26]

* *
*

With this decision, the Court further clarified the scope of the 'private copying' exception. Recognising the dynamic nature of the digital environment, it emphasised the importance of the principle of technological neutrality in ensuring that legal interpretations do not hinder innovation or favour one technology over another.[27]

---

22 Rec. 27 in the preamble to Dir. 2001/29 states that: '*This Directive should harmonise further the author's right of communication to the public. This right should be understood in a broad sense covering all communication to the public not present at the place where the communication originates. This right should cover any such transmission or retransmission of a work to the public by wire or wireless means, including broadcasting. This right should not cover any other acts.*'

23 Para. 63 of the annotated judgment.

24 Para. 65 of the annotated judgment. See also Opinion of Advocate General Szpunar of the annotated judgment, para. 54.

25 See e.g. Case C-775/21 and C-826/21, 20 April 2003, *Blue Air Aviation* and Case C-265/16, 29 November 2017, *VCAST*.

26 Para. 67 of the annotated judgment.

27 See, to that effect, Case C-433/20, 24 March 2022, *Austro-Mechana*, paras. 26-27 and Case C-515/19, 15 April 2021, *Eutelsat*, para. 48.

As Advocate General Szpunar[28] emphasised in his Opinion, the Court concluded that it is the service provider that reproduces and then makes the protected works available to the public through the reproductions made. This decision is grounded in the understanding that the system employed by service providers grants access to recorded broadcasts to an indeterminate number of individuals for commercial purposes, posing a potentially unreasonable prejudice to the legitimate interests of rightholders.[29] Consequently, there is no justification for applying the 'private copying' exception for the benefit of the service provider.

Regarding the second part of the ruling, the Court further strengthened its jurisprudence[30] by reiterating that the involvement of the service provider in granting end users access to protected works remains a crucial element for establishing an act of communication to the public.[31]

It is worth noting the link between this judgment and the earlier case C-753/18, Stim and SAMI, in which the CJEU was asked to interpret Article 3(1) of the InfoSoc Directive. In that case, the Court considered whether the hiring out of motor vehicles equipped with radio receivers constituted a communication to the public. It concluded that such a scenario did not amount to an 'act of communication' to the public of protected works, since the supply of a radio receiver, which is an integral part of a hired motor vehicle and enables it to receive, without any additional intervention by the leasing company, the terrestrial radio broadcasts available in the area in which the vehicle is located, does not in itself amount to a communication within the meaning of the Directive.[32] Similarly, in the annotated judgment, the Court upheld this interpretation and confirmed the importance of the 'indispensable role' of the service provider in the establishment of an act of communication.

---

[28] Opinion of Advocate General Szpunar of the annotated judgment, para. 37. See also Opinion of Advocate General Szpunar in Case C-775/21 and C-826/21, *Blue Air Aviation*, 15 December 2022, para. 25.

[29] Paras. 40-49 of the annotated judgment.

[30] See for example Case C-775/21 and C-826/21, 20 April 2003, *Blue Air Aviation* and Case C-265/16, 29 November 2017, *VCAST*.

[31] See also Case C-610/15, 14 June 2017, *Stichting Brein*, para. 26 and Case C-775/21 and C-826/21, 20 April 2003, *Blue Air Aviation*, para. 49.

[32] Case C-753/18, 2 April 2020, *Stim and SAMI*, paras. 33-34.

COURT OF JUSTICE 11 JANUARY 2024

ON THE LIMITATION OF THE EFFECTS OF A TRADE MARK, USE OF A TRADE MARK TO INDICATE THE INTENDED PURPOSE OF A PRODUCT OR SERVICE

Case C-361/22

Summary and Analysis by Lucia Martin-Sanz Barrachina[1]

Parties:

Industria de Diseño Textil SA (Inditex)

v

Buongiorno Myalert SA

1. Background and History

In 2010, the company Buongiorno Myalert SA, ('Buongiorno') launched an advertising campaign for a paid subscription to a multimedia messaging service, marketed under the name 'Club Blinko'. The subscription to this service allowed for participation in a prize draw, in which one of the prizes was a 'ZARA gift card' worth EUR 1,000. After clicking on a banner to access the prize draw, on the next screen the subscriber was shown the 'ZARA' sign in a rectangle, reminiscent of the design of the gift cards.

The Spanish company Industria de Diseño Textil SA (Inditex), owner of the ZARA brand, decided to bring an infringement action before the Commercial Court Madrid, Spain against Buongiorno claiming infringement of the exclusive rights conferred by a national trade mark protecting the 'ZARA' sign ('the ZARA trade mark').

In this action, the defendant denied that rights conferred by the ZARA trade mark were infringed, arguing that the use made was not for branding purposes but to refer to the prizes for the winners of the prize draw. This precise use, it argued, was among those contemplated as 'lawful uses of third parties' in Article 37 of the Trade Mark Law 17/2001 (the 'Trade Mark Law').[2]

---

1 Digital & Tech Law Manager at Herrero & Asociados Abogados, S.L.

2 In its original version, Art. 37(1)(c) of the Trade Mark Law, which transposed Art. 6(1)(c) of First Directive 89/104 into Spanish law, stated:
'The rights conferred by the trade mark shall not entitle the proprietor to prohibit a third party from using, during trade, the elements stated below, provided that that use is in accordance with honest practices in industrial or commercial matters:
(c) the trade mark where it is necessary to indicate the intended purpose of a product or service, in particular as accessories or spare parts.'

The court of first instance dismissed the action on the basis that the conditions set out in Article 34(2)(b) and (c)[3] of the Trade Mark Law were not met, and that the use of the ZARA trade mark did not constitute a 'referential' use covered by Article 37 of the Trade Mark Law.

Inditex appealed against this decision, but without any success: the Superior Court confirmed that the use of the ZARA trade mark by Buongiorno did not damage the reputation of that trade mark or take unfair advantage of that reputation.

Faced with this outcome, Inditex decided to file a cassation appeal before the Spanish Supreme Court.[4]

In these circumstances, the Spanish Supreme Court decided to stay the proceedings and to refer the following question to the Court of Justice for a preliminary ruling:

> *'Must Article 6(1)(c) of [First Directive 89/104] be interpreted as implicitly including within the limitation on trade mark rights the more general conduct now referred to in Article 14(1)(c) of [Directive 2015/2436], namely the use of "the trade mark for the purpose of identifying or referring to goods or services as those of the proprietor of that trade mark"?'*[5]

2. Decision

Article 6(1)(c) of Directive 2008/95/EC of the European Parliament and of the Council of 22 October 2008 to approximate the laws of the Member

---

[3] *'The registered trade mark proprietor shall be entitled to prohibit all third parties not having his or her consent from using in the course of trade: (b) any sign which, because of its identity with, or similarity to, the trade mark and the identity or similarity of the goods or services, gives rise to a likelihood of confusion on the part of the public; the likelihood of confusion includes the likelihood of association between the sign and the trade mark;*
(c) any sign which is identical with, or similar to, goods or services which are not similar to those for which the trade mark is registered, where that trade mark is well known or has a strong reputation in Spain and the use of the sign without due cause may indicate a connection between those goods or services and the trade mark proprietor or, generally, where that use takes unfair advantage of, or is detrimental to, the distinctive character, well-known nature or strong reputation of the registered trade mark.'

[4] Tribunal Supremo.

[5] The Court found it necessary to reformulate the question to the effect that the referring court was asking whether Art. 6(1)(c) Dir. 2008/95 must be interpreted as meaning that it covers any use of the trade mark in the course of trade by a third party for the purpose of identifying or referring to, in accordance with honest practices in industrial or commercial matters, goods or services as those of the proprietor of that trade mark, or only use of that trade mark which is necessary to indicate the intended purpose of a product marketed by that third party or of a service offered by that party.

States relating to trade marks must be interpreted as meaning that it covers use of the trade mark in the course of trade by a third party for the purpose of identifying or referring to, in accordance with honest practices in industrial or commercial matters, goods or services as those of the proprietor of that trade mark only when such use of the trade mark is necessary to indicate the intended purpose of a product marketed by that third party or of a service offered by that party.

3. Motivation and Analysis

As a preliminary question, the Court clarified that the provision applicable *ratione temporis* at the time of the facts in the main proceedings was Article 6(1)(c) of Directive 2008/95, and not Article 6(1)(c) of First Directive 89/104, the latter provision having been replaced by the former. It should, however, be pointed out that the wording of these two provisions is identical.

On the one hand Article 6(1)(c) of Directive 2008/95 provides that a trade mark must not entitle its proprietor to prohibit a third party from using the mark in the course of trade where it is necessary to indicate the intended purpose of a product or service, in particular as accessories or spare parts.

On the other hand, Article 14(1)(c) of Directive 2015/2436 states, first of all, that it covers the use of the trade mark for the purpose of identifying or referring to goods or services as those of the proprietor of the trade mark, and then reproduces the normative content of Article 6(1)(c) of Directive 2008/95, preceded by the expression 'in particular'.

A literal comparison of these two provisions is provided below:

Article 6(1)(c) of Directive 2008/95:

> *'The trade mark shall not entitle the proprietor to prohibit a third party from using, in the course of trade:*
>
> *(c) the trade mark where it is necessary to indicate the intended purpose of a product or service, in particular as accessories or spare parts;'*

Article 14(1)(c) of Directive 2015/2436:

> *'A trade mark shall not entitle the proprietor to prohibit a third party from using, in the course of trade:*
>
> *(c) the trade mark for the purpose of identifying or referring to goods or services as those of the proprietor of that trade mark, in particular, where the use of the trade mark is necessary to indicate the intended purpose of a product or service, in particular as accessories or spare parts'*

The Court noted that a use that is capable of limiting the effects of a trade mark under Article 6(1)(c) of Directive 2008/95 now constitutes one of the situations of lawful use which the proprietor of a trade mark cannot oppose under Article 14(1)(c)of Directive 2015/2436.[6] The scope of Article 6(1)(c) of Directive 2008/95 is more limited than that of Article 14(1)(c) of Directive 2015/2436, in that Article 6(1)(c) covers only the use, in the course of trade, of the trade mark where that is necessary to indicate the intended purpose of a product or service.[7]

Such an understanding of Article 6(1)(c) of Directive 2008/95, it observed, is backed both by the directive's objectives – particularly the intent behind that provision as interpreted through case-law – and by reviewing the legislative development that led to its successor, Article 14(1)(c) of Directive 2015/2436.[8]

Thus, the interpretation of Article 6(1)(c) of Directive 2008/95 is supported by two key points.

Firstly, case-law has established that Article 6(1)(c) aims to reconcile trade mark protection with the free movement of goods and services. It allows third parties to use a trade mark when necessary to provide clear and accurate information about the practical link between their products or services and those of the trade mark owner, provided this use is limited to what is strictly required.[9]

Secondly, the legislative history of Article 14(1)(c) of Directive 2015/2436, which replaced Article 6(1)(c), highlights a consistent intent to limit permissible uses of a trade mark to cases where it is necessary, ensuring alignment with market interests and competition principles.[10]

These elements, the Court stated, confirm the directive's focus on balancing trade mark rights with broader market objectives.

Moreover, and as the Advocate General rightly pointed out in his Opinion[11] according to the Court:

(a) the Commission's intention to propose the introduction of a limitation of the effects of a trade mark covering referential use in general and to extend

---

6 Para. 46 of the annotated judgment.

7 Para. 47 of the annotated judgment.

8 Para. 48 of the annotated judgment.

9 Paras. 49-52 of the annotated judgment, referring *inter alia* to *Gillette*, C-228/03; *Portakabin*, C-558/08.

10 Paras. 53-54 of the annotated judgment.

11 Opinion of advocate general Szpunar delivered on 7 September 2023, Case C-361/22 Industria de Diseño Textil SA (Inditex) v Buongiorno Myalert SA https://eur-lex.europa.eu/legal-content/EN/TXT/HTML/?uri=CELEX:62022CC0361

the scope of the limitation now provided for in Article 14(1)(c) of Directive 2015/2436, is apparent from the term 'appropriate to provide [...] for'[12];

(b) the Commission's intention to extend the scope of the limitation previously contained in Article 6(1)(c) of Directive2008/95 is also apparent from the wording: '*the proprietor should not be entitled to prevent the general fair and honest use of the mark for identifying or referring to the goods or services as those of the proprietor.*'[13]

Therefore, the Court noted, the legislative history of Article 14(1)(c) of Directive 2015/2436 reinforces the interpretation that the scope of Article 6(1)(c) of Directive 2008/95 is narrower than that of its successor.[14]

The Court concluded its judgment by stating that the answer to the question referred was that Article 6(1)(c) of Directive 2008/95 must be interpreted as meaning that it covers use of the trade mark in the course of trade by a third party for the purpose of identifying or referring to, in accordance with honest practices in industrial or commercial matters, goods or services as those of the proprietor of that trade mark only when such use of the trade mark is necessary to indicate the intended purpose of a product marketed by that third party or of a service offered by that party.[15]

* *
*

Following the CJEU's decision, the Supreme Court finally resolved the main dispute in a judgment issued on 10 April 2024.[16] In this judgment, the Supreme Court held that the wording of Article 37[17] in force at the time of the facts only covered the use of a third party's trade mark, in accordance with fair practices, when it was necessary to indicate the purpose of a product or service. It found that this was not the case here.

---

12 Proposal for a Directive of the European Parliament and of the Council to approximate the laws of the Member States relating to trade marks (COM(2013)162 final)

13 Recital 25 of the Proposal for a Directive of the European Parliament and of the Council to approximate the laws of the Member States relating to trade marks (COM(2013)162 final).

14 Para. 56 of the annotated judgment.

15 Para. 58 of the annotated judgment.

16 STS 485/2024, Civil, of 10 April 2024, www.poderjudicial.es/search/AN/openDocument/bdc9d1a15af44d02a0a8778d75e36f0d/20240419.

17 Art. 37(1)(c) of the Law on Trade Marks, which transposed Art. 6(1)(c) of First Directive 89/104 into Spanish law, stated: '*The rights conferred by the trade mark shall not entitle the proprietor to prohibit a third party from using, in the course of trade, the elements stated below, provided that that use is in accordance with honest practices in industrial or commercial matters:*
(c) the trade mark where it is necessary to indicate the intended purpose of a product or service, in particular as accessories or spare parts.'

For this reason, the Supreme Court upheld the trade mark infringement on the understanding that the use made of the ZARA trade mark was not covered by the wording of Article 37, and that it entailed '*taking unfair advantage of the reputation and prestige of said trade mark*.' The use of the ZARA trade mark as part of a marketing strategy to promote its mobile phone and internet services was not 'necessary' to designate the destination of these services.

This ruling significantly strengthens the position of established brands in the marketplace and provides crucial guidance on the conditions under which the use of third-party trade marks is deemed lawful.

While the Supreme Court analysed an earlier version of Article 37(1)(c) of the Trade mark Law, which has undergone minor revisions in its current wording, it is reasonable to assume that the Supreme Court would have reached the same conclusion even if the events in question had occurred after 14 January 2019, when the updated regulation came into force. Notably, the unchanged provision in Article 37(2), which requires that referential use of a third-party trade mark adhere to 'fair industrial or commercial practices,' reinforces this consistency. Interestingly, the Supreme Court did not find it necessary to rely on this requirement in granting Inditex's appeal, underscoring the robustness of its decision.

This case thus sets a decisive precedent for interpreting the lawful boundaries of trade mark use, offering clarity for future disputes.

COURT OF *JUSTICE* 11 *JANUARY* 2024

ON THE INTERPRETATION OF ARTICLE 9(7) OF DIRECTIVE 2004/48/EC OF THE EUROPEAN PARLIAMENT AND OF THE COUNCIL OF 29 APRIL 2004 ON THE ENFORCEMENT OF INTELLECTUAL PROPERTY RIGHTS

Case C-473/22

Summary and Analysis by Åsa Krook and Felix Suihko[1]

Parties:

Mylan AB

v

Gilead Sciences Finland Oy
Gilead Biopharmaceutics Ireland UC
Gilead Sciences Inc.

1. Background and History

On 3 December 2009, the Finnish Patent and Registration office granted Gilead Sciences Finland Oy, Gilead Biopharmaceutics Ireland UC and Gilead Sciences Inc. (together 'Gilead') a supplementary protection certificate No 266 for an antiretroviral medicine indicated for the treatment of people with HIV ('SPC'), on the basis of European Patent No EP 0 915 894, designated in Finland. The basic patent of the underlying European Patent expired on 25 August 2017.

Mylan AB ('Mylan') offered a generic medicine in a public procurement procedure organised by two hospital districts in spring 2017 and won the tenders in both cases. On 15 September 2017, as the holder of the SPC, Gilead brought an action against Mylan before the Finnish Market Court for infringement of the SPC. Gilead also filed an application for provisional measures against Mylan. Mylan opposed the infringement action and the application for provisional measures. Later, on 30 November 2017, Mylan also brought an action to the Market Court seeking a declaration of invalidity of the SPC at issue.

In December 2017, the Finnish Market Court upheld Gilead's application for provisional measures on the basis of the SPC and prohibited Mylan, on pain of a fine of EUR 500.000, from offering, placing on the market and using the generic medicine at issue and from importing, manufacturing and possessing the

[1] Åsa Krook is an IP partner at the Finnish law firm Waselius Attorneys Ltd and is a member of the Finnish Bar Association. Felix Suihko is an Associate Lawyer at the Finnish law firm Waselius Attorneys Ltd.

generic medicine for those purposes. The provisional measures were ordered to remain in force until a decision was delivered in the main proceedings or until further notice.[2]

However, following an appeal by Mylan, the provisional measures were revoked by order of the Supreme Court of Finland on 11 April 2019.[3] The Finnish Market Court found the SPC at issue to be invalid in its decision on 25 September 2019.[4]

Upon the invalidation of the SPC, Mylan filed a lawsuit with the Finnish Market Court claiming compensation for the injury caused by the provisional measures unnecessarily obtained.[5] The claim for compensation was based on paragraph 11 of Chapter 7 of the Code of Judicial Procedure, transposing Article 9(7) of Directive 2004/48 (the 'Enforcement Directive') into Finnish law. The said paragraph provides for liability without fault, according to which the principle of strict liability is applied to any damage claim arising from an unjustified provisional measure.

In its response to the lawsuit, Gilead referred to the Court's interpretation of Article 9(7) in the judgment of 12 September 2019, *Bayer Pharma* ('the judgment in *Bayer Pharma*')[6] claiming that Article 9(7) precludes strict liability. Therefore, it argued, imposing an obligation to pay compensation solely on the grounds that the SPC – the infringement of which justified the order of provisional measures – was later declared invalid, should be deemed contrary to Article 9(7).

The key issue that the Finnish Market Court considered was whether Article 9(7) of the Enforcement Directive and its interpretation in the judgment in *Bayer Pharma* precluded the application of the principle of strict liability as provided for by Finnish law.

In Finland, the principle of strict liability provides that a person who obtains a provisional measure is liable to pay compensation if the intellectual property right on the basis of which the provisional measure was granted is subsequently found to be invalid. In addition, the principle of strict liability, as applied within the Finnish legal system, is also taken into account when granting a provisional measure. Before a provisional measure is granted, it is necessary to assess the likelihood of the intellectual property right on which that measure is based being declared invalid following a possible action seeking a declaration of invalidity. Consequently, the loss caused to the subject of the order for the provisional

---

[2] Case number MAO:830/17.

[3] Case number KKO:2019:34.

[4] Case number MAO:421/19.

[5] Case number MAO:31/2022.

[6] Case C-688/17, EU:C:2019:722, *Bayer Pharma*.

measure, on the one hand, should be weighed against the loss that would be caused to the applicant if the provisional measure is not granted.

In these circumstances, the Finnish Market Court decided to stay the proceedings and to refer the following question to the Court of Justice for a preliminary ruling:

> '(1) *Is a compensation regime based on strict liability, such as that [...] in force in Finland, to be regarded as compatible with Article 9(7) of [Directive 2004/48]?*
>
> *(2) If the first question is answered in the negative, what then is the nature of the liability for compensation on which the liability under Article 9(7) of [Directive 2004/48] is based? Is that liability to be regarded as a form of liability based on fault, an abuse of rights, or some other ground?*
>
> *(3) In relation to the second question, what circumstances must be taken into account in assessing the existence of liability?*
>
> *(4) In particular, as regards the third question, must the assessment be made solely on the basis of the circumstances known at the time when the provisional measure was obtained, or is it permissible to take into account, for example, the fact that the intellectual property right on whose alleged infringement the provisional measure was based was subsequently, after that measure was obtained, found to be invalid ab initio and, if so, what significance is to be attached to that circumstance?*'

2. Decision

Article 9(7) of Directive 2004/48/EC of the European Parliament and of the Council of 29 April 2004 on the enforcement of intellectual property rights must be interpreted as not precluding national legislation which provides for a mechanism for compensation for any injury caused by a provisional measure, within the meaning of that provision, based on a system of strict liability of the applicant for those measures, in the context of which the court is entitled to adjust the amount of damages by taking into account the circumstances of the case, including whether the defendant played a part in the occurrence of the injury.

3. Motivation and Analysis

To reach its decision, the Court first pointed out that it is for the national authority to which such an application has been made to examine whether the three conditions laid down in Article 9 of the Enforcement Directive are satisfied. First, it must ascertain whether the provisional measures have been revoked or have lapsed due to any act or omission by the applicant, or whether there has been no infringement or threat of infringement of that applicant's intellectual property right. Second, it must assess the existence of injury. Third, it must determine whether there is a causal link between that injury and those measures.[7]

Furthermore, the Court pointed out that the said provision does not mention among those three conditions the existence of fault on the part of the applicant for provisional measures.[8]

In order to determine whether Article 9(7)[9] of the Enforcement Directive imposes on Member States a specific liability regime, the CJEU took into consideration the context of that provision, the objectives pursued by the legislation of which it forms part and the origin of that legislation.

The Court pointed out that, according to previous case law,[10] the EU legislature chose to provide for minimum harmonisation concerning the enforcement of intellectual property rights in general. Furthermore, the Court sought support from the TRIPS Agreement. The wording of Article 9(7) corresponds, in essence, to that of Article 50(7) of the TRIPS Agreement. Thus, by reproducing in Article 9(7) of the Enforcement Directive the broad wording of Article 50(7) of the TRIPS Agreement, the EU legislature expressed its intention, first, not to harmonise the rules on compensation for defendants beyond what is required by that agreement and, second, to allow the Member States discretion as to the specific implementation of the rules governing the applicant's liability.[11]

Therefore, the Court interpreted Article 9(7) as laying down a minimum standard concerning the enforcement of intellectual property rights, while leaving the Member States leeway to opt for a strict liability regime or a fault-based liability regime as the case may be.

Moreover, the Court held that it cannot be inferred from the judgment in *Bayer Pharma* that Article 9(7) of the Enforcement Directive provides for compensation to be paid to the defendant only in the event of fault on the part of the

---

[7] Para. 30 of the annotated judgment.

[8] Para. 31 of the annotated judgment.

[9] Art. 9(7) of the Enforcement Directive provides that '*Where the provisional measures are revoked or where they lapse due to any act or omission by the applicant, or where it is subsequently found that there has been no infringement or threat of infringement of an intellectual property right, the judicial authorities shall have the authority to order the applicant, upon request of the defendant, to provide the defendant appropriate compensation for any injury caused by those measures.*'

[10] See e.g. the judgment of 28 April 2022, *Koch Media*, C-559/20, EU:C:2022:317, paras. 31 and 32 and the case law cited.

[11] Paras. 34-35 of the annotated judgment.

applicant for the provisional measures. The Court merely intended to point out that it is for the national authority to assess the particular circumstances of the case in order to decide whether the applicant should be ordered to pay the defendant appropriate compensation.[12]

In essence, the Court held that it follows from the *Bayer Pharma* case that Article 9(7) provides that the national court must be able to take into account all the circumstances of the case at issue – irrespective of the liability regime adopted. Therefore, it was established that Article 9(7) of the Enforcement Directive does not, as such, preclude the application of strict liability regime.

However, the Court further pointed out that the adopted liability regime is also subject to the requirements of Article 3 of the Enforcement Directive. In order to comply with Article 3, the Court considered it necessary to examine whether a system of strict liability is equitable, proportionate and applied in such a manner as to avoid the creation of barriers to legitimate trade.[13]

First, the Court noted that the proportionality and equitable nature of the system ensure the protection of a defendant by providing for legal instruments which make it possible to mitigate comprehensively the risk that the defendant will suffer loss as a result of provisional measures. The purpose here is to strike a balance between a high level of protection of intellectual property rights and the rights and freedoms of the defendant.[14]

The Court held that it cannot be argued that a strict liability mechanism such as that at issue in the main proceedings would upset the balance described. The fact that the defendant did not have to demonstrate fault committed by the applicant in the system of strict liability is a counterweight to the fact that, on the other hand, the applicant was able to obtain such measures without having to provide definitive evidence of any infringement.[15] Therefore, the rights of the applicant and of the defendant appeared to be in balance in the strict liability system at issue.

Moreover, the Court pointed out that the strict liability mechanism at issue allowed the court to adjust the amount of damages and thereby mitigate any deterrent effect for the applicant.[16] The possibility of adjusting the amount of damages was in line with the requirement of balance between the applicant's and the defendant's rights, but also consistent with the judgment in *Bayer Pharma*, in which it was held that the court must be able to take into account all the circumstances of the case at issue.

---

[12] Para. 38 of the annotated judgment.

[13] Paras. 41-42 of the annotated judgment.

[14] Para. 44 of the annotated judgment.

[15] Para. 45 of the annotated judgment.

[16] Para. 46 of the annotated judgment.

Second, in this situation, the high level of protection of intellectual property intended by the EU legislature could not be invoked since the intellectual property right that had been declared invalid retroactively was deemed never to have existed. Therefore, the Court further stated that a system of provisional measures incorporating a strict liability regime such as that at issue does not create a barrier to legitimate trade.[17]

Lastly, the Court considered that the dissuasive nature of a system of provisional measures, as provided for under Article 9 of the Enforcement Directive, is not undermined by the incorporation of a strict liability regime. In the case at issue, the court could take into account all relevant factors, including the defendant's conduct, to determine the appropriate amount of damages. Importantly, the Court held that the right to compensation is narrowly confined to the harm directly caused by the unjustified provisional measures and does not extend to any additional damage resulting from the defendant's own actions that may have aggravated the initial injury.[18]

In the light of the above, the Court ruled that Article 9(7) of the Enforcement Directive must be interpreted as not precluding a system of strict liability for compensation for any injury caused by a provisional measure, provided that the court is able to adjust the amount of damages taking into account all circumstances of the case.

The judgment confirmed the permissibility of strict liability mechanisms that hold applicants liable for unjustified provisional measures. However, the Court emphasised, first, that there must be a balance between the rights of the applicant and of the defendant and, second, that courts have to be able adjust compensation based on the specifics of the case. In general, the Enforcement Directive provides that while national courts have leeway in implementing liability regimes, they must ensure that these regimes are equitable, proportionate, and do not create barriers to legitimate trade.

The essential impact of the Court's judgment is that it provides clarity with regard to the current compensation systems based on strict liability following a somewhat ambiguous decision in the judgment in *Bayer Pharma*. The outcome further enables a fair balance to be struck between the rights of the applicant and that of the defendant. As such, strict liability is not comparable to automatic liability, and it is up to national courts to determine on a case-to-case basis what constitutes appropriate compensation.

---

[17] Para. 49 of the annotated judgment.

[18] Para. 50 of the annotated judgment.

COURT OF *JUSTICE 18 JANUARY 2024*

ON THE BURDEN OF PROOF OF THE EXHAUSTION OF THE RIGHTS CONFERRED BY AN EU TRADE MARK

Case C-367/21

Summary and analysis by Ewa Nagy[1]

Parties:

Hewlett Packard Development Company LP

v

Senetic S.A.

1. Background and History

The main proceedings concerned claims brought by Hewlett Packard against Senetic, a company operating in Poland, for infringement of Hewlett Packard's EU trade marks. Senetic purchased computer equipment bearing Hewlett Packard's EU trade marks from sellers established in the EEA who were not official distributors of Hewlett Packard's products, and placed those goods on the Polish market. When purchasing the goods, Senetic obtained assurances from the sellers that the marketing of those goods in the European Economic Area ('EEA') would not infringe Hewlett Packard's exclusive rights. Senetic also sought confirmation from Hewlett Packard's authorised agents but was unsuccessful. Hewlett Packard sued Senetic for infringement of its EU trade marks, claiming that the goods sold by Senetic had not been put on the market in the EEA with Hewlett Packard's consent. Hewlett Packard sought an order restraining Senetic from importing, exporting, advertising and storing for the above purposes computer equipment bearing Hewlett Packard's EU trade marks which had not previously been put on the market in the EEA by Hewlett Packard or with its consent. Hewlett Packard also sought an order requiring Senetic to withdraw the goods from the market. Senetic's defence was that the goods in question had previously been put on the market in the EEA by Hewlett Packard or with its consent and that the trade marks were therefore exhausted. The marking system used by Hewlett Packard did not allow third parties (such as Senetic) to determine whether the goods were intended to be marketed in the EEA. Nor could Senetic obtain such information from its suppliers.

The IP Court in Warsaw (the referring court) noted that, in the absence of a marking system which would allow an independent distributor to verify whether the

[1] Ewa Nagy is a senior associate at the Wardyński & Partners law firm in Poland.

product was intended for the EEA market, it was very difficult for a distributor to ensure that the product had been placed on the market by the right holder or with its consent. The Court also noted that suppliers were generally reluctant to disclose their source of supply, and it was, therefore, unlikely that Senetic would be able to obtain information about previous distributors in the distribution chain. The Court referred to the CJEU judgment in *Van Doren + Q* (CJEU judgment of 8 April 2003, C-244/00).

The Court noted that the practice of the Polish courts was to refer in the operative part of the judgment to '*goods which have not previously been placed on the market within the [EEA] by the applicant (the proprietor of the EU trade mark) or with its consent.*' Such a formulation made it difficult, at the stage of enforcement proceedings, to determine which goods were or were not covered by the exhaustion of the trade mark rights exception. The Court noted that this practice most often led to the seizure of all goods in the defendant's possession, including those put on the market by the right holder or with its consent. According to the referring court, the defendant was confronted with a number of difficulties in defending itself against the measures ordered.

In addition, the referring court noted that the protection of intellectual property rights in the EU was not absolute and had some limitations.

The Regional Court in Warsaw decided to stay proceedings and to refer the following questions to the Court of Justice for a preliminary ruling:

> *'(1) Must the second sentence of Article 36 TFEU, read in conjunction with Article 15(1) of Regulation [2017/1001] and with the [second subparagraph] of Article 19(1) [TFEU], be interpreted as precluding the practice of the national courts of the Member States, which is that the courts:*
>
> - *when upholding claims by right holders to prohibit the importation, exportation and advertising of goods bearing the EU trade mark or to order their withdrawal from the market;*
> - *when ruling, in protective proceedings relating to the seizure of products bearing an EU trade mark, refer in their rulings to "goods which have not been put on the market within the [EEA] by the right holder or with his consent", with the result that it is left to the enforcement authority, in view of the general wording of the ruling, to determine which items bearing the EU trade mark are subject to the injunctions and prohibitions granted (that is to say, which items have not been put on the market within the [EEA] by the right holder or with his consent) [and the authority relies, in making the findings set out, on statements of the right holder or tools supplied by him (including IT tools and databases)], while the possibility of challenging the aforementioned findings of the enforcement authority before a court in declaratory proceedings is excluded or limited*

by the nature of the legal remedies available to the defendant in proceedings to secure claims and in enforcement proceedings?

(2) Must Articles 34, 35 and 36 [TFEU] be interpreted as precluding the holder of the registration of a Community (now EU) trade mark from relying on the protection provided for in Articles 9 and 102 of Regulation [No 207/2009] (now Articles 9 and 130 of Regulation [2017/1001] in a situation where:

- *the holder of the registration of the Community (EU) trade mark distributes, within and outside the [EEA], goods bearing that mark through authorised distributors, who may resell the goods bearing the trade mark to persons who are not the final recipients of those goods [only if they belong] exclusively to the official distribution network – and at the same [time] the authorised distributors are required to purchase the goods only from other authorised distributors or from the right holder;*
- *the goods bearing the trade mark have no other markings or distinctive characteristics which would make it possible to determine where they have been put on the market by the right holder or with his consent;*
- *the defendant acquired the goods bearing the mark in the [EEA];*
- *the defendant collected statements from the sellers of goods bearing the mark to the effect that they may be marketed, in accordance with the law, in the [EEA];*
- *the holder of the registration of the EU trade mark does not provide any IT tool (or other tool) or use a system of markings – which enables the potential purchasers of the goods bearing the mark to verify independently the legality of marketing those goods in the [EEA] before purchasing them – and refuses to carry out such verification at the purchaser's request?'*

In simple terms, the referring court sought to ascertain whether, in the factual circumstances of the dispute before it, it was possible to reverse the burden of proof or even to exclude the possibility of the trade mark proprietor claiming protection.

The proceedings in the case were stayed pending delivery of the judgment of the Court of Justice on 17 November 2022 in the *Harman International Industries* case (C-175/21). In its judgment in case C-175/21, the CJEU held that the operative part of a decision upholding an action for infringement of an EU trade mark may be worded in terms which, owing to their general nature, leave it to the authority with competence to enforce that decision to determine the products to which that decision applies, provided that, in the course of the enforcement proceedings, the defendant may contest the determination of the goods covered by the proceedings and that a court may, in accordance with the provisions of Directive 2004/48, examine and decide which goods have actually been placed on the market in the EEA by the proprietor or with its consent.

Following this decision, the IP Court in Warsaw decided to withdraw the first question and to uphold only the second.

2. Decision

Article 13(1) of Council Regulation (EC) No 207/2009 of 26 February 2009 on the [European Union] trade mark and Article 15(1) of Regulation (EU) 2017/1001 of the European Parliament and of the Council of 14 June 2017 on the European Union trade mark, read in conjunction with Articles 34 and 36 TFEU, must be interpreted as precluding the burden of proof of exhaustion of the rights conferred by an EU trade mark being borne exclusively by the defendant to the action for infringement where the goods bearing that trade mark, which do not bear any marking enabling third parties to identify the market on which they are intended to be marketed and which are distributed through a selective distribution network whose members may resell them only to other members of that network or to end users, have been purchased by that defendant in the European Union, or in the European Economic Area, after having obtained an assurance from the sellers that they could be marketed legally there, and the proprietor of that trade mark refuses to carry out that verification at the purchaser's request.

3. Motivation and Analysis

The CJEU first held that Article 13 of Regulation No 207/2009 and Article 15 of Regulation No 2017/1001 comprehensively regulate the question of exhaustion of trade mark rights in respect of goods put on the market in the EEA.[2]

Article 13(1) of Regulation No 207/2009, now Article 15(1) of Regulation No 2017/1001, provide that the trade mark proprietor's rights are exhausted when goods bearing the trade mark have been put on the market in the European Union or the EEA by the proprietor or with its consent. The CJEU noted that the purpose of this provision is to reconcile the fundamental interest in protecting the rights conferred by the trade mark with the fundamental interest in the free movement of goods within the European Union or the EEA.[3]

The CJEU went on to point out that, in order to ensure a fair balance between these two principles, the principle of exhaustion is limited only to the goods put on the market in the European Union or the EEA by the proprietor or with its consent.[4]

---

2 Para. 46 of the annotated judgment.

3 Para. 50 of the annotated judgment.

4 Paras. 51-52 of the annotated judgment.

The CJEU explained that the question of which party bears the burden of proof of exhaustion is not governed by any of the above-mentioned regulations and that the procedural aspects of the enforcement of intellectual property rights are, in principle, governed by national law. The CJEU also stated that a provision of the national law of a Member State under which exhaustion of the rights conferred by a trade mark constitutes a plea in defence is consistent with EU law, but also noted that, in accordance with paragraphs 35 to 37 of the judgment of 8 April 2003, *Van Doren + Q*, C-244/00, the requirements arising from the protection of the free movement of goods may mean that those rules of evidence need to be qualified, in particular in a situation where they are likely to enable the proprietor of that trade mark to partition national markets and thus help to maintain price differences between Member States.[5]

The CJEU therefore concluded that, in a situation where the defendant succeeds in proving that there is a real risk of partitioning of national markets where the burden of proof is on the defendant, the national court should qualify the burden of proof of exhaustion of the rights conferred by the trade mark.[6]

In a situation such as that in the present case, where the right holder had implemented a selective distribution system, placing the burden of proof exclusively on the defendant could enable the right holder to oppose parallel imports of goods even though that would not be justified. Therefore, in circumstances such as those described in the case referred by the IP Court in Warsaw, it is for the national court to decide who bears the burden of proving exhaustion of rights. The court may shift the burden of proof and expect the right holder to prove that the goods in question were first put on the market outside the EU or the EEA. The defendant will then have to prove that the goods were subsequently imported into the EEA by the right holder or with its consent.[7]

* *
*

The CJEU judgment is in line with its earlier judgment of 17 November 2022 in the *Harman International Industries* case (C-175/21). In both cases, the CJEU accepted the possibility of shifting the burden of proof from the defendant to the right holder if there is a risk of partitioning national markets and maintaining price differences between Member States. The *Harman International Industries* case concerned an exclusive distribution system, whereas the *Hewlett Packard* case concerned selective distribution. However, it appears that the nature of the distribution system is irrelevant for the national court or for the competent enforcement authority when deciding whether the burden of proof should be reverse. What matters is whether it is clear from the circumstances of the case

---

5 Paras. 58-59 of the annotated judgment.

6 Para. 60 of the annotated judgment.

7 Paras. 63-66 of the annotated judgment.

as a whole that it would be difficult for the defendant to prove that the goods were placed on the market in the EEA by the trade mark proprietor or with its consent, and whether placing the burden of proof exclusively on the defendant would lead to a risk of partitioning of national markets and the maintenance of price differences between Member States.

COURT OF JUSTICE 25 JANUARY 2024

ON THE LIMITATIONS OF TRADE MARK USE IN AUTOMOTIVE SPARE PARTS

Case C-334/22

Summary and Analysis by Emma Dekeuwer[1]

Parties:

Audi AG

v

GQ

1. Background and History

Audi AG, a manufacturer of motor vehicles, holds the exclusive rights to the figurative EU trade mark, shown below, registered under number 000018762 ('the Audi AG trade mark'):

This trade mark primarily applies to Class 12 of the Nice Classification, covering land, air and water vehicles and constituent parts thereof (not included in other classes), including engines for vehicles[2].In the dispute giving rise to the main proceedings, a Polish trader, known under the name GQ, advertised and sold through a website non-original radiator grilles adapted and designed for older Audi car models. These grilles featured a component specifically designed for attaching the emblem of the Audi motor vehicle brand ('the Audi emblem').[3]

Clarification from the author: These grilles contain a cut-out space, just like the original grilles, on which the Audi emblem can be inserted and fitted. An

[1] Emma Dekeuwer is an IP/IT lawyer at the law firm & DE BANDT in Brussels, Belgium.

[2] Para. 7 of the annotated judgment.

[3] Para. 8 of the annotated judgment.

example of an Audi A5 grille in which a cut-out and the outlines of the Audi trade mark can be clearly seen:[4]

Starting in 2017, Audi AG pursued legal action against GQ to stop him from selling non-original spare parts, whose shapes partially or fully resembled those of the Audi AG trade mark.

In May 2020, Audi AG initiated proceedings before the Sąd Okręgowy w Warszawie (Regional Court in Warsaw, Poland, the referring court), alleging that GQ's production of radiator grilles with elements corresponding to the Audi AG trade mark infringed its EU trade mark rights. More precisely, Audi AG sought an injunction to prohibit GQ from importing, advertising, and offering for sale non-original radiator grilles that displayed a sign identical or similar to the Audi AG trade mark. Additionally, Audi AG demanded the destruction of 70 units of these infringing products, which had been seized by Polish customs authorities.[5]

In response, GQ contested the allegations, claiming that his actions were in line with an established industry practice among car manufacturers of not opposing the sale of non-original radiator grilles containing a space for attaching the brand emblem that reflects the protected trade mark.[6]

The referring court believed that to resolve the dispute, it must first determine whether the scope of protection of the Audi AG trade mark – widely recognised in Poland, highly distinctive and strongly associated with Audi AG – also extends to spare parts designed for attaching the Audi emblem to radiator grilles that

---

[4] M. Pemsel, Four rings on a car grille infringe Audi's trade mark, *the IPKat* 2024, https://ipkitten.blogspot.com/2024/02/four-rings-on-car-grille-infringe-audis.html.

[5] Para. 10 of the annotated judgment.

[6] Para. 11 of the annotated judgment.

are identical in shape to the Audi AG trade mark and could create a likelihood of confusion with the Audi AG trade mark.[7]

In that regard, the referring court raised concerns about the consequences of the absence of a provision in trade mark law similar to the 'repair clause' provided for in Community design law.[8] The referring court also questioned whether such spare parts could have the ability to fulfil the function of indicating the commercial origin and inquired whether Article 14(1)(c) Regulation (EU) 2017/1001 of the European Parliament and of the Council of 14 June 2017 on the European Union trade mark ('EUTMR')[9] should be interpreted as preventing the owner of an EU trade mark from prohibiting a third party from using a sign that is identical or confusingly similar to that trade mark in relation to motor vehicle spare parts, such as radiator grilles, where that sign is a component designed for attaching the manufacturer's emblem.

Finally, the referring court sought guidance on the appropriate criteria for determining whether the use of an EU trade mark is consistent with honest practices in industrial and commercial matters.[10]

In these circumstances, the referring court decided to stay the proceedings and refer the following questions to the Court of Justice of the European Union for a preliminary ruling:

> *'(1) Must Article 14(1)(c) of Regulation [2017/1001] be interpreted as precluding the trade mark proprietor [or] court from prohibiting a third party from using in the course of trade a sign which is identical or confusingly similar to an EU trade mark, in relation to automotive spare parts (radiator grilles) where that sign constitutes a mounting element for an automotive accessory (an emblem reflecting the EU trade mark), and:*
>
> – *where it is technically possible to affix the original emblem reflecting the EU trade mark to an automotive spare part*

---

7 Para. 12 of the annotated judgment.

8 The referring court stated that, while the case did not involve the protection of a Community design, the so-called 'repair' clause could not be applied by analogy in trade mark law, as established in the 6 October 2015 *Ford Motor Company* judgment, because a trade mark cannot confer broader protection than the combined rights granted by both the trade mark and a Community design; Art. 110 Council Regulation (EC) No 6/2002 of 12 December 2001 on Community designs reads as follows: '*Until such time as amendments to this Regulation enter into force on a proposal from the Commission on this subject, protection as a Community design shall not exist for a design which constitutes a component part of a complex product used within the meaning of Article 19(1) for the purpose of the repair of that complex product so as to restore its original appearance.*'

9 Art. 14 EUTMR.

10 Paras. 14-17 of the annotated judgment.

(radiator grille) without reproducing on that part a sign identical or confusingly similar to the EU trade mark;

or in a situation

- *where it is technically impossible to affix the original emblem reproducing the EU trade mark to an automotive spare part (radiator grille) without reproducing on that part a sign identical or confusingly similar to the EU trade mark?*

If the answer to [the first question, first or second indent] is in the affirmative:

(2) What evaluation criteria should be used in such cases to determine whether the use of an EU trade mark is consistent with honest practices in industrial and commercial matters?

(3) Must Article 9(2) and Article 9(3)(a) of Regulation [2017/1001] be interpreted as meaning that, where the trade mark is included in the shape of an automotive part and in the absence in Regulation 2017/1001 of a clause that would be similar to the repairs clause in Article 110(1) of Regulation [No 6/2002], the trade mark does not fulfil a designation function in that situation?

(4) Must Article 9(2) and Article 9(3)(a) of Regulation [2017/1001] be interpreted as meaning that, where the mounting element for a trade mark, which reflects the shape of the trade mark or is confusingly similar to it, is included in the shape of an automotive part and in the absence in Regulation 2017/1001 of a clause that would be similar to the repairs clause in Article 110(1) of Regulation [No 6/2002], that mounting element cannot be regarded as a trade mark with a designation function even if it is identical to the trade mark or confusingly similar to it?'

2. Decision

1. Article 9(2) and (3)(a) to (c) of Regulation (EU) 2017/1001 of the European Parliament and of the Council of 14 June 2017 on the European Union trade mark must be interpreted as meaning that a third party who, without the consent of the manufacturer of motor vehicles which is the proprietor of an EU trade mark, imports and offers for sale spare parts, namely radiator grilles for those motor vehicles, containing an element which is designed for the attachment of the emblem representing that trade mark and the shape of which is identical with, or similar to, that trade mark, is using a sign in the course of trade in a manner liable to affect one or more of the functions of that trade mark, which is a matter for the national court to ascertain.

2. Article 14(1)(c) of Regulation 2017/1001 must be interpreted as meaning that it does not preclude the manufacturer of motor vehicles which is the proprietor

of an EU trade mark from prohibiting a third party from using a sign identical with, or similar to, that trade mark in relation to spare parts for those motor vehicles, namely radiator grilles, where that sign consists of the shape of an element of the radiator grille designed for the attachment thereto of the emblem representing that trade mark, regardless of whether or not there is a technical possibility of attaching that emblem to the radiator grille without affixing that sign to it.

3. Motivation and Analysis

i) Third and fourth preliminary questions – could this use constitute an infringement?

Dealing with the third and fourth questions first, the Court stressed that use in the course of trade should be considered before assessing whether there is a likelihood of confusion under Article 9(2)(b) EUTMR.[11]

The Court dispelled any doubts the Polish court had about whether a 'repair clause', as it is known in design law,[12] could restrict the rights of the trade mark owner. The Court primarily recalled that such a repair clause does not exist in trade mark law, and that this clause applies without prejudice to the provisions of trade mark law.[13] For trade marks, the objective of maintaining undistorted competition – which the designs repair clause seeks to enable – is met by Article 14 EUTMR concerning the referential use of trade marks.[14] Because of this, there is no need to include, even by analogy, the repair clause in the interpretation of Article 9 EUTMR.[15]

In contrast to the Court, Advocate General Medina ('the AG') sought an interpretation of EU trade mark law that, in cases where it converges with other IP domains, avoids neutralising the shared objectives of those domains, particularly in preserving undistorted market competition.[16]

---

11 Art. 9(2)(b) EUTMR; para. 22 of the annotated judgment.

12 Art. 110 Regulation (EC) No 6/2002 on Community designs.

13 Case C-500/14, 6 October 2015, *Ford Motor Company*, paras. 39 and 41-42.

14 Art. 14 EUTMR.

15 Para. 26-29 of the annotated judgment.

16 Opinion of Advocate General Medina 21 September 2023 of the annotated judgment, para. 42; The AG referred to Case C-48/09 P, 14 September 2010, *Lego Juris A/S* concerning the distinction between trade mark and patent law.

Furthermore, the Court noted that the concept of 'using' within the meaning of Article 9(2) EUTMR is not defined by that Regulation.[17] Instead, case law confirms that '*it refers exclusively to active conduct on the part of the third party*,'[18] and that use occurs in the course of trade '*if it is in the context of a commercial activity intended to obtain an economic advantage and not in the private sphere*.'[19]

The Court stressed that the referring court deemed the shape of the component for attaching the Audi emblem to be identical or similar to the Audi AG trade mark, qualifying it as a sign under Article 9(2) EUTMR. This was not affected by the fact that it was a radiator grille, which is a component of a spare part for a car. Moreover, the use of the sign on radiator grilles for marketing purposes falls under Article 9(3)(a) EUTMR, and GQ's import and sale of these grilles was considered to constitute use under Articles 9(3)(b) and (c) EUTMR, capable of creating an association in the public's eyes with the Audi AG trade mark.[20]

The Court went on to consider the various functions of a trade mark, emphasising that its essential function is to guarantee origin.[21] Additionally, the Court highlighted other key functions, such as the investment function, which allows the proprietor to attract and retain consumers through various commercial techniques, along with the functions of communication, advertising and guaranteeing the quality of the product or service.[22]

The Court further reiterated fundamental principles of EU trade mark law, noting that for 'double identity' infringement under Article 9(2)(a) EUTMR, it must be established that the third party use adversely affects or is likely to adversely affect one of the trade mark functions, such as origin, quality, communication, investment or advertising.[23] For a double identity infringement to take place, a likelihood of confusion is required, meaning that the public might believe the goods or services come from the same undertaking or economically linked

---

[17] Para. 30 of the annotated judgment; Case C-148/21 and C-184/21, 22 December 2022, *Louboutin*, para. 25.

[18] Para. 33 of the annotated judgment; Case C-129/17, 25 July 2018, *Mitsubishi Shoji Kaisha and Mitsubishi Caterpillar Forklift Europe*, para. 38.

[19] Para. 34 of the annotated judgment; Case C-206/01, 12 November 2002, *Arsenal Football Club*, para. 40; Case C-236/08 and C-238/08, 23 March 2010, *Google France*, para. 50.

[20] Paras. 38-40 of the annotated judgment.

[21] Para. 35 of the annotated judgment; Case C-206/01, 12 November 2002, *Arsenal Football Club*, para. 48; Case C-129/17, 25 July 2018, *Mitsubishi Shoji Kaisha and Mitsubishi Caterpillar Forklift Europe*, para. 35.

[22] Paras. 31 and 36 of the annotated judgment; Case C-129/17, 25 July 2018, *Mitsubishi Shoji Kaisha and Mitsubishi Caterpillar Forklift Europe*, paras. 33-34 and 36.

[23] Art. 9(2)(a) EUTMR; para. 42 of the annotated judgment; Case C-323/09, 22 September 2011, *Interflora and Interflora British Unit*, para. 33; Case C-179/15, 3 March 2016, *Daimler*, para. 26.

undertakings.[24] The likelihood of confusion therefore refers to origin, meaning that the trade mark's essential function must be adversely affected or be likely to be adversely affected for this type of infringement to be established.[25]

Finally, the Court also addressed infringement under Article 9(1)(c) EUTMR concerning trade marks with a reputation. When a trade mark enjoys a reputation in the EU, the proprietor also has the right to prohibit a third party from using a sign that is identical or similar to that trade mark in the course of trade, but the exercise of this right *does not* require the existence of a likelihood of confusion among the relevant public. [26]

In those circumstances, the Court consequently ruled that affixing a component to a non-original spare part, intended to insert and attach the car manufacturer's original emblem, constitutes use of a sign in the course of trade that is liable to infringe the functions of the trade mark. The Court left it to the national court to determine whether the radiator grille element was identical with or similar to the Audi AG trade mark and whether the grilles were identical with or similar to one or more of the goods for which the trade mark was registered.[27]

Nonetheless, the Court pointed out that, if the national court considered that the Audi AG trade mark has a reputation within the EU, it would benefit from the enhanced protection. The Court also clarified that the average consumer's perception of the grilles as non-original was irrelevant.[28]

ii) First preliminary question – is this referential use?

Dealing with the first preliminary question, the Court looked at whether GQ's use could be said to fall within the scope of Article 14(1)(c) EUTMR, and whether Audi AG could therefore be stopped from seeking to prohibit GQ's use, having ascertained that GQ's use of the Audi AG logo in the course of trade was liable to affect the functions of the trade mark, and therefore constituted an infringement of trade mark rights.

Under Article 14(1)(c) EUTMR, a trade mark owner cannot prevent a third party from using that trade mark if the use is necessary to indicate the intended purpose of a product or service – particularly when used as an accessory or spare part – provided the use is in line with honest practices in industrial or

---

[24] Para 43 of the annotated judgment; Case C-342/97, 22 June 1999, *Lloyd Schuhfabrik Meyer*, para. 17; Case C-558/08, 8 July 2010, *Portakabin*, para. 51.

[25] Para 43 of the annotated judgment; Case C-179/15, 3 March 2016, *Daimler*, para. 27.

[26] Para. 44 of the annotated judgment; Case C-323/09, 22 September 2011, *Interflora and Interflora British Unit*, paras. 70-71.

[27] Paras. 45-47 of the annotated judgment.

[28] Para. 48 of the annotated judgment.

commercial matters.[29] However, in this case, the Court did not deem the use to be necessary and noted that GQ's use of the sign was motivated by the *commercial aim* of resembling the original radiator grille as closely as possible.[30]

Furthermore, the Court clarified that a distinction must be made between on the one hand, the current case, where a sign was affixed to spare parts intended for incorporation into goods of the trade mark owner, and on the other hand, a different scenario, where the sign indicated that the spare parts were intended to be incorporated into those goods, but was not affixed to the spare parts. The latter situation falls into Article 14(1)(c) EUTMR, while the former does not.[31] Therefore, the Court held that the use of the trade mark lay outside the scope of referential use.[32]

The Court added that it did not matter whether it was technically feasible to affix the original emblem to the grille without reproducing the mark. The mounting element itself was capable of infringing, allowing Audi AG to seek to prevent such use.[33]

As regards the second question, the Court chose not to respond, as there was no need to assess whether GQ's use aligned with honest practices in industrial or commercial matters.[34]

* *
*

The key takeaway from the judgment is that a spare part cannot feature the original manufacturer's trade mark, even if the sign is integral to the design or is necessary to mount the trade mark. While the precise interpretation and implementation by national courts of this ruling remains to be seen, it could lead spare parts manufacturers to steer clear of incorporating automotive brands into their designs to avoid infringement. The decision therefore strengthens the position of car manufacturers in trade mark disputes with suppliers of spare parts using their trade marks.

---

29 Para. 53 of the annotated judgment; see also Case C-361/22, 11 January 2024, *Inditex*, paras. 44-46.

30 Para. 56 of the annotated judgment.

31 The Court referred to and agreed with the arguments set out in para. 57 of the Advocate General Medina's Opinion, 21 September 2023.

32 Para. 57 of the annotated judgment.

33 Para. 59 of the annotated judgment. The Court continued that: '*GQ's use of that shape, which in the present case is considered by the referring court to be a sign identical with, or similar to, the AUDI trade mark, must be assessed in the light of the rules set out in Article 9 of Regulation 2017/1001, as interpreted by the Court in the case-law referred to in paragraphs 42 to 48 of this judgment.*'

34 Para. 61 of the annotated judgment.

Furthermore, this judgment highlights the differences between design rights and trade marks in regulating the spare parts market. The Court made it clear that the repair clause in design law does not apply to trade mark law, not even by analogy. However, the ruling seems to overlook the European Commission's recent efforts[35] to revise the EU designs regime, which aims to liberalise design protection for spare parts and provide consumers with more choices for affordable repairs. If, under that new regime, the repair clause continues to apply only to spare parts that are visually identical to the original,[36] this judgment could significantly restrict the application of the repair clause. From a trade mark perspective, if a spare part cannot incorporate elements necessary to attach the original manufacturer's emblem, it will fail to meet the 'must match' criteria set by design law.

In addition, the Court did not extend the scope of the referential use exception to allow spare parts suppliers to include a space in the spare part, the shape of which is identical or similar to a trade mark, in order to attach the car manufacturer's emblem for the purpose of marketing the spare part. This narrow interpretation of referential use also seems to strengthen the protection of EU trade mark holders.

---

[35] Art. 20(a) of the Proposal for a Regulation of the European Parliament and of the Council amending Council Regulation (EC) No 6/2002 on Community designs and repealing Commission Regulation (EC) No 2246/2002 and Art. 19 of the Proposal for a Directive of the European Parliament and of the Council on the legal protection of designs.

[36] Case C-397/16 and C-435/16, 20 December 2017, *Acacia and D'Amato*, para. 75. The Court also stated in para. 89 that: '*In the light of all the foregoing considerations, the answer to the third question in Case C-397/16 and the third and fourth questions in Case C-435/16 is that Article 110(1) of Regulation No 6/2002 must be interpreted as meaning that, in order to rely on the 'repair' clause contained in that provision, the manufacturer or seller of a component part of a complex product are under a duty of diligence as regards compliance by downstream users with the conditions laid down in that provision.*'

Court of Justice 24 October 2024

On copyright protection for the subject matter of applied art of which the country of origin is not a Member State and the criterion of material reciprocity of the Berne Convention

Case C-227/23

Summary and Analysis by Bram Woltering[1]

Parties:

Kwantum Nederland BV,
Kwantum België BV

v

Vitra Collections AG

1. Background and History

This request for a preliminary ruling concerns the interpretation of Articles 2 to 4 of Directive 2001/29/EC of the European Parliament and of the Council of 22 May 2001 on the harmonisation of certain aspects of copyright and related rights in the information society (*OJ 2001 L 167*, p. 10), of Article 17(2) and Article 52(1) of the Charter of Fundamental Rights of the European Union ('the Charter'), read in the light of Article 2(7) of the Convention for the Protection of Literary and Artistic Works, signed in Berne on 9 September 1886 (Paris Act of 24 July 1971), as amended on 28 September 1979 ('the Berne Convention'), and of the first paragraph of Article 351 of the Treaty on the Functioning of the European Union ('TFEU').

It was made in proceedings between Vitra Collections AG ('Vitra'), a company governed by Swiss law, on the one hand, and Kwantum Nederland BV and Kwantum België BV (together, 'Kwantum'), which operate, in the Netherlands and in Belgium, a chain of shops selling interior design articles, including furniture, on the other, on the ground that Kwantum marketed a chair which, according to Vitra, infringed copyright held by it.

Vitra invoked copyright in relation to the so-called (Eames) Dining Side Chair Wood (the 'DSW' chair) designed by the since-deceased spouses, Charles and Ray Eames, as an entry for a furniture design competition at the Museum of Modern Art in New York (United States) in 1948 and exhibited in that museum

[1] Bram Woltering is an attorney at law at AKD, the Netherlands, and works within the Intellectual Property & Technology practice group.

from 1950. The spouses were nationals of the United States of America. Vitra obtained the copyright.

In 2014, Vitra ascertained that Kwantum was marketing a chair called the 'Paris chair', in breach, according to Vitra, of the copyright which it held in the DSW chair.[2]

In an action brought by Vitra, the Rechtbank Den Haag (District Court, The Hague, Netherlands) held that Kwantum was not infringing Vitra's copyright in the Netherlands or in Belgium and that it was not acting unlawfully by marketing the Paris chair. The court therefore dismissed Vitra's claims and largely upheld Kwantum's claims.

That judgment was set aside by the Gerechtshof Den Haag (Court of Appeal, The Hague, Netherlands), which held that, by marketing the Paris chair, Kwantum was infringing Vitra's copyright in the DSW chair in the Netherlands and in Belgium.

On appeal, the referring court, the Hoge Raad der Nederlanden (Supreme Court of the Netherlands), considered that the dispute concerned the applicability and scope of the second sentence of Article 2(7) of the Berne Convention which, with respect to works protected in the country of origin solely as designs and models, provides, *inter alia*, that such works are to be entitled in another country of the Union established by that convention only to such special protection as is granted in that country to designs and models, thereby laying down a criterion of material reciprocity.[3]

In that regard, the referring court noted, first, that, although the European Union is not a party to the Berne Convention, it has, through international treaties, undertaken to comply with Articles 1 to 21 of that convention. Moreover, it observed that EU legislation does not contain any provision relating to the criterion of material reciprocity referred to in the second sentence of Article 2(7) of that convention, raising the question as to whether the Member States may themselves determine whether or not they will disapply that criterion with respect to a work the country of origin of which is a third country and the author of which is a national of a third country.[4]

Second, the referring court stated that copyright in a work of applied art is an integral part of the right to protection of intellectual property enshrined in Article 17(2) of the Charter. It considered that the judgment of 8 September 2020, *Recorded Artists Actors Performers* (C-265/19, EU:C:2020:677) ('*RAAP*'), in which the Court of Justice interpreted a provision of the WIPO

---

[2] Para. 24 of the annotated judgment.

[3] Para. 27 of the annotated judgment.

[4] Para. 28 of the annotated judgment.

Performances and Phonograms Treaty, to which the European Union is a party, raises the question whether EU law, in particular Article 52(1) of the Charter, requires, with respect to the limitation on the exercise of copyright in a work of applied art by the criterion of material reciprocity referred to in the second sentence of Article 2(7) of the Berne Convention, that such a limitation be provided for by law, namely by means of a clear and precise rule. In that regard, the referring court observed that it could be inferred from that judgment that it is for the EU legislature alone, and not for the national legislatures, to determine whether, in the European Union, copyright in a work of applied art may be limited by the application of Article 2(7) of the Berne Convention in respect of a work of applied art which comes from a third country and the author of which is not a national of a Member State of the European Union, and, if so, to define that limitation clearly and precisely. In its view, as EU law currently stood, the EU legislature had not provided for such a limitation.[5]

Third, it noted that Kwantum argued before the referring court that the criterion of material reciprocity referred to in the second sentence of Article 2(7) of the Berne Convention falls within the scope of the first paragraph of Article 351 TFEU. In the referring court's view, it was necessary to determine to what extent that provision is capable of affecting the application of the second sentence of Article 2(7) of that convention with regard to the claims relating to the Kingdom of Belgium.[6]

In those circumstances, the Supreme Court of the Netherlands decided to stay the proceedings and to refer the following questions to the Court of Justice for a preliminary ruling:

> '*(1) Does the situation at issue in these proceedings fall within the material scope of EU law?*
>
> *Should the preceding question be answered in the affirmative, the following questions are also submitted.*
>
> *(2) Does the fact that copyright [in] a work of applied art forms an integral part of the right to protection of intellectual property enshrined in Article 17(2) of the Charter mean that EU law, in particular Article 52(1) of the Charter, in order to limit the exercise of copyright (within the meaning of Directive [2001/29]) [in] a work of applied art by application of the [criterion of] material reciprocity [provided for in] Article 2(7) [of the Berne Convention], requires this limitation to be provided for by law?*
>
> *(3) Must Articles 2, 3 and 4 of Directive [2001/29] and Articles 17(2) and 52(1) of the Charter, read in the light of Article 2(7) [of the Berne Convention], be interpreted as meaning that it is solely for the EU legislature (and not for national legislatures) to determine whether the exercise*

5 Para. 29 of the annotated judgment.

6 Para. 30 of the annotated judgment.

of copyright (within the meaning of Directive [2001/29]) in the European Union can be limited by application of the [criterion of] material reciprocity provided for in Article 2(7) [of the Berne Convention] in respect of a work of applied art whose country of origin within the meaning of [that convention] is a third country and whose author is not a national of an EU Member State and, if so, to define that limitation clearly and precisely ?

(4) Must Articles 2, 3 and 4 of Directive [2001/29], read in conjunction with Articles 17(2) and 52(1) of the Charter, be interpreted as meaning that[,] as long as the EU legislature has not provided for a limitation [on] the exercise of copyright (within the meaning of Directive [2001/29]) [in] a work of applied art by application of the [criterion of] material reciprocity [provided for in] Article 2(7) [of the Berne Convention], EU Member States may not apply that [criterion] in respect of a work of applied art whose country of origin within the meaning of [that convention] is a third country and whose author is not a national of an EU Member State?

(5) In the circumstances at issue in the present proceedings and given the time of the establishment of (the predecessor of) Article 2(7) [of the Berne Convention], are the conditions of the first paragraph of Article 351 TFEU satisfied for [the Kingdom of] Belgium, meaning that [that Member State] is therefore free to apply the [criterion of] material reciprocity provided for in Article 2(7) [of that convention], taking into account the fact that[,] in the present case[,] the country of origin acceded to the Berne Convention on 1 May 1989?'

2. Decision

1. A situation in which a company claims copyright protection for a subject matter of applied art marketed in a Member State, provided that that subject matter may be classified as a 'work' within the meaning of Directive 2001/29/EC of the European Parliament and of the Council of 22 May 2001 on the harmonisation of certain aspects of copyright and related rights in the information society, falls within the material scope of EU law.

2. Article 2(a) and Article 4(1) of Directive 2001/29, read in conjunction with Article 17(2) and Article 52(1) of the Charter of Fundamental Rights of the European Union, must be interpreted as meaning that, as EU law currently stands, they preclude Member States from applying, in national law, the criterion of material reciprocity laid down in the second sentence of Article 2(7) of the Convention for the Protection of Literary and Artistic Works, signed in Berne on 9 September 1886 (Paris Act of 24 July 1971), as amended on 28 September 1979, in respect of a work of applied art the country of origin of which is a third country and the author of which is a national of a third country. It is

for the EU legislature alone, in accordance with Article 52(1) of the Charter of Fundamental Rights, to provide, by means of EU legislation, whether the grant in the European Union of the rights laid down in Article 2(a) and Article 4(1) of that directive should be limited.

3. The first paragraph of Article 351 TFEU must be interpreted as not permitting a Member State to apply, by way of derogation from the provisions of EU law, the criterion of material reciprocity contained in the second sentence of Article 2(7) of the Convention for the Protection of Literary and Artistic Works, signed in Berne on 9 September 1886 (Paris Act of 24 July 1971), as amended on 28 September 1979, in respect of a work the country of origin of which is the United States of America.

3. Motivation and Analysis

With its first question, the referring court asked whether the situation at issue in the main proceedings fell within the material scope of EU law.

It was common ground in the case that the dispute in the main proceedings concerned an action brought by Vitra before the Netherlands courts, by which that company claimed copyright protection in the Netherlands and in Belgium for the DSW chair – designed by nationals of the United States of America and originating in that third country – in respect of which Kwantum was allegedly marketing imitations. The Court noted that it was apparent that Directive 2001/29 concerns the legal protection of copyright and related rights in the framework of the internal market. The Court observed that the directive is defined not in accordance with the criterion of the country of origin of the work or of the nationality of its author, but by reference to the internal market, which equates to the territorial scope of the treaties as set out in Article 52 TEU.[7] Subject to Article 355 TFEU, and comprising the territories of the Member States.[8]

It maintained that, in accordance with Article 10(1) of the Directive 2001/29, the provisions of that directive, which harmonises certain aspects of copyright and related rights in the information society, are to apply in respect of all works and other subject matter referred to therein which, on the date laid down for its transposition, meet the criteria for protection under the provisions of that directive. In particular the Court recalled that Article 2(a) and Article 3(1) of Directive 2001/29 define a copyright holder's exclusive rights in the European Union of reproduction and communication to the public in unequivocal terms, those provisions forming a harmonised legal framework that ensures a high and

[7] Paras. 44-45 of the annotated judgment.

[8] Case C-265/19 of 8 September 2020, *Recorded Artists Actors Performers*, para. 59 and the case law cited. Paras. 44-45 of the annotated judgment.

even level of protection for the rights of reproduction and communication to the public and constituting measures of full harmonisation of the corresponding substantive law. Furthermore, as regards Article 4(1) of Directive 2001/29, it was clear from its wording that that provision also defines in unequivocal terms the exclusive right of distribution to the public referred to therein, that measure constituting, like the abovementioned provisions, a measure of full harmonisation of the corresponding substantive law.[9]

Consequently, the Courts concluded that a situation in which a company claims copyright protection for a subject matter of applied art marketed in a Member State, provided that that subject matter may be classified as a 'work' within the meaning of Directive 2001/29, falls within the material scope of EU law.[10]

The Court noted that the referring court's second to fourth questions in essence asked whether Article 2(a) and Article 4(1) of Directive 2001/29, read in conjunction with Article 17(2) and Article 52(1) of the Charter, must be interpreted as precluding Member States from applying the criterion of material reciprocity laid down in the second sentence of Article 2(7) of the Berne Convention in respect of a work of applied art the country of origin of which is a third country and the author of which is a national of a third country.

In order to answer those questions, it was necessary to determine, first, whether the abovementioned provisions apply to a work of applied art the country of origin of which is a third country or the author of which is a national of a third country, and, second, whether those provisions preclude the application, in national law, of the criterion of material reciprocity laid down in the second sentence of Article 2(7) of the Berne Convention.[11]

As a preliminary point, the Court recalls that the terms of a provision of EU law which makes no express reference to the law of the Member States for the purpose of determining its meaning and scope must normally be given an autonomous and uniform interpretation throughout the European Union; that interpretation must take into account the wording of that provision, its context and the objectives pursued by the rules of which it forms part.[12]

In the first place, the Court noted that, as regards the wording of Article 2(a) and Article 4(1) of Directive 2001/29, according to those provisions, Member States are to provide authors with exclusive rights to authorise or prohibit, first, direct or indirect, temporary or permanent reproduction by any means and in any form, in whole or in part, of their works, and, second, in respect of

[9] Paras. 46-47 of the annotated judgment.

[10] Paras. 50-51 of the annotated judgment.

[11] Para. 55 of the annotated judgment.

[12] Case C-265/19 of 8 September 2020, *Recorded Artists Actors Performers*, para. 46 and the case law cited. Para. 56 of the annotated judgment.

the original of their works or of copies thereof, any form of distribution to the public by sale or otherwise. In that regard, it stated, it must be observed that those provisions do not expressly specify whether the concept of 'work' referred to therein covers a work of applied art originating in a third country, or whether the concept of 'author', within the meaning of those provisions, covers the author of such a work who is a national of a third country. The Directive, it added, does not lay down any condition relating to the country of origin of the work in question or to the nationality of the author of that work. In the second place, in defining the scope of the Directive by means of a territorial criterion, the EU legislature had necessarily taken into account all the works for which protection is sought in the territory of the European Union, irrespective of the country of origin of those works or the nationality of their author.[13]

Second, it noted that certain instruments of the harmonised copyright legislation provide for a specific regime for works in respect of which the country of origin, within the meaning of the Berne Convention, is a third country and the author of which is not a national of a Member State. Thus, Directive 2006/116, in particular Article 7(1) thereof, provides that the copyright protection granted by the Member States to such works is to expire on the date of expiry of the protection granted in the country of origin of the work, but may not exceed the term laid down in that directive. Such a regime, which specifically concerns the protection of the rights of authors and of works the country of origin of which is a third country, would serve no purpose if the protection of the works in question were not ensured under Directive 2001/29.[14]

Thirdly, it stated, such an interpretation is also consistent with the objectives of the Directive 2001/20. The directive seeks, *inter alia*, to avoid significant differences in protection and thereby restrictions on the free movement of services and products incorporating, or based on, intellectual property, leading to a refragmentation of the internal market and legislative inconsistency, and any harmonisation of copyright must, according to recital 9 of that directive, take as a basis a high level of protection. Such an objective would be disregarded if Directive 2001/29 regulated only offers copyright protection for works originating in a Member State or works the author of which is a national of a Member State. Furthermore, recital 15 of Directive 2001/29 states that that directive also serves to implement a number of the international obligations arising from the WCT. In that regard, in accordance with Article 9(1) of the TRIPS Agreement and Article 1(4) of the WCT, the European Union must comply, first, with Articles 1 to 21 of the Berne Convention, as stated in paragraph 40 of the present judgment, and second, with the appendix to that convention. The Court pointed out that it is apparent from Article 5(1) of the Berne Convention that authors are to enjoy, in respect of works for which they are protected under that convention, in countries of the Union established by that convention other

[13] Paras. 57-60 of the annotated judgment

[14] Para. 61 of the annotated judgment.

than the country of origin of the work, the rights which their respective laws do now or may hereafter grant to their nationals. Thus, it would be contrary to the international obligations of the European Union implemented by Directive 2001/29 in the field of intellectual property for that directive to harmonise copyright in respect of works the country of origin of which is a Member State or the author of which is a national of a Member State, while leaving it to the national law of the Member States to determine the legal regime applicable to works the country of origin of which is a third country or the author of which is a national of a third country.[15]

Accordingly, it found that Article 2(a) and Article 4(1) of Directive 2001/29 apply to works of applied art originating in third countries or the authors of which are nationals of such countries.

The Court deems that those provisions preclude Member States from applying, in national law, the criterion of material reciprocity laid down in the second sentence of Article 2(7) of the Berne Convention in respect of a work of applied art the country of origin of which is a third country or the author of which is a national of a third country.[16]

First, the Court noted that application by a Member State of that criterion of material reciprocity would not only be contrary to the wording of those provisions but would also undermine the objective of that directive, which consists in the harmonisation of copyright in the internal market. This is because such a criterion could lead to inconsistent treatment of works from third countries across different Member States, which would undermine the objective of harmonising copyright within the EU.[17]

Second, in any event, since intellectual property rights are protected under Article 17(2) of the Charter, any limitation on the exercise of those rights must, in accordance with Article 52(1) of the Charter, be provided for by law and respect the essence of those rights and freedoms. The application by a Member State of the criterion of material reciprocity laid down in the second sentence of Article 2(7) of the Berne Convention might constitute such a limitation, inasmuch as that application is liable to deprive the potential holder of those rights of the enjoyment and exercise thereof in a part of the internal market, namely in the territory of the Member State applying that clause.[18]

The Court held that such a limitation must be provided for by law under Article 52(1) of the Charter. In the case at hand there was no such limitation. Where a rule of EU law harmonises copyright protection, it is for the EU legislature

---

[15] Paras. 62-65 of the annotated judgment.

[16] Para. 67 of the annotated judgment.

[17] Para. 68 of the annotated judgment.

[18] Paras. 69-70 of the annotated judgment.

alone, and not the national legislatures, to determine whether the grant in the European Union of that copyright should be limited in respect of works the country of origin of which is a third country or the author of which is a national of a third country (see, to that effect, the judgment of 8 September 2020, *Recorded Artists Actors Performers*, C-265/19, EU:C:2020:677, para. 88). The Court highlighted that by adopting Directive 2001/29, the EU legislature is deemed to have exercised the competence previously devolved on the Member States in the field concerned. Thus, within the scope of that directive, the European Union must be regarded as having taken the place of the Member States, which are no longer competent to implement the relevant stipulations of the Berne Convention (judgment of 26 April 2012, *DR and TV2 Danmark*, C-510/10, EU:C:2012:244, para. 31 and the case law cited).[19]

Although Directive 2001/29 aims to harmonise copyright law, it also allows some discretion for Member States in its implementation. However, this discretion does not extend to applying the material reciprocity criterion. The list of exceptions and limitations, contained in Article 5 of Directive 2001/29, to the exclusive rights provided for in Articles 2 to 4 of that directive is exhaustive, so as not to undermine the effectiveness of the harmonisation of copyright and related rights effected by that directive and the objective of legal certainty pursued, as well as the requirement of consistency in the implementation of those exceptions and limitations (see, to that effect, the judgment of 29 July 2019, *Funke Medien NRW*, C-469/17, EU:C:2019:623, paras. 56, 62 and 63 and the case law cited).[20]

The Court pointed out that, while the EU legislature had decided to apply a criterion of material reciprocity, first, to Article 7(1) of Directive 2006/116 as regards the term of protection, and, second, to Article 7(1) of Directive 2001/84 as regards the resale right, in accordance with Article 7(8) and Article 14(3)(2) of the Berne Convention, that legislature had not, by contrast, included in Directive 2001/29 or in any other provision of EU law a limitation of the exclusive rights granted to authors by Article 2(a) and Article 4(1) of that directive in the form of a criterion of material reciprocity such as that laid down in the second sentence of Article 2(7) of the Berne Convention.[21]

It is for the EU legislature alone, the Court concluded, in accordance with Article 52(1) of the Charter, to provide, by means of EU legislation, whether the grant in the European Union of the rights laid down in Article 2(a) and Article 4(1) of that directive should be limited.

By its fifth question, the referring court asked, in essence, whether the first paragraph of Article 351 TFEU must be interpreted as permitting a Member State

---

[19] Paras. 71-73 of the annotated judgment.

[20] Paras. 74-76 of the annotated judgment.

[21] Para. 79 of the annotated judgment.

to apply, by way of derogation from the provisions of EU law, the criterion of material reciprocity contained in the second sentence of Article 2(7) of the Berne Convention in respect of a work the country of origin of which is the United States of America.

Article 351 TFEU states that agreements made before a Member State's accession to the EU will not be affected by EU law. This includes agreements made with third countries prior to 1 January 1958, or the accession of new Member States.

The Court noted that the Berne Convention is an international agreement under Article 351 TFEU. The purpose of Article 351 TFEU is to ensure that a Member State respects its prior international agreements and obligations, even after joining the EU, in line with international law principles. The Court's case law states that if an international agreement concluded by a Member State prior to its accession to the EU allows a Member State to adopt a measure that contradicts EU law, the Member State must refrain from adopting such a measure. Furthermore, in a situation where, because of a development in EU law, a legislative measure adopted by a Member State in accordance with the power offered by an earlier international agreement appears contrary to EU law, the Member State concerned cannot rely on that agreement in order to exempt itself from the obligations that have arisen subsequently from EU law (judgment of 9 February 2012, *Luksan*, C-277/10, EU:C:2012:65, paragraph 63).[22]

* *
*

The CJEU's ruling was highly anticipated and further harmonises copyright law in the EU. Relying on its previous judgments on copyright, the Court confirmed that 'originality' is the sole condition for copyright protection under EU law, and that there is a single system that treats all original works equally, regardless of their country of origin. This is an important next step towards further harmonisation of copyright law across the EU.

This landmark decision by the Court must be applauded from the perspective of all creators in 'third countries', and in particular those where a stricter approach to copyright protection applies in comparison with EU law. All can now benefit from the more generous EU copyright protection towards their creations that are marketed in the EU, which allows them to protect their interests in the EU market in relation to their works, including works of applied art.

In Dutch practice at least, the material reciprocity clause of the Berne Convention had sometimes proved to be a serious copyright hurdle for works of applied art originating from outside the EU. The claimant needed to show that the work of applied art was eligible for copyright protection in the country of origin, and the courts had to make an assessment based on foreign law.

---

22 Paras. 83-87 of the annotated judgment.

The complexities of such cases are also revealed by this case. The parties were able to rely on opposing legal opinions of US professors and US lawyers as to the question whether the DWS chair would be eligible for copyright protection in the US. In the first instance the District Court of The Hague held that the Eames chair was not eligible for copyright protection in the US and rejected the claims of Vitra that were based on copyright. The Court of Appeal in The Hague – in light of new case law in the US – on the other hand concluded that the DSW chair was eligible for copyright protection in the US.

The referral by the Supreme Court was remarkable considering that neither of the parties, nor the Advocate-General appointed to the case, questioned that the application of the material reciprocity of the Berne Convention would have to be applied. It was common practice to apply the material reciprocity clause of the Berne Convention.

The Supreme Court took the initiative of seeking to ascertain whether the Member States were still free to apply the material reciprocity clause contained in the Berne Convention to works of applied art originating in third countries. The referral was made in light of the Court's earlier decision in *RAAP*. The Court in this case also relied heavily on its earlier *RAAP* judgment. In *RAAP* the Court had decided that Member States may not unilaterally invoke material reciprocity regarding the remuneration right accorded to phonogram producers and performing artists under Article 8(2) of Directive 2006/115/EC. The Court emphasised in that case that the Information Society Directive, which harmonises the main rights of exploitation, does not comprise a rule of material reciprocity. Allowing individual Member States to individually apply Article 2(7) Berne Convention would undermine the Information Society Directive's aim of reducing fragmentation of the internal market.

The Court also further confirmed that where harmonised copyright protection is concerned, it is for the EU legislature alone, and not the national legislatures, to determine whether the copyright may be limited. Unless the EU legislature has granted explicit discretion in relation to certain aspects of copyright protection, there is no room to deviate for Member States. As a result, the material reciprocity rule of the Berne Convention may no longer be applied.

This decision of the Court should also be welcomed for the reason that it will lead to more predictable and more cost-efficient enforcement, given that only the EU copyright test will have to be applied and legal opinions on protection in the country of origin are no longer needed.

Court of Justice 14 November 2024

On the direct effect of Article 5(2)(a) and (b) of the InfoSoc Directive

Case C-230/23

Summary and Analysis by Karel Janssens and Emma Dekeuwer[1]

Parties:

Reprobel CV

v

Copaco Belgium NV

1. Background and History

Reprobel CV ('Reprobel'), a copyright collecting society authorised by the Belgian State to collect and distribute the remuneration for authors and publishers as fair compensation for reprography activities, initiated legal proceedings against Copaco Belgium NV ('Copaco'), a distributor of IT products and reproduction devices such as photocopiers and scanners.

As a distributor of reproduction devices, Copaco was liable to pay Reprobel a flat-rate remuneration for the reproduction of works protected by copyright or related rights ('remuneration by way of fair compensation').[2] However, Copaco claimed that, by its *Hewlett-Packard Belgium* judgment of 12 November 2015,[3] the Court of Justice of the European Union ('CJEU') had ruled that Article 5(2)(a) and (b) of Directive 2001/29 ('InfoSoc Directive') precluded the 'flat-rate' portion of the remuneration system laid down by Belgian legislation, and suspended payment of Reprobel's invoices issued from November 2015 to January 2017. Copaco invoked the direct effect of Article 5(2)(a) and (b) and stated that it would continue to suspend the payments until Belgian legislation was aligned with the provisions of the InfoSoc Directive. Belgium introduced a new system for remuneration by way of fair compensation in March 2017.[4]

In December 2020, Reprobel initiated legal proceedings against Copaco before the Ondernemingsrechtbank Gent, afdeling Dendermonde (Ghent Business

---

[1] Karel Janssens specialises in IP and IT law and is a partner at the Belgian law firm & DE BANDT. Emma Dekeuwer also focuses on IP/IT law at the law firm & DE BANDT.

[2] Para. 13 of the annotated judgment.

[3] Case C-572/13, 12 November 2015, *Hewlett-Packard Belgium*; Para. 14 of the annotated judgment.

[4] Para. 14 of the annotated judgment.

Court, Dendermonde Division, Belgium). In an interim judgment of 4 March 2022, the case was transferred to the Ondernemingsrechtbank Gent, afdeling Gent (Ghent Business Court, Ghent Division).[5]

The referring court noted that the CJEU judgment in *Hewlett-Packard Belgium* had concluded that the Belgian remuneration system in effect until December 2016 was, at least partially, incompatible with Article 5(2)(a) and (b) of the InfoSoc Directive. Among other things, the system provided for the application of a flat-rate remuneration which lacked an objective quantitative correlation with the actual use of the reproduction devices. As such, the remuneration presented a risk of being more than purely compensatory.[6]

Before the referring court, Copaco submitted that Article 5(2)(a) and (b) of the InfoSoc Directive had direct effect and could be invoked against Reprobel, given the latter's status as a State entity entrusted with the task of collecting and distributing remuneration by way of fair compensation.[7] Reprobel, on the other hand, contested this claim and asserted that Article 5(2)(a) and (b) was not unconditional, clear, or precise, since Member States retained the discretion to (i) provide for the exceptions and limitations referred to in that provision as they saw fit, and (ii) define the fairness of the compensation under that provision. Reprobel further maintained that it was an association governed by private law, so that the InfoSoc Directive could not be relied on against it.[8]

In these circumstances the referring court decided to stay the proceedings and refer the following questions to the Court of Justice for a preliminary ruling:

> '*(1) Is an entity such as Reprobel, in so far as it has been entrusted by the State, by means of a royal mandate, to collect and distribute the fair compensation, set by the State, within the meaning of Article 5(2)(a) and (b) of Directive 2001/29, and over which the State exercises control, an entity against which an individual may rely, in his or her defence, on the incompatibility with EU law of a national provision which that entity seeks to impose on that individual?*
>
> *(2) Is it relevant to the answer to that question that the control exercised by the State over that entity includes:*
>
> - *The obligation for that entity to always forward to the competent minister a copy of the requests for data it sends to the persons liable to pay the remuneration, required both for the collection and distribution of the remuneration for reprography, in such a way that the minister is in a position to know how the entity exercises the right of supervision and decide whether it*

[5] Paras. 15 and 16 of the annotated judgment.

[6] Para. 17 of the annotated judgment. See also para. 18 of the annotated judgment.

[7] Para. 20 of the annotated judgment.

[8] Paras. 21 and 22 of the annotated judgment.

is advisable to stipulate, by means of a ministerial decree, the content, number and frequency of the requests for data in such a way as not to impede, more than is necessary, the activities of the persons receiving those requests;

- *The obligation for the entity to call upon the minister's representative to send a request for data, required for the collection of the proportional remuneration for reprography, to the persons liable to pay the remuneration, the dealers, whether wholesalers or retailers, the leasing companies or equipment maintenance companies if the person liable to pay the remuneration has not cooperated in the collection, on the understanding that the entity also has the obligation to send a copy of this request to the competent minister in such a way that the latter can determine that the content, number and frequency of the requests do not impede, more than is necessary, the activities of the persons receiving those requests;*
- *The obligation for the entity to submit to the competent minister for approval the rules for the distribution of reprography remuneration and any amendment it makes to them;*
- *The obligation for the entity to submit the declaration form it has prepared to the competent minister for approval, without which it cannot be issued[?]*

(3) Is it also relevant to the answer to the question referred that the entity has the following powers:

- *The power to request all data necessary for collecting the remuneration for reprography from all persons who are liable to pay the remuneration, liable to pay a contribution, dealers, whether wholesalers or retailers, leasing companies and equipment maintenance companies. Every request must always state the criminal penalties applicable in the event of failure to comply with the time limit set or provision of incomplete or inaccurate information;*
- *The power to require all persons liable to pay remuneration to provide all data relating to copied works necessary for the distribution of the remuneration for reprography;*
- *The power to obtain all information necessary for the performance of its task from the Administratie der Douane en Accijnzen (Belgian Customs and Excise), the Administratie van de btw (Belgian VAT Administration) and the Rijksdienst voor Sociale Zekerheid (Belgian National Office for Social Security)?*

(4) Does Article 5(2)(a) and (b) of Directive 2001/29 have direct effect?

(5) Is a national court required, on the application of an individual, to disapply a national provision where that provision, imposed by the State, contravenes Article 5(2)(a) and (b) of Directive 2001/29, referred to above, in particular because that provision, contrary to the aforementioned article, obliges that individual to pay charges?'

2. Decision

1. Article 5(2)(a) and (b) of Directive 2001/29/EC of the European Parliament and of the Council of 22 May 2001 on the harmonisation of certain aspects of copyright and related rights in the information society must be interpreted as meaning that an individual may rely, before a national court, against an entity entrusted by a Member State with collecting and distributing the fair compensation established under that provision, on the fact that the national legislation laying down that compensation contravenes provisions of EU law which have direct effect, provided that such an entity has, in order to perform that task in the public interest, special powers beyond those which result from the normal rules applicable in relations between individuals.

2. Article 5(2)(a) and (b) of Directive 2001/29 must be interpreted as having direct effect, and that therefore, in the absence of a correct transposition of that provision, an individual may rely on it for the purposes of disapplying national rules under which that individual is obliged to pay remuneration by way of fair compensation imposed in contravention of that provision.

3. Motivation and Analysis

i) Regarding Questions 1, 2 and 3

The Court addressed the first, second, and third questions together, and examined whether an individual may challenge, before a national court, the compensation claimed by an entity tasked by a Member State with collecting and distributing the fair compensation under Article 5(2)(a) and (b) of the InfoSoc Directive, on the ground that the national legislation laying down that compensation violates EU law. The referring court asked if this may be the case where the entity in question performs a task in the public interest, is subject to State control, and possesses special powers beyond those which result from the normal rules applicable to relations between individuals.[9]

The Court emphasised, with reference to the *Foster and Others*[10] and *Farrell*[11] cases, that individuals may invoke provisions of a directive with direct effect not only against Member States and their organs but also against organisations which are subject to State control, perform tasks in the public interest, and are granted special powers. Such organisations may be treated as comparable to the State. It suffices that the organisation is either subject to the authority or control

9 Para. 24 of the annotated judgment.

10 Case C-188/89, 12 July 1990, *Foster and Others*.

11 Case C-413/15, 10 October 2017, *Farrell*.

of the State, or is entrusted with the performance of a task in the public interest and, for that purpose, possesses special powers.[12]

In this case, the Court found that Reprobel, a cooperative governed by private law, was neither governed by public law nor controlled by the Belgian State. The Court therefore had to assess whether Reprobel performed a public interest task and had been entrusted with special powers to do so.[13]

The Court noted that Reprobel had been entrusted by the Belgian State with the task of collecting and distributing remuneration by way of fair compensation. The Court then recalled the principles and case-law relating to Article 5(2)(a) and (b) of the InfoSoc Directive, entitling Member States to establish exceptions to the reproduction right and requiring them, for that purpose, to establish fair compensation and a system to finance that compensation.[14]

The Court emphasised, among other things, that through the task entrusted to an entity responsible for collecting and distributing remuneration by way of fair compensation, a Member State gives effect to its obligation to ensure, for the benefit of those rightholders, the effective collection of fair compensation intended to preserve a fair balance between the interests involved, which is entirely a matter of the public interest.[15]

Turning to the powers granted to Reprobel, the Court confirmed that these included the power to collect remuneration by way of fair compensation from manufacturers and distributors of copying devices and media. According to the Court, these powers went beyond those resulting from the normal rules applicable in relations between individuals.[16]

The Court also clarified that it was irrelevant that the Belgian State determined the amount of the remuneration,[17] and referred to Reprobel's other specific powers, in particular the power to request information from the persons liable to pay remuneration and other operators active on the market for copying equipment, on pain of criminal penalties, and even from customs, tax and social security authorities.[18]

In light of the above, the Court ruled that an individual may indeed rely on Article 5(2)(a) and (b) of the InfoSoc Directive before a national court, against an entity such as Reprobel, based on the fact that the national legislation governing

---

[12] Paras. 26 and 27 of the annotated judgment.

[13] Para. 28 of the annotated judgment.

[14] Paras. 29-30 of the annotated judgment.

[15] Paras. 31-36 of the annotated judgment.

[16] Paras. 37-39 of the annotated judgment.

[17] Para. 40 of the annotated judgment.

[18] Paras. 41-44 of the annotated judgment.

fair compensation contravenes provisions of EU law with direct effect, provided that such an entity is entrusted with special powers beyond the normal rules applicable in relations between individuals to perform the task in the public interest.[19]

ii) Regarding Questions 4 and 5

The referring court's fourth and fifth questions sought to ascertain whether Article 5(2)(a) and (b) of the InfoSoc Directive should be interpreted as having direct effect. Specifically, the referring court queried whether, in the absence of a proper transposition of these provisions into national law, individuals could invoke them before national courts to disapply national rules requiring the payment of remuneration by way of fair compensation, where such rules contradict the provisions of the InfoSoc Directive.[20]

The Court of Justice reaffirmed its settled case law that a provision of a directive has direct effect whenever it is both unconditional and sufficiently precise. In case of direct effect, the provision may be relied upon before the national courts by individuals against the State where this State has either failed to implement the directive in national law within the prescribed time frame or has implemented it incorrectly. A provision is unconditional where it establishes an obligation without being qualified by any condition or contingent on further actions by either EU institutions or Member States. It is sufficiently precise where it sets forth an obligation in unequivocal terms.[21]

The Court acknowledged the argument put forth by Reprobel and the Belgian and French Governments, which maintained that the broad discretion granted to Member States in organising fair compensation systems rendered these provisions insufficiently precise and unconditional.[22] The Court, however, disagreed and noted that a provision of a directive may be regarded as unconditional and precise even though the directive leaves Member States a degree of discretion in its implementation.[23]

With regard to Article 5(2)(a) and (b) of the InfoSoc Directive, the Court noted that while Member States are not obliged to adopt these exceptions, if they do, they must provide for the payment of fair compensation to the authors harmed by the application of those exceptions and respect the requirements relating to

---

[19] Para. 45 of the annotated judgment.

[20] Para. 46 of the annotated judgment.

[21] Paras. 47-48 of the annotated judgment. See also Case C-684/16, 6 November 2018, *Max-Planck-Gesellschaft zur Förderung der Wissenschaften*, para. 63; Case C-205/20, 8 March 2022, *Bezirkshauptmannschaft Hartberg-Fürstenfeld (Direct effect)*, para. 18.

[22] Para. 49 of the annotated judgment.

[23] Para. 50 of the annotated judgment.

the structure and level of that compensation which flow from the interpretation of that provision.[24]

As part of these requirements, the Court referred to the detailed arrangements for calculating the remuneration by way of fair compensation as established in the *Hewlett-Packard Belgium* judgment. In that judgment, the Court held that while Article 5(2)(a) and (b) of the InfoSoc Directive allows Member States discretion in structuring fair compensation, such systems must ensure that the amount of the levies reflect actual harm suffered by the rightholders and must include reimbursement mechanisms to address overcompensation and to preserve the InfoSoc Directive's requirement for a fair balance between right holders and users.[25]

In this case, the national legislation at issue was incompatible with Article 5(2)(a) and (b) of the InfoSoc Directive, as established in *Hewlett-Packard Belgium*. The Court recalled that, on the basis of the principle of primacy, the national court must give full effect to a provision of EU law with direct effect and, where it is unable to interpret national legislation in compliance with the EU law, if necessary disapply the legislation without having to request or await the prior setting aside thereof by the legislator.[26]

In conclusion, the Court held that Article 5(2)(a) and (b) of the InfoSoc Directive did indeed have direct effect, enabling individuals to invoke that provision before national courts and to let national rules imposing payment obligations in contravention of that provision to be set aside.[27]

* *
*

The Court's *Reprobel* judgment puts an end to a debate that has been ongoing for many years in Belgium as to whether Article 5(2)(a) and (b) of the InfoSoc Directive has direct effect and whether the incompatibility of the (old) Belgian system on fair compensation[28] can be invoked against Reprobel.

---

[24] Paras. 52-54 of the annotated judgment. See also Case C-467/08, 21 Oktober 2010, *Padawan*, para. 36.

[25] Paras. 55-56 of the annotated judgment. See also Case C-572/13, 12 November 2015, *Hewlett-Packard Belgium*, paras. 83-87 and Case C-110/15, 22 September 2016, *Microsoft Mobile Sales International and Others*, paras. 37, 54 and 55.

[26] Paras. 51 and 57 of the annotated judgment. See also Case C-205/20, 8 March 2022, *Bezirkshauptmannschaft Hartberg-Fürstenfeld (Direct effect)*, para. 37.

[27] Para. 58 of the annotated judgment.

[28] Artt. 59-61 of the Law of 30 June 1994 on Copyright and Related Rights, *BS* 27 July 1994.

In recent years, Belgian courts have repeatedly ruled[29] that Article 5(2)(a) and (b) of the InfoSoc Directive does not have direct effect, with the Supreme Court (Cour de Cassation) even expressing this very firmly as follows:

> *'It follows without any doubt from these statements that, while the principle of fair compensation is established, the content itself of the right granted to the copyright holder and its essential condition, fall under the power of the Member States, so that Article 5(2)(a) and (b) does not constitute, with regard to the form of, arrangements for and level of fair compensation, a provision that is sufficiently clear and unconditional.'*[30]

The Court has now taken an entirely opposite stance and clearly affirmed that Article 5(2)(a) and (b) of the InfoSoc Directive *is* sufficiently unconditional and precise to give it direct effect. Surprisingly though, the Court mainly refers to the *Hewlett-Packard Belgium* judgment to come to that conclusion, rather than to the text of the provision itself.

The Court has also put an end to the question of whether an entity like Reprobel should be considered as an 'emanation of the State'. Reprobel is held to perform a task in the public interest and to possess special powers beyond those which result from the normal rules applicable to relations between individuals. Individuals may invoke the direct effect of Article 5(2)(a) and (b) of the InfoSoc Directive against Reprobel.

Undoubtedly, this judgment will often be invoked in proceedings in the coming years, and if the Court maintains this case-law, other provisions of copyright law may also be granted direct effect, with possibly far-reaching consequences. Could this be a solution for advancing the harmonisation of national copyright laws and, consequently, for achieving a true EU internal market for copyright?

---

29 See, *inter alia*, Cass. 3 December 2021, *Annuaire Pratiques du marché* 2021, liv. 1, p. 466-476; Brussel 17 April 2018, AR no. 2014/AR/2722, *AM* 2018-2019/3, p. 343-357; Court of Appeal of Brussels (9th Chamber) 12 May 2017, *J.L.M.B.* 2017/30, p. 1426-1448. As far as we know, there is one brave ruling by a lower court, namely the District Court of Antwerp, 16 June 2022, AR no. A/21/3648, unpublished, in which direct effect was accepted.

30 Cass. 24 September 2020, RG C. 18.0039.F, C.18.0468, *AM* 2022, afl. 4, 389 (free translation of: '*Il suit, sans aucun doute possible, de ces énonciations que, si le principe d'une compensation équitable est établi, le contenu même du droit conféré au titulaire des droits d'auteur ainsi que ses conditions essentielles relèvent du pouvoir des États membres, en sorte que l'article 5, paragraphe 2, a) et b), ne constitue pas, en ce qui concerne la forme, les modalités et le niveau de la compensation équitable, une disposition suffisamment claire et inconditionnelle.*').

Index Case Number

Index Case Name